THE FAITH EXPLAINED

THE

FAITH

EXPLAINED

LEO J. TRESE

FIDES PUBLISHERS, INC.

NOTRE DAME, INDIANA

53205

Library of Congress Catalog Card No.: 59-7820

Nihil Obstat:
Louis J. Putz, C.S.C., University of Notre Dame

Imprimatur:
Leo A. Pursley, D.D., Bishop of Fort Wayne, Indiana

Copyright: 1959, Fides Publishers
Association, Chicago, Illinois

Manufactured by American Book–Stratford Press,
New York, N.Y.

⬤55

First Edition, March 1959
Second Printing, January 1960
Third Printing, June 1961
Fourth Printing, February 1962
Fifth Printing, October 1962
Sixth Printing, October 1963

Published and copyrighted originally by The Confraternity
of Christian Doctrine in a series of six discussion club
booklets under the general title of THIS WE BELIEVE.

Contents

PART ONE : THE CREED

I. The Purpose of Man's Existence 3
Why Am I Here? 3
What Must I Do? 8
Who Will Tell Me? 13

II. God and His Perfections 18
Who Is God? 18

III. The Unity and Trinity of God 25
How Are There Three? 25

IV. Creation and the Angels 31
How Did Creation Begin? 31
Is the Devil Real? 36

V. The Creation and the Fall of Man 42
What Is Man? 42
How Did God Make Us? 47
What Is Original Sin? 52
After Adam, What? 57

VI. Actual Sin 62
Can My Soul Die? 62
What Are the Roots of Sin? 67

VII. The Incarnation 73
Who Is Mary? 73
Who Is Jesus Christ? 78

VIII. The Redemption 85
How Does It End? 85

IX. The Holy Ghost and Grace   91
 The Unknown Person   91
 What Is Grace?   96
 The Grace that Comes and Goes   101
 Wellsprings of Life   106
 What Is Merit?   112

X. The Virtues and the Gifts of the Holy Ghost   118
 What Is Virtue?   118
 Hope and Love   124
 Wonders Within Us   130
 The Moral Virtues   135

XI. The Catholic Church   142
 The Holy Ghost and the Church   142
 We Are the Church   148

XII. The Marks and Attributes of the Church   154
 Where Do We Find It?   154
 Holy and Catholic   159
 Reason and Faith—and Myself   165

XIII. The Communion of Saints
and the Forgiveness of Sins   171
 The End of the Road   171

XIV. The Resurrection and Life Everlasting   175
 The End of the World   175

PART TWO : THE COMMANDMENTS

XV. The Two Great Commandments   187
 Faith Proven by Deeds   187
 Accenting the Positive   192
 The Greater Good   199

XVI. The First Commandment of God   205
 Our First Duty   205
 Sins Against Faith   211

Hope and Love 217
Sacrilege and Superstition 223

XVII. The Second and Third
Commandments of God 230
Holy Is His Name 230
"Bless and Do Not Curse" 236
Why Sunday Mass? 241

XVIII. The Fourth and Fifth
Commandments of God 248
Parents, Children and Citizens 248
Life Belongs to God 254

XIX. The Sixth and Ninth
Commandments of God 260
Commandments Six and Nine 260

XX. The Seventh and Tenth
Commandments of God 267
Mine and Thine 267

XXI. The Eighth Commandment of God 274
Nothing But the Truth 274

XXII. The Commandments of the Church 280
Laws of the Church 280

PART THREE : THE SACRAMENTS
AND PRAYER

XXIII. The Sacraments 289
We Begin the Sacraments 289
Why Seven Sacraments? 294

XXIV. Baptism 300
The Beginning of Life 300
The Mark of a Christian 305
Getting Baby Baptized 310

viii / CONTENTS

Before Childbirth and After 315
The Birth of a Soul 320
Who Can Baptize? 325

xxv. Confirmation 331
The Sacrament of Confirmation 331
The Meaning of Confirmation 336

xxvi. The Eucharist 343
The Greatest Sacrament 343
The Promise Is Kept 348
Bread No Longer 354
Bread and Wine and Priest 359

xxvii. The Mass 366
We Begin the Mass 366
What Makes a Sacrifice 371
Every Mass is Our Mass 377
The Mass is a History 382
The Mass of the Faithful 388
Why Have Vestments? 393
The Roman Missal 399
Participating in the Mass 404

xxviii. Holy Communion 411
So Close to Christ 411
Who May Receive? 416
The Eucharistic Fast 422
Practical Pointers for Communicants 426

xxix. Penance 433
The Sacrament of Penance 433
Preparing for Confession 439

xxx. Contrition 445
When Is Sorrow Real? 445
Thank God for Confession 451

XXXI. Confession 457
    Telling Our Sins 457
    Sin and Punishment 463

XXXII. Temporal Punishment and Indulgences 469
    Indulgences 469
    Plenary Indulgences 474

XXXIII. Extreme Unction 481
    Sacrament of the Sick 481
    When to Call a Priest 486

XXXIV. Holy Orders 493
    What Is a Priest? 493
    What Is Holy Orders? 499
    Bishops—and Others 505

XXXV. Matrimony 511
    God Made Marriage 511
    Matrimony Has Special Graces 517
    Foresight Makes Happy Marriages 522

XXXVI. The Sacramentals 528
    Agents of Grace 528

XXXVII. Prayer 535
    The What and Why of Prayer 535
    Prayer that Reaches God 541
    For Whom Shall I Pray? 546

XXXVIII. The Our Father 552
    The Best Prayer 552

XXXIX. The Bible 558
    Do You Read the Bible? 558

Cross Reference to the Baltimore Catechism
Number 3

The Faith Explained	Baltimore Catechism No. 3
Chapter I: page 3	Lesson 1: page 1
Chapter II: page 18	Lesson 2: page 9
Chapter III: page 25	Lesson 3: page 22
Chapter IV: page 31	Lesson 4: page 28
Chapter V: page 42	Lesson 5: page 38
Chapter VI: page 62	Lesson 6: page 47
Chapter VII: page 73	Lesson 7: page 55
Chapter VIII: page 85	Lesson 8: page 67
Chapter IX: page 91	Lesson 9: page 77
Chapter X: page 118	Lesson 10: page 87
Chapter XI: page 142	Lesson 11: page 102
Chapter XII: page 154	Lesson 12: page 115
Chapter XIII: page 171	Lesson 13: page 132
Chapter XIV: page 175	Lesson 14: page 137
Chapter XV: page 187	Lesson 15: page 148
Chapter XVI: page 205	Lesson 16: page 163
Chapter XVII: page 230	Lesson 18: page 181
Chapter XVIII: page 248	Lesson 19: page 193
Chapter XIX: page 260	Lesson 20: pages 208-212; 225-226
Chapter XX: page 267	Lesson 20: pages 212-218; 227
Chapter XXI: page 274	Lesson 20: pages 218-225
Chapter XXII: page 280	Lesson 21-22: pages 228; 236
Chapter XXIII: page 289	Lesson 23: page 245
Chapter XXIV: page 300	Lesson 24: page 254
Chapter XXV: page 331	Lesson 25: page 265

Cross Reference to the Baltimore Catechism
Number 3

The Faith Explained	*Baltimore Catechism No. 3*
Chapter XXVI: page 343	Lesson 26: page 273
Chapter XXVII: page 366	Lesson 27: page 281
Chapter XXVIII: page 411	Lesson 28: page 291
Chapter XXIX: page 433	Lesson 29: page 300
Chapter XXX: page 445	Lesson 30: page 305
Chapter XXXI: page 457	Lesson 31: page 315
Chapter XXXII: page 469	Lesson 33: page 332
Chapter XXXIII: page 481	Lesson 34: pages 340-345
Chapter XXXIV: page 493	Lesson 34: pages 345-355
Chapter XXXV: page 511	Lesson 35: page 355
Chapter XXXVI: page 528	Lesson 36: page 369
Chapter XXXVII: page 535	Lesson 37: page 374
Chapter XXXVIII: page 552	Lesson 38: page 387
Chapter XXXIX: page 558	Appendix 1: pages 398-400

PART ONE ————————————————

THE

CREED

CHAPTER I

The Purpose of Man's Existence

Why Am I Here?

Is man just a biological accident? Is the human race just another stage in the process of blind and purposeless evolution? Is this human life just a brief flash of light between the long darkness that preceded the womb, and an everlasting darkness that will follow the grave? Am I just a meaningless speck in the universe, tossed off by the creative power of an uncaring God much as a baseball fan might toss a peanut shell over his shoulder? Is there any design or plan to life, any significance? Where did I come from, anyway? And why am I here?

These are questions that any intelligent person is bound to ask himself, once he is old enough to do any serious thinking. The *Catechism of Christian Doctrine*, then, is eminently logical when it proposes as its very first question, "Who made us?"; and, having answered that, immediately asks, "Who is God?" But it seems preferable to delay, for the moment, in discussing these two questions, and to begin rather with a consideration of the third. It is equally basic, equally urgent, and is for us a better starting point. The question is, "Why did God make us?"

There are two ways of answering that question. It depends on whether we look at it from God's point of view or from our own. Looking at it from God's point of view, the answer is, "God made us to show forth His goodness." Since God is a Being infinitely perfect, the main reason why He does anything must be an infinitely perfect reason. But there is only one infinitely perfect reason for doing anything, and that is to do it for God. So it would be unworthy of God, it would be contrary to His infinite perfection, if He were to do something for a reason less than Himself.

Perhaps we can see that better if we apply it to ourselves. Even for us, the highest and the best reason for doing anything is to do it for God. If I do something for another human being—even something noble, like feeding the poor —and I do it mainly just for that person, without referring it to God in any way, then it is an imperfect thing that I do. Not a *bad* thing, but a less perfect thing. That would be true even if I did something for an angel or for our Blessed Mother herself, and left God out of the reckoning. There just is no higher motive for doing anything than to do it for God. That is true of the things that God does, as well as it is true of the things that we do.

The first reason, then—the big reason why God made the universe and us—was to give glory to Himself, by showing forth His infinite power and goodness. His infinite power is shown forth by the fact that we exist. His infinite goodness is shown by the fact that He wills to share His own infinite love and happiness with us. And if it seems to us that God is egotistical to make things just for His own honor and glory, it is because we can't help thinking of God in human terms. We think of Him as a creature like ourselves. But the fact remains that there just isn't anything or anyone else that is more deserving of God's thought and God's love than is God Himself.

However, when we say that God made the universe (and us) for His own greater glory, we do not mean of course that God *needed* any of it. The glory that is given to God by the works of His creation is what we call an "external glory." It is something outside of God. It doesn't actually add anything to God. It is very much like an artist who has a great talent for painting and a mind full of beautiful images. If the artist puts some of those images on canvas for people to look at and admire, it still hasn't added anything to the artist himself. It hasn't made him any better or more wonderful than he was before.

So, God made us primarily for His own honor and glory. That is why our first answer to the question "Why did God make us?" is, "God made us to show forth His goodness." But the principal way in which God's goodness is demonstrated is in the fact that He made us with spiritual and immortal souls, capable of sharing His own happiness. Even in human affairs we feel that the goodness of a person is shown by the generosity with which that person shares himself and his possessions with others. Likewise is the goodness of God shown, above all, by the fact that He shares His own happiness, He shares *Himself* with us.

That is why, in answering from our own point of view the question "Why did God make us?", we say that He made us "to share with us His everlasting happiness in heaven." The two answers are like the two sides of the same coin, front and back. It is God's goodness that caused Him to share His happiness with us, and it is God's sharing His happiness with us that shows forth His goodness.

Well, what *is* this happiness that we keep talking about, this happiness for which God made us? To answer that, let us begin with the example of an American soldier who is stationed at an army base overseas. One day, while reading a copy of his hometown paper, mailed to him by his mother, the soldier runs across the picture of a girl. The soldier doesn't know the girl. He has never even heard about her before. But as he looks at the picture the soldier says to himself, "Gee, but I like that girl's looks. There's a girl I'd like to marry."

The girl's address is under her picture, and the soldier gets up nerve enough to write to her, hardly expecting an answer. Yet an answer does come, and the boy and girl begin a regular correspondence. They exchange pictures, they tell one another all about themselves. Every day the soldier grows more and more in love with this girl he has never seen.

Then, finally, the soldier is shipped home. For two years he has been worshiping his girl from afar. Because of his love for her, he has been a better soldier and a better man. He has tried to be the sort of fellow that girl would want him to be. He has done the things she would like him to do, and has kept from doing anything that would displease her if she knew about it. It is actually a hunger for the girl that he has had in his heart—and now he is coming home.

Can we imagine the happiness that will tingle in every fiber of that boy's being as he steps off the train and at long last takes his girl in his arms? "Oh!" he exclaims as they embrace, "oh, if only this moment could last forever!" His happiness is the happiness of *love fulfilled*, love finding itself at last in complete possession of the person loved. We call it the *fruition* of love. The boy always will look back to this moment—this moment when his distant longing suddenly is rewarded with the first actual meeting—he will look back to this as one of the happiest moments of his life upon earth.

It is the best example, too, that we can give of the nature of the happiness of heaven. It is a woefully imperfect example, a most inadequate example, but it is the best that we can find. For the primary happiness of heaven exists exactly in this, that we shall possess the infinitely perfect God, and be possessed by Him, in a union so utterly complete that we cannot now even faintly imagine the ecstasy of it.

It will not be a human being, however wonderful, that we

possess. It will be to God Himself that we shall be personally and consciously united; God Who is infinite Goodness and Truth and Beauty; God Who is *everything*, and Whose infinite love can (as no human love possibly can) fulfill every craving and desire of the human heart. We shall then know a ravishing happiness such as "Eye has not seen nor ear heard, nor has it entered into the heart of man," to quote St. Paul (1 Cor. 2:9). And it is a happiness which, once achieved, we can never lose.

This does not mean that it will continue on and on, through hours and months and years. Time is something that belongs to the perishable world of matter. Time is a measure of change. Once we leave this world behind us, we also leave time as we know it. For us, eternity will not be "a long time." The succession of moments which we shall experience in heaven—the type of duration to which theologians have given the name of *aevum*—will not be a clock-measured cycle of minutes and hours. There will be no feeling of "waiting," no sense of monotony, no looking ahead to tomorrow. For us, "NOW" will be all that matters.

That is the wonderful thing about heaven—that it never ends. We shall be absorbed in the possession of the greatest Love that exists, of which the keenest human love is but a pale shadow. And our ecstasy will not be marred by the thought that one day we must surrender it, as is the case with all merely human happiness.

Of course, no one is perfectly happy in this life. Sometimes people think that they will be perfectly happy if they can get everything they want. But when they get it—health and wealth and fame, loving family and loyal friends—they find that there still is something missing. They still aren't genuinely happy; there still is something that the heart hungers for. There are wiser people who know that worldly well-being is a deceptive source of happiness. Too often, worldly goods are like salt water to a thirsty man, increasing instead of satisfying the craving for happiness. These wiser people have discovered that there is no happiness so deep and so abiding as that which grows out of a living faith in God, and an active, fruitful love for God. But even these wiser ones find that their happiness in this life is never perfect, never complete. Indeed, it is they more than anyone else who feel the inadequacy of this world's happiness.

And it is right here—in the fact that no human ever is perfectly happy in this life—that we have one of our proofs for the existence of everlasting happiness beyond the grave. God, Who is infinitely good, would not place in human hearts this desire for perfect happiness if there were no way in which that desire could be satisfied. God does not torture with frustration the souls whom He has made.

But even if the material or spiritual riches of this life *could* satisfy every human want, there would still be the knowledge that one day death would take it all from us— and our happiness would be incomplete. In heaven, on the contrary, not only shall we be happy to the utmost capacity of our heart, but we also shall have that final perfecting happiness of knowing that nothing can take our happiness from us. It is eternally secure.

What Must I Do?

Many people, it is to be feared, look forward to heaven as a place where they will see their departed loved ones, rather than as a place where they will see God. It is true that we shall know our loved ones in heaven, and shall rejoice at their presence. When we are with God, we are with everyone else who is with God. We shall be happy that our loved ones are there, as God is happy that they are there. We shall want those we have left behind to reach heaven too, as God wants them to reach heaven.

But heaven is something more than a family reunion. God is the one Who will matter, to all of us. On an infinitely higher scale, it will be something like having an audience with the Holy Father. Each member of the family who are visiting the Vatican is glad that the others are there. But when the Pope steps through the door into the audience chamber, it is to him that all eyes and thoughts are mainly directed. Similarly, we shall know and love each other in heaven—but we shall know and love each other *in God*.

It cannot too often be emphasized that the happiness of heaven consists essentially in the intellectual vision of God —the final and complete possession of the God Whom we have desired and loved weakly at a distance. And if that is to be our destiny—to be eternally united with God in love —then it follows that we must begin to love God here in this life.

God cannot fulfill something that does not even exist. If there is no beginning of love for God in our hearts here upon earth, then there can be no *fruition* of love in eternity. That indeed is why God has placed us here upon earth: so that, by loving Him, we may lay the necessary foundation for the happiness of heaven.

In the previous chapter we talked about a soldier who, at a distant post, sees a girl's picture in the paper and falls in love with her. He begins writing to the girl, and ends up by having her for his very own when he eventually returns home. It is evident that if the boy had not been impressed by the girl's picture in the first place, or if he had lost interest after the exchange of a few letters and had stopped writing—it is evident that the girl would have meant nothing to the boy when he got back home. Even if she happened to be on the station platform when the train arrived, she would be just another face in the crowd to him. His heart would not jump at the sight of her.

Similarly, unless we begin to love God in this life, there is no way in which we can be united with God in eternity. For one who would go into eternity with no love for God in his heart, heaven would simply not exist. Just as a man without eyes cannot see the beauty of the world around him, so the man without love for God cannot see God; he goes into eternity blind. It is not a case of God's saying to the un-

repentant sinner (sin being simply a denial of love to God):
"You do not love Me. I want no part of you. Go to hell!"
The man who dies without love for God—that is, in unrepented sin—has made his own choice. God is there, but
he cannot see God; just as the sun still shines, though the
blind man cannot see it.

It is evident that we cannot love someone we do not know.
That brings us to another duty which we have in this life.
We must learn all that we can about God, so that we may
love Him, and keep our love alive, and grow in love for
Him. Going back again to our imaginary soldier: If the boy
had never seen that girl's picture, he certainly never would
have loved her. He could not love someone he had never
heard of. Even after seeing the picture and being impressed
with the girl's appearance, if the boy had not written and
found out through correspondence what a swell girl she
was, his first impulse of interest would never have developed
into an ardent love.

That is why we "study religion." That is why we have
catechism lessons in school, religion courses in high school
and college. That is why we listen to sermons on Sunday
and read Catholic books and periodicals. That is why we
have religious discussion clubs. It is all part of what we
might call our "correspondence" with God. It is all part of
our effort to know Him better, so that we may develop a
love for Him, grow in love for Him, and preserve our love
for Him.

There is, of course, only one rock-bottom way of proving our love for anyone. That is by doing the things that
will please the one we love, by doing what the loved person
wants us to do. Taking once more the example of our soldier boy: If, while claiming to love his girl and wanting to
marry her, he at the same time spent his time and money on
prostitutes and drunkenness, he would be a liar of the first
water. It would not be real love at all, else he would try to
be the kind of a man his girl wanted him to be.

Likewise, there is only one way in which we can prove our love for God. That is by doing what God wants us to do, by being the kind of human being He wants us to be. Love for God does not reside in the emotions. Love for God does not mean that our heart must turn handsprings when we think of Him. Some people *may* feel their love for God in an emotional way, but that is not at all essential. Because love for God resides in our *will*. It is not in how we *feel* toward God, but in what we are willing to *do* for God that our love for Him proves itself.

And the more we do for God here, the greater will be our happiness in heaven. That may seem like a paradox, to say that some in heaven will be happier than others, when already we have said that everyone will be *perfectly* happy in heaven. But there is no contradiction. Those who have loved God more in this life will find greater joy in the fulfillment of that love in heaven. A man who loves a girl a little will find happiness in marrying the girl. But a man who loves a girl a lot will find even greater happiness than the first man, in the fulfillment of his love. Similarly, as our love for God increases (and our obedience to His will) so also does our capacity for happiness-in-God increase.

Consequently, while it is quite true that every soul in heaven will be perfectly happy, it also is true that some will have a greater *capacity* for happiness than others. To use an old example: a quart bottle and a pint bottle may both be full—but the quart bottle will hold more than the pint bottle. Or to use another example: six different people may listen to a symphony concert, and each be happily absorbed in the music. But there will be six different degrees of enjoyment, depending upon the musical knowledge and musical appreciation of each person.

All of this, then, is what the catechism means when it asks, "What must we do to gain the happiness of heaven?" and answers by saying, "To gain the happiness of heaven we must know, love and serve God in this world." That middle word, "love," is the key word, the essential word. But there is no love without knowledge, so we must know God in order to love Him. And there is no true love unless it manifests itself in action—in the doing of what the loved one wants. So we must also *serve* God.

However, before we leave the question of "What Must I Do?" it is well to recall that God does not leave us to our own human weakness in this matter of knowing, loving and serving Him. The happiness of heaven is itself a supernatural happiness. It is not something to which our human nature has any right. It is a happiness that is above (super) nature. Even though we love God, it still would be impossible for us to see God in heaven if God did not give us a special power. This special power which God gives to the souls in heaven, a power that is not a part of our human nature, a power to which we have no right, is called the "light of glory." If it were not for the light of glory, the highest happiness to which we could aspire would be the natural happiness of limbo. That would be a happiness very much like the happiness a saint enjoys in this life, when he is in close and ecstatic union with God but does not see God.

The happiness of heaven, then, is a *supernatural* happiness. That we may achieve it, God gives us the supernatural helps which we call grace. If God left us to our own purely natural strength, we never could achieve the kind of love that will merit heaven for us. It is a special kind of love. We call it "charity," and God implants the seed of it in our will at Baptism. So long as we do our part, by seeking, accepting and using the successive graces which God provides, this supernatural love for God will grow in us, and will bear fruit.

Heaven is a supernatural reward, to be achieved through the living of a supernatural life. To know, love and serve God, under the impulse of God's grace—that *is* a supernatural life. It is the whole plan, the whole philosophy of a truly Christian life.

Who Will Tell Me?

Here is a little scene that easily could happen: The manager of a manufacturing plant takes one of his workers over to a new machine that has just been installed. It is a huge and complicated machine. The manager says to the workman, "Now I am going to put you in charge of this machine. If you do a good job with it, you'll get a bonus of five thousand dollars at the end of the year. But it is an expensive machine; if you mess it up, out you go on your ear. Here is a book that explains the machine. Now get to work!"

"Wait a minute!" the worker well might say. "If this is going to mean the difference between a pile of money and no job at all, I want more than a book. A book is too easy to misunderstand. And besides, you can't ask questions of a book. How about getting somebody over here from the place where they make these machines? He can tell me all about it and see that I get it straight."

It is a reasonable request that the workman makes, and a sensible one too. Likewise we, when we are told that our whole job on earth is "to know, love and serve God," and that our eternal happiness depends upon how well we do that, we also very reasonably ask, "Who is going to tell me how, who is going to tell me the things I need to know?"

God already has anticipated that question and has answered it. And God has not merely put a book in our hands, to let us puzzle over it as best we can. God has sent us Someone from "Headquarters" to tell us the things we need to know and to do in order to work out our destiny. God has sent no one less than His own Divine Son, in the Person of Jesus Christ. Jesus did not come upon earth for the single purpose of dying upon the Cross to atone for our sins. Jesus came also to teach, and to demonstrate. He came to teach us the truths about God that will lead to love for God —and to *show* us how to live so as to prove that love.

Jesus, in His physical, visible presence returned to heaven on Ascension Thursday. Nevertheless He contrived a means by which He still could remain with us as our Teacher, until the end of time. With His twelve Apostles as the core, the nucleus, Jesus fashioned a new kind of Body for Himself. It is a Mystical rather than a physical Body by means of which He remains upon earth. The cells of this Body are people, rather than protoplasm. The Head of the Body is Jesus Himself, and the Soul of the Body is the Holy Spirit. The Voice of the Body, continuing to speak to us, to teach us and to guide us, is the Voice of Christ Himself. This Body, the Mystical Body of Christ, we call the Church.

As Peter and the other Apostles were the core of the Church in the beginning, so Peter's successor, the Pope, and the other bishops who have succeeded the Apostles, are the core of the Church today. It is into their hands that Jesus has entrusted the fullness of His teachings. It is through them that the Voice of Jesus comes to us. It is they whom Jesus preserves from error when they tell us, "This is what Jesus Christ teaches; this we must believe, this we must do!"

That is what the catechism means when it asks, as we also ask, "From whom do we learn to know, love and serve God?" and answers: "We learn to know, love and serve God from Jesus Christ the Son of God, Who teaches us through the Catholic Church." And, that we may have at our finger tips the principal truths taught by Christ, the Church has compacted those truths together in the declaration of faith which we call the Apostles' Creed. These are the fundamental truths upon which a Christian life is built.

The Apostles' Creed is such an ancient prayer that no one knows exactly when it was first formulated in its present wording. It goes back to the early days of Christian beginnings. The Apostles, before they separated after Pentecost and set out on their missionary journeyings through the world, certainly drew up some kind of a summary of the essential truths which Christ had entrusted to them. By doing so, they all would be sure to cover these essential truths in their preaching. It would be also a declaration of belief to which all prospective converts would be required to subscribe before being admitted by Baptism to Christ's Mystical Body.

We, then, can be very sure that when we begin, "I believe in God, the Father Almighty . . ." we are reciting in substance the very same profession of faith which the first converts to Christianity—Cornelius and Apollos and Aquila and Priscilla and all the rest—so proudly recited and so joyfully sealed with their blood.

Some of the truths which we have in the Apostles' Creed are truths which, under ideal conditions, we could figure out for ourselves. Such are the fact that God exists, that He is almighty, that He is the Creator of heaven and earth. Other truths are known to us only because God has made them known—such as the fact that Jesus Christ is the Son of God, and that there are three Persons in one God. The whole body of truths which God has made known to us (some of them things which we could have figured out by ourselves, some of them things beyond the reach of our reason)—this whole body of truth is called "divine revelation." That is, it is truth which has been revealed to us by God. ("To reveal" comes from a Latin word which means "to draw back the veil.")

God's unveiling of Himself to mankind began with the truths He made known to our first father, Adam. Down through the centuries God kept drawing the veil back a little farther, a little farther. He made revelations concerning Himself—and us—to the Patriarchs, such as Noe and Abraham; to Moses and the prophets who followed after Moses, such as Jeremias and Daniel.

From Adam until the coming of Christ, the truths revealed to us by God are called "pre-Christian revelation." They were a bit-by-bit preparation for the grand unfolding of divine truth which God was to make through His Son Jesus Christ. The truths made known to us by our Lord, whether directly or through His Apostles under the inspiration of the Holy Ghost, we call "Christian revelation."

Through Jesus Christ, God completed the public revelation of Himself to mankind. He has told us, now, all that we need to know in order to get to heaven. He has told us all we need to know in order to fulfill our destiny and to achieve eternal union with God Himself. Consequently, after the death of the last Apostle (St. John), there were no "new" truths which the virtue of faith would require us to believe.

With the passing years, men would make use of their God-given intelligences to examine, compare and study the truths revealed by Christ. Like a bud unfolding, the deposit of Christian truth would respond to the thought and examination of great minds in each generation.

Naturally, then, we in the twentieth century *understand* Christ's teachings much better than did the Christians of the first century. But faith does not depend upon fullness of understanding. So far as the truths themselves are concerned, we today believe exactly the same truths which the first Christians believed—the truths which they received from Christ and His spokesmen, the Apostles.

When St. Peter's successor, the Pope, solemnly defines a dogma—such as the dogma of the Assumption—he is not suddenly presenting us with a new truth to be believed. He is simply giving us public notice that here is a truth which goes back to the Apostles, and that consequently we must believe it.

Since the time of Christ there have been many times when God has made things known privately to individual saints or holy people. These messages are classified as "private" revelations. Unlike the "public" revelations made to us through Christ and His Apostles, they command the assent only of those for whom they are made. Even such famous apparitions as those at Lourdes and Fatima, or the apparitions of the Sacred Heart to St. Margaret Mary, are not what we call "matters of divine faith." If clear and certain evidence tells us that the apparitions are genuine, we should be foolhardy to question them. But even if we denied them, we should not be guilty of heresy. Such private revelations are not a part of the "deposit of faith."

While we are on the subject of divine revelation, we might take note of the volume in which many of God's revelations have been written down for us: the Holy Bible. We call the Bible the Word of God, because it was God Himself Who inspired the writers of the various "books" which make up the Bible. God inspired them to write down the things which He wanted written, *and nothing else*. By His direct action upon the mind and the will of the writer (whether Isaias or Ezechiel or Matthew or Luke), God the Holy Ghost dictated what He wanted written. It was, of course, an interior and silent dictation. The writer would write in his own style of expression. He might not even realize what was moving him to put down the things he was writing. He might not realize that he was writing under the influence of divine inspiration. Yet the Holy Ghost would be guiding every stroke of his pen.

It is evident, then, that the Bible is not free from error because the Church, after a searching examination, has declared it free from error. The Bible is free from error because God Himself is its author, the human writer being merely God's instrument. The Church's role has been to tell us which of the ancient writings *are* the inspired ones, and to preserve them, and to interpret them for us.

We know, of course, that not all of what Jesus taught is contained in the Bible. We know that many of the truths which make up the deposit of faith have come down to us through the oral teaching of the Apostles, transmitted from generation to generation through the bishops, who are the Apostles' successors. This is what we call the Tradition of the Church: truths handed on from age to age through the living Voice of Christ in His Church.

It is in these twin sources—the Bible and Tradition—that we find the completeness of divine revelation, the truths which we *must* believe.

CHAPTER II

God and His Perfections

Who Is God?

I once read of a Sunday-school teacher who claimed to have lost his faith because a little child asked him, "Who made God?" and the teacher suddenly realized that he had no answer to that question. I find it hard to believe the incident, because it does seem that anyone intelligent enough to teach a Sunday-school class would know that the answer is "Nobody."

The principal proof for the existence of God lies in the fact that nothing happens unless something causes it to happen. Cookies don't disappear from the cooky jar unless someone's fingers snitched them. An oak tree doesn't grow up out of the ground unless an acorn was dropped there. The philosophers express it by saying, "Every effect must have a cause."

So if we trace the development of the physical universe back to its beginnings (a million years or a billion years, whatever the scientists want to make it), we eventually come to the point where we have to ask, "All right, but who started it all off? *Somebody* had to start things, or there would be no universe. From nothing, nothing comes." Babies come from parents, and flowers grow from seeds, but there has to be a starting point. There must be someone who wasn't made by anyone else. There must be someone who *always* existed, someone who never had a beginning. There must be someone of limitless power and intelligence whose very *nature* it is to exist.

There is such a someone—and that Someone is exactly He Whom we call God. God is He Who exists by His very nature. The only exact description we can give of God is to say, "He is Who is." So that the answer to the child who asks, "Who made God?" is simply, "No one made God. He always was, and He always will be."

We express this concept of God, this fact that He is the source of all being, above and beyond all else that exists, by saying that He is the Supreme Being. It follows that there can be but *one* God. To speak of two (or more) supreme beings would be a contradiction. The very word "supreme" means "above all others." If there were two equally powerful Gods side by side, then neither of them would be supreme. Neither would have the infinite power which God by His nature must have. The "infinite" power of the one would cancel out the "infinite" power of the other. Each would be limited by the other. As St. Athanasius puts it, "To speak of several equally powerful Gods is like speaking of several equally powerless Gods."

There is but one God—and He is a Spirit. To understand that we must know that philosophers distinguish two kinds of substances: spiritual substances and physical substances. A physical substance is one that is made up of parts. The air that we breathe, for example, is made up of nitrogen and oxygen. The nitrogen and oxygen in turn are made up of molecules, and the molecules of atoms, and the atoms of neutrons and protons. Every bit of the material universe is made up of physical substances. Physical substance has within itself the elements of its own dissolution, since its parts can be separated through corruption or destruction.

In a spiritual substance, however, there are no parts. There is nothing that can ever be broken up, or corrupted, or separated, or divided. This is expressed in philosophy by saying that a spiritual substance is a *simple* substance. And this is why a spiritual substance is immortal. Outside of a direct act of God, there is no way in which it can cease to exist.

There are three classes of spiritual substances which we know about. First of all there is God Himself, the infinitely perfect Spirit. Then there are angels, and finally there are human souls. In each case there is an intelligence without dependence upon *physical* substance for its actions. It is true that in this life our soul is united with a physical body, and is dependent upon the body for its activities. But this is not an *absolute* and permanent dependence. When disunited from the body at death, the soul still will function. It still will know and love, even more freely than during its mortal life.

If we want to try to imagine what a spirit is "like" (pretty difficult, since "to imagine" means "to picture," and there is nothing to picture); if we want to grasp for an idea of a spirit, we can think of what we would be like if our body suddenly melted away. We still would be conscious of our own identity and personality; we still would retain all the knowledge that we have, all the loves that we have. We still would be ME—but the body would be gone. We then would be a spirit.

If "spirit" is a hard word to deal with, "infinite" is even more difficult. "Infinite" means "not finite," and "finite" in turn means "limited." A thing is limited if there is an outermost boundary or capacity beyond which there is no passing. Everything created is limited in some fashion. There is a limit to the amount of water that the Pacific Ocean will hold. There is a limit to the energy of the hydrogen atom.

There is a limit even to the holiness of the Blessed Virgin Mary. *But with God there is no limit of any kind*, no limit in any direction.

The catechism tells us that God is "an infinitely perfect Spirit." This means that there is nothing good or desirable or worth while that is not found in God to an absolutely limitless degree. Indeed, it would be better to turn it around and say that there is nothing good or desirable or worth while in the universe that is not a reflection (a little "splinter" may we say?) of that same quality as it exists immeasurably in God. The beauty of a flower, for example, is a tiny reflection of God's unbounded beauty—much as a fugitive moonbeam is a tiny reflection of the blazing light of the sun.

The perfections of God are of the very *substance* of God. If we wish to speak with precise accuracy, we do not say that "God is good." Rather we say, "God IS goodness." God, strictly speaking, is not wise; God IS wisdom.

We cannot hope to discuss here all of the wonderful perfections of God, but at least let us look at a few of them. We already have touched upon one of God's perfections— His eternity. Men and angels may be said to be eternal, in so far as they will never die. But they did have a beginning and are subject to change. Only God is eternal in the absolute sense; not only will He never die, but never was there a time when He did not exist. He always will be—as He always was, without change forever.

God, as we have said, is infinite goodness. There is absolutely no limit to His goodness. Such is His infinite goodness that to see Him will be to love Him with an irresistible love. And His goodness pours itself out continually upon us.

Someone may ask, "If God is so good, why does He allow so much suffering and evil in the world? Why does He allow wars and crimes and sickness and misery?" Whole books have been written on the problem of evil, and we cannot hope to do justice to the subject here. We can point out, however, that evil—physical as well as moral—as it affects human beings, came into the world as a consequence of man's sin. Having set His plan for mankind in motion, having given man a free will, God does not keep constantly stepping in to snatch back His gift of freedom. With the free will that God has given us, we must work out our destiny together until the end—with the help of God's grace if we will accept and use it—toward everlasting happiness if we so direct ourselves, but freely to the end.

Evil is man's idea, not God's. And if the innocent and the good must suffer from the depravity of the wicked, their reward in the end will be the greater. Their pains and their tears will be as nothing in the joy that will come. Meanwhile, God has always in His keeping those who have God in their hearts.

Next there is the fact of God's infinite knowledge. All of time—past, present and future; all things that are and all things that even *could* be; all possible knowledge, is what we might call "just one big thought" in the mind of God. All of Time and all of Creation is encompassed within the mind of God, somewhat as the infant is encompassed within the mother's womb.

Does God know what I am going to do tomorrow? Yes. And next week? Yes. Then doesn't that mean that I *have* to do it? Isn't that the end of free will? If God knows that I am going to visit Aunt Gussie on Tuesday, how can I help doing it?

That apparent difficulty, which a moment's thought will resolve, stems from confusing God as a *knower* with God as a *causer*. God's knowing that I shall go to Aunt Gussie's isn't what makes me go there. It is the other way around. It is my choosing to go to Aunt Gussie's that provides the occasion for God's knowing it. The fact that the weather man, studying his maps, knows that it is going to rain tomorrow is not what makes the rain fall. On the contrary, it is the fact that rain is going to fall that provides the weather man with the occasion, the indispensable condition for knowing it.

To be theologically exact, we should take note of the fact that, *absolutely* speaking, God is the cause of all that is and of all that happens. He is, by His very nature, the First Cause. That means that nothing exists and nothing happens that does not have its origin in God's infinite power. Here, however, there is no need to enter into a discussion of the philosophical question of causality. It is enough for our purpose to know that God's foreknowledge does not oblige me to do what I freely will to do.

Another perfection of God is that there is no limit to His presence; we say that He is "omnipresent." He is everywhere, all the time. How could it be otherwise, since there is no place outside of God? He is here in my room as I write, He is in your room as you read. If ever a space ship succeeds in reaching Mars or Venus, the pilot will not find himself alone when he gets to his planet; God will be there.

This limitless presence of God, be it noted, has nothing to do with size. Size is concerned only with physical matter. "Big" and "little" are meaningless terms when applied to any spirit, much less to God. No, it is not that one part of God is in one place and part in another. *All* of God is *everywhere*. In reference to God, space is as meaningless as size.

Another perfection of God is His infinite power. He is almighty; He can do or make anything. "Can He draw a square circle?" someone asks. No, because a square circle is not a something, it is a no-thing, a contradiction in terms, like a daylight night. "Can God commit a sin?" Again no, because sin too is a no-thing, a failure to give obedience to God. In short, God can do anything, but He does not do no-things.

God is infinitely wise too. He made all things in the first place, so certainly He knows best how to use the things which He has made, how best to plan for His creatures. One who is tempted to complain, "Why does God do that?"

or "Why doesn't God do so-and-so?" should remember that an ant has more right to criticize an Einstein than has man with his limited intelligence to question the infinite wisdom of God.

The infinite holiness of God scarcely needs remarking. The spiritual beauty of Him from Whom all human holiness flows, we take for granted. We know that even the spotless holiness of the Blessed Virgin Mary, when compared to the dazzling splendor of God, would be like a match flame compared to the sun.

And God is all-merciful. As often as we repent, so often will God forgive. There is a limit to your patience and mine, but no limit to the infinite mercy of God. Yet He also is infinitely just. God is not a doting grandmother, closing His eyes to our sins. He wants us in heaven, but His mercy cannot defeat His justice if we refuse Him the love which is the purpose of our being.

All of this, and more, is what we mean when we say that "God is an infinitely perfect Spirit."

CHAPTER III

The Unity and Trinity of God

How Are There Three?

None of us, I am sure, would care to have the task of explaining a problem in nuclear physics to a five-year-old child. Yet the gap between a five-year-old's intelligence and the upper reaches of science are as nothing compared to the gap between the most brilliant human mind and the true nature of God. There is a limit to what the human mind, even at its best, can grasp and understand. Since God is an infinite Being, no created intellect, however gifted, can plumb His depths.

That is why God, in revealing to us the truth about Himself, often has to be content with simply telling us what the truth is; the how of the truth is so far beyond our grasp in this life that even God doesn't try to explain it to us.

One such truth is the fact that although there is only one God, yet in that one God there are three divine Persons—the Father, the Son, and the Holy Spirit. There is only one divine nature, but there are three divine Persons. In human affairs, nature and person are practically one and the same thing; we say that nature and person are "coterminous." If there are three persons in a room, then there are three human natures; and if there is only one human nature present, then there is only one human person. So when we try to think of God as three Persons possessing one and the same nature, we find ourselves batting our head against the ceiling.

That is why we call such truths of faith as that of the Blessed Trinity a "mystery" of faith. We believe it is so because God says it is so; and He is all-wise and all-truthful. As to just how it can be so, we must await God's full unveiling of Himself in heaven, to discover.

Theologians do of course cast some light upon the mystery for us. They explain that the distinction between the three Persons in God is based upon the relationship that exists between the three Persons. There is God the Father, Who looks into His divine mind and sees Himself as He really is, and forms a thought about Himself. You and I do the same thing, often. We turn our gaze inward, and see ourselves, and form a thought about ourselves. It is a thought which expresses itself in the silent words "John Smith" or "Mary Jones."

But there is this difference between our knowledge and God's knowledge of Himself: Our knowledge of ourselves is imperfect, incomplete. (Our friends could tell us things about ourselves that would surprise us—not to mention what our enemies could tell us!) Yet even if we did know ourselves perfectly; even if the thought we had about ourselves as we silently spoke our own name was a complete thought, a perfect reproduction, it still would be only a thought remaining inside us. The thought would have no existence of its own, no life of its own. The thought would cease to exist, even in my own mind, the minute I turned my attention to something else. The reason is that existence, or life, is not a necessary part of the picture of myself. There was a time when I did not exist at all. And I immediately would fall back into nothingness if God did not keep me in existence.

But with God things are very different. It is of the very nature of God to exist. There is no other way of thinking straight about God, except to think of Him as the Being Who never had a beginning, the Being Who always was and always will be. The only real definition we can give of God is to say, "He is Who is." That is the way, you will remember, that God described Himself to Moses: "I am Who am."

If the thought that God has of Himself, then, is to be an infinitely complete and perfect thought, it must include existence, since to exist is of the very nature of God. The image that God sees of Himself, the silent Word that He eternally speaks of Himself, must have a distinct existence of Its own. It is this Living Thought which God has of Himself, this Living Word in which He perfectly expresses Himself, Whom we call God the Son. God the Father is God, knowing Himself; God the Son is the expression of God's knowledge of Himself. Thus the second Person of the Blessed Trinity is called the Son precisely because, from all eternity, He is generated, He is begotten, in the divine mind of the Father. He also is called the Word of God, because He is the "mental word" in which the divine mind gives utterance to the thought of Himself.

Now God the Father (God knowing Himself) and God the Son (God's knowledge of Himself) contemplate the divine nature which They possess in common. As they gaze (we speak of course in human terms), they behold in that nature all that is beautiful and good—all, in short, that commands love—to an infinite degree. And so the divine will moves in an act of infinite love—for the divine goodness and beauty. Since God's love for Himself, like God's knowledge of Himself, is of the very nature of God, it must be a living love. This infinitely perfect, infinitely intense, living love which flows eternally from Father and Son is He Whom we call the Holy Ghost, "proceeding from the Father and the Son." He is the third Person of the Most Blessed Trinity.

God the Father is God, knowing Himself.

God the Son is the expression of God's knowledge of Himself.

God the Holy Spirit is the result of God's love for Himself.

This is the Blessed Trinity—three divine Persons in one God, one divine nature.

Here is a little illustration that may make somewhat clearer the relationship that exists between the three divine Persons: Father, Son and Holy Spirit.

Suppose you look at yourself in a full-length mirror. You see there an image of yourself that is perfect except for one thing: it is not a living image; it is just a reflection in the glass. But if that image were to step out of the mirror and stand beside you, living and breathing like yourself—then it would be a perfect image indeed. There would not be two of you. There would be just one YOU, one human nature. There would be two "persons," but only one mind and one will, sharing the same knowledge and the same thoughts.

Then, since self-love (the right kind of self-love) is natural to an intelligent being, there would flow between you and your image an ardent love, one for the other. Now give your fancy free rein, and think of this love as being so much a part of yourself, so deeply rooted in your very nature, as to be a living, breathing reproduction of yourself. This love would be a "third person" (still only one YOU, remember; only one human nature), a third person standing between you and your image, the three of you linked hand in hand, three persons in one human nature.

Perhaps this flight of imagination may help us toward a faint understanding of the relationship that exists between the three Persons of the Blessed Trinity: God the Father "looking at" Himself in His divine mind and beholding there the Image of Himself Which is so infinitely perfect that It is a living image, God the Son; and God the Father and God the Son loving the divine nature which they possess in common as a living love, God the Holy Ghost. Three divine Persons, one divine nature.

If the example which I used does not help us at all in our thinking about the Blessed Trinity, we should not let ourselves feel frustrated. We are dealing with a mystery of faith; no one, not even the greatest theologian, can hope in this life to really understand it. At best, there will merely be varying degrees of ignorance.

Neither should we feel frustrated that there are mysteries of faith. Only a person suffering from consummate pride of intellect would expect to fully understand the infinite, the inexhaustible depth of God's nature. Rather than resenting our human limitations, we should be moved to gratitude that God has chosen to tell us as much as He has about Himself, about His own inner nature.

One error we must guard against in our thinking about the Blessed Trinity: We must not think of God the Father as having "come first," and God the Son a little later, and God the Holy Ghost later still. All three are equally eternal, possessing as They do the one divine nature; God's Thought and God's Love are equally timeless with God's Nature. And God the Son and God the Holy Spirit are not in any way subordinate to God the Father; one is not more powerful, nor wiser, nor greater than the other. All three possess the same infinite perfection, an equality rooted in the one divine nature which They equally possess.

However, we do attribute to the individual divine Persons certain works, certain activities that seem most suitable to the particular relationship of this or that divine Person. For example, it is to God the Father that we attribute the work of creation, since we think of Him as the "generator," the instigator, the starter of things, the seat of the infinite power which God possesses.

Similarly, since God the Son is the Knowledge or the Wisdom of the Father, we ascribe to Him the works of wisdom; it was He Who came upon earth to make truth known to us, and to heal the breach between God and man.

Finally, since the Holy Ghost is infinite Love, we appropriate to Him the works of love, particularly the sanctification of souls, since sanctification results from the indwelling of God's Love within the soul.

God the Father is the Creator, God the Son is the Redeemer, God the Holy Spirit is the Sanctifier. And yet what One does, All do; where One is, All are.

That is the mystery of the Most Blessed Trinity—the infinite variety in absolute unity Whose beauty will ravish us in heaven.

CHAPTER IV

Creation and the Angels

How Did Creation Begin?

Sometimes a dress designer or a pastry cook or a per-fume manufacturer will boast of a "new creation." When they do so, they are using the word "creation" in a very loose way. No matter how fresh a new style of dress may be, it began with a fabric of some kind. No matter how delectable a dessert, or how delightful a fragrance may be, they began with some kind of ingredients.

To "create" means to "make out of nothing." Only God, Whose power is infinite, can do that. Accurately speaking, only God can create.

There are scientists today who labor patiently in labora-tories, hoping to "create" new life in a test tube. Over and over again, through repeated failures, they mix their chemi-cals and rearrange their molecules. Whether or not they may someday be successful in synthesizing a living cell, I do not know. But even if their patience should be so re-warded, they still will not have "created" new life. They will have been working, all along, with materials which God has provided.

When God creates He has no need of materials or tools to work with. He simply WILLS that a thing should be—and there it is. "Let there be light," said God in the beginning, "and there was light. . . . Let there be a firmament in the midst of the waters," said God, "and so it was" (Gen. 1:3, 6).

Not only is it God's creative will that has brought all things into existence, it is God's will also that KEEPS them in existence. If God were to withdraw His sustaining will from any of His creatures, that very instant the creature would cease to exist; it would fall back into the nothingness from which it came.

The earliest works of God's creation which are known to us (He hasn't necessarily told us everything) are the angels. An angel is a spirit—that is, a being with an intelligence and a will, but without a body, without any dependence at all upon matter. The human soul, too, is a spirit, but the human soul will not be an angel, even during the time after death when it is separated from the body, awaiting the resurrection.

The human soul was made to be united to a physical body. We say that the soul has an "affinity" for its body. A human person, composed of body and soul, is not complete without the body. We may talk more of that when we come to discuss the resurrection of the body. At the moment we wish only to emphasize that an angel is a complete person without a body or need for a body, and that an angel is a being far superior to a human being.

Nowadays there is much fanciful talk about "men from Mars." These supposed inhabitants of our neighboring planet usually are represented as being much more intelligent and powerful than we earth-bound mortals. But even the most ingenious writer of science fiction could never do justice to the breath-taking beauty, the surpassing intelligence, and the tremendous power of an angel. If this is true of the lowest order of the angelic host—the angels properly so-called—what shall we say of the ascending orders of pure spirits who are above the angels? They are identified for us in the Bible as archangels, principalities, powers, virtues, dominations, thrones, cherubim and seraphim. It is quite possible that an archangel is as much above an angel in perfections as an angel is above man.

Actually, of course, we know little about the angels, about their inner nature or the degree of distinction between them. We do not even know how many of them there are, although the Bible indicates their number is very great: "Thousands of thousands ministered to Him, and ten thousand times a hundred thousand stood before Him," says the Book of Daniel (7:10).

Only three of the angels have been named for us: Gabriel ("Hero of God"), Michael ("Who is like God?"), and Raphael ("God hath healed"). With regard to the angels, it almost seems that God has been content to give us a quick peek into the marvels and the magnificence that await us in the world beyond time and space. Like the lines of perspective which in a painting draw attention to the picture's central theme, so do the rising choirs of pure spirits draw our vision irresistibly to the supreme Majesty Who is God —to God Whose infinite perfection is immeasurably beyond that of even the exalted seraphim.

And this, let us remember, is not a world of fantasy and imagination that we are talking about. It is a world far more real than the planet Mars, more substantial even than the sod we tread. Best of all, it is a world to which we can go without benefit of interplanetary spaceships. It is a world to which we shall go if we wish.

When God made the angels, He made each with a will that was supremely free. We know that the price of heaven is love for God. It is by making an act of love for God that a spirit, whether an angel or a human soul, fits itself for heaven. The love must be proved in the only way in which love for God *can* be proved—by a free and voluntary submission of the created will to God, by what we commonly call an "act of obedience" or an "act of loyalty."

God made the angels with free wills so they might be capable of making their act of love, their choice of God. Only after they had done so would they see God face to face; only then would they enter into that everlasting union with God which we call "heaven."

God has not made known to us the nature of the test to which the angels were put. Many theologians think that God gave the angels a preview of Jesus Christ, the Redeemer of the human race and commanded that they adore Him . . . Jesus Christ in all His humiliations, a babe in the manger, a criminal on a cross. According to this theory, some of the angels rebelled at the prospect that they would have to adore God in the guise of a man. Conscious of their own spiritual magnificence, their beauty and their dignity, they could not bring themselves to the act of submission that adoration of Jesus Christ would demand of them. Under the leadership of one of the most gifted of all the angels, Lucifer ("Light-bearer"), the sin of pride turned many of the angels away from God, and there rang through heaven the awful cry, "We shall not serve!"

And thus hell began. Because hell is, essentially, the eternal separation of a spirit from Almighty God. Later on, when the human race would sin in the person of Adam, God would give the human race a second chance. But there was no second chance for the sinning angels. Because of the perfect clarity of their angelic minds and the unhampered freedom of their angelic wills, even the infinite mercy of God could find no excuse for the sin of the angels. They understood (to a degree that Adam never did) what the full consequence of their sin would be. With them there was no "temptation," in the sense in which we ordinarily understand the word. Theirs was what we would call a cold-blooded sin. By their deliberate and fully aware rejection of God, their wills were fixed against God, fixed forever. For them there was no turning back; they did not want to turn back. Their choice was made for eternity. There burns in them an everlasting hatred for God and all His works.

We do not know how many angels sinned; this is another point upon which God has not chosen to inform us. From references made to them in the Bible, we infer that the fallen angels (or "devils," as we commonly call them) are numerous. But it seems more probable that the great majority of the heavenly host remained faithful to God, made their act of submission to God, and are with God in heaven.

Frequently the devils are referred to as "Satan." Satan is a Hebrew word which means "adversary." The devils are, of course, the adversary, the enemy of mankind. In their undying hatred for God, it is natural that they should hate God's creature, man. Their hatred is even more understandable in the light of the belief that God created the human race precisely to replace the angels who sinned—to fill the gap in heaven left by their defection.

When they sinned, the fallen angels lost none of their natural endowments. The devils possess a keenness of intellect and a power over nature such as is unknown to mere man. All their cleverness and power are directed now toward keeping from heaven the souls which are destined for that place. The efforts of the devils are ceaselessly directed toward leading humans into their own path of rebellion against God. In other words, we say that the devils tempt us to commit sin.

We do not know exactly the limit of their power. We do not know how much control they have over nature, how much they may be able to steer the course of natural events so as to bring us up against a temptation—the point at which we must make a decision between God's will and our own will. We do know that the devil can never force us to commit sin. He cannot get inside the human soul and manipulate it to suit himself. He cannot destroy our freedom of choice. He cannot, so to speak, make us say "Yes" when we really want to say "No." But he is an adversary healthily to be feared and respected.

Is the Devil Real?

Someone has said that even the worst sinner spends more time doing things that are good and harmless than in doing things that are bad. In other words, there is some good even in the worst of us.

That is what makes it so hard for us really to understand the true nature of devils. The fallen angels are pure spirits without bodies. They are completely immaterial. When they set their wills against God by their act of rebellion, they embraced evil (which is rejection of God) with their entire nature. A devil is 100 percent evil, 100 percent hatred, without even the faintest pinpoint of good anywhere in his being.

Not the least of the horrors of hell will be the soul's constant and inescapable association with these spirits whose unrelieved malice is a living and an active force. In this life we are uncomfortable and unhappy if we find ourselves even briefly in the company of a manifestly evil person. We hardly can bear to think what it would be like to be linked for all eternity with a living depravity whose completeness and driving force are immeasurably beyond those of the most corrupt human.

We can hardly bear to think of it—but we should do so, at least occasionally. Our great present danger from the devil is that we may let ourselves forget that he is a living and active force in the world. An even greater danger is that we may let ourselves be influenced by the intellectual pride of unbelievers. Reading "clever" books and listening to "smart" people who patronizingly assume that the devil is a "medieval superstition" long since outgrown, we may unconsciously begin to think of the devil as a figure of speech, as an abstract symbol of evil without real existence.

And that would be a fatal mistake. Nothing would suit the devil better than to have us forget about him, or ignore him—above all, stop believing in him. An enemy whose presence is unsuspected, who can strike from ambush, is a doubly dangerous enemy. The devil's chances of victory increase in proportion to the blindness and the overconfidence of his victim.

What God has made, He does not unmake. What God has given, He does not take back. Having given the angels intelligence and powers of a high order, God did not revoke those gifts, not even from the angels who sinned. If a mere human can tempt us to sin: if a fellow worker can say, "Come on, Joe, let's go out tonight and hit the hot spots"; and if a neighbor woman can say, "Here is something I wish you'd try, Mary—you owe it to yourself not to have another baby for a while"—then certainly the devil can set before us temptation much more devious and much less obvious.

But the devil cannot make us sin. There is no power on earth or in hell that can make us sin. We still have our free will. It still remains with us to make the choice—and no one can force that choice upon us. Joe can say "No!" to the fellow worker who wants to paint the town red; Mary can say "No!" to the neighbor who recommends the contraceptive. And the temptations that the devil may place in our path, however enticing they be, can be just as firmly rejected. There can be no sin unless and until our will freely turns from God, and chooses a lesser good in preference to God. No one, ever, can truthfully say, "I sinned because I couldn't help it."

Not all temptations come from the devil, of course. Many temptations come from the world around us—even from our very friends and acquaintances, such as those mentioned above. Temptations can come also from the deep-seated forces within us which we call passions, passions that often are rebellious and imperfectly controlled as a result of original sin. But from whatever source the temptation may come, we know that we can conquer it if we have the will to do so.

God does not demand the impossible from anyone. He would not demand of us unyielding love and absolute loyalty unless it were possible for us to give them. Now, should we be troubled or frightened by the fact that we are tempted? It is by conquering temptation that we acquire merit before God. It is through temptation, met and defeated, that we grow in holiness. There would be little credit in being good if it were easy to be good. The great saints were not men and women who had no temptations; in most cases they were men and women who had tremendous temptations—and became saints by their victories.

We shall not, of course, win our battles by ourselves. We must have God's help to re-inforce our weakened wills. "Without Me you can do nothing," Jesus tells us. His help, His grace, is available to us in limitless abundance if we want it, if we seek it. Frequent confession, frequent Holy Communion and prayer (particularly in time of temptation) will make us proof against any temptation—provided we do our part.

We have no right to expect God to do it all. Unless we avoid unnecessary danger, unless we avoid those circumstances, so far as we can—those people, places and things that might entice us to sin—then we are not doing our part. If we go looking for danger, God's hands are tied. We have choked off grace at its very source.

Sometimes it is said of a person whose life or actions are particularly evil, "He must be possessed by the devil!" In most cases the words "possessed by the devil" are not meant literally; they simply indicate an abnormal degree of malice.

But there is such a thing as being possessed by the devil, really and literally. As we have pointed out previously, the full extent of the devil's power over the created universe, including mankind, is unknown to us. We do know that the devil can do nothing unless God permits. Yet we also know that God, having set His creative plan in motion, does not normally take back (either from the angels or from humans) any of the powers He originally bestowed.

In any case, both the Bible and human history, as well as the continuing experience of the Church, make it very plain that diabolical possession does happen. Diabolical possession means that the devil enters into the body of a person and takes control of that person's physical activities: his speech, his movements, his actions. But the devil cannot take over control of the person's soul; the freedom of the human soul remains inviolate, and not all the demons of hell can force it. During diabolical possession a person loses control over his own physical actions to a stronger power—the power of the devil. What the body does, is being done by the devil, not by the person himself.

There is another form of influence which the devil may exert. This is called diabolical obsession. In this case, the devil attacks a person from without rather than from within. He may pick the person up and dash him to the ground; cast him out of bed; torment him with hideous noises and other manifestations. St. John Vianney, the beloved Curé of Ars, was one who suffered much from this type of demoniac influence.

Both diabolical possession and obsession are rarely encountered nowadays in Christian lands; it seems that Christ's redeeming blood has shackled Satan's power. But they still do occur in pagan lands, as missionaries frequently testify; although not so noticeably as before Christ's redeeming Sacrifice.

The religious rite by which the devil is cast out of a person possessed or obsessed is called exorcism. In the ritual of the Church there is a special ceremony for this purpose, in which the Mystical Body of Christ calls upon the name and the power of her Head, Jesus Himself, to break Satan's hold upon a person. The office of exorcist belongs to every priest, but it may not be officially exercised except with special permission from the bishop, and then only after careful investigation has established that it really is a case of possession and not just mental illness.

There is, of course, nothing to prevent a priest from using his power of exorcism in a private, unofficial capacity. On a railroad train, for example, a priest listened unhappily to a torrent of blasphemy and profanity from the man in the seat ahead. Finally the priest said silently, "I command you, Satan, in the name of Jesus Christ the Son of God, to go back to hell and leave this man alone!" The blasphemous language stopped at once.

Another time the same priest spoke a similar private exorcism in the presence of a married couple who were quarreling bitterly—and immediately their anger subsided. The devil often is present and at work, even outside the extreme cases of possession and obsession.

We have talked at considerable length about the fallen angels only because of the grave danger involved should we take lightly their presence or their power. (God defend us from the devil's own most subtle trap—that is, ignoring his existence because it happens to be intellectually unfashionable to believe in him.) It seems much easier and much pleasanter to believe in the reality of the good angels; and of course their power for good is much greater than Satan's power for evil.

The angels who remained faithful to God are now with Him in heaven, engaged in the eternal love and adoration of God which one day (we pray) will be our lot also. Their will now is God's will. Like our Blessed Mother and the saints, the angels are intensely interested in our welfare, in seeing us come safely to heaven. They pray for us, as do the saints. They use their angelic power (whose extent again is unknown to us) to aid those who want and will accept their aid.

That the angels do help us is a matter of faith. If we do not believe that, we do not believe the Church, nor do we believe the Bible. That each of us has an individual guardian angel is not a matter of faith, but it is the commonly held belief of all Catholics. And as we honor God by our devotion to His friends and heroes, the saints, we shall make a great mistake if we fail to honor and to invoke His earlier masterpieces, the angels who people heaven and protect earth.

CHAPTER V

The Creation and the Fall of Man

What Is Man?

Man is the bridge between the world of spirit and the world of matter. (It is obvious, surely, that we use the word "man" to designate all members of the human race, male and female.)

The soul of man is a spirit and is similar to the nature of an angel; the body of a man is physical matter, similar in nature to an animal. Yet man is neither an angel nor a beast; he is a being in his own right, a being with one foot in time and one foot in eternity. Philosophers define man as "a rational animal"—the word "rational" indicating man's spiritual soul, the word "animal" indicating his physical body.

Considering how prone we humans are to pride and vanity, it is strange that we give so little thought to the fact that we *are* such marvelous beings. The body alone is sufficient cause for wonderment. The skin that covers our body, for example, is a protective sheath that would be worth millions to the scientist who could produce it for commercial use. It is elastic, it is self-renewing, it will not let in a particle of air or matter or water, and yet it will let all these things out. It maintains the body at a constant temperature of 98.6 degrees, regardless of weather and outside temperature.

When we look inside, the marvels of the body are even greater. There are the tissues and membranes and muscles that make up the organs: the heart and the lungs and the stomach and all the rest. Each organ is made up of a galaxy of parts like a cluster of stars, and each part of the organ, each cell, concentrates its labors on doing the work of that particular organ—circulating blood, or breathing air, or digesting air, or digesting food. The various organs carry on their work twenty-four hours a day, without conscious thought or direction from the mind. And (most amazing of all!) although each organ seems exclusively intent on its own work, yet all constantly work together for the good of each other and for the good of the whole body.

Giving support and protection to the whole organism that we call the body is the skeleton. It gives us the rigidity we need to be able to stand and sit and walk. The bones provide the anchoring posts for the muscles and tendons that make movement and action possible. They also provide protection for the most vulnerable of the organs; the cranium protects the brain, the vertebrae protect the spinal cord, the ribs protect the heart and lungs. Besides doing all this, the ends of the longer bones also help in the making of red blood corpuscles.

Another awesome thing about our body is the manufacturing processes that it is carrying on all the time. We put food and water into our mouths and then forget about them; the body takes over from there. By a process that biology can explain but cannot reproduce, the digestive system changes our bread and meat and beverages into a liquid of living cells that constantly bathes and nourishes every part of the body. This liquid food, which we call blood, contains sugars and fats and proteins and many other elements. It flows through the lungs and picks up oxygen, which it carries, along with nourishment, to every other part of the body.

The nervous system is another object for our admiration. Really there are two nervous systems—the motor nervous system, by which the brain controls the movements of the body (my brain commands, "Walk," and my feet obediently pick themselves up), and the sensory nervous system by which we feel pain (the body's vigilant sentinel against sickness or injury) and by which the outside world is brought into the brain through the sensory organs of sight, hearing, touch, taste and smell.

These organs themselves are further prodigies of design and precision. Again the scientist—the anatomist, the biologist, the oculist—can tell us how these organs work; yet the greatest scientists cannot make a human eye, or build an organ of hearing, or manufacture a single taste bud.

The litany of the body's marvels could be prolonged indefinitely—we have touched only a few of them here. If a person were to make a guided tour of his own physical self, he would find more wonders to admire than he would find in a trip to Grand Canyon and Yosemite and all the tourist attractions of the world.

Our body is only one half of us, and the lesser half by far. But it is a gift to be valued, a gift to be grateful for, a fitting habitation for the spiritual soul which gives it life and power and meaning.

Like the animals, man has a physical body, yet he is more than an animal. Like the angels, man has an immortal spirit, yet he is less than an angel. In man, the world of matter and the world of spirit meet. Body and soul are fused into the one complete substance which we call a human being.

Man's body and soul are not joined together in any casual sort of way. The body is not merely an instrument which the soul uses in the way that an automobile is the instrument of its driver. The body and soul were MADE FOR each other.

They are fused and linked together so intimately that, in this life at least, neither can get along without the other.

If a piece of copper and a piece of zinc are welded together, they form one piece of metal. However, their union in that case is what we call an "accidental" union. No new substance has resulted. Anyone can see that it still is a piece of copper and a piece of zinc. But if the copper and zinc are melted down and then mixed together, we get a new substance, which is called brass. Brass is neither zinc nor copper; it is a new substance composed of both. In somewhat the same way (no example is perfect) are man's body and soul united in the one substance which we call a human being.

The closeness of the union that binds body and soul into one personality is seen from the way body and soul interact upon each other. If I cut my finger, it is not just my body that suffers; my soul, too, suffers. *All of me* feels the pain. And if my soul is afflicted with worry, my body takes part in the worry, and may develop ulcers or some other disorder. If my soul is struck with fear or anger, the body will reflect the emotion: my face will flush or grow pale, my heart will beat faster; in a dozen ways my body will share the emotion with my soul.

The human body, then, is not to be despised as a mere accessory to the soul. At the same time we do recognize that the soul is the more important part of the complete person. It is the soul that is deathless; and it is due to this immortality of the soul that the body will, in the end, be delivered from the death which is its due.

The fact that the body is such a marvelous work of divine planning and power, with millions of tiny cells formed into the various organs and all the organs working together in such wonderful harmony for the good of the whole body—this fact should give us a faint idea of what a magnificent piece of God's handiwork the soul must be. It is, we know, a spirit. In considering the nature of God, we discussed the nature of a spirit. A spirit, we saw, is a conscious and intelligent being that is not merely invisible (as air is invisible) but absolutely immaterial: that is, with no physical matter in its makeup. There are no molecules in a spirit; there are no atoms in the soul.

There are no measurements to a spirit; there is neither length nor breadth nor depth, any more than there is weight. That is why the entire soul is in every part of the body at one and the same time; not part of the soul in the head, and part in the hand, and part in the foot. If I were to lose an arm or a leg through surgery or accident, I would not lose part of my soul. The soul simply would cease to be present in what is no longer a part of my living body. And when, finally, my body is so damaged by disease or injury that it can no longer sustain its function, then my soul will leave the body and I shall be adjudged dead. But my soul shall not be dead. Since it is completely immaterial (what philosophers call a "simple substance"), there is nothing about my soul that can be damaged or destroyed. Since there are no parts, no basic elements into which the soul can be resolved, there is no way in which it can decompose or cease to be what it is.

It is no wonder then that we say that God has made us to His own image and likeness. While our body, like all things which God has made, reflects the power and wisdom and greatness of God, yet it is our soul which is very especially a portrait of its Maker. It is a portrait in miniature, and an imperfect one at that. But the spirit that gives us life and being is an image of the infinitely perfect Spirit Who is God. The power of intelligence, by which we can know and understand truth, and reason to new truths, and make judgments as to what is right and wrong—in all this we mirror the all-wise and all-knowing God. The power of free will by which we deliberately choose to act or not to act, is a likeness of the Infinite Freedom which God possesses. And of course our immortality reflects the eternal deathlessness of God.

Since God's inner life consists in knowing Himself (God the Son) and in loving Himself (God the Holy Spirit), we approach most closely to the divine Image when we use our intelligence to know God—by reason and by the grace of faith now, and by the "light of glory" in eternity; and when we use our free will to love the Giver of our freedom.

How Did God Make Us?

The entire human race is descended from one man and one woman. Adam and Eve were the first ancestors of every human being. No truth in the Bible is more clearly taught than this. The Book of Genesis definitely establishes our common descent from that single pair of first parents.

What, then, of the theory of evolution in its extreme form: that the human race developed from a lower form of animal life, from some species of ape?

This is not the place to examine in detail the theory of evolution, the theory that all which exists—the world and everything in it—has evolved from a formless mass of primitive matter. So far as the world itself is concerned, the world of mineral and rock and lifeless matter, there is solid scientific evidence that the fashioning of the world was a slow, gradual process extending over a long period of time. Some guesses run as high as two billion years.

There is nothing contrary to the Bible or contrary to the faith in such a theory. If God chose to form the world by creating an original mass of atoms, at the same time establishing the natural laws by which that primitive mass would develop, step by step, into the universe as we know it today, He could have done so. He still would be the Creator of all things.

Indeed, such a gradual unfolding of His plan, working through secondary causes, would really reflect His creative power more than if He made, in one single flash, the universe as we see it now. The manufacturer who produces his wares by training supervisors and foremen to take care of details, really is a more able man than the boss who personally attends to every step of the fabrication.

This phase of creative progress, the development of lifeless matter, is called "inorganic" evolution. When we apply the same theory to living matter, we have what is called the theory of "organic" evolution. Here the picture is by no means so clear; the evidence is full of gaps and the theory still is in need of much more scientific proof. The theory is that all life as we know it today, even the human body, has developed through eons of time from some very simple form of living cell—up through plants and fish and birds and reptiles to man.

This theory of organic evolution still is far from being scientifically proved. Father Brennan, in his excellent book *The Image of His Maker*, will afford the interested reader a well-balanced examination of the whole question. For our purpose it is enough to note that exhaustive scientific search has so far failed to discover the remains of any creature that would be halfway between ape and man. The organic evolutionists make much of the similarities between the bodies of apes and those of human beings, but a really impartial judgment will note that the differences are as great as the similarities.

The search for the "missing link" goes on. Every now and then ancient bones are discovered in caves and excavations. For a little while there is great excitement—and then it is found that the bones are definitely human or definitely those of an ape. We have had the "Peking man" and the "Java ape man" and the "Foxhall man," and a host of others. But the halfway creature, a little more than an ape and a little less than a human, has still to be unearthed.

The whole point of interest to us, however, is that it will not, in the end, matter to us so far as our faith is concerned.

God could have fashioned man's body, if He so chose, through a process of evolution. He could have guided the development of a particular species of ape until it reached the point of perfection that He wanted. God then could have created spiritual souls for a male and a female of that species and we would have had the first man and woman: Adam and Eve. It still would be true that God made man out of the slime of the earth.

What we must believe, and what the Book of Genesis unqualifiedly teaches, is that the human race is descended from one original pair, and that the souls of Adam and Eve (like the individual souls of every one of us) were directly and immediately created by God. The soul is a spirit; it cannot possibly "evolve" from matter, no more than a soul can be inherited from our parents. Husband and wife co-operate with God in the formation of the human body. But the spiritual soul which makes that body a human being must be directly created by God and infused into the embryonic body within the mother's womb.

The search for the "missing link" will go on, and Catholic scientists will take part in that search. They know that since all truth comes from God, there can be no clash between scientific fact and religious fact. Meanwhile, the rest of us are not disturbed. However God may have chosen to make our bodies, we know that it is the soul that matters most. It is the soul that lifts the animal's eyes from the ground—from the limited search for food and sex, for pleasure and avoidance of pain. It is the soul that lifts our eyes to the stars so that we may see beauty and know truth and love what is good.*

* In his encyclical letter, *Humani Generis*, Pope Pius XII has pointed out to us the caution needed in the investigation of such matters of science. "The teaching authority of the Church," Pope Pius says, "does not forbid that in conformity with the present state of human sciences and sacred theology research and discussions on the part of men experienced in both fields take place with regard to the doctrine of evolution in as far as it inquires into the origin of the human body as

Some people like to talk about their ancestors. Especially if back in the family tree there was a nobleman or a great statesman or a famous person of some kind—especially then do people like to brag a bit.

All of us could boast, if we wanted to, about the first ancestors on our family tree, Adam and Eve. As God made them, they were wonderful persons indeed. God did not make them just ordinary human beings subject to the usual laws of nature, such as inevitable decay and finally death, a death that would be followed by a merely natural happiness in which there would be no vision of God. Neither did God make them subject to the usual limitations of human nature, such as the necessity to acquire knowledge by laborious study and investigation, and the necessity to maintain by painful vigilance the control of the spirit over the flesh.

In the gifts which God bestowed upon Adam and Eve in the very first moment of their existence, our first parents were wealthy beyond all compute. First of all there were the gifts which we classify as "preternatural" gifts, as distinguished from "supernatural" gifts. Preternatural gifts are those that do not belong, by right, to human nature—and yet they are not entirely beyond the capacity of human nature to receive and to possess.

To use a homely example from a lower order of creation, we might say that if a horse were given the power to fly, that ability would be a preternatural gift. It does not belong to the nature of a horse to fly, and yet there are creatures

---

coming from pre-existent and living matter—for Catholic faith obliges us to hold that souls are immediately created by God. However, this must be done in such a way that the reasons for both opinions, that is, those favorable and those unfavorable to evolution, be weighed and judged with the necessary seriousness, moderation and measure, and provided that all are prepared to submit to the judgment of the Church to whom Christ has given the mission of interpreting authentically the Sacred Scripture and of defending dogmas of faith." (Paulist Press translation, p. 19, No. 64.)

that do fly—the birds. The word "preternatural," then, means "outside of, or beyond the usual course of nature."

Now if a horse were given the power to THINK, and to understand abstract truths, that would be not preternatural, that would be, in a sense, SUPERNATURAL. It is not merely beyond the ordinary nature of a horse to think, it is absolutely and entirely ABOVE the nature of a horse, or any animal. That is exactly the meaning of the word "supernatural"— something which is completely above the nature of a creature; not merely a horse or a human, but *any* creature.

Perhaps this example will help us a little in understanding the two kinds of gifts which God conferred on Adam and Eve. First of all, there were preternatural gifts. These included wisdom of an immensely high order—a clear and flawless natural knowledge of God and of the world that otherwise could have been gained only by painstaking research and study. Then there were a remarkable strength of will and perfect control of the passions and senses, resulting in a perfect interior tranquillity and lack of self-conflict. These two endowments, of mind and of will, were the two principal preternatural gifts on the spiritual level.

On the physical level, their great gifts were freedom from suffering and freedom from death. As God made Adam and Eve, they would have lived out their allotted span upon earth wholly free from pain and suffering—pain and suffering which ordinarily would have been inevitable for a physical body in a physical world. When their years of temporal life were completed, they would have entered into eternal life body and soul, without having to experience the dreadful separation of soul from body which we call death.

But greater than any of these preternatural gifts was the supernatural gift that God bestowed on Adam and Eve. This was nothing less than a sharing, by God, of His own nature with Adam and Eve. In a marvelous way which we shall never fully understand until we see God as He is in heaven, God let His Love (which is the Holy Spirit) flow into, and occupy, the souls of Adam and Eve. It is a very inadequate example, of course, but I like to think of this flow of God's love into the soul as somewhat like the flow of blood in transfusion. Somewhat as the patient is joined to the blood donor by the flow of the donor's own blood, so were the souls of Adam and Eve joined to God by the flow of God's own Love into their souls.

The new kind of life which Adam and Eve possessed as a result of their union with God, this supernatural life, is what we call "sanctifying grace." Later on we shall talk more at length about sanctifying grace, since it plays such an all-important part in our own spiritual lives.

But we can see at once that if God chooses to share His own life with a soul here upon earth, in time—it also means that God will share His own divine life with that soul eternally, in heaven.

As a consequence of this supernatural gift of sanctifying grace, Adam and Eve were no longer destined to an eternal happiness that would be merely a natural happiness; that is, a happiness based upon a purely natural knowledge of God, Who still would be invisible, and a purely natural love of God, Who still would be unseen. Now, with sanctifying grace, Adam and Eve would know God as He is, face to face, after their life on earth had ended. Seeing Him face to face, they would love God with an ecstatic love of such intensity as man could never, by his own nature, hope to achieve.

And that is the kind of ancestors you and I had. That is Adam and Eve as God made them.

What Is Original Sin?

A devoted father is not content merely to fulfill his bare duty toward his children. He is not content to feed them and clothe them and give them the minimum of education the law demands. In addition, the benevolent father will supply his children with every possible comfort and convenience; he will give them every advantage his means will permit.

God likewise was not content to give to His creature, man, simply those gifts to which a human being is entitled by his nature. Marvelously designed though the human body be, and wonderfully endowed though the human soul is, with intelligence and free will—this still was not enough for God. These were the things which human beings, by their very nature, were entitled to. God went far beyond these and conferred on Adam and Eve such preternatural gifts as freedom from suffering and death and the supernatural gift of sanctifying grace. In God's original plan, if we may call it that, these gifts were to be passed on by Adam to his posterity. They were gifts which you and I ought to be enjoying today.

Just one thing was required of Adam in order that he might confirm these gifts, and make these gifts secure to his descendants—he must, by a free act of choice, give his love irrevocably to God. It was for this that God made all human beings: that they might give glory to God by their love for God. And their love for God was to be, in a sense, the coin by which they would make secure the supernatural destiny of face-to-face union with God in heaven.

It is of the very nature of genuine love to make a complete surrender of self to the one who is loved. In this life, there is only one way in which love for God can prove itself—by the doing of God's will, by obedience to Him. That is why God gave to Adam and Eve a commandment, one single commandment: They must not eat of the fruit that grew on a certain tree. It probably was no different (except in its effects) from any of the other fruits which Adam and Eve could reach out and pick. But there had to be a commandment so that there could be an act of obedience; there had to be an act of obedience so that there could be a proof of love, a free and deliberate choosing of God in preference to self.

We know what happened. Adam and Eve failed the test. They committed the first sin, the original sin. And their sin was not simply one of disobedience. Like the sin of the fallen angels, it too was a sin of pride. The tempter whispered to them that if they ate of this fruit, they would be as great as God, they themselves would be gods.

Yes, we know that Adam and Eve sinned. But what is hard for us to realize is the enormity of their sin. Today we look upon sin as something that is, to a degree, inevitable—considering human ignorance and human weakness. Sin is lamentable, yes, but not surprising. We are likely to forget that before the fall there was no ignorance, there was no weakness. It was with complete clarity of mind, and with complete control of reason over passion, that Adam and Eve sinned. There were no extenuating circumstances; there was positively no excuse. It was with their eyes wide open, we might say, that Adam and Eve chose self in preference to God.

And in sinning, they brought the temple of creation crashing down around their ears. Lost in an instant were all those special gifts which God had bestowed upon them—the lofty wisdom, the perfect self-control, freedom from suffering and death—above all, that bond of intimate union with God which we call sanctifying grace. They were stripped right down to the bare essentials which belonged to them by virtue of their human nature.

The tragedy of it is that it was not Adam's sin alone. Because all of us were present, potentially, in our common father Adam. All of us suffered when he sinned. By God's decree, he was the ambassador-at-large of the entire human race. What Adam did, we all did. He had the opportunity to put us, his family, spiritually on easy street. He refused to do so, and all of us must suffer the consequences. Because our human nature fell from grace in its very *origin*, we say that we are born "in the state of original sin."

When I was a child and first heard about the "stain of original sin," my child mind pictured original sin as a big black blot on the soul. I had seen plenty of stains on table-cloths and clothing and blotters—coffee stains and berry stains and ink stains. So of course it was easy for me to picture a nice white soul covered with an ugly splotch of black.

Growing older, I learned (as we all do learn) that the word "stain" is a very broad metaphor when applied to original sin. Aside from the fact that there could be no actual "stain" on a spirit, I came to understand that our heritage of original sin is not something that is "on" the soul or "in" the soul. On the contrary, it is something which is absent from the soul, something that ought to be there—the supernatural life which we call sanctifying grace.

In other words, original sin is not a something, it is a "no-thing," just as darkness is a "no-thing."

We can't put a quart of darkness into a jar and take it in-side to examine it under the light. Darkness has no existence of its own at all; it simply is the absence of light. When the sun rises in the morning, the darkness of night necessarily disappears.

Similarly, when we say that "we are born in the state of original sin," we mean that we are born with a soul that is spiritually dark, a soul that is lifeless so far as supernatural life is concerned. Then when we are baptized the light of God's love pours into the soul. Our soul becomes bright and beautiful, vibrantly alive with the supernatural life which is the result of God's indwelling, the result of our union with Him—the life which we call sanctifying grace.

Although Baptism does restore to us the greatest of God's gifts to Adam—the supernatural gift of sanctifying grace—it does not restore the preternatural gifts, such as freedom from suffering and death. These latter gifts are lost to us forever in this life. But that thought should not disturb us. We should dwell rather on the thought that God did restore to us the big gift, the really important gift of supernatural life. If His infinite justice were not balanced by His infinite mercy, God could so easily have washed His hands of the human race after the sin of Adam. God could so easily have said, "All right, you've had your chance! Now make the best of things as you are."

Here is a question I once heard asked: "Why must I suffer for something that Adam did? I didn't personally commit original sin. Why should I be punished for it?"

With a moment's thought, the question answers itself. We have not lost, any of us, anything which we are by right entitled to. The gifts—preternatural and supernatural —which God bestowed on Adam were not qualities which were due to us by reason of our human nature. They were gifts beyond our deserts, gifts which Adam could have passed on to us had he made his act of love, but nothing which we can claim as our due.

If, before I was born, some wealthy man had offered my father a million dollars in return for doing some small job the millionaire asked him to do—and my father turned the offer down, then surely today I could not blame the millionaire because I was poor. It would be my father's fault, not the fault of the rich man.

In the same way, if I am born into the world without the gifts which Adam could so easily have earned for me, I cannot blame God for the failure that was Adam's. On the contrary, I should bless the infinite mercy of God which did, in spite of everything, restore the greatest of those gifts—through the merits of God's own Son, Jesus Christ.

Since Adam, only one human being (besides Christ) has possessed a perfectly balanced human nature: the Blessed Virgin Mary. Because Mary was destined to be the Mother of the Son of God, and because it was repugnant that God should have any contact, however indirect, with sin, Mary was preserved, FROM THE VERY FIRST MOMENT OF HER EXISTENCE, from the spiritual darkness of original sin.

From the very instant of her conception in Anna's womb, Mary was in union with God, her soul was flooded with His love, she was in the state of sanctifying grace. This unique privilege of Mary's—the first step in our redemption—we call her Immaculate Conception.

After Adam, What?

It once happened that a man was walking along the edge of an abandoned stone quarry. Absent-mindedly the man stepped too near the brink and plunged headlong into the water that filled the bottom of the quarry. When he tried to climb out, he found that there was no toe hold or hand hold in the perpendicular rock cliffs which enclosed the quarry.

Good swimmer though he was, the man would have drowned from exhaustion if a passer-by had not seen his plight and rescued him with a rope. As he sat emptying the water out of his shoes, the near victim philosophized a bit. "It's amazing," he said, "how impossible it was to get out of there, considering how easy it was to get in."

The story illustrates rather well the plight of the human race after the sin of Adam. We know that the higher the dignity of a person is, the more serious is an offense committed against that person. If a man throws a rotten tomato at his next-door neighbor, he probably will suffer nothing more than a black eye. But if a man were to throw a rotten tomato at the President of the United States, the F. B. I. would close in and the man might not be at home for his meals for a long time.

It is plain, then, that the seriousness of an offense depends in some degree upon the dignity of the one offended. Since God, the infinitely perfect Being, is of limitless dignity, it follows that the malice of an offense against God is an infinite malice—an evil without limit or measure.

That is why the sin of Adam left the human race in much the same predicament as the man at the bottom of the quarry. There we were, down at the bottom, with no possible way of getting back out by ourselves. Whatever a human being may do, is finite, or measurable, in its value. If the greatest of saints were to lay down his life to atone for sin, the value of his sacrifice would still be a limited value.

Indeed, if every member of the human race, from Adam until the last survivor at the end of the world, were to offer his life to pay humanity's debt to God, the payment still would be inadequate. Collectively it would be a great payment, but it still would not be an infinite payment. It just is not within the power of man to do anything of infinite worth.

After Adam's sin, our fate would have been a hopeless one if no one had come along to throw us a rope. It was God Himself Who threw us that rope; it was God Himself Who solved our dilemma. The dilemma was that, since only God is infinite, only God would be capable of an act of atonement which would repair the infinite malice of sin. Yet he who would undertake to pay for human sin, would need to be human if he were really to take our sins upon himself, really to represent us.

God's solution is an old story to us now—but it never can become a trite story or a tiresome story. The man of faith can never cease to gasp at the infinite love and mercy displayed by God, Who decreed, from all eternity, that His own Divine Son should come into the world and unite Himself to a human nature like ours, in order to pay the price for our sins.

As a genuine human being like ourselves, our Redeemer thus could truly represent us and act for us. Yet, being genuinely God also, the least of His actions would be of infinite value—sufficient to atone for all the sins that ever had been or could be committed.

At the very beginning of man's history, when He expelled Adam and Eve from the Garden of Paradise, God said to Satan: "I will put enmity between you and the woman, between your seed and her seed; he shall crush your head, and you shall lie in wait for his heel." Many long centuries were to elapse before Mary's seed, Jesus Christ, would crush the serpent's head. But the ray of hope and of promise, like a distant light in the darkness, would always be there.

When Adam sinned and Christ, the second Adam, atoned for that sin, the story wasn't ended. Christ's death upon the Cross did not mean that henceforth men would be compelled to be good. Christ by His atonement did not take away the freedom of the human will. If we are to be capable of proving our love for God by our obedience to God, then we must be left free for the choice that obedience involves.

In addition to original sin, under whose shadow all of us are born, we must reckon with another kind of sin, the kind that we ourselves commit. This sin, which is not inherited from Adam but which is actually our own, we call "actual sin." Actual sin may be either mortal or venial, depending upon the degree of malice in the sin.

We know there *are* degrees of gravity in disobedience. A son who disobeys his parents in things that are petty or ways that are thoughtless is not thereby convicted of lack of love for his parents. His love may be a less perfect love, but the love still is there. However, if that same son should disobey his parents deliberately in a matter that is of grave importance to them, a matter which would hurt them and grieve them deeply—then we would have good reason to conclude that the boy does not really love his parents. At least we could conclude that he loves himself more than he loves them.

The same thing may be said of our relationship to God. If we disobey God in a matter of lesser importance, then it is not necessarily a denial of our love for God. Such an act of disobedience, in which the matter is not grave, we call a venial sin. For example, to tell a simple lie, which harms no one—"Where were you last night?" . . . "I was out bowling," when really I was at home watching TV— would be a venial sin.

Even in a matter that of itself is grave, my sin might be a venial one because of ignorance or lack of full consent.

For example, it is a mortal sin to tell a lie under oath. But if I *think* that perjury is a venial sin, and commit perjury, that would be a venial sin for me. Or, if I were to swear falsely because my questioner took me by surprise and I was rattled (lack of sufficient reflection), or because great fear of the consequences lessened my freedom of choice (lack of full consent), then again it would be venial sin.

In all these instances we can see that the malice of a conscious, deliberate rejection of God is lacking. In none of these cases do we convict ourselves of lack of love for God.

Such sins are called "venial" from the Latin word "*venia*," which means "forgiveness." Venial sins are readily forgivable by God, even without the sacrament of Penance; a genuine act of sorrow and purpose of amendment will suffice for forgiveness.

This does not mean that venial sin "doesn't matter." Any sin is at least a partial failure in love, an act of ingratitude toward God, Who loves us so much. In all creation there is no evil so great as a venial sin, excepting only mortal sin. Venial sin is by no means a harmless laxity. Every venial sin brings punishment in its train, here or in purgatory. Every venial sin lessens a little the love of God in our hearts and weakens our resistance to temptation.

No number of venial sins will ever add up to a mortal sin, but carelessness about venial sin will surely pave the way for mortal sin. If we keep saying "Yes" to ourselves in little things, we shall end up by saying "Yes" when a really big temptation comes along. For one who truly loves God, the habitual resolution will be to avoid all deliberate sin, venial as well as mortal.

It might be well to point out also that just as a sin that is objectively mortal might subjectively be a venial sin, due to special circumstances, such as ignorance or lack of full advertence, so also a sin which on the surface seems venial might become a mortal sin under special circumstances.

For example, if I thought it was a mortal sin to steal a dime, and stole the dime anyway, then for me it would be a mortal sin. Or if I stole the dime from a newsboy and ran the risk of disgracing myself and my family, the evil possibilities of my act would make it a mortal sin. Of if I kept stealing a dime or a quarter at a time until I had accumulated a large amount—maybe a hundred dollars—then my sin would be a mortal sin.

But if complete obedience to God and His will is our intention and our desire, we shall have to worry about none of these things.

CHAPTER VI

Actual Sin

Can My Soul Die?

If a man drives a knife into his heart, that man is dead. If a man commits a mortal sin, he is spiritually dead. The story of mortal sin is as simple as that—and as real as that.

By Baptism we are rescued from the spirtiual death into which we were plunged by the sin of Adam. In Baptism God united our soul to Himself. God's Love—the Holy Spirit—poured into our soul to fill the spiritual vacuum that was the result of original sin. As a result of this intimate union with God, our soul was elevated to a new kind of life, a supernatural life, a sharing in God's own life. From then on, it becomes our duty to preserve this divine life (we call it "sanctifying grace") within us; not only to preserve it, but to deepen and intensify it.

Once He has united us with Himself by Baptism, God will never, Himself, abandon us. After Baptism, the only way in which we can be separated from God is by our own deliberate rejection of God. That happens when, in the full consciousness of what we are doing, deliberately and of our free choice, we refuse God our obedience in a serious matter. If we do that, then we have committed a mortal sin, which means simply a "death-dealing" sin. This conscious and willful disobedience of God in a serious matter, which we call mortal sin, is at the same time a rejection of God. It severs the union between our soul and God just as definitely as a pair of wire cutters would sever the union between your home and the electric light company's generators if the wire cutters were applied to the power line outside your house. In the latter event, your house would instantly be plunged into darkness; in the case of mortal sin, the same thing happens to our soul—with far more terrible consequences, because our soul is plunged not merely into darkness, but into death.

It is a death the more horrible because outwardly there is no semblance of death, no odor of corruption, no chilling cold. It is indeed a living death, in which the sinner stands naked and alone in the midst of divine love and abundance. God's grace flows over and around him, but cannot enter; God's love touches him, but cannot penetrate. All the supernatural merits that the sinner had acquired previous to his sin now are lost. All the good deeds he has done, all the prayers that he has said, and Masses offered, and pains suffered for Christ—all are swept away in the moment of his sin.

He has lost heaven, of course, this soul in mortal sin; he has lost heaven if he should die thus cut off from God. There is no way of establishing union with God beyond the grave.

The very purpose of this life upon earth is to prove our love for God by our obedience to God. Death ends our time of opportunity, our time of trial. There is no chance for a change of heart hereafter. Death "freezes" the soul forever in the state in which death finds the soul—God loved, or God rejected.

With heaven lost, there is no alternative for the soul but hell. All sham is stripped away. The mortal sin which seemed, at the time of its commission, but a simple bit of temporizing with self, now shows up in the cold light of God's justice for what it really is: an act of pride and rebellion, an act of hatred for God which is implicit in every mortal sin. And there bursts upon the soul the awful, burning, torturing hunger and thirst for the God for Whom the soul was made, the God whom that soul shall never find. The soul is in hell.

We sometimes talk about God "sending" a soul to hell. That, let us make clear, is figurative language only. Strictly speaking, God does not "send" any soul to hell. The soul in hell is there because it freely chose hell for itself. The choice of hell is part of the choice involved in every mortal sin—and the choice is plain: "Love God and have God as your portion forever; reject God, and risk losing God for all eternity!" In his act of disobedience the sinner may try to evade facing that choice, but the choice is there in spite of him; the choice goes with the sin.

And all this is what it means, a little bit of what it means, to disobey God knowingly and willfully in a serious matter, to commit a mortal sin.

A sin is a refusal to give God our obedience, a refusal to give God our love. Since every bit of us belongs to God, and the whole purpose of our existence is to love God, it follows that every bit of us owes obedience to God. Not only in our outward words and actions, but in our innermost thoughts and desires as well, does this obligation to obedience apply.

Indeed, we may sin not only by doing what God has forbidden (sin of commission), but we may sin also by failing to do what God has commanded (sin of omission). It is a sin to steal—but it also is a sin to fail to pay our just debts. It is a sin to work unnecessarily on Sunday, but it also is a sin to fail to worship God on Sunday in the Mass.

It may seem an almost insultingly simple question to ask: "What makes a thing right or wrong?" And yet, time and again I have asked that very question of children, even children in the upper grades of Catholic schools, without getting the right answer. We know that it is God's will that makes rightness and wrongness. An action is right if it is something that God wants us to do. It is wrong if it is something God does not want us to do. But I have had children tell me that a thing is wrong "because the priest says so, or the catechism says so, or the Bible says so, or the Church says so."

It may not be out of place, then, to point out to parents how necessary it is to get this point across to children as soon as they are old enough to distinguish between right and wrong: that rightness or wrongness is what God does want or doesn't want; that doing what God wants is our way, our only way, of proving to God that we love Him. That will make sense to the child, as it makes sense to us. And the child will obey God much more willingly and cheerfully than he would obey a mere parent, or priest, or book.

Of course, it is through the Bible (God's Written Word) and the Church (God's Living Voice) that we know God's will. But neither the Bible nor the Church makes God's will. Even the so-called "commandments of the Church" are merely particularized explanations to us of God's will, detailed interpretations to us of duties that otherwise might not be obvious and clear.

Parents need to exercise caution, too, lest in the moral training of their youngsters they exaggerate the difficulties of virtue. If every little sin of a child is magnified into a Great Big Sin; if the child who uses a "swear" word or says, "I won't!" is told that he has committed a mortal sin and that God doesn't love him any more—well, that child is likely to grow up with a picture of God as a very severe and unreasonable taskmaster. If every sin is represented to him as a grievous sin, the child may grow discouraged at the plain impossibility of being good, and may give up trying. That has happened.

We know that for a sin to be a mortal sin, three things are necessary. If any of the three are missing, it is not a mortal sin.

First of all, the matter must be serious, whether it be a thought, word or action. It is not a mortal sin to tell a childish lie; it *is* a mortal sin to seriously hurt another's reputation by a lie. It is not a mortal sin to steal an apple or a nickel; it *is* a mortal sin to steal a hundred dollars, or to set a building on fire.

Secondly, I must know that the thing I am doing is wrong, seriously wrong. I cannot sin through ignorance. If I did not know that it is a mortal sin to take part in non-Catholic religious services, then it would not be a sin for me if I went with my friend to his church. If I forgot that it was Friday, and ate meat, then it would not be a sin for me. This presupposes, of course, that my ignorance is not my own fault. If I purposely tried to avoid learning the truth, for fear that it would interfere with what I wanted to do, then I still would be guilty of the sin.

Finally, I cannot commit a mortal sin unless I freely choose the action or omission which God has forbidden. I cannot be made to commit a sin by force if, for instance, someone physically stronger than I actually forces me to throw a brick through a store window. And I cannot commit a sin by accident, as when I unintentionally bump into someone and knock him down and fracture his skull. Nor can I commit a sin in my sleep, no matter how evil my dream might be.

It is important that we understand these things ourselves. It is important that our children be made to understand them, in proportion to their ability to grasp them. Mortal sin, which means a complete separation from God, is too horrible a thing to be taken lightly; too horrible a thing to use as a weapon in child training; much too horrible a thing to equate with childish thoughtlessness and misbehavior.

What Are the Roots of Sin?

It is easy to say that this action or that action is sinful. It is not so easy to say that this person or that person has committed a sin. If a man forgets, for example, that it is a holyday of obligation, and misses Mass as a consequence of his forgetfulness, then his sin is an outward sin only. There is no interior intention to do wrong. In such a case we say that the man has committed a *material* sin, but it has not been a *formal* sin. There was an evil deed, but no evil intent. It would be pointless and needless to mention it in confession.

The opposite also is true. A person can commit a sin interiorly without actually doing anything wrong. To use the same example, if a man believes that the day is a feast day of obligation, and willfully decides to miss Mass for no good reason, then he is guilty of the sin of missing Mass, even though he is mistaken, even though it is not a holyday at all. Or, to give another illustration, if a man steals a large amount of money and later finds out that it was his own money that he took—again he has committed the sin of stealing interiorly, even though there has been no actual theft. In both of these cases we say there has been no *material* sin, but there has been a *formal* sin. And of course these sins, both of them, would have to be confessed.

We can see, then, that it is the intention which exists in the mind and will of a person which finally determines the malice of a sin. It is the intention to do what self wants, rather than what God wants, that constitutes the evil.

That is why I become guilty of a sin the moment I make up my mind that I am going to commit the sin—even though actually I do not get the chance to commit the sin, or even though I later change my mind. If I decide that I am going to lie about a certain matter when asked about it, but as it happens nobody does ask me about it—nevertheless I already have been guilty of the sin of lying, because of my evil intention. If I decide to steal some tools from the shop where I work, but get laid off before I have a chance to take the tools—I already have been guilty, interiorly, of the sin of theft. These would be real sins, sins to be confessed, if the matter were grave.

Even a change of mind cannot wipe out the sin. If a man decided today that he was going to commit fornication tomorrow; and then tomorrow had a change of heart and decided not to—there still would be yesterday's mortal sin upon his soul. Today's good resolution cannot wipe out yesterday's evil intent. We are supposing, of course, that his mind in the first instance was definitely made up. We are not talking here of a person who may be undergoing severe temptation, a person who may struggle with himself for hours or even days. If such a person finally gains the victory over self and says a definite "No!" to the temptation, he has committed no sin.

On the contrary, he has shown great virtue and has acquired great merit before God. There is no need to feel guilty because temptation has been strong or stubborn; anyone could be good if it was easy to be good. There would be no credit in that. No, the person we have been talking about is the person who positively decides to commit a sin, although a change of mind or lack of opportunity actually prevents him from carrying out his intention.

This is not to say that the outward action doesn't matter. It would be a mistake to infer that once a person has made up his mind to sin he might as well go through with it. On the contrary, putting the evil intent into practice and really doing the deed does add to the gravity of the sin, does intensify its malice. This is especially true when the outward sin causes harm to another, as by theft; or causes another to commit sin, as in unchaste relations.

And while we are on the subject of "intention," it may be worth while to recall that we cannot change a bad deed into a good or harmless deed simply by having a good purpose in mind. If I steal from a rich man in order to give to a poor man, it still is stealing, it still is a sin. If I tell a lie in order to help a friend out of a tight spot, it still is a lie that I tell and a sin that I commit. If parents make use of contraceptives in order to give their present children more advantages, the guilt of their deed remains. In short, a good purpose can never justify an evil means. God's will may not be forced and twisted to make it coincide with ours.

Just as sin is, essentially, the opposing of our will to God's will; so too the practice of virtue consists simply in the wholehearted effort to identify our will with God's. That is difficult only if we depend upon our own strength, instead of depending upon God's grace. An old theological axiom puts it this way: "To him who does what in him lies, God's grace will not be wanting."

If we do "what in us lies" by regular daily prayer, frequent confession and Holy Communion; by recalling often what a grand thing it is to have God Himself dwelling within us, what a glorious thing it is to know that at whatever moment God may call us, we are ready to open our eyes upon Him in eternity (even though purgatory may come first); if we keep ourselves occupied with useful work and wholesome play, and avoid the persons and places and things which might put a strain upon our human weakness —then there can be no doubt about our victory.

It helps, too, to know our own weaknesses. How well *do* you know yourself? Or, to put it negatively, do you know what your outstanding fault is?

You may have several faults; most of us do. But you may be sure that there is some one fault, more prominent than the others, that is your greatest obstacle to spiritual growth. Spiritual writers describe such a fault as one's "predominant passion."

First of all, it is well to be clear as to the difference between a fault and a sin. A fault is what we might call "a weak streak" in us, which makes it more easy for us to commit certain kinds of sins, more difficult to practice certain virtues. A fault is a more or less permanent (until we eliminate it) flaw in our character, whereas a sin is a transient act, a "one-shot" affair, which flows from the fault. If we compare sin to a weed, then a fault would be the root from which the weed grows.

We all know that in cultivating a garden it does little good to break the weeds off at the soil line. Unless we dig up the root, the weed will grow again and again. Similarly, certain sins are very likely to keep repeating themselves in our lives unless we get at the root of such sins, the fault from which they spring.

Theologians list for us seven principal faults or character flaws, to one or the other of which almost every actual sin can be traced. These seven human weaknesses are commonly called the "seven capital sins." The word "capital" in this instance has the significance of outstanding, or most frequent; it is not intended necessarily to mean the biggest or the worst.

What are these seven dominating vices of human nature? The first is *pride*, which is defined as an inordinate seeking after one's own honor and excellence. It would take too much space to list all the sins that can stem from pride. Excessive ambition, over-reliance on one's own spiritual strength, vanity, boastfulness—these are only a few. Or, in contemporary language, "keeping up with the Joneses," social climbing, "be the first to own one"—and others of like ilk.

The second capital sin is *covetousness*, or plain avarice. This is an immoderate desire for temporal goods. Not only do outright sins of stealing and fraud spring from it, but also less acknowledged sins of injustice on the part of employers or employees, sharp business practices, stinginess and indifference to the needs of the poor—to mention only a few specimens.

Next on the list is the vice of *lust*. It is easy to recognize that the gross sins against chastity have their origin in lust; but it nourishes other sins too. Many acts of dishonesty, injustice and deceit can be traced to lust; loss of faith in one's religion, or despair of God's mercy frequently are the fruit of lust.

Then there is *anger*, that disordered emotional state in which we seek revenge upon others, or range in unreasonable opposition to persons and things. Murder, quarreling and profanity are a few of the obvious sins to which anger gives rise. Hatred, malicious gossip, and property damage are some others.

Gluttony is another of the capital sins. It is an intemperate love for food and/or drink. It seems the most ignoble of all the vices; there is something so animal-like about the glutton. Gluttony can result in sinful abuse of one's health, gross and blasphemous speech, injustice to one's family or other persons—and a whole host of evils too evident to need enumerating.

Envy is another dominant vice. It takes an honest and a humble person to admit its existence within himself. Envy does not consist in wishing that we were as well off as someone else. That is a perfectly natural feeling, unless it goes to the extreme of covetousness. No, envy is, rather, a sadness of mind that another should be better off than ourselves, as though we ourselves suffered because of another's good fortune. We wish that we had what he has, instead of his having it. At least we wish that he didn't have it, so long as we cannot have it too. Envy is the classical "dog-in-the-manger" state of mind. It leads to hatred, slander, detraction, resentment, sullenness and kindred ills.

Finally there is *sloth*, or laziness. This is not merely a dislike for work; very few people do like to work. Sloth is rather a surrender to one's dislike for work. It is a distaste for, and a sluggishness in doing, one's duty, particularly one's duty to God. If we are on a low level of attainment in our quest for sanctity, and particularly if we are content with spiritual mediocrity, then almost certainly sloth is the cause. Missing Mass on Sunday, laxity in prayer, neglect of work or family—all of these can result from sloth.

These, then, are the seven capital sins: pride, covetousness, lust, anger, gluttony, envy and sloth. Doubtless we have the laudable habit of examining our conscience before we go to bed at night, and certainly before going to confession. Hereafter it would be profitable to ask ourselves not merely "What sins, and how many," but "Why?"

CHAPTER VII

The Incarnation

Who Is Mary?

On March 25 we celebrate the great event which we term the "Annunciation"—the archangel Gabriel's announcement to Mary that God had chosen her to be the mother of the Redeemer.

On the day of the Annunciation God bridged the infinite distance between Himself and us. By an act of His almighty power, God did something that, to our human minds, seems impossible. He united His own divine nature to a true human nature, to a body and soul like ours. What leaves our heads really whirling is the fact that this union did not result in a being with two personalities—the personality of God and the personality of man. On the contrary, the two natures are united in one single Person, the God-Man Jesus Christ.

Because this union of the divine and the human in one Person is such a unique union, with no counterpart in human experience to which we can compare it, it is therefore completely beyond our comprehension. It ranks with the

Blessed Trinity as one of the great mysteries of faith. We call this particular mystery the Incarnation (from the Latin word "*caro*," which means "flesh"). In St. John's Gospel we read that "*Verbum caro factum est*—The Word was made flesh." That is, the Second Person of the Most Blessed Trinity, God the Son, was incarnated, was made man. This union of the two natures in the one Person, Jesus Christ, has a special name; it is called the "hypostatic union" (from the Greek word "hypostasis," which means "that which lies underneath").

To provide the human nature of the Redeemer, God chose a fifteen-year-old Hebrew maiden named Mary, a descendant of the great King David, who lived quietly with her parents in the village of Nazareth. Mary had vowed her virginity to God, under an impulse of grace which was part of God's plan for her.

This was but a further beautifying of a soul that had received a still greater grace in its very beginning. When God created the soul of Mary, at the instant of her conception in Anna's womb, He had exempted her soul from the otherwise universal law of original sin. To Mary was given the heritage that Adam had lost. From the first moment of her beginning her soul was united with God. Not for a single instant would she whose Son would crush Satan's head be under his dominion.

Although Mary had made what we today would call a vow of perpetual chastity, she had nevertheless been pledged to marry her kinsman Joseph. Two thousand years ago there were no "bachelor girls" or "career women." In a world that was strictly a man's world, any girl aspiring to virtue needed a man to provide for her and to protect her. Moreover, it was not a part of God's plan that Mary, in mothering His Son, should suffer disgrace as an unwed mother. So, through the quiet workings of His grace, God saw to it that Mary had a husband.

The young man whom God chose for this role of Mary's

champion and Jesus' guardian was a saint in his own right. The Gospel describes Joseph by saying simply that he was "a just man." This word "just" in its original Hebrew connotation meant a man possessed of all the virtues. It was the equivalent of our modern word "saintly."

It is not surprising, then, that Joseph, approached by Mary's parents, happily consented to be Mary's legal and true husband, even though he was apprised of Mary's vow of virginity, and knew that the marriage could never be consummated. Mary, incidentally, remained a virgin, not only in giving birth to Jesus, but throughout the rest of her life. When we read references in the Gospels to "brothers and sisters" of Jesus, we must remember that we are reading an English translation of the Greek translation of the Hebrew. In the original, these words meant simply "blood relatives"—about the same as our word "cousin."

It was while she was still with her parents, before she had taken up residence with Joseph, that the angel appeared to Mary. It had been by the free choice of Adam that sin had come into the world; God willed now that it should be by the free choice of Mary that salvation should come. The God of heaven and earth waited upon a maiden's consent.

When, having heard the angel's message, Mary bowed her head and said, "Be it done to me according to thy word," at that instant God the Holy Ghost (to Whom are ascribed the works of love) conceived within her womb the body and soul of a male child to which God the Son immediately united Himself.

Because it was by her own free consent that Mary chose to be the mother of the Redeemer, and because it was freely (and so intimately!) that she shared in His Passion, Mary is acclaimed by the Church as the Co-Redemptress of the human race.

It is this grand moment of Mary's consent and our own salvation that we commemorate each time that we recite the Angelus.

And it is no wonder that God preserved her body, from whom His own body was taken, from the corruption of the grave. In the fourth mystery of the Rosary, and annually on the feast of the Assumption, we celebrate the fact that Mary's body, after death, was reunited with her soul in heaven.

"I wish that I were twins, so that I could get my work done." Many of us probably have made a remark something like that at times when we have been especially busy. It is an idea that can lead us to an interesting bit of fantasy.

Supposing that I were really twins, with two bodies and two souls under the direction of the one single personality which is me. Both bodies would work together as a unit on whatever task might engage me. It would be especially convenient if there were a ladder to be carried or a table to be moved. And both minds would always be working together on whatever problem might face me. This would be particularly nice in disposing of worries and arriving at decisions.

The whole idea is fantastic, of course. We know that in God's plan there is only one human nature (body and soul) for each human person (the self-conscious identity which marks me off from everyone else). But perhaps the imagery will help me to understand, just a little bit better, the personality of Jesus. The hypostatic union, the union of a human nature and a divine nature in the one Person, Jesus Christ, is a mystery of faith. That means that we cannot hope fully to understand it; but it does not mean that we cannot understand it at all.

As the second Person of the Blessed Trinity, God the Son, Jesus existed from all eternity. From all eternity He was generated or "begotten" in the mind of the Father. Then, at a certain point in time, God the Son united Himself, in the womb of the Virgin Mary, not merely to a body like ours, but to a body and soul—a complete human nature. The result was one single Person, acting always in harmony, acting always together, acting always as one identity.

The Son of God did not merely push a human nature around as a workman might push a tool. The Son of God was (and is) in and with His human nature with a personality as single and undivided as we, in our fantasy, were in and with the twin human natures which we imagined.

Jesus plainly showed the "twoness" of His natures by doing, on the one hand, things that only God could do: such as raising the dead to life by His own power. On the other hand, Jesus did the things that men must commonly do, such as eating and drinking and sleeping. And let it be noted that Jesus did not merely "go through the motions" of eating and drinking and sleeping and suffering. When He ate it was because He was really hungry; when He slept He was really fatigued; when He suffered He really felt the pain.

Equally plainly did Jesus show the "oneness" of His personality. In all that He did, there was complete unity of Person. He did not say to the widow's son, for example, "The God part of Me says to thee, Arise!" Jesus commanded simply, "I say to thee, Arise!" On the Cross Jesus did not say, "My human nature thirsts." He cried out, "I thirst."

Perhaps none of this will help us much in understanding the union of the two natures in Christ. At best, the truth will remain a mystery still. But at least it will remind us that we are not indulging in poetic fancy when we call the Virgin Mary by her glorious title of "Mother of God."

Sometimes our non-Catholic friends are moved to rebuke us for what they call the "over-glorification" of Mary. They are quite willing to call Mary the Mother of Christ, but they would rather be caught dead than to call her the Mother of God. And yet, unless they are ready to deny the divinity of Christ (in which case they cease to be Christians), they have no right to distinguish between "Mother of Christ" and "Mother of God."

A mother is not just the mother of her child's physical body; she is the mother of the complete person whom she bears. The complete Person Whom Mary bore is Jesus Christ, God as well as man. The Child Whom she bore, in the stable at Bethlehem nineteen and a half centuries ago, in a certain sense has God as His Father twice. The second Person of the Blessed Trinity had God as His Father from all eternity. Jesus Christ had God as His Father also when, at the Annunciation, the Holy Ghost conceived a Child within Mary's womb.

Anyone who has a dog fancier for a friend knows that there is considerable truth in the old saying, "Love me, love my dog." Silly as such a state of mind may seem to us, I am sure that any man or woman would subscribe to the statement, "Love me, love my mother."

How then could anyone profess to have a genuine love for Jesus Christ without also having a love for His Mother? The objection that honor given to Mary is honor taken from God; the criticism that Catholics have added a second mediator to the "one mediator between God and man, the Man Christ Jesus," shows how little understood is the truth of Christ's genuine humanness. Because Jesus loves Mary not merely with the impartial love which God has for every soul, not merely with the special love which God has for holy souls; Jesus loves Mary with the perfect human love which only the Perfect Man could have for the perfect Mother. He who belittles Mary does Jesus no service. On the contrary, he who dishonors Mary by reducing her to the stature of a "good woman," dishonors God in one of his most noble works of love and mercy.

Who Is Jesus Christ?

The greatest single fact in our lives is our Christian faith. Our entire lives, indeed the culture of the whole Western World, is built around our firm conviction that Jesus Christ lived and died. It would seem obvious that we should want to know all that we can about the life of Him

Who has so influenced us personally, and the world as well.

Yet there are Catholics who have read book-length biographies of Thomas Jefferson or Abraham Lincoln or the Little Flower, who still have never read a book-length life of Christ. In view of His importance to us, it seems pitiable that our knowledge of Jesus, in so many cases, should be confined to the fragmentary bits which are read in the Sunday Gospels.

At the very least, we should have read the complete story of Christ's life as it is told to us in the New Testament by Matthew, Mark, Luke and John. After doing that, the Gospel narrative will take on much more meaning for us if we read a book-length biography of Jesus.

There are many such volumes available at any Catholic bookstore or lending library. In these books the authors have drawn upon their scholarly knowledge of the times and customs amid which Jesus lived, in order to flesh out the bare skeleton of the Gospel account. Among the many fine biographies of Jesus which have been written, there is the semi-classic *The Christ, the Son of God*, by the Abbé Constant Fouard, a favorite of my own. More recent works are the *Life of Christ* as written by Father Giuseppe Ricciotti, and translated from the Italian. Then there is the very good and inexpensive *Life of Christ* written by the late Father Isidore O'Brien, O. F. M., and a more recent one entitled *Only Son*, written by the Dominican Father Walter Farrell. Any one of them is well worth the reading.

For our purpose here it must suffice to touch very briefly upon some of the high lights in the earthly career of Jesus Christ, Son of God and Son of man. After the birth of Jesus in the stable cave at Bethlehem on the first Christmas day, the next great event was the coming of the Wise Men from the East, guided by a star, to adore the newborn King.

It was a very significant event for us who are not Jews. It was the means which God took to show, publicly and clearly, that the Messias, the Promised One, had not come merely to save the Jews. That was the almost universal belief among the Jews themselves: that when the Messias came, He would be the exclusive property of the children of Israel, and would lead their nation to greatness and glory. But with the calling of the Wise Men to Bethlehem, God made it plain that Jesus was to be the Savior of the Gentiles, or non-Jews, as well as the Savior of His chosen people. That is why the coming of the Magi is called by the Greek name "Epiphany," which means "a public showing." That is why, too, the event was of such importance for you and for me. Although the feast of the Epiphany, January 6, is not a holyday of obligation in the United States,* nevertheless the Church ranks it in dignity even ahead of Christmas.

After the visit of the Magi, the subsequent flight of the Holy Family into Egypt to escape Herod's murderous plans, and their return from Egypt to Nazareth—the next glimpse we have of Jesus is when He accompanies Mary and Joseph to celebrate the great Jewish feast of the Passover at Jerusalem. The story of the Child's separation from His parents, and their discovery of Him three days later in the Temple, is familiar to us. Then the Evangelist St. Luke brings us up short before dropping the veil of silence upon the youth and young manhood of Jesus. "And Jesus advanced in wisdom," says St. Luke, " and age and grace before God and men" (2:52).

That phrase, "Jesus advanced in wisdom," brings up a question that might be worth discussing for a moment; the question of whether Jesus, in growing up, had to learn things as other children do. To answer that we have to remember that because Jesus had two natures, human and divine, He also had two kinds of knowledge. He had the infinite knowledge which God has: the knowledge of all things. Jesus had this knowledge, of course, from the very beginning of His existence in Mary's womb. As a human

* The feast of the Epiphany is a holyday of obligation by the law of the Church, but we are dispensed from it in the United States.

being, Jesus had another kind of knowledge, His human knowledge. His human knowledge, in turn, was of three kinds.

First there was the beatific knowledge which His human nature had from the moment of His conception, a knowledge which was the result of His human nature being united to a divine nature. This is similar to the knowledge which you and I will have when we see God in heaven. But there also was in Jesus an infused knowledge, such as God gave to the angels and to Adam. It is a knowledge directly conferred by God, a complete knowledge of created things, a knowledge that does not have to be laboriously reasoned out from the evidences supplied by the senses.

There also was in Jesus the experimental knowledge, the knowledge-by-experience, which He acquired as He grew and developed.

A navigator may know, by his charts and his instruments, that he will encounter a certain island at a certain point in the ocean. Yet when he finds the island, the navigator adds experimental knowledge to his previous theoretical knowledge. In somewhat the same way Jesus knew from the beginning what it would be like, for example, to walk. But He acquired the experimental knowledge of what it is like to walk only when His legs were strong enough to bear Him. . . . And so, at the age of twelve, St. Luke leaves the Child for another eighteen hidden years at Nazareth.

We might be tempted to wonder why Jesus Christ "wasted" so much of His life in the humble obscurity of Nazareth. From the time He was twelve until He was thirty, the Gospel tells us absolutely nothing about Jesus except that "Jesus advanced in wisdom and age and grace before God and men."

Then, on second thought, we see that Jesus was teaching us during His hidden years at Nazareth one of the most important lessons that man has need of. By quiet year piled upon quiet year, He was impressing upon us the fact that before God no person is unimportant and no task is trivial.

It is not by the size of our job that God measures us, but rather by the fidelity with which we try to do the thing that He has placed in our hands to do—the wholeheartedness with which we try to make His will ours.

Actually the quiet years He spent in Nazareth were as much a part of our redemption as were the three years of active ministry with which Christ's life ended. While He was wielding a hammer and driving nails in Joseph's workshop, Jesus was redeeming us just as truly as when other hands were driving other nails through His own palms on Calvary.

"To redeem" means to buy back something that has been lost, or sold or given away. By sin, man had lost—cast away —his birthright of eternal union with God, eternal happiness in heaven. The Son of God made man undertook to purchase that birthright back for us. That is why He is called the Redeemer; that is why His work is called the work of redemption.

And just as man's betrayal of himself had been caused by his refusal to give God his love (a refusal expressed in the act of disobedience, which is sin), so also Christ's work of redemption was in the form of an act of infinitely perfect love, expressed in the act of infinitely perfect obedience that comprised His whole life upon earth. Christ's death upon the Cross was the climax of this act of obedience; all that went before Calvary, and all that followed after, was a part of His Sacrifice too.

Whatever God does is of infinite value. Because He was God, the very least of Christ's sufferings was sufficient to satisfy for man's sin, sufficient to compensate for man's rejection of God. The least chill suffered by the Infant Jesus in Bethlehem's cave was enough to pay for all the sins that man could heap upon the other side of the scales.

But, in the plan of God, that was not enough. God's Son would carry His act of infinitely perfect obedience to the point of completely "emptying" Himself, to the point of death on Golgotha, or Calvary—which means the "Place of the Skull." Calvary was the peak, the summit, of the redemptive act. Nazareth, like Bethlehem, was a part of the slope that led to it. By the very fact that Christ's sufferings and death were so far beyond the price that really needed to be paid for sin, God has made unforgettably plain to us the twin lessons of sin's infinite evil, and God's infinite love for us.

It was when He was about thirty years old that Jesus began that phase of His work which we commonly call His public life. This began with His first public miracle at the wedding feast at Cana and continued through the ensuing three years. During these three years Jesus traveled up and down the countryside, preaching to the people, teaching them the truths which they must know, and the virtues which they must practice, if they wished to benefit by His redemption.

For although Christ's sufferings were sufficient to atone for every human sin, that did not mean that everyone, automatically, would be freed from sin. It still would be necessary for each one, individually, to apply to himself the merits of Christ's atoning Sacrifice or, in the case of infants, to have them applied through Baptism by another.

As He traveled and preached, Jesus worked countless miracles. Not only because of His infinite compassion did He work miracles, but also (and mainly) to prove His right to speak as He did. He was asking a lot from His hearers when He asked them to believe that He was the Son of God. But He left them no room for honest doubt when they saw Him cleanse lepers, restore sight to the blind, and raise the dead to life.

During these three years, too, Jesus kept reminding his listeners that the kingdom of God was at hand. This kingdom of God upon earth—which we now know as the Church—would be man's preparation for the eternal kingdom of heaven. The old Jewish religion, which God had established to prepare the way for Christ's coming, now would end. The old law of fear now would be replaced by the new law of love.

Very early in His public life Jesus chose the twelve men who were to be the first rulers in His new kingdom, the first bishops and priests of His Church. For three years Jesus instructed and trained His twelve Apostles for the task that was to be theirs—the task of solidly establishing the kingdom which He was founding.

CHAPTER VIII

The Redemption

How Does It End?

The present ambition of the Russian dictators is to conquer the world. They have made a good start at it, as the
enslaved peoples of a dozen countries can testify.

Two thousand years ago the emperors of Rome had
actually succeeded in doing what the Russians would like
to do today—the armies of Rome actually had conquered
the whole world—a much smaller world than the one we
know today. It comprised the known countries in southern
Europe, northern Africa, and western Asia. The rest of the
globe was as yet unexplored.

Rome was much easier on her satellite countries than
Russia is on hers. As long as the subject peoples behaved
themselves and paid their taxes to Rome, they were bothered
very little. A force of Roman soldiers was stationed in each
country and there was a proconsul or governor to keep an
eye on things. But otherwise the people were allowed to
retain their own local governments, and follow their own
laws and customs.

That was the position of Palestine in the time of our Lord Jesus Christ. Rome was top boss, but the Jews had their own king, Herod, and were governed by their own parliament, or council, which was called the Sanhedrin. There were no political parties as we know them today, but there was something very much like our modern political "machine." This political machine was made up of the Jewish priests, to whom politics and religion were one and the same thing; the Pharisees, who were the "blue bloods" of their day; and the Scribes, who were the lawyers. While there were some exceptions, most of these men were the type whom we would nowadays classify as "crooked politicians." They had nice soft jobs for themselves, and they were lining their pockets at the expense of the common people, whom they oppressed in a thousand ways.

That was the situation as Jesus walked the highways and by-ways of Judea and Galilee, preaching His message of God's love for man, and man's hope in God. As He worked His miracles and spoke of the kingdom of God that He had come to establish, many of His hearers took his words literally—they thought in terms of a political kingdom rather than a spiritual kingdom. They talked of making Jesus their king right then and there, a king who would subdue the Sanhedrin and throw out the hated Romans.

Word of all this reached the ears of the priests and the Scribes and the Pharisees. These corrupt men began to fear that the people might indeed stage a revolution, might indeed cast them out of their cozy and profitable offices. Their fear was turned to bitter hatred when Jesus publicly condemned them for their covetousness, their hypocrisy, their hardness of heart. They plotted among themselves as to how they might silence this Jesus of Nazareth Who was such a threat to their peace of mind. Several times they sent out lynching parties with the purpose of stoning Jesus to death or casting Him over a cliff. But each time Jesus (Who was not yet ready to die) slipped easily through the cordon of would-be assassins. Finally they began to search for a "finger man"—someone who would be close enough to Jesus to deliver Him safely into their hands without any slip-up, someone whose loyalty they could buy.

Judas Iscariot was their answer. And, unfortunately for Judas, Jesus now was ready to die. His task of revealing the fullness of God's truths to mankind was completed; His work of training the Apostles was finished. And so He waited, lying in the pool of His own bloody sweat, for Judas to come. The bloody sweat was forced from His physical organism by His divine knowledge of the agony that awaited Him.

But even more than the knowledge of the agony was the accompanying knowledge that for so many His blood would be shed in vain. There in Gethsemani His human nature was allowed to taste and to know, as only God can know, the infinite evil of sin in all its awful horror.

So Judas came, and His enemies took Jesus away to a trial that was a mockery of justice. Sentence of death already had been passed by the Sanhedrin even before the paid and contradictory witnesses were heard. The charge was simple: Jesus claimed to be God. That was a blasphemous thing for a man to claim. Blasphemy was punishable by death; to death Jesus must go. Then on to Pontius Pilate, the Roman governor. He must confirm the death sentence, since the infliction of capital punishment was not permitted to the subject nations. Only Rome could take a man's life.

When Pilate objected to sending Jesus to His death, the Jewish leaders threatened to make trouble for Pilate at Rome by reporting him as incompetent. The weakling Pilate succumbed to the blackmail—after vainly trying to assuage the rabble's blood thirst by having Jesus brutally scourged and crowned with thorns. It is on these things that we meditate as we tell the Sorrowful Mysteries of the Rosary, or make the Way of the Cross. We meditate, too, on what happened the next day at noon as the sound of hammers was heard on

Calvary, and the tortured Jesus hung for three hours upon the Cross, and finally died that we might live, on the Friday that we call Good.

Until Jesus died upon the Cross and paid the price of man's sin, no human soul could enter heaven, none could see God face to face. And yet, in the many centuries that had elapsed since Adam, there surely had been great numbers of men and women who had believed in God and His mercy and obeyed God's laws. Since such souls were not deserving of hell, they existed (until the Crucifixion) in a state of purely natural happiness, without any direct vision of God. They were happy very much as we on earth would be happy if everything were just perfect for us.

The state of natural happiness in which these souls awaited the full unveiling of God's glory is called limbo. It was to these souls that Jesus appeared, while His body lay in the tomb, to announce to them the glad tidings of their redemption; to escort them personally, we might say, as His first fruits to God the Father.

That is what we are referring to when we say in the Apostles' Creed that Jesus "descended into hell." Nowadays we use the word "hell" to designate only the state of the damned, those who have lost God forever. But the old English of the Creed uses the word "hell" to translate the Latin word *"inferus,"* which means "lower regions," or, simply, "the place of the dead."

Since Christ's death upon the Cross was a real death, it was His soul that appeared in limbo; His lifeless body, from which His soul was separated, lay in the tomb. During this time, however, His divine Person remained united both to His body and to His soul, ready to draw them together again on the third day.

Because Christ had promised that He would, He rose from the dead on the third day. He had promised, also, that it would be by His own power, and not by that of another, that He would return to life. It was this that would give the final and inescapable proof of the fact that He was, as He claimed to be, God Himself.

The story of the Resurrection, the event which we celebrate on Easter Sunday, is too familiar to need repeating here. There was the blind obstinacy of the Jewish leaders who thought to defeat the plans of God by placing a guard at the sepulcher to keep the body of Jesus safely shut up. There was the early-morning stupor of the guards, and the rolling back of the stone from the sepulcher's entrance, as Jesus walked out.

It was in a glorified body that Jesus rose from the dead, a body glorified even as our bodies will be after our own resurrection. It was a body that was "spiritualized," freed from the limitations of the physical world. It was (and is) a body that could no longer suffer or die; a body that radiated the brightness and beauty of a soul united with God; a body that physical matter could not impede, and which could pass through a solid wall as if the wall did not exist; a body which had no need to travel by laborious steps, but which could pass from place to place with the speed of thought; it was a body free from such organic necessities as food and drink and sleep.

Having risen from the dead, Christ did not, as we might have expected, ascend immediately into heaven. Had He done so, the skeptics who disbelieved (and they still are with us) in His Resurrection would have been even harder to convince. It was partly for this reason that Jesus chose to remain forty days upon earth. During this time He appeared to Mary Magdalen, to the disciples on the road to Emmaus, to His Apostles several times. But we may be sure that our Lord made many other appearances besides the ones mentioned in the Gospels: to individuals (His Blessed Mother, surely?) and to whole crowds of people (St. Paul mentions one such appearance, when more than five hundred were present). No one ever would be able to ask, in honesty, "How do we know that He is risen? Who saw Him?"

Besides proving the reality of His Resurrection, Jesus had another aim to fulfill during those forty days—to complete the training and commissioning of His twelve Apostles. At the Last Supper on Holy Thursday night He had made them priests. Now on Easter Sunday night He complements their priesthood with the power to forgive sins. When He appears to them at another time He fulfills His promise to Peter, to make Peter the head of His Church. He explains to them the Holy Ghost, Who will abide as the life-giving Spirit in His Church. He outlines to them their future course of action. And finally, on Mt. Olivet, on the day we commemorate as Ascension Thursday, He gives His Apostles their final command to go and preach the Gospel to the whole world; He gives them His final blessing, and ascends into heaven.

There He "sits at the right hand of God, the Father Almighty." Being Himself God, He is in all things the Father's equal; and as man He is above all the saints in the closeness of His union with God the Father, with supreme authority as King over all creatures. Like converging rays of light focused in a lens, all creation became focused in Him, became His, when He took our human nature for His own. Through His Church He rules souls in matters spiritual; but even in matters purely civil and temporal, His will and His law must come first. And His title to supreme ruler over men was made doubly secure when He redeemed them, purchased them, with His precious blood.

Since He has ascended to His Father, mankind's next view of their Risen King will come at the end of the world. He came once in helpless weakness to Bethlehem; at the end of the world He will come in glorious strength to judge the world which His Father has given to Him, and which He Himself bought so dearly. "He shall come to judge the living and the dead!"

CHAPTER IX

The Holy Ghost and Grace

The Unknown Person

In the Bible, in the Acts of the Apostles (19:2), we read that St. Paul came to the city of Ephesus, in Asia. There he found a small group of people who already believed in the teachings of Jesus. Paul asked them, "Did you receive the Holy Spirit when you became believers?" Their answer was, "We have not even heard that there is a Holy Spirit."

Certainly none of us today is ignorant of the Holy Spirit —or if we prefer the Old English, the Holy "Ghost." We know well that He is one of the three divine Persons who, with the Father and the Son, constitute the Blessed Trinity. We also know that He is called the Paraclete (the Greek word for "Comforter"), the Advocate (pleading God's cause with mankind), the Spirit of Truth, the Spirit of God, and the Spirit of Love. We also know that He "comes to us" when we are baptized, and that He continues to dwell within us as long as we do not shut Him out by mortal sin.

That, for many Catholics, is just about the sum of their knowledge of the Holy Spirit. And yet we can have but little understanding of the work of sanctification that goes on within our souls unless we know the place of the Holy Spirit in the divine scheme of things.

The existence of the Holy Spirit—indeed the doctrine of the Blessed Trinity—was all but unknown until Christ unveiled the truth to us. In Old Testament times the Jews were surrounded by idolatrous nations. More than once the Jews turned from the worship of the one God who had made them His chosen people, to the worship of many gods as practiced by their neighbors. As a consequence, God, through His prophets, hammered away at the idea of the *oneness* of God, the *unity* of God. He did not complicate things by revealing to pre-Christian man that there are three Persons in God. It remained for Jesus Christ to give us this marvelous insight into the inner nature of the Deity.

It might be well to recall here, briefly, the essence of the divine nature so far as we can understand it. God's knowledge of Himself, we know, is an infinitely perfect knowledge. That is, the "picture" that God has of Himself in His own divine mind is an absolutely perfect representation of Himself. But it would not be a *perfect* representation unless it were a *living* representation. To live, to exist, belongs to the very nature of God. A mental image of God that was not a living image would not be a perfect representation.

This living image of Himself which God has in His mind, this idea of Himself which God has been generating (or "giving birth to") in His divine mind from all eternity, we call God the Son. God the Father we might say is God in the eternal act of "thinking about" Himself. God the Son is the living (and eternal) "thought" which results from that thinking. Both the Thinker and the Thought are of course within one and the same divine nature; there is only one God, but these are two Persons.

And it does not stop there. God the Father and God the Son behold, each of them, the infinite lovableness of the other. And so there flows between these two divine Persons a divine Love. It is a love so perfect, of such infinite ardor, as to be a *living* love, and we call this Love the Holy Spirit, the third Person of the Blessed Trinity. Like two volcanoes exchanging a single stream of fire, Father and Son eternally reciprocate this Living Flame of Love. That is why we say, in the Nicene Creed, that the Holy Spirit proceeds from the Father *and* the Son.

This, then, is the internal life of the Most Blessed Trinity —God knowing, God known, and God loving-and-loved. Three divine Persons, each distinct from the other two in his relationship to each of the others and yet possessing one and the same divine nature, possessing that nature, too, in absolute unity. Since they possess the divine nature equally, there is no subordination of one to the other. God the Father is not wiser than God the Son. God the Son is not more powerful than God the Holy Spirit.

We must guard too against thinking of the Blessed Trinity in terms of time. God the Father did not "come first," and then God the Son a little later, with God the Holy Ghost "coming" last of all. This process of knowing-loving that constitutes the inner life of the Blessed Trinity has been going on from all eternity; it had no beginning.

There is one other point of interest before we go on to discuss the Holy Spirit in particular. That is the fact that the three divine Persons are not only united in one divine nature; they also are united in *each other*. Each one of them is in each of the others in an inseparable unity—somewhat as the three primary colors of the spectrum are (by nature) inseparably united in the one colorless radiation which we call light. It is of course possible to break up a ray of light by artificial means, such as a prism, to make a rainbow. But if the ray of light is left to itself, the red is in the blue and the blue is in the yellow and the red is in them both; just one ray of light.

No example, of course, is perfect when applied to God. But by analogy we might say that just as the three colors of the spectrum are inseparably present, each in the other, so also in the Blessed Trinity the Father is in the Son, and the Son in the Father, and the Holy Spirit in both. Where one is, all are. This inseparable unity of the three divine Persons —in case you are interested in theological terms—is called "circumincession."

Most of us, when we were in school, studied physiology or biology. As a consequence we have a pretty good idea of what goes on inside our bodies. But not so many of us have a clear idea as to what goes on inside our souls. We talk rather easily of grace—actual grace and sanctifying grace— and of supernatural life and of growth in holiness. The question is, what do these words *mean?*

To answer that question adequately, we need first to understand the part which the Holy Spirit plays in the sanctification of the human soul. We know that the Holy Spirit is the infinite Love flowing eternally between God the Father and God the Son. He is Love in person, a *living* love. Since it is God's love for us that has led Him to make us sharers in His own divine life, it is quite natural for us to ascribe to the Spirit of Love—the Holy Ghost—the operations of grace in our souls.

However, we have to keep in mind that the three divine Persons are inseparable. In terms that are human (but not theologically exact) we might say that none of the three divine Persons does anything separately or alone, outside the divine nature. Within that divine nature, within the Godhead, each Person has His own particular activity, His own particular *relationship*, one to the other. God the Father is God knowing Himself, God "seeing" Himself; God the Son is God's living image of Himself; and God the Holy Ghost is God's love for Himself.

But "outside Himself" (if we may speak so loosely), God acts only in His perfect unity; no divine Person does anything by Himself. What one divine Person does, all three do. Outside the divine nature, it is the Blessed Trinity always who acts. To use a very homely and inadequate example, I might say that the only place my brain and heart and lungs do anything by themselves is inside me; each of them doing its own proper job for the good of the other. But *outside* me, brain and heart and lungs work inseparably together. Wherever I may go, whatever I may be doing, brain and heart and lungs are in on it as a unit. None of the three goes off on a separate activity of its own.

But we often speak as though they did. We say that a man is "long-winded," as if it were only his lungs which did all the talking. We say that a man is "stout-hearted," as though courage were entirely a matter of the heart. We say that a man is "brainy," as though a brain could think without blood and oxygen. We ascribe to one particular organ a job that all of them are working on together.

Now let us make the tremendous jump from our own lowly physical organs to the three living Persons who constitute the Blessed Trinity. Then perhaps we can understand a little better why it is that the work of sanctifying souls is assigned to the Holy Spirit.

Since God the Father is the source of principle of the divine activity which goes on within the Blessed Trinity (the knowing-and-loving activity), He is considered to be the beginning of everything. That is why we assign to the Father the work of creation. Actually, of course, it is the Blessed Trinity who creates—whether it be the universe or an individual soul. What one divine Person does, all Three do. But we *appropriate* to the Father the act of creation. Because of His relationship to the other two Persons, the role of Creator fits the Father best.

Then, since it was through the second Person, God the Son, that God united a human nature to Himself in the Person of Jesus Christ, we attribute the work of redemption to God the Son, the living Wisdom of God the Father. Infinite Power (the Father) decrees redemption; Infinite Wisdom (the Son) puts the decree into execution. However, when we refer to God the Son as the Redeemer, we remain conscious of the fact that God the Father and God the Holy Spirit were also inseparably present in Jesus Christ. Absolutely speaking it was the Blessed Trinity who redeemed us. But we *appropriate* to the Son the act of redemption.

Finally, since the work of sanctifying souls is pre-eminently a work of divine love (as distinguished from a work of power or a work of wisdom) we refer this work of sanctification to the Holy Spirit. He is, after all, divine Love personified. Basically it is the Blessed Trinity who sanctifies us. It is God the Blessed Trinity who dwells within the sin-free soul. But we *appropriate* the action of grace to the Holy Spirit.

In the preceding paragraphs I have italicized the word "appropriate." I have done so because it is the exact word used in the science of theology. It is the word used to describe this way of "dividing up" the work of the Blessed Trinity among the three divine Persons. What one Person does, all do. And yet certain activities seem more *appropriate* to one Person than to another. As a consequence theologians say that God the Father is the Creator, by appropriation; God the Son is the Redeemer, by appropriation; and God the Holy Ghost is the Sanctifier, by appropriation.

All this may seem unnecessarily technical to the average reader. And yet it may help us to understand what is meant when the catechism, for example, says, "The Holy Ghost dwells in the Church as the source of its life and sanctifies souls through the gift of grace." God's Love is at work, but His wisdom and power also are there.

What Is Grace?

The word "grace" has many meanings. It may mean "attractiveness," as when we say, "She moved with grace across the room." It may mean "benevolence," as when we say, "I sought his good graces in the matter." It may mean "thanksgiving," as when we speak of saying "grace after meals." Any one of us probably can think of half a dozen other ways in which the word "grace" is commonly used.

In the science of theology, however, *grace* has a very definite and restricted meaning. It means, first of all, a gift from God. Not just any kind of gift; on the contrary, a very special sort of gift. Life itself is a gift of God. God was under no compulsion to make the human race to begin with, much less to make you or me as individuals. All that accompanies human life is likewise a gift of God. The power of sight and of speech; physical health; such abilities as we may possess—to sing or draw or bake a cake; all of these are gifts of God. But such gifts as these we call *natural* gifts. They are a part of our nature as human beings. There are certain things that necessarily go with being a human creature, as God has designed human nature. These gifts of God we cannot accurately call *graces*.

The word "grace" is reserved in theology to describe those gifts to which man is not even remotely entitled, not even by virtue of his nature as a human being. The word "grace" is used to identify those gifts which are *above* human nature. And so we take the Latin word "super," which means "above," and we say that grace is a *supernatural* gift of God.

The definition, however, still is incomplete. There are gifts of God which are supernatural but which cannot, strictly speaking, be called graces. For example, a person with an incurable cancer might be miraculously cured at Lourdes. In such a case that person's health would be a supernatural gift, restored by a means which is above and beyond nature. If we want to be precise, we do not call this cure a *grace*. There are other gifts, too, which are supernatural in their origin but which do not qualify to be called graces. The Bible, for example, is a supernatural gift of God; so is the Church, so are the sacraments.

Such gifts as these, supernatural though they be, operate

outside us. It would not be incorrect to call them "external graces." The word "grace," however, when it is used simply and by itself, refers to those *invisible* gifts which reside in the soul, or operate in the soul. So we build up our definition of grace a little more, by saying that it is an *interior* supernatural gift of God.

That immediately brings up another question. Sometimes God gives to chosen souls the power to foretell the future. This is an interior supernatural gift. Would we call it a grace, this power of prophecy? Or again, a priest has the power to change bread and wine into Christ's body and blood, and to forgive sins. These certainly are interior supernatural gifts. Are they graces? To both questions the answer is no. Powers such as these, although they are interior and supernatural gifts, are given for the benefit of other people, not for the benefit of the one who has the power. A priest's power to offer Mass is not for his own sake, but for the sake of Christ's Mystical Body. A priest might conceivably be in the state of mortal sin himself, and yet his Mass would be a true Mass and would gain grace for others. He might have sin on his own soul, and yet his words of absolution would forgive the sins of others. This brings us then to another point which must be added to our definition of grace: grace is an interior supernatural gift of God bestowed on us *for our own salvation*.

Finally we raise this question: If grace is a gift of God to which we have absolutely no shadow of right or claim, how is it that we have been given grace? The first creatures (that we know of) to whom grace was given were the angels and Adam and Eve. It perhaps is not so surprising, in view of God's infinite goodness, that the angels and our first parents were given grace. They didn't *deserve* it, true enough; but, although they had no *right* to grace, at the same time they were not positively unworthy of the gift.

However, once Adam and Eve had sinned, they (and we their descendants) were not only undeserving of grace; they (and we) became actually *unworthy* of anything beyond the ordinary natural gifts pertaining to human nature. How could God's infinite justice, outraged by original sin, be satisfied so that His infinite goodness might operate once again to mankind's benefit?

The answer to that question rounds out for us the definition of grace. It was Jesus Christ, we know, whose life and death made satisfaction to the divine Justice for mankind's sin. It was Jesus Christ who merited for us, earned for us, the grace which Adam had so lightly tossed away. And so we complete our definition by saying: *Grace is an interior supernatural gift of God bestowed on us through the merits of Jesus Christ for our salvation.* Who would have thought that so few words could contain so much meaning!

When we were born our soul was, spiritually speaking, dark and empty—spiritually dead. There was no bond of union between our soul and God. There was no intercourse, no communication, between our soul and God. If, without Baptism, we had reached the use of reason and had died without committing a single personal sin (a purely imaginary hypothesis, actually impossible), we still would not have gone to heaven. We would have entered into a state of natural happiness which, for want of a better name, we call limbo. But we never would have seen God, face to face, and as He really is.

This is a point that bears repeating—the fact that by our nature as human beings we have no *right* to that direct vision of God which constitutes the essential happiness of heaven. Not even Adam and Eve, before their fall, had any *right* to heaven. In fact, the human soul, in what we might call its purely natural state, simply has not got the power to see God; it has not got the capacity for intimate, personal union with God.

But God did not leave man in this purely natural state. When He created Adam, God gave Adam all that he was entitled to as a human being. But God went further; He gave to the soul of Adam a certain quality or power which would make it possible for Adam to live in close (although invisible) union with Him in this life. Because this special quality of soul—this power of union and intercommunication with God—was completely *above* the *natural* powers of the soul, we call it a *super*natural quality of the soul, a supernatural gift.

The way that God imparted this special quality or power to the soul of Adam was by the indwelling of Himself in Adam's soul. In a wonderful manner that must remain a mystery to us until Judgment Day, God "took up residence" in Adam's soul. And much as the sun in the sky imparts light and warmth to the surrounding atmosphere, so also did God in Adam's soul impart this supernatural quality which is nothing less than a sharing, to a degree, in God's own life. Sunlight is not the sun; but it flows from the sun, it is the result of the sun's presence. So also this supernatural quality of soul that we speak of is distinct from God, yet flows from Him and is the result of His presence in the soul.

This supernatural quality of the soul has another effect. It not only enables us to live in close union and communication with God in this life; it also prepares the soul for another gift which God will add after death. That gift will be the gift of supernatural vision, the power to see God face to face, as He really is.

The reader will have recognized already that this "supernatural quality of soul" of which I have been talking, is that gift of God to which theologians have given the name "sanctifying grace." I have described it first, instead of naming it, in the hope that the name might mean more when we got to it. And the added gift of supernatural vision after death, is what theologians call (in Latin) the "Lumen Gloriae." In English, it is the "Light of Glory." Sanctifying grace is a necessary preparation, a prerequisite to the Light of Glory. Much as an electric lamp is useless without a socket into which to fit, so also the Light of Glory could find no place in a soul that was not possessed of sanctifying grace.

I have talked of sanctifying grace in terms of Adam. In the very act of creating Adam, God raised him above a merely natural level, raised him to a supernatural destiny by conferring sanctifying grace upon him. By original sin, Adam lost that grace for himself and us. Jesus Christ healed the breach between man and God by His death on the cross. Man's supernatural destiny is restored. To each man individually sanctifying grace is imparted in the sacrament of Baptism.

When we are baptized we receive sanctifying grace for the first time. God (the Holy Ghost by "appropriation") takes up His abode within us. By His presence He imparts to our soul that supernatural quality which makes it possible for God, in a grand and mysterious manner, to see Himself in us and therefore to love us. And, because this supernatural quality of soul, this sanctifying grace, was purchased for us by Jesus Christ, we are bound by it to Christ, we share it with Christ—and God consequently sees us as He sees His Son—and we become, each of us, a child of God.

Sanctifying grace is sometimes called habitual grace, because it is intended to be a habitual or permanent condition of the soul. Once we are united with God in Baptism, it is intended that we remain united with Him forever—invisibly here, visibly hereafter.

The Grace that Comes and Goes

God made us for the beatific vision—for the person-to-person union with Himself which is the happiness of heaven. In order that we may be capable of this direct vision of God, He will give us a supernatural power which we call the Light of Glory. The Light of Glory, however, can be bestowed only on a soul which already is united with God by means of that earlier gift which we call sanctifying grace. If we go into eternity deprived of sanctifying grace, then we have lost God forever.

Once we have received sanctifying grace in Baptism, it

then becomes a matter of life-and-death importance that we preserve this supernatural gift to the very end. Or, if self-sought catastrophe does strike in the form of mortal sin, then it is of dreadful urgency that we recover the precious gift which our sin has lost, the spiritual life of sanctifying grace which we have extinguished in our soul.

It is important, too, that we increase sanctifying grace within our soul. And it *is* capable of increase. The more the soul is purified of self, the more responsive does it become to the action of God. As self diminishes, sanctifying grace increases. And it is the *degree* of sanctifying grace that will determine the degree of our happiness in heaven. Two men looking at the ceiling of the Sistine Chapel will both find complete enjoyment in the sight of Michelangelo's master-piece, but the man with the cultivated eye will find more enjoyment in it than the other man, whose artistic tastes are of a low order. The man with little artistic appreciation will be quite satisfied; he will not be aware that he is missing any-thing, but he will be missing a lot. Similarly, we all shall be perfectly happy in heaven. But the *degree* of our happi-ness will depend upon the spiritual sharpness of our vision. That in turn will depend upon the degree to which sancti-fying grace has permeated our soul.

These, then, are our three needs with regard to sanctify-ing grace: first, that we preserve it permanently and until the end; secondly, that we recover it immediately if we have lost it by mortal sin; thirdly, that we seek to grow in sanctifying grace with an eagerness that sees the sky as the limit.

Now none of these three things is easy to do. In fact, by our human wisdom and strength alone, none of these three things is even possible. Like a bombed victim wandering dazed and weakened from the ruins, so has human nature staggered down through the centuries from the explosive rebellion of original sin—judgment permanently warped, will permanently weakened. It is so hard to recognize danger in time; so hard to look honestly at the greater good that needs doing; so hard to turn our gaze from the hypnotic beckoning of sin.

That is why sanctifying grace, like a king surrounded by a retinue of servants, is preceded by and accompanied by a whole train of special helps from God. These special helps we call actual graces. An actual grace is a momentary, transient *impulse*, a spurt of spiritual energy with which God touches the soul—somewhat as the hand of a mechanic might touch a spinning wheel in order to keep the wheel in motion.

Actual grace may work upon the mind or upon the will; usually upon both. Actual grace is given by God always for one of the three purposes mentioned above: either to prepare the way for the first infusion of sanctifying grace (or to restore it when lost); to preserve sanctifying grace in the soul; and to increase it. The operation of actual grace may be clearer if we trace its work in an imaginary person who has lost sanctifying grace through mortal sin.

First God illumines the mind of the sinner so that he may see the evil of what he has done. If the sinner accepts this grace, he admits to himself, "I have offended God in a serious matter; I have committed a mortal sin." The sinner can, of course, reject this first grace; he can say, "What I did wasn't so awfully bad; lots of people do worse things than that." If he does reject the first grace, there probably will be no second. In the normal course of God's providence, one grace begets another. This is the meaning of Christ's words when He says, "To everyone who has shall be given, and he shall have abundance; but from him who does not have, even that which he seems to have shall be taken away" (Matt. 25:29).

But supposing the sinner to have accepted the first grace, then the second grace follows. This time it is a strengthening of the will, which enables the sinner to make an act of contrition: "Dear God," he groans inwardly, "if I die like this, I'll lose heaven and go to hell, and it's a shabby way I've treated You, in return for all Your love. Dear God, I'll *not* do that again!" If the sinner's sorrow is perfect (stemming mainly from his love for God), then sanctifying grace is at once restored to his soul; God at once reunites the soul to Himself. If the sorrow is imperfect, based mainly on fear of God's justice, then there will be a further impulse of grace. His mind enlightened, the sinner will say, "I *must* go to confession." His will strengthened, he will resolve, "I *shall* go to confession." And, in the sacrament of Penance, sanctifying grace is restored to his soul. That is a concrete instance of how actual grace works.

Without God's help we cannot succeed in getting to heaven. The story of grace is as simple as that. Without sanctifying grace we are not *capable* of the beatific vision. Without actual grace we are not *capable* of receiving sanctifying grace in the first place (once we have reached the use of reason). Without actual grace we are not capable of remaining for any long period in the state of sanctifying grace. Without actual grace we cannot recover sanctifying grace if we should lose it.

In view of the absolute necessity of grace, it is comforting to recall another truth which also is a matter of faith—something we must believe. That is the fact that God gives to every soul He creates sufficient grace to get to heaven. No one ever will lose heaven except through his own fault, through his own failure to *use* God's grace.

For it is possible, of course, to reject grace. God's grace works in and through our human will. God's grace does not destroy our freedom of choice. It is true that grace does most of the work, but God requires of us our co-operation. At the very least, our part is to place no obstacle to the operation of grace in our soul.

We are speaking mainly of actual graces, those divine impulses which move us to judge what is right and to do what is good. Perhaps an example will help to illustrate the operation of grace with respect to free will.

Let us suppose that I have been bedridden with a long illness. Now I am recuperating, but I have to learn to walk again. If I try to walk alone, I shall fall on my face. So a good friend undertakes to help me. He puts his arm around my waist, and I lean heavily on his shoulder. Gently he propels me across the floor; I am walking again! Actually, as I walk my friend is doing most of the work, but there is one thing my friend cannot do for me; he cannot pick up my feet. If I will not even try to put one foot in front of the other; if I just let myself hang, a dead weight, clinging to my friend, then my friend's help is wasted. In spite of him, I will not walk.

In much the same way we can let God's grace go unused. By our own indifference or sloth—and even worse, by our positive resistance—we can frustrate the operation of God's grace in our soul. Of course, God can, if He chooses, give us so much grace that our human will is carried along with almost no effort on our part. This is what theologians call *efficacious* grace, as distinguished from merely sufficient grace. Efficacious grace actually accomplishes its purpose. It not only is *sufficient* to our spiritual needs, but in addition is strong enough to overcome the weakness or obduracy which might cause us to neglect or resist the grace.

All of us, I am sure, at one time or another have had experiences like this: We are faced with a strong temptation; perhaps we even know by past experience that this is a temptation which usually defeats us. We breathe a half-hearted prayer for help, not even sure in our own mind that we *want* to be helped. And lo and behold! the temptation disappears. Thinking about it afterwards, we can't honestly say that we *conquered* the temptation; rather, it just seemed to evaporate.

We have had the experience, too, of doing an action that is, for us, unexpectedly generous or self-sacrificing or compassionate. We feel a shock of pleased surprise. "Really," we admit secretly to ourselves, "that wasn't like me at all."

In both of these examples we have had graces that were

not merely *sufficient*, but graces that were efficacious. These examples are of the more striking kind. But actually, any time that we do good or abstain from evil, our grace has been efficacious; it has accomplished its purpose. This is true even when we are conscious of some effort on our part, even when we feel that we have been through a struggle.

Indeed, I think that one of our biggest surprises on Judgment Day will be to discover how *little* we have had to do with our own salvation. We shall be amazed to learn how continually and completely God's grace has surrounded us and accompanied us all through life. During this life we do occasionally recognize God's hand. Once in a while we can say, "God's grace surely was with me," but on Judgment Day we shall see that for every grace which we have recognized, there have been a hundred or ten thousand other, more hidden, graces of which we have been totally unconscious.

Our surprise too will be mixed with shame. We go through life, most of us, patting ourselves on the back for our little victories. We said no to that drink which would have been one too many; we changed our mind about going out with that person who might have meant sin for us. We held our tongue when we wanted to make a biting and angry reply. We rolled out of bed for weekday Mass when our body was crying in protest.

And then on Judgment Day we shall get our first square look at ourselves. We shall see the full picture of the workings of grace in our life. We shall see how little we ourselves had to do with our heroic decisions and our supposedly noble deeds. Almost, we can imagine God smiling at us in loving amusement as He sees our chagrin; as He hears us exclaim in confusion, "Why God! It was You all the time!"

Wellsprings of Life

There are, as we well know, two sources of divine grace: prayer and the sacraments. Once we have received sanctifying grace through Baptism, then it is by means of prayer and the other six sacraments that sanctifying grace is increased in the soul. If we lose sanctifying grace through mortal sin, then it is by means of prayer (disposing us for forgiveness) and the sacrament of Penance that sanctifying grace is restored to the soul.

Prayer is defined as "the lifting of the mind and heart to God." We may lift our mind and heart to God through the use of words. We may say, "O my God, I am sorry for my sins," or "O my God, I love You," speaking to God quite naturally in our own words. Or we can raise our mind and heart to God by means of words which someone else has written, trying to *mean* the words which we speak.

These "set" prayers may be the privately composed (but officially approved) prayers which we find in many prayer books and devotional leaflets; or they may be liturgical prayers, the official prayers of the Church, of the Mystical Body of Christ. These are the prayers of the Mass, of the Breviary, and of various sacred functions. Most of these prayers, such as the Psalms and the Canticles, have been taken from the Holy Bible, and so are words inspired by God Himself.

We may pray, then, in our own words or in the words of another. We may use privately composed prayers or liturgical prayers. Whatever the sources of our words may be, so long as the use of words figures prominently in our prayer, then our prayer is classified as *vocal prayer*. This would be true even though the words are not spoken aloud, even though we say the words silently to ourselves. It is not the tone of voice, but the use of words that determines vocal prayer. This is a type of prayer that is universally used, by saint and not-so-saintly, alike.

But there is a higher type of prayer which is called *mental prayer*. In this kind of prayer, the mind and heart do *all* the work, without benefit of words. Almost everyone makes use of mental prayer at one time or another, oftentimes without realizing it. If you have ever looked at a crucifix and have thought to yourself of how much Jesus suffered for you, of how petty your own troubles are, and have resolved to be more patient hereafter—then you have practiced mental prayer. If you have ever (perhaps after Communion?) thought about how good God has been to you, of how little you have done for Him, and have resolved to be more generous with God in the future, then you have practiced mental prayer.

This kind of mental prayer, in which the mind thinks about some divine truth—perhaps about some word or action of Christ—with the result that the heart (really the *will*) is moved to greater love and fidelity to God—this kind of prayer is commonly called meditation. While it is true that almost any practical Catholic will, at least intermittently, practice a certain amount of meditation, yet it needs pointing out that normally there will be no notable spiritual growth unless a person gives some of his prayer time regularly to mental prayer. That is why the Canon Law of the Church requires that every priest devote some time daily to mental prayer. Most religious orders prescribe a full hour of mental prayer daily for their members.

For the average person, a very simple and fruitful form of meditation would be to read a chapter of the Gospels each day. It should be at a time and in a place that is as free as possible from noise and distractions. It should be read thoughtfully and slowly. Then a few minutes should be given to turning over in one's mind what has been read; giving it a chance to sink in, applying it to one's own life; letting it lead, as it normally will, to a resolution of some kind.

Besides meditation, of which we have been speaking, there is another form of mental prayer—a still higher form of prayer—which we call contemplation. We are accustomed to thinking of the saints as "contemplatives." We are likely to think that contemplation is something reserved to convents and monasteries. Actually, the prayer of contemplation is a form of prayer at which every sincere Christian ought to aim. It is a form of prayer to which, usually, our prayer of meditation will lead if we meditate *regularly*.

It is hard to describe the prayer of contemplation because there is so little to describe. We might say that it is that type of prayer in which the mind and heart are raised to God— period. The mind and heart are raised to God and rest there. The mind, at least, is inactive. What movement there is is of the heart (or *will*) only, towards God. Whatever "work" is done is done by God Himself. He can operate now quite freely in this heart which has fastened itself so firmly to Him.

Before anyone says, "Oh, I never could contemplate!" let me ask this: "Have you never knelt (or sat) in a quiet church, perhaps after Mass or on your way home from work; have you never remained there for a few minutes, without conscious thought, perhaps just looking at the tabernacle, not thinking, just sort of *yearning;* and left church finally, with a strange feeling of renewed strength and courage and peace? Then you *have* practiced the prayer of contemplation, whether you knew it or not. So let us not say that contemplation is beyond our reach. It is the kind of prayer that God wants *all* of us to reach for; it is the kind of prayer that all other prayer—vocal prayer (whether private or liturgical) and meditation—is designed to lead us to. It is the kind of prayer that will most richly contribute to growth in grace.

This wonderful inner life which is ours—this sharing in God's own life which we call sanctifying grace—is increased through prayer. It is increased also by means of the sacraments, the sacraments which follow after Baptism. The life of an infant increases with every breath he draws, with every ounce of food he takes, with every movement of his unformed muscles. So too do the other six sacraments build upon the life-beginning, the first accession of sanctifying grace which Baptism gives.

That is true even of the sacrament of Penance. We usually

think of Penance as the sacrament of forgiveness. We think of it as the sacrament which restores life when sanctifying grace has been lost through mortal sin. That is, indeed, the primary purpose of the sacrament of Penance. But the sacrament is a life-building medicine as well as a life-restoring medicine. It would be a most unfortunate ignorance to suppose that the sacrament of Penance is to be reserved only for the forgiveness of mortal sin. It has a secondary purpose. For the soul which already is in the state of sanctifying grace, Penance is just as truly an increaser of life as is the Holy Eucharist. That is why those who aim at more than mediocrity in their spiritual lives love to receive the sacrament of Penance frequently.

It is the Holy Eucharist, however, which is pre-eminently the sacrament of life. It is the Holy Eucharist which above all other sacraments, enriches and intensifies the life of grace within us. The very form of the sacrament would tell us that. In the Holy Eucharist God comes to us, not through the cleansing washing with water, not through the strengthening anointing with oil, not through the power-giving imposition of hands, but as the very food and drink of our souls, under the appearances of bread and wine.

The dynamic upward-thirsting life which we call sanctifying grace is the result of the soul's union with God, the result of God's personal indwelling in the soul. There is no other sacrament which unites us so directly and so intimately with God as does the Holy Eucharist. This is true whether we think of the Holy Eucharist in terms of the Mass or in terms of Holy Communion. In the Mass our soul reaches up, like an infant seeking the breast of his mother, to the very bosom of the Most Blessed Trinity. As we unite ourselves with Christ in the Mass, Christ integrates our love with His own infinite love for God. We become a part of the gift of Himself which He is offering, in this endless Calvary, to the Triune God. He carries us, we might say, along with Himself and introduces us into that mysterious depth which is the eternal life of the Godhead. In such immediate contact with God it is no wonder that the Mass is for us such an abounding source of life, such a multiplier of sanctifying grace.

But the flow of life does not end as, at the Consecration of the Mass, we touch divinity. Now the process reverses itself. As we, with and through Christ, have reached up to God, so God in turn, in and through Christ, reaches down to us. In a mystery of union which must leave even the angels gasping, God comes to us. This time God does not use water or oil or gesture or spoken word as the carrier of His grace. This time it is Jesus Christ Himself, God's own Son, really and personally present under the appearances of bread, who skyrockets the level of sanctifying grace within us.

The Mass itself, even without Holy Communion, is a limitless sources of grace for every member of Christ's Mystical Body who is already spiritually alive. For each of us individually the graces of the Mass increase to the degree in which we consciously and actively unite ourselves with Christ in His offering of Himself. When circumstances make quite impossible the actual reception of Holy Communion, a sincere and fervent spiritual communion will still more increase the grace we receive from Mass. Christ is quite capable of bridging a gap that is not of our own making.

But it should be quite evident that any Catholic genuinely interested in his own spiritual growth will want to complete the cycle of grace with actual Holy Communion. "Every Mass a Communion Mass" should be the aim of all of us. There is a sad waste of grace in any Mass for one who fails through lethargy or indifference to open his heart to the gift of Himself which God offers. And it is a misunderstanding that is close to stupidity to look upon Holy Communion as a periodic "duty" to be fulfilled once a month or once a year.

There is a point that bears noting here with regard to the life-giving power of prayer and the sacraments alike.

It has been emphasized that grace, in all its forms, is a free gift of God. Whether it be the beginning of holiness in Baptism or growth in holiness through prayer and the other sacraments—every bit of it is the work of God. No matter what heroic acts I might perform, without God's grace I never could save myself.

However, this must not lead me to think that prayer and the sacraments are magic formulas which will save me and sanctify me in spite of myself. If I think that, then I shall be guilty of that religious "formalism" of which Catholics often are accused. Religious formalism results when a person thinks that he becomes "good" simply by going through certain motions, speaking certain prayers and taking part in certain ceremonies. Against Catholics in general the accusation is most unjust, but the charge would rightly be leveled against an individual Catholic whose spiritual life was limited to the automatic and unthinking recitation of certain fixed prayers—with no lifting of the mind and heart to God; and to the force-of-habit or sense-of-duty reception of the sacraments, with no conscious striving for closer union with God. In short, God can penetrate the soul only insofar as *self* will let Him.

What Is Merit?

In the news dispatches I once read of a man who built a new house for his family. He did most of the work himself and put all his savings into the materials. When the house was completed after many months of labor, the man found to his horror that he had built it on the wrong lot, another man's lot. The owner of the lot calmly took possession of the house, while the builder could only weep for his wasted time and money.

Pitiable as was that poor man's loss, it is as nothing compared to the pitiableness of the man—or woman—who lives without sanctifying grace. No matter what grand or noble deeds such a person may perform, not one of his actions has any value in the eyes of God. Whether it be through lack of Baptism or because of subsequent mortal sin, the soul which is cut off from God lives his days in vain. His sorrows and his pains, his sacrifices and his goodnesses—all are without eternal value, all are wasted so far as God is concerned. There is no *merit* in anything he does. What, then, *is* merit?

Merit has been defined as that property of a good work which entitles the doer to a reward. All of us, I am sure, will agree that generally speaking it requires an effort to do what is right, what is good. Whether it is feeding the poor, or giving aid to the sick, or doing a kind turn for a neighbor, it is easy to see that there is some sacrifice of *self* involved. It is easy to see that such actions have a *value*, that they can lay claim, at least potentially, to a reward. But they can lay no claim to a reward from God if God has had no part in the doing of the deeds. They can lay no claim to a reward from God if there is no communication between God and the doer. No matter how hard a workman might labor, he cannot claim compensation for his work if he has neglected to put his name on the payroll.

That is why it is only the soul that is in the state of sanctifying grace which can gain merit for its actions. Indeed, it is *being* in the state of sanctifying grace that *gives* eternal value to an action. Human deeds, so long as they are purely human, have no supernatural significance at all. It is only when these deeds become the work of God Himself that they have a divine worth. And our deeds *are* in a sense the work of God Himself present in the soul when the soul is living the supernatural life which we call sanctifying grace.

This is so true that even the *least* of our actions has a supernatural value when it is performed in union with God. Whatever God does, even when He does it through us as His free and willing instruments, has a divine worth. That is why even the least of our actions, provided it be a morally good action, is meritorious so long as we have the intention, at least habitual, of doing all for God.

It is no surprise to anyone that helping the needy, practicing penances, or giving to the missions, are meritorious actions when performed in the state of sanctifying grace. But many persons are surprised to learn that beating a rug, getting a haircut, or weeding a garden are meritorious actions too when performed by one who is living his life on a supernatural level—in the state of sanctifying grace. Any free and conscious action which is not sinful is a morally good action, no matter how simple and unpretentious it may be. Therefore, *everything* which we freely do which is not sinful, and which we do in the state of sanctifying grace, is a source of merit, with the further proviso that there must be at least a virtual intention of doing all for love of God.

Since merit is "that property of a good work which entitles the doer to a reward," we next ask, logically, what our reward is to be? Our supernaturally good actions will merit, but *what* will they merit? They will merit a triple reward: an increase in sanctifying grace, eternal life, and an increase of glory in heaven. With regard to the second phase of this reward—eternal life—it might be of interest to note this point: for the baptized infant, heaven is a heritage by virtue of the infant's being an adopted child of God incorporated in Christ, but for the adult Christian, heaven is a recompense as well as a heritage, a reward we can earn, because God has promised it to those who serve Him.

With regard to the third item of reward—increase of heavenly glory—we can see that it flows from the first. Our degree of glory in heaven will be proportionate to the degree of our union with God, the extent to which sanctifying grace has permeated our soul. As grace increases, so does our prospective glory in heaven also increase.

However, to achieve the eternal life and the increased glory that we have merited, we must, of course, die in the state of sanctifying grace. Mortal sin wipes out all merit, just as a bank crash can wipe out one's life savings. And there is no merit to be gained beyond the grave. There is no merit that we can gain in hell or in purgatory—not even in heaven. This life and this life only is the time of testing, the time of merit.

It is consoling, however, to know that merits which have been lost by mortal sin are restored as soon as the soul turns back to God by an act of perfect contrition or the sacrament of Penance. Merits revive the moment that sanctifying grace returns to the soul. The repentant sinner, in other words, does not have to begin all over again; his former treasure of merits is not wholly lost.

For you and for me, and in practical everyday terms, what does it mean to live in the state of sanctifying grace? To answer that question, let us take two men who work side by side in the same office (or it could be a factory, a store, a farm). To the casual observer, the two men are very much alike. Both do the same kind of work, both are married, both have families; both of them lead what might be called "respectable" lives. One of the men, however, is what we would term a "secularist." He practices no religion, he gives little, if any, thought to God. His philosophy is that it is up to him to make his own happiness, to get all that he can out of life. "If you don't get it yourself," he will say, "no one else is going to get it for you."

He is not a *bad* man. On the contrary, he is admirable in many ways. He is a bear for work, both because he wants to get ahead in the world and because he wants to give his family the best of everything. He is genuinely devoted to his family, proud of his pretty wife, who is such a capable helpmate, and wrapped up in his children, whom he sees as an extension of himself. "They are the only immortality I ask for," he tells his friends. He is a friendly fellow, well liked by those who know him, reasonably generous, and active in civic affairs. His industry, truthfulness, honesty, thoughtfulness are not based on any religious principles.

"It's the *decent* thing to do," he will explain. "I owe it to myself as a civilized human being."

There, very much condensed, is a picture of the "naturally" good man. All of us have met him, at one time or another. Outwardly at least, he puts many a professing Christian to shame. And yet we know that he is failing in the biggest thing of all. He is *not* doing the decent thing, he is *not* being a credit to himself as a human being so long as he ignores the one big thing for which he was made: to love God, and to prove that love by doing God's will, doing God's will for God's *sake*. Precisely because he is so good in all the lesser things, our pity is the greater, our prayers for him the more agonized.

Now we turn our attention to the other man, who works at the next desk or machine or counter. The second man seems almost the identical twin of the first: in family status, home, work, personality. But there is an incalculable difference which the casual eye will not easily spot. The difference lies first of all in *intention*. The second man's life is not based on a philosophy of "common decency" or "owe it to myself." At least not *mainly*. The natural loves and human urges which he shares in common with all mankind have been transformed in him by a higher love and a higher urge: the love of God, and the desire to do God's will.

His wife is not merely his companion of the fireside. She also is his companion of the altar. He and she are partners with God, helping one another on to holiness, co-operating with God in the creation of new human beings destined for eternal life. His love for his children is not a mere extension of himself; he sees his children as a solemn trust from God; he sees himself as a steward who one day will have to answer for their souls. His love for them, as for his wife, is part of his love for God.

His job is not merely a chance for advancement and for material gain. It is a part of his priestly fatherhood, the means of providing for the material needs of his family, a part of the pattern of God's plan for him. He gives his job the best he has got because he understands that he is an instrument in God's hands for the completion of God's creative work in the world. For God, only the best will do. And so it goes through his day. His natural friendliness is imbued with a spirit of charity. His generosity is perfected by detachment. His thoughtfulness partakes of the compassion of Christ. Not perhaps that he thinks of such things often; certainly not that he goes through his day in self-conscious righteousness. But he has begun his day by pointing it where it should be pointed—towards God and away from self. "O my God," he has said, "I offer up to Thee all my thoughts, words, actions and sufferings of this day. . . ." He has perhaps made the best beginning of all by starting his day with Mass.

But there is one other thing necessary to make this man a truly *supernatural* man. His right intention is necessary, but alone it is not enough. His day must not only be directed to God, it also must be lived in union with God if it is to have any everlasting value. In other words, he must be in the state of sanctifying grace.

In Christ, even His most insignificant action was of infinite value, because His human nature was united with His divine nature. Whatever Jesus did, God was doing. It is somewhat (only somewhat) the same with us. When we are in the state of sanctifying grace we do not *possess* the divine nature, but we do *participate* in God's own nature, we do share in a special way in God's own life. As a consequence, whatever we do—sin excepted—God is doing in and through us. God-in-us gives an eternal value to all that we do. Even our homeliest actions, such as wiping the baby's nose or scouring the sink, merit an increase in sanctifying grace and a higher degree of glory in heaven, if our life is centered on God. This is what it means to live in the state of sanctifying grace. This is what it means to be a *supernatural* man.

CHAPTER X

The Virtues and the Gifts of the Holy Ghost

What Is Virtue?

Are you a virtuous person? Modesty probably would move you to answer, "No, not particularly so," to that question. Yet, if you are baptized and are in the state of sanctifying grace, you do possess the three greatest virtues of all—the divine virtues of faith and hope and charity. If you were to commit a mortal sin you would lose the virtue of charity (or love for God), but you still would retain the virtues of faith and hope.

Before going any further, perhaps we should recall what the word "virtue" means. In religion virtue is defined as a "habit or permanent disposition which inclines a person to do good and to avoid evil." For example, if you have the habit of always telling the truth, then you have the virtue of veracity or truthfulness. If you have the habit of being strictly honest with regard to the rights of others, then you have the virtue of justice.

If we acquire a virtue by our own efforts, by consciously developing a certain good habit, then we call that virtue a *natural* virtue. Suppose that we decide to develop the virtue of veracity. We become watchful of our speech, careful not to say anything which we know is at variance with the truth. In the beginning perhaps we find it difficult, especially when telling the truth causes us embarrassment or inconvenience. A habit, however (good or bad), is strengthened by repeated acts. Little by little we find it easier to tell the truth, even when the results are painful. It becomes almost second nature for us to tell the truth; it "goes against the grain" for us to tell a lie. At that point, we definitely have acquired the virtue of veracity. Because we have accomplished it by our own efforts, we term it a *natural* virtue.

God may, however, directly infuse a virtue into our soul without any effort on our part. By His almighty power God may confer upon the soul the power and the inclination to perform certain actions that are supernaturally good. A virtue of this kind, a habit bestowed upon the soul directly by God, is called a *supernatural* virtue. Chief among the supernatural virtues are those three which we call the *theological* virtues: faith, hope, and charity. They are called theological (or divine) virtues because they pertain directly to God: it is in God that we believe, in God that we hope; it is God that we love.

These three virtues are infused into our soul along with sanctifying grace, in the sacrament of Baptism. Even the baptized infant possesses these three virtues, although he will not be able to exercise them until he reaches the age of reason. Once we receive these three virtues they are not easily lost. The virtue of charity, the ability to love God with a supernatural love, will be lost only if, by mortal sin, we deliberately separate ourselves from God. When sanctifying grace goes, charity goes also.

But even with charity gone, faith and hope may still remain. We lose the virtue of hope only by a sin against hope —by the sin of despair, in which we no longer trust in God's goodness and mercy. Hope also would be lost, of course, if faith were lost. We certainly will not trust in a God in whom we do not believe. And faith itself will be lost only by a grievous sin directly against faith, by a refusal to believe what God has revealed.

Besides the three great virtues which we call the theological or divine virtues, there are four other supernatural virtues which are infused into the soul at Baptism along with sanctifying grace. Because these virtues do not pertain directly to God but rather concern our attitude towards persons and things in relation to God, they are called moral virtues. Aside from faith, hope and charity, all other virtues are moral virtues. The four of which we speak, the four supernatural moral virtues which are infused into the soul with sanctifying grace, are prudence, justice, fortitude and temperance.

These four virtues have a special name of their own; they are called the four cardinal virtues. The word "cardinal" comes from the Latin word "cardo," which means "a hinge." Prudence, justice, fortitude and temperance are called cardinal virtues because they are the "hinge" virtues, the key virtues upon which all the other moral virtues depend. If a man is truly prudent, just, spiritually strong and temperate, then he will possess all the other moral virtues too. We might say that these four contain within themselves the seeds of all the other virtues. For example the virtue of religion, which disposes us to offer to God the worship which is His due, stems from the cardinal virtue of justice. Religion, incidentally, is the highest of all the moral virtues.

It may be of interest to point out two notable differences between natural and supernatural virtues. A natural virtue, because it has been acquired by repeated practice and by repeated self-discipline, makes it *easy* for us to perform an act of that particular virtue. We reach the point, for an illustration, where it is more pleasurable to be truthful than to be untruthful. On the other hand, a supernatural virtue, since it is directly infused and not acquired by repeated acts, does not necessarily make it *easy* for us to practice the virtue. I can imagine a person who might possess the virtue of faith to a very high degree and yet be tempted by doubts against faith his whole life long.

Another difference between natural and supernatural virtue is the manner in which each increases. A natural virtue, such as an acquired patience, is increased by repeated and persevering practice. A supernatural virtue, however, receives its increase only from God—an increase which God gives in proportion to the moral goodness of our actions. In other words, whatever increases sanctifying grace, also will increase the infused virtues. We grow in virtue as we grow in grace.

What do we mean, exactly, when we say, "I believe in God," "I hope in God," "I love God"? In our everyday conversation we are likely to use words rather loosely; it is good occasionally to recall the strict and original meaning of the words we use.

"Faith" is a good word to start with. Of the three divine virtues which are infused into our soul at the time of our Baptism, faith is the most basic. It is obvious that we cannot hope in nor love a God in whom we do not believe.

Divine faith is defined as "the virtue by which we firmly believe all the truths God has revealed, on the word of God revealing them, who can neither deceive nor be deceived." There are two key phrases there: "firmly believe," and "word of God." They will merit examination.

To believe means to accept as true. We believe something when we give it our definite and unquestioning assent. We can see how loosely we are using the word when we say, "I believe it will rain tomorrow," or "I believe this is the nicest summer we ever had." In both these cases we merely are expressing an opinion; we *surmise* that it may rain tomorrow; we *have an impression* that this is the nicest summer we've had. This is one point to bear in mind—an opinion is not really a belief. Faith means certainty.

But not all certainty is faith. I do not say that I believe something if it is something I can plainly see and understand. I do not say that I believe that two plus two equals four. I *know* that two plus two equals four. It is something which I can understand and prove to my own satisfaction. Knowledge of this kind, concerning facts which I can perceive and grasp, is called *understanding* rather than belief.

Belief then—or faith—is the acceptance of something as true *on the authority of someone else*. Personally I have never been in China, but many persons who have been there assure me that there is such a country as China. Because I have confidence in those people, I believe that China exists. Similarly, I know little about the science of physics and absolutely nothing about nuclear fission. Yet, despite the fact that I never saw an atom, I believe that the atom can be split, because I trust the competency of the men who say it can be and has been done.

This kind of knowledge is the knowledge of faith: facts accepted on the authority of others in whom we have confidence. Since there is so much that we do not understand in life, and so little time for investigating things for ourselves, we can see that most of our knowledge is based upon faith. If we did not have confidence in our fellow human beings, life would stand still. If the man who says, "I only believe what I can see," or "I don't believe it unless I can understand it," really lives up to his words, he will accomplish very little.

This kind of faith of which we have been talking—the acceptance of a truth on the say-so of another human being —is termed *human* faith. The adjective "human" distinguishes it from the faith which accepts a truth on the authority of God. When our mind gives adherence to a truth simply because God has said that it is so, our faith is called *divine* faith. It is plain that divine faith is a much more certain knowledge than merely human faith. It is not likely, but it is possible, for all human witnesses to be mistaken about some fact—as, for instance, all scholars once taught that the world was flat. It is not likely but it is possible for all available human witnesses to be deceivers—as, for instance, the Communist dictators have deceived the Russian people. But God cannot be mistaken, He cannot deceive; He is infinite Wisdom and infinite Truth. Concerning the truths that God has made known to us, there never can be the faintest shadow of a doubt. That is why true faith is always a firm faith. To entertain doubts about a truth of faith willingly is to question either God's infinite knowledge or His infinite truthfulness. To speculate, "I wonder whether there really are three Persons in God," or "I wonder whether Jesus really is present in the Holy Eucharist," is to question the credibility of God and to deny His authority. It is, in effect, to reject divine faith.

For the same reason, true faith must be *complete*. It would be folly to suppose that we can pick and choose among the truths God has revealed, according to our taste. To say, "I believe in heaven, but not in hell"; or "I believe in Baptism but not in confession," is to say, in effect, "God can be wrong." The logical conclusion then is, why believe God at all?

The faith of which we have been speaking is *supernatural* faith, the act of faith which springs from the infused virtue of divine faith. It would be possible to have a purely *natural* faith in God and in many of His truths. Such a faith might result from the evidence of nature, which witnesses to a Supreme Being of infinite power and wisdom. Such a faith might result from acceptance of the testimony of countless wise and great men, or from evidence of divine Providence in one's own life. A *natural* faith of this kind is a preparation for the genuinely supernatural faith which will be infused, with sanctifying grace, at the baptismal font. But it is only this supernatural faith, this virtue of divine faith which is infused at Baptism, that makes it possible for us to believe firmly and completely *all* the truths, even the most ineffable and mysterious truths, which God has revealed. Without such a faith we who have reached the use of reason cannot be saved. The *virtue* of faith alone will save the baptized infant, but with the age of reason there must be the *act* of faith as well.

Hope and Love

It is a doctrine of our Christian faith that God gives to every soul He creates sufficient grace to get to heaven. It is upon this teaching of Christ's Church that the divine virtue of hope, infused into our soul at Baptism, feeds and grows with the passing years.

Hope is defined as "the virtue by which we firmly trust that God, who is all-powerful and faithful to His promises, will in His mercy give us eternal happiness and the means to obtain it." In other words, no one loses heaven except by his own fault. So far as God's part is concerned, our salvation is certain. It is only our part—our co-operation or non-co-operation with God's grace—that is uncertain.

It is this confidence that we have in God's goodness and power and fidelity that sweetens and makes bearable the hardships of life. If the practice of virtue at times demands of us self-discipline and self-renunciation, perhaps even the self-immolation of martyrdom, we find the needed strength and courage in the assurance of our final victory.

The virtue of hope is implanted in the soul at Baptism, along with sanctifying grace. Even the infant, once baptized, has the virtue of hope. But the virtue must not be allowed to lie dormant. With the advent of reason, the virtue must find expression in the *act* of hope. This is the inner conviction and the conscious expression of trust in God and reliance upon His promises. The act of hope should figure prominently in our daily prayers. It is a form of prayer particularly pleasing to God since it expresses simultaneously our admission of complete dependence upon God and our absolute confidence in His love for us.

It is evident that the act of hope is absolutely necessary for salvation. To entertain doubts as to God's fidelity in keeping His promises, or as to the effectiveness of His grace in overcoming our human weakness, would be to offer blasphemous insult to God. Nor would it be possible to weather the rigors of temptation, to practice self-forgetful charity towards others, in short to lead a truly Christian life, if we had no confidence in the eventual outcome. How few of us would have the fortitude to persevere in good if we thought we had only once chance in a million of getting to heaven!

It follows, too, that our hope must be a *firm* hope. Hope that is weak belittles God, either His almighty power or His infinite goodness. This does not mean that we should not have a wholesome fear of losing our soul. But the fear should stem from lack of confidence in ourselves, not from lack of confidence in God. If even a Lucifer could reject grace, then we also have within us the capacity for failure —but the failure will not be God's. It is only a stupid person who will say, in repenting of sin, "O God, I am so ashamed of being so weak!" The hopeful person would say, "O my God, I am so ashamed of forgetting how weak I am!" A saint might be described as one who has the utmost distrust of his own strength, and the utmost confidence in God.

It is well to bear in mind also that the basis of Christian hope applies to others as well as to ourselves. God wills the salvation, not just of *me*, but of all men. That is why we never should weary in our prayers for sinners and unbelievers, especially for those who may be close to us by blood or friendship. It is the teaching of Catholic theologians that God never entirely withdraws His grace even from the most obdurate sinners. When the Bible speaks of God hardening His heart against a sinner (for example, Pharao who resisted Moses), it is really only a poetic way of describing the sinner's own reaction. It is the sinner who hardens his own heart by resisting God's grace.

And if someone dear to us has died, apparently unrepentant to the end, we still should not lose heart and "grieve as those who have no hope." What thunderbolts of grace God may have unleashed upon that stubborn soul in the last split-second of consciousness—graces gained by our own hopeful prayers—we shall not know until we meet in heaven.

Although trust in God's providence is not exactly the same thing as the divine virtue of hope, yet it is enough allied to hope to merit attention here. Trust in God's providence simply means that we do believe that God loves each of us with an infinite love—a love that could not be more direct and personal even if we were the only soul on the face of the earth. To that faith is added our belief that God wills only what is best for us—that in His infinite wisdom He knows best what *is* best for us—and that in His infinite power He can bring about what is best for us.

On that solid foundation of God's love and care and wisdom and power, we stand secure. We do not fall into a black mood of despondency when "things go wrong." When our plans are upset, our expectations thwarted and failure seems to dog our every step, we know that in some way God is working this all out to our ultimate good. Even the terror of the hydrogen bomb and the shadow of Communist threats will leave us unshaken, because we know that the very evils which men fashion God will somehow work into His plan.

It is this same trust in God's providence that comes to our aid when we are tempted (as who is not, sometimes?) to think that we are smarter than God; that we know better than He, under these circumstances, what is best for us. "Maybe it is a sin, but we just can't afford another baby"; "Maybe it isn't quite honest, but I've got to stay in business"; "I know it seems a bit crooked, but politics is like that." It is when alibis like these start to rise to our lips that we beat them down with our trust in God's providence. "It looks as if doing the right thing is going to be rough on me," we say, "but God knows all the circumstances. He's smarter than I am. And He cares. I'll string along with Him."

The only one of the three divine virtues which will remain with us forever is the virtue of charity. In heaven faith will give way to knowledge; there is no longer any need to "believe in" the God whom we actually see. Hope also will disappear, as we actually possess the happiness for which we hoped. But charity will not disappear. On the contrary, only in that breathless ecstatic moment when we see God face to face will the virtue of charity which was infused into our soul at Baptism reach the fullness of its capabilities. It is then that our love for God, so muted and so weak in this life, will blaze up like an exploding rocket. Finding ourselves united with the infinitely lovable God who alone can fulfill the human heart's capacity for love, our charity will express itself forever in an act of love.

Divine charity, the virtue which is implanted in our soul at Baptism, along with faith and hope, is defined as "the virtue by which we love God above all things for His own sake, and our neighbor as ourselves for the love of God." It is called the Queen of virtues. Other virtues, both divine and moral, carry us *towards* God, but it is charity which fastens us *to* God. Where there is charity, the other virtues *must* be. "Love God and do as you please!" one of the saints has said. It is evident that if we truly love God, it will please us only to do what will please Him.

It is, of course, the *virtue* of charity which is infused into our soul in the sacrament of Baptism. It still remains for us, when we have reached the use of reason, to exercise that virtue, to make acts of love. It is the power to make such acts of love, easily and in a supernatural manner, that is given us in Baptism.

A person could have a natural love for God. Contemplating God's goodness and mercy and His endless benefits to us, we could be moved to love Him as we love any other lovable person. Indeed, a person who had no opportunity to be baptized (or a person in mortal sin with no chance for confession) could not save his soul unless he did make an act of perfect love for God. That means a selfless love, loving God just because He is so infinitely lovable, loving God for Himself alone. Even for such an act of love as this, we would need God's help, in the form of actual grace, but it still would be a *natural* love.

It is only through the indwelling of God in the soul, with the accompanying supernatural life called sanctifying grace, that we become capable of an act of supernatural love for God. The reason that our love then is a supernatural love is because *it really is God Himself loving Himself through us.* To clarify that, we might use the example of a son who buys a birthday present for his father, using (with the father's permission) the father's own charge account to buy the present. Or, like a child writing a letter to his mother, with the mother herself guiding the child's inexperienced hand. Similarly, it is by the divine life within us that we are able to love God adequately, proportionately, with a love that is worthy of God. With a love also that is *pleasing* to God, in spite of the fact that it is God, in a sense, who is doing the loving.

It is this same virtue of charity (which always accompanies sanctifying grace) which makes it possible to love our neighbor with a supernatural love. We love our neighbor then not with a merely natural love because he is a likable person, because he is congenial to us, because we get along well with him, because he in some way appeals to us. Such natural love is not bad, but there is no supernatural merit in it. By means of the divine virtue of charity, we make ourselves a vehicle, an instrument, by means of which God, *through us,* can love our neighbor. Our part is simply to lend ourselves to God, to put no obstacle to the flow of

God's love. Our part is to have a good will towards our neighbor because of our own love for God, because we know that is what God wants. "Our neighbor," incidentally, includes everyone whom God has made: the angels and saints in heaven (easy), the souls in purgatory (easy), and all living human beings, *even our enemies* (ouch!).

It is right here that we touch the very heart of Christianity. It is right here that we come up against the cross. It is right here that we prove or disprove the reality of our love for God. It is easy to love our family and friends. It is not hard to love "everybody" in a vague and general sort of way, but to wish well to (and to pray for, and to be ready to help) that fellow at the next desk who stole your girl, or that woman across the street who told lies about you, or that double-crossing relative who got all of Aunt Minnie's money, or that criminal in the newspaper who raped and killed the six-year-old child—well, it's hard enough to forgive them, let alone love them. In fact, *we just couldn't do it* naturally speaking. But with the divine virtue of charity we can do it; in fact we *must* do it, or our love for God is a fake and a sham.

Let us remember, though, that supernatural love, whether for God or for neighbor, need not be an *emotional* love. Supernatural love resides primarily in the *will*, not in the emotions. We might have a very deep love for God, as proved by our fidelity to Him, without particularly *feeling* that love. To love God simply means that we are willing to give up *anything* rather than offend God by mortal sin. Similarly we may have a genuine supernatural love for our neighbor, even though on the natural level we feel a strong distaste for him. Do I forgive him, for God's sake, the wrong he has done? Do I pray for him, and hope that he will get the grace he needs and save his soul? Do I stand ready to help him if he should be in need, in spite of my own natural repugnance? Then I do have a supernatural love for my neighbor. The divine virtue of charity is function-

ing within me. I can pray an act of love (as I ought frequently to do) without hypocrisy or sham.

Wonders Within Us

A young man whom I had just baptized said to me
afterwards, "You know, Father, all those wonderful things
you told me would happen when I got baptized? I don't
seem to feel any of them. I do feel relieved to know that
my sins are forgiven, and happy at the thought that I am
a child of God and a member of the Mystical Body of
Christ, but as for the indwelling of God in my soul and
sanctifying grace and the virtues of faith and hope and
charity, and the gifts of the Holy Ghost—well, I just don't
feel any of that."

And, of course, we *don't* feel any of that, at least not
usually. The awesome transformation that takes place in us
in Baptism does not take place in our body—in our brain or
nervous system or emotions. It takes place in the inner core
of our being, in our soul. It is beyond the reach of intellectual analysis or emotional reaction. But what if by some
miracle we could be fitted with a pair of glasses that would
enable us to see our soul as it really is in the state of sanctifying grace, adorned with all its supernatural gifts? Then I
am sure that we would walk about in a daze of perpetual
wonderment at the lavishness with which God has equipped
us to deal with life here and to prepare for life hereafter.

Included in the rich dowry which accompanies sanctifying grace, are the seven gifts of the Holy Ghost. These
gifts—wisdom, understanding, counsel, fortitude, knowledge,
piety, and fear of the Lord—are qualities imparted to the
soul which make the soul responsive to the movements of
grace and give facility in the practice of virtue. They make
the soul alert to the silent voice of God within, docile to
His gently guiding hand. We might say that the gifts of

the Holy Ghost are the "lubricant" of the soul, as grace is the power of the soul.

Taking them one by one, there is first the gift of wisdom. Wisdom gives us a right sense of proportion so that we esteem the things of God; we value goodness and virtue at their true worth and see the goods of the world as stepping-stones to sanctity, not as ends in themselves. The man, for example, who misses his weekly bowling night in order to attend the parish mission is being guided by the gift of wisdom, whether he realizes it or not.

Next is the gift of understanding. This gift gives us a spiritual perception which enables us to understand the truths of faith in accordance with our needs. All things else being equal, a priest would much prefer to explain a point of doctrine to a person who is in the state of sanctifying grace rather than to one who is not. The former, having the gift of understanding, will be much quicker in grasping the point at issue.

The third gift, that of counsel, sharpens our judgment. By its aid we perceive—and choose—the course of action that will be most conducive to God's honor and our own spiritual good. It is a dangerous step he takes who makes a major decision in the state of mortal sin, whether it be a decision as to vocation, job, family problem, or any of the other choices that constantly face us. Without the gift of counsel, human judgment is all too fallible.

The gift of fortitude almost explains itself. Every good life must be to some degree a heroic life. There always is the hidden heroism required for the conquest of self. Sometimes a still higher heroism is called for, when the doing of God's will means the risk of losing friends or money or health. And there is the highest heroism of the martyrs, when life itself is sacrificed for love of God. It is not without purpose that God strengthens our human weakness with His gift of fortitude.

The gift of knowledge gives us spiritual "know-how."

It disposes us to recognize, under the impulse of God's grace, whatever will be helpful or hurtful to us spiritually. It is closely allied with the gift of counsel. Counsel moves us to *choose* what is helpful and to reject what is harmful. But before we can choose we must *know*. As an example, by the gift of knowledge I might perceive that too much secular reading is dulling my taste for things spiritual. Then the gift of counsel might guide me to stop buying so many slick periodicals, and inspire me to begin doing some regular spiritual reading.

The gift of piety is one that may easily be misunderstood by anyone who thinks of piety in terms of folded hands and downcast eyes and lengthy prayers. The word "piety" in its original meaning describes the attitude of a child towards his parents: a mixture of love, confidence, and reverence. When we habitually manifest this attitude towards our Father, God, we are practicing the virtue of piety. It is the *gift* of piety which impels us to practice the *virtue*—to maintain this attitude of childlike intimacy with God.

Finally there is the gift of fear of the Lord. This balances the gift of piety. It is right that we look to God with eyes in which there is love and trust and tender reverence. But it equally is right that we should never forget that God is our all-just Judge to whom we shall one day have to answer for the graces that He has given us. Remembering that, we shall have a wholesome fear of offending Him by sin.

Wisdom, understanding, counsel, fortitude, knowledge, piety, and fear of the Lord. These are the "lubricants," the auxiliaries to graces. These are the predispositions to holiness which, with sanctifying grace, are infused into the soul in Baptism.

Every catechism that I have ever seen lists the "twelve fruits of the Holy Ghost"—charity, joy, peace, patience, benignity, goodness, long-suffering, mildness, faith, modesty, continency and chastity. But, so far as I have been able to observe, it is seldom that the twelve fruits get more than a passing mention in religious instruction classes. Even more rarely are they explained in sermons.

It seems unfortunate that it should be so. If a teacher of science undertook to explain an apple tree to his class, he would, of course, describe the roots and the trunk, and would tell how the sun and moisture made the tree grow. But he would not dream of ending his explanation with a brusque statement that, "on this tree apples grow." A description of the fruit of the tree would be considered a very important part of the learning experience. Similarly it would be illogical to talk about sanctifying grace and the virtues and gifts which accompany sanctifying grace without more than a casual mention of the *results*. The fruits of the Holy Ghost are just that: the outward fruits of the inner life, the external product of the indwelling Spirit.

Or, turning to another figure of speech, we might say that the twelve fruits are the broad brush-strokes which outline for us the portrait of a truly Christian man—or woman. Perhaps the simplest procedure would be to see what that portrait looks like. What kind of person is it who lives habitually in the state of sanctifying grace, and who tries perseveringly to subordinate self to the working of grace?

First of all he is an unselfish person. He sees Christ in his neighbor and is considerate of others and helpful to others, even at the cost of inconvenience and hardship to himself. This is charity.

Then he is a cheerful and pleasant sort of person. He seems to radiate an inner glow which makes itself felt in any group of which he is a part. When he is around, the sun seems to shine a little brighter. People smile more easily, speak more gently. This is joy.

He is a quiet and relaxed person. Psychologists would call him "well-adjusted." His brow may be puckered with thought, but seldom with worry. He is a *steady* sort of person, a wonderful man to have around in an emergency. This is peace.

He is not easily angered, he is not resentful of slights. He is not upset or frustrated when things go wrong or people are stupid. He can fail six times and still start over the seventh time without grinding his teeth and cursing his luck. This is patience.

He is a kind person. People come to him with their troubles, and find in him a sympathetic listener; they go away feeling better just for having talked with him. He is interested in the enthusiasms and the problems of others; he is especially considerate of children and the aged, of the unhappy and the unfortunate. This is benignity.

He stands solidly for what is right, even when it means standing alone. He is not self-righteous; he does not judge others; he is slow to criticize and still slower to condemn; he is forbearing with the ignorance and the weakness of others. But he will not compromise principle, he will not temporize with evil. In his own religious life he is invariably generous with God, never seeking the easiest way out. This is goodness.

He is uncomplaining under pain and disappointment, in sickness and in sorrow. Self-pity is unknown to him. He will raise his tear-stained eyes to heaven in prayer but never in rebellion. This is long-suffering.

He is a gentle person, a restful sort of person to have around. He gives of his best to whatever task comes to hand, but without any of the aggressiveness of the "go-getter." He does not seek to dominate others. He will reason persuasively, but he never is argumentative. This is mildness.

He is proud of his membership in Christ's Mystical Body. He does not try to ram his religion down anyone's throat, but neither is he apologetic for what he believes. He does not try to conceal his religion in public; he is quick to defend the truth when it is attacked in his presence; his religion is the most important thing in life to him. This is faith.

His love for Jesus Christ makes him recoil from the thought of being an ally of the devil, from the thought of occasioning sin to another. In dress and deportment and speech, there is a decency about him—or her—which fortifies rather than weakens others in their virtue. This is modesty.

He is a temperate person, with his passions firmly ruled by reason and by grace. He is not up in the clouds today and down in the depths tomorrow. Whether in eating or drinking, whether at work or at play, he manifests an admirable self-control in all that he does. This is continency.

He has a great reverence for the procreative power that God has given him, a holy awe that God should have so shared His creative power with humankind. He sees sex as something precious and sacred, a bond of union to be used only within the limits of wedlock and for the purpose established by God; never as a plaything, as a source of self-gratification. This is chastity.

And there we have the profile of the Christian man—or woman: charity, joy, peace, patience, benignity, goodness, long-suffering, mildness, faith, modesty, continency and chastity. We might try the profile on for size and see where the bulges are.

The Moral Virtues

"Grace builds upon nature." That is an axiom of the spiritual life. It means simply that when God gives us His grace He does not first exterminate our human nature and then put grace in its place. God *adds* His grace to what we already are. The effect that grace will have upon us, and the use we make of it, will be conditioned to a great extent by our individual make-up—physical, mental, and emotional. Grace will not make a genius out of a moron any more than grace will straighten a bent back; nor will grace, normally, make a well-adjusted person out of a neurotic.

It becomes our responsibility, then, to do our best in removing obstacles to the operation of grace; to do our best to facilitate the effects of grace. We are not talking now of such moral obstacles as sin and self-love; their hindrance to grace is quite apparent. We are talking rather of what we might call *natural* obstacles; such obstacles as ignorance or faulty temperament or ill-formed habits. It is an obstacle to grace, certainly, if our intellectual fare is confined to the daily newspapers and popular magazines. It is an obstacle to grace if our over-aggressiveness provokes us to easy anger. It is an obstacle to grace if habits of untidiness or unpunctuality offend charity by inconveniencing others.

These considerations are particularly pertinent when we turn to an examination of the moral virtues. The moral virtues, as distinguished from the theological virtues, are those virtues which dispose us to lead moral or good lives by aiding us to treat persons and things in the right way—that is, according to the will of God. We possess these virtues, in their supernatural form, when we are in the state of sanctifying grace. That is, sanctifying grace gives us a certain predisposition, a certain *readiness* for the practice of these virtues—together with a supernatural merit when we do practice them. This readiness is something like the readiness of a child, at a certain age, to learn to read and write. The child still has to acquire, by practice, the technique of reading and writing, but meanwhile the organism is ready, the power is there.

This may be plainer if we make an individual examination of some of the moral virtues. The four chief moral virtues, we know, are those which we call the cardinal virtues: prudence, justice, fortitude and temperance. Prudence is the power to make right judgments. A person who is temperamentally impulsive, given to rash and unthinking action and snap judgments, will have a job to do in removing those obstacles before the virtue of prudence can operate in him effectively. It is obvious, too, that in any particular circumstance one's knowledge and experience will facilitate the exercise of prudence. A child has the virtue of prudence in root form, but in matters that pertain to the adult world a child could not be expected to make prudent judgments with knowledge and experience lacking.

The second cardinal virtue is justice, which perfects our will (as prudence perfects our intelligence) and safeguards the rights of our fellow man: his right to life and freedom, to the sanctity of the home, to his good name and honor, and to his material possessions. An obstacle to justice that readily comes to mind is prejudice. Prejudice denies a man his human rights, or hampers him in the achievement of those rights because of his color or race or nationality or religion. Another obstacle might be a natural stinginess, close-fistedness—a temperamental defect that might be the result of childhood deprivation. It would be our duty to labor at the removal of such barriers as these, if the supernatural virtue of justice were to have full play within us.

Fortitude, the third cardinal virtue, disposes us to do what is good in spite of every difficulty. The perfection of fortitude is exemplified in the martyrs, who have accepted death rather than sin. Few of us are likely to be called upon for such an extreme degree of fortitude. But the virtue will never be able to operate, even in the small demands made upon our courage, unless we chop away at the barriers. Such barriers as an exaggerated desire to conform, to belong, to be "one of the crowd." Such barriers as an unreasonable fear of public opinion (we call it human respect); the fear of being criticized or belittled; or, worst of all, ridiculed.

The fourth of the cardinal virtues is temperance, which disposes us to control our desires and especially to use rightly the things which appeal to our senses. Temperance is especially necessary in moderating the use of food and drink, and in regulating the enjoyment of sex in the married state. The virtue of temperance will not remove an allergy to alcohol. With some, the only true temperance will be abstinence, just as the only true temperance in matters of sex for the unmarried lies in abstinence. Temperance does not eliminate, it *regulates* desire. In this case, the removal of obstacles consists mainly in the avoidance of circumstances which would excite desires which may not, in conscience, be gratified.

There are other moral virtues besides the four cardinal ones. Here we shall mention but a few, and each of us, if he be honest with himself, can discover his own obstacles. There is filial piety (and its extension, patriotism), which disposes us to honor, love and respect our parents and our country. There is obedience, which disposes us to do the will of our superiors as a manifestation of God's will. There are veracity and liberality and patience and humility and chastity and others besides. But on the whole, if we are prudent and just and courageous and temperate, the other virtues will pretty well follow, like children behind Mother and Dad.

What, then, does it mean to have a "Christian spirit"? It is not an easy term to define. It means, of course, having the spirit of Christ. That in turn means viewing the world as Christ views it; reaching to the circumstances of life as Christ would react. The truly Christian spirit is nowhere summarized for us better than in the eight beatitudes with which Jesus began His surpassingly beautiful Sermon on the Mount.

The Sermon on the Mount, incidentally, is a passage of the Bible which everyone ought to read occasionally in its entirety. It is contained in chapters five, six and seven of St. Matthew's Gospel, and is the very distillation of our Saviour's teaching.

But to return to the beatitudes: they get their name from the Latin word "beatus," which means "blessed," the word with which each of the beatitudes begins. "Blessed are the poor in spirit," Christ tells us, "for theirs is the kingdom of heaven." This is the first of the eight beatitudes, and it reminds us that heaven is for the humble. The poor in spirit are those who never forget that all that they are and all that they have is from God. Whether it be talents or health or possessions, whether it be even a child of their own flesh, they have nothing, in the absolute sense, which they can rightly call their own. Because of this poverty of spirit, this willingness to surrender back to God whatever of His gifts He may choose to take, their very adversity, when it comes, is a claim upon God for grace and merit. It is a pledge that the God whom they value above all things else, will indeed be their everlasting reward. With Job they say, "The Lord gave, and the Lord has taken away; blessed be the name of the Lord!" (1:21).

Jesus emphasizes this point by repeating the same thought in the second and third beatitudes. "Blessed are the meek," He says, "for they shall possess the earth." "The earth" to which Jesus refers is, of course, simply poetic imagery for heaven. This is true of all the beatitudes; heaven is the reward which is promised, under figurative language, in each of them. "The meek" of whom Jesus speaks in the second beatitude are not the spineless milk-and-water characters whom the world would describe as meek. The truly meek are anything but weaklings. It takes great inner strength to accept disappointment, misfortune and even disaster, and to keep one's face turned all the while in undimmed hope to God.

"Blessed are they who mourn," Jesus continues in the third beatitude, "for they shall be comforted." Here again, as in the first and second beatitudes, we are impressed with the infinite compassion of Christ towards the poor, the unfortunate, the sorrowful and the suffering. These, who see their pain as the rightful lot of sinful humanity, and accept it without repining and without complaint, in union with the cross of Christ Himself; it is these who hold first place in the mind and the heart of Jesus. They are the ones who say with St. Paul, "I reckon that the sufferings of the present time are not worthy to be compared with the glory to come that will be revealed in us" (Romans 8:18).

But, right as it is that we should bear our own burdens in courage and in hope, it is not right that we should acquiesce complacently in the injustices done to others. However willing we may be to surrender our own material happiness, we are nevertheless bound, by a divine paradox, to labor for the happiness of others. Injustice not only destroys the temporal happiness of the one who suffers it; it imperils his eternal happiness too. This is true whether it be an economic injustice which oppresses the poor (the hapless migrant, agricultural laborer, the city slum-dweller are cases in point); or whether it be the racial injustice which degrades our brother (and how do *you* feel about the Negro and segregation?); or whether it be a moral injustice which stymies the workings of grace (are you disturbed by some of the literature on your neighborhood newsstand?). We must have a zeal for justice, whether it be the justice of a square deal for our fellow man or the higher justice towards God which is sinlessness, in others as well as in ourselves. These are some of the implications of the fourth beatitude: "Blessed are they who hunger and thirst for justice, for they shall be satisfied." Satisfied in heaven, but never satisfied here.

"Blessed are the merciful," Christ continues, "for they shall obtain mercy." It is so hard to forgive those who have hurt us; so hard to be patient with the weak and the ignorant and the disagreeable. But the very essence of the Christian spirit is here. There can be no forgiveness for him who will not forgive.

"Blessed are the clean of heart, for they shall see God." The sixth beatitude does not primarily refer, as many think, to chastity. It refers to selflessness; everything viewed first of all from God's viewpoint, rather than my own. It means singleness of purpose; God first, without self-deceit or compromise.

"Blessed are the peacemakers, for they shall be called the children of God." As I listen to Christ saying that, I must ask myself whether I am a center of peace and harmony in my own home, an island of good will in my neighborhood, a mender of discord in the place where I work. It is a sure path to heaven.

"Blessed are they who suffer persecution for justice' sake, for theirs is the kingdom of heaven." And with the eighth beatitude we hang our head in shame as we recall the small inconveniences our own religion costs us—and think of (and pray for) the tortured souls of our brethren behind the Iron and the Bamboo Curtains.

CHAPTER XI

The Catholic Church

The Holy Ghost and the Church

When he is instructing a prospective convert, the priest usually explains, very early in the course of the instruction, the meaning of perfect love for God. He explains what it means to make a perfect act of contrition. Just because the convert must wait for several months before he receives the sacrament of Baptism, there is no reason why he should live those weeks or months in the state of sin. An act of perfect love for God, which includes a desire for Baptism, will cleanse the soul from sin even before Baptism is received.

The prospective convert is happy to know this, of course, and I am sure that I have poured the water of Baptism on the heads of many adults whose souls already were in the state of sanctifying grace. They had already made acts of perfect love for God; they had already received baptism of desire. And yet in every such case, the convert has expressed his relief and joy at receiving, actually, the sacrament of Baptism. Because, up to that moment he could not be *sure* that his sins were gone. No matter how hard he might try to make an act of perfect love, he never could be sure that he had succeeded. But when the saving water had flowed upon his head, he knew then with certainty that God had come to him.

St. Paul tells us, of course, that not even the best of us can ever be *absolutely* sure that we are in the state of sanctifying grace. But moral certitude is all we ask for; the kind of certitude we have when we have been baptized or (in the sacrament of Penance) absolved. The peace of mind, the happy confidence which such assurance brings indicate to us one of the reasons why Jesus Christ established a visible Church. The graces which He purchased for us on Calvary Jesus could have dispensed to each individual soul directly and invisibly, without need of outward sign or ceremony. However, being mindful of our human need for visible assurance, Jesus chose to channel His graces through visible symbols. He instituted the sacraments so that we might know when and how and what kind of grace we were receiving. Visible sacraments necessitated a visible agency in the world to be the custodian and the dispenser of the sacraments—and that visible agency is the Church which Jesus established.

The need for a Church was not, obviously, limited to a need for a keeper of the sacraments. No one could be expected to *want* the sacraments unless he first *knew* about them. No one could be expected to *believe* in Christ, even, unless he *knew* about Christ. Unless Christ's whole life—and death— were to be in vain, there had to be a living voice in the world which would proclaim Christ's teachings down through the centuries. It would have to be an audible voice, it would have to be a visible speaker whom all men of good will could recognize as one having authority. Consequently Jesus founded His Church not merely to sanctify mankind by means of the sacraments but first of all to *teach* mankind the truths which Jesus taught, the truths necessary for salvation. A moment's reflection will bring home to us the fact that if Jesus had not founded a Church even the name of Jesus Christ would be unknown to us today.

But it is not enough for us to have grace available to us in the visible sacraments of the visible Church. It is not enough to have the truth proclaimed to us by the living voice of the teaching Church. We also want to know what we must *do* for God; we want a dependable guide to point out to us the path we must follow in accordance with the truth we know and the graces we receive. Just as it would be useless for us here in the United States to have a Constitution unless we had a government to interpret and enforce the Constitution by appropriate laws, so also must the body of Christian revelation be implemented by pertinent laws. How does one become a member of the Church and how does one remain a member of the Church, who may receive this sacrament or that, and when and how; it is such questions as these that the Church answers when it promulgates its laws; when it fulfills, under Christ, its third duty: to *govern* as well as to teach and sanctify.

The Church, we know, is defined as "the congregation of all baptized persons united in the same true faith, the same sacrifice, the same sacraments, under the authority of the Sovereign Pontiff and the bishops in communion with him." A person becomes a member of the Church by receiving the sacrament of Baptism. A person remains a member of the Church as long as he does not cut himself off from membership by schism (denying or defying the authority of the Pope), or by heresy (denying one or more of the truths of faith as proclaimed by the Church), or by excommunication (being ejected from membership because of certain grave and unrepented sins). But even such persons as these, having been validly baptized, are still basically subjects of the Church and are obliged by her laws unless specifically exempted.

Having said all this, we yet realize that we have been looking at the Church only from the outside. Just as a man is more than his visible, physical body, so also is the Church infinitely more than a mere outward visible organization. It is the soul of a man that makes him a human being. And it is the soul of the Church which makes the Church a living *organism* as well as an organization. Just as the indwelling of the three divine Persons gives to the soul that supernatural life which we call sanctifying grace; so also does the indwelling of the Blessed Trinity give to the Church her unquenchable life, her everlasting vitality. Since the work of salvation (which is the work of divine Love) is ascribed to the Holy Ghost by appropriation, it is therefore the Holy Ghost whom we acknowledge as the *soul* of the Church— of the Church of which Christ is the Head.

From the dust of the earth did God fashion the body of Adam, and then—in the beautiful imagery of the Bible— God breathed a soul into the body, and Adam became a living man. In much the same way did God create His living Church.

In the Person of Jesus Christ, God first designed the Body of His Church. This was a task spread over three years, from Jesus' first public miracle at Cana until His ascent into heaven. It was during this time that Jesus chose His twelve Apostles, destined to be the first bishops of His Church. For three years He instructed them and trained them for their duties, their task of establishing the kingdom of God. During this same time Jesus designed the seven sacraments—the seven channels through which would flow into men's souls the graces Jesus would gain for men upon the cross.

Concurrently, Jesus imparted to the Apostles their threefold mission, the threefold mission of His Church. The mission to teach: "Go, therefore, and make disciples of all nations, . . . teaching them to observe all that I have commanded you" (Matt. 28:19–20). The mission to sanctify: "Baptizing them in the name of the Father, and of the Son, and of the Holy Spirit" (Matt. 28:19). "This is My body.

. . . Do this in remembrance of Me" (Luke 22:19). "Whose sins you shall forgive, they are forgiven them; and whose sins you shall retain, they are retained" (John 20:23). The mission to govern in His name: "If he refuse to hear even the Church, let him be to thee as the heathen and the publican. . . . Whatever you bind on earth shall be bound also in heaven; and whatever you shall loose upon earth shall be loosed also in heaven" (Matt. 18:17–18). "He who hears you, hears Me; and he who rejects you, rejects Me" (Luke 10:16).

Another task of Jesus, as He formed the Body of His Church, was to provide leadership for His Kingdom upon earth. It was to the Apostle Simon, son-of-John, that Jesus assigned this post of leadership—and in doing so Jesus changed Simon's name to Peter, which means rock. Here is the promise: "Blessed art thou, Simon Bar-Jona. . . . I say to thee, thou art Peter, and upon this rock I will build My Church, and the gates of hell shall not prevail against it. And I will give thee the keys of the kingdom of heaven" (Matt. 16:17, 18–19). This was the promise. After His resurrection, Jesus fulfilled the promise, as we read in the twenty-first chapter of St. John's Gospel. After first extracting from Peter a thrice-repeated avowal of love ("Simon, son of John, dost thou love Me?"), Jesus made Peter the supreme shepherd of His flock. "Feed My lambs," Jesus says, "Feed My sheep." The entire flock of Christ—the sheep and the lambs; the bishops, priests and people—were to be under the jurisdiction of Peter. Of Peter and his successors, because, of course, Jesus did not come upon earth just to save the souls who were contemporaries of the Apostles. Jesus came to save all souls, so long as there would be souls to be saved.

The triple duty (and power) of the Apostles—to teach, sanctify and govern—was to be passed on by them, through the sacrament of Holy Orders, to the men whom they would ordain and consecrate to carry on their work. The bishops of today are the successors of the Apostles. Each bishop of today has received his episcopal power in an unbroken continuity from Christ through the Apostles. And the supreme power of Peter, whom Christ made the head of *all*, resides today in the Bishop of Rome, whom we lovingly call our Holy Father. That came about, in the designs of Providence, by reason of the fact that Peter traveled to Rome and died there as the first bishop of that city. Consequently, whoever is Bishop of Rome is automatically the successor of Peter and therefore possesses Peter's special power as teacher and ruler of the entire Church.

This, then, is the Body of His Church as Jesus Christ created it: not merely an invisible brotherhood of men united only by bonds of grace; but a *visible society* of men with authoritative leadership and governance. It is what we call a *hierarchical* society, with the admirable and solid proportions of a pyramid. At the top is the Pope, the spiritual monarch with supreme spiritual authority. Immediately below him are the other bishops, whose jurisdiction, each in his own diocese, flows from union with Peter's successor. Below them are the priests, to whom the sacrament of Holy Orders has given the power to sanctify (as in the Mass and the sacraments), but not the power of jurisdiction (the power to teach and govern). A priest possesses the power of jurisdiction only to the extent that it is delegated to him by the bishop whom he was ordained to assist. Finally, there is the broad base of God's people—the baptized souls for whose sake all the rest of it exists.

Again, this is the Body of the Church as Jesus constituted it during His three years of public life. Like the body of Adam, it awaited only its soul. That soul Christ promised when He told His Apostles before His Ascension: "But you shall receive power when the Holy Spirit comes upon you, and you shall be witnesses for Me in Jerusalem and in all Judea and Samaria and even to the very ends of the earth" (Acts 1:8). We know well the story of Pentecost Sunday—the tenth day after our Lord's Ascension, the fiftieth day after Easter (Pentecost means "fiftieth"). "And there appeared to them [the Apostles] parted tongues as of fire, which settled upon each of them. And they were all filled with the Holy Spirit" (Acts 2:3–4). And now the body so marvelously fashioned by Jesus through three patient years suddenly comes to life. The Living Body rises and begins to walk abroad. It is the birthday of Christ's Church.

We Are the Church

What is a human being? We might answer that question by saying that a human being is an animal that walks on its hind legs and can reason and talk. Our definition would be correct, but it would not tell the whole story. It would tell what a man is like, looking at him from the outside. But it would leave out of the reckoning the most wonderful thing about a man: the fact that he has a spiritual, immortal soul.

What is the Church? We can answer that question also by looking at the Church from the outside. We can define the Church (and frequently do so) by saying that it is the society of all baptized persons united in the one true faith under the authority of the Pope, the successor of St. Peter.

But when we describe the Church in these terms, and when we describe her hierarchical organization of Pope, bishops, priests and laity, we must remember that we are describing what is called the *juridical* Church. That is, we are looking at the Church as an *organization*, as a public society whose members and leaders are bound together by visible and legal bonds of unity. It is somewhat similar to the manner in which the citizens of a nation are bound together by visible legal bonds of citizenship. The United States of America, for example, is a *juridical* society.

Jesus Christ did indeed establish His Church as a juridical society. It had to be a visible organization if it was to fulfill its purpose of teaching, sanctifying, and ruling mankind. Pope Pius XII, in his encyclical letter *On the Mystical Body*

of Christ, pointed out this fact. The Holy Father also emphasized that as a visible organization the Church is the most
perfect juridical society that exists. It is the most perfect of
all societies because it has the noblest of all purposes: the
sanctifying of its members for the glory of God.

Then the Holy Father went on, in his encyclical, to make
plain that the Church is far more than just a juridical organization. It is the very Body of Christ, a body so special that
it must have a special name—the Mystical Body of Christ.
Christ is the Head of the Body; each baptized soul is a living
part, a *member* of the Body; and the Soul of that Body of
the Mystical Body of Christ, is the Holy Ghost.

The Holy Father warned us: "There is question here of a
hidden mystery, which during this earthly exile can only be
dimly seen." But let us try to see it, at least in its dimness.
We know that our own human body is made up of millions
of individual cells, all working together for the good of the
whole body, under the direction of the head. The various
parts of the body do not occupy themselves with private
business of their own. Each is working all the time for the
good of the whole. The eyes and ears and other senses
gather knowledge for the use of the entire body. The feet
carry the entire body wherever it may wish to go. The
hands carry food to the mouth, the stomach absorbs nourishment for the whole man. The heart and lungs send blood
and oxygen to every part of the anatomy. All live and labor
for all.

And it is the soul, of course, that gives life and unity to
all these separate parts, to all these individual cells. When
the digestive tract changes food into our bodily substance,
the new cells are not added *onto* the body in casual fashion
like a plaster stuck onto the skin. The new cells become a
living part of the living body, because the soul has become
present in the new cells just as it is in the rest of the body.

We can apply this now, by analogy, to the Mystical Body
of Christ. When we are baptized, the Holy Spirit takes

possession of us, very much as our soul takes possession of newly formed cells of our body. This same Holy Spirit is at one and the same time the Spirit of Christ who, to quote Pope Pius XII, "delights to dwell in the beloved soul of our Redeemer as in His most cherished shrine; this Spirit Christ merited for us on the cross by shedding His own blood. . . . But after Christ's glorification on the cross, His Spirit is communicated to the Church in an abundant outpouring, so that she, and her individual members, may become daily more and more like to our Saviour." The Spirit of Christ becomes, in Baptism, our Spirit too. The "Soul of the Soul" of Christ becomes the Soul of our soul too. "Christ is in us through His Spirit," continues the Holy Father, "whom He gives to us and through whom He acts within us in such a way that all divine activity of the Holy Spirit within our souls must also be attributed to Christ."

That, then, is the Church as seen from "inside." A juridical society, yes, with a visible organization provided by Christ Himself. But more than this, it is a living *organism*, a living Body, with Christ as the Head, us (baptized) as the members, and the Holy Spirit as the Soul. It is a living Body from which we could be cut off by heresy or schism or excommunication as a finger might be cut off by a surgeon's knife. It is a Body in which mortal sin, like twine twisted around a finger, may temporarily cut off the flow of life to a member until the tourniquet is removed by repentance. It is a Body in which every member profits by every Mass that is offered, every prayer that is said and every good deed done by every member throughout the world. It is the Mystical Body of Christ.

The Church is the Mystical Body of Christ. I am a member of that Body. What does this mean for me? I know that in the human body every part has a duty to perform: the eye to see, the ear to hear, the hand to grasp, the heart to pump blood. In the Mystical Body of Christ is there a duty for *me* to perform? We all know that the answer to that question is "YES." We know, too, there are three sacraments by means of which Jesus Christ assigns our duties to us.

First there is the sacrament of Baptism, by which we are made members of Christ's Mystical Body. We say that by Baptism we are "*incorporated*" in Christ. The word "incorporated" comes from the Latin word "corpus," which means "body." In Latin the complete word is "in-corporatus," which means "made a part of the body." Food is incorporated in us when it is changed to living cells and becomes a living part of our body. That, by analogy, is what happens to us when we are baptized; we are *incorporated* in Christ.

Having united us to Himself in this so-intimate union, Jesus makes us sharers, according to our human limitations, in all that He is and all that He has. He makes us sharers especially in His eternal priesthood. We share with Christ in His awesome task of offering adequate worship to the Most Blessed Trinity. The baptized Christian, consciously exercising the common priesthood which he shares with Christ, participates in the Mass in a way that an unbaptized person never could.

But we adore God in other ways besides the Mass. We adore God by prayer and by sacrifice, and by the practice of the virtues of faith, hope and charity, *especially* by the virtue of charity. Charity means love, love for God, and love for the souls whom God has made and for whom Jesus has died. As members of Christ's Mystical Body, as sharers in His eternal priesthood, we are driven by a zeal to labor actively with Christ in His work of redemption. To be true to our vocation as baptized Christians, we *must* have this zeal for souls. We must be apostles, all of us, and if we belong to the laity we are called "lay apostles."

Both of those words come from the Greek language. In Greek, the word "apostle" means "someone who is sent." The twelve men whom Jesus sent into the world to establish His Church are called the Twelve Apostles, written with capital letters. But they were not to be the only apostles. At the baptismal font Jesus sends every one of us forth to continue what the Twelve Apostles began. We too are apostles, with a small "a."

The word "lay" also originates in the Greek language. Quite simply, it means "people." We know that in the Church there are three broad classifications of members. There are the *clergy*. This term includes the bishops, priests and all seminarians who have received the tonsure, their first step on the way to the priesthood. Then there are the *religious*—men and women who live in community life and make the vows of poverty, chastity and obedience. Thirdly, there are the *laity*, the people. This term embraces everyone baptized who is neither a cleric nor a religious.

All three classes of members in the Church *together* make up the Mystical Body of Christ. Not the clergy alone; not the clergy and religious; but clergy, religious and laity—all three united in one Body constitute the Church of Christ. In that Body each of the three classes has its own function. But all have this in common: no matter to which class we belong, each of us has, through Baptism, the call to be an apostle, each according to his state.

His eternal priesthood which Jesus shared with us in Baptism, He still more fully shares with us in Confirmation. Having shared with us in Baptism His office of worshiper of the Trinity, Christ in Confirmation shares with us His "prophetic" office, His office of teacher. As we were marked at Baptism with the indelible seal of membership in His Body and sharer in His priesthood, we are marked again in Confirmation with the indelible seal of channel of divine truth. We now have the right to whatever graces we may need to be strong in our own faith, and whatever enlightenment we may need to make that faith intelligible to others, always supposing, of course, that we do our part to learn the truths of our faith, and are guided by the teaching authority of the Church, which resides in the bishops. Once confirmed, we have a *double* responsibility to be lay apostles—and a double source of grace and strength to fulfill that charge.

There is, finally, the third of the "priesthood-sharing" sacraments: Holy Orders. This time Christ *fully* shares His priesthood—fully with the bishops and only a little less with the priests. In Holy Orders there is not only a calling, there is not only grace, but there is *power* as well. To the priest is given the power to consecrate and forgive, to sanctify and bless. To the bishop is given, in addition, the power to ordain other priests and bishops, and the jurisdiction to rule souls and to define the truths of faith.

But we are all called to be apostles. We are all expected to help the Mystical Body of Christ grow and be healthy. Christ expects each of us to labor for the salvation of the world—the little part of the world in which we live: our own home, our neighborhood, our parish, our diocese. He expects us in our own lives to make Him visible to those with whom we live and work and recreate. He expects us to feel a sense of responsibility for the souls of others, to be saddened by their sins, to be worried at their unbelief. Christ expects us to give support and active assistance to our bishops and priests in their gigantic task.

All this is only a little bit of what it means to be a lay apostle. And when our apostolate is carried on by us not as private individuals or as members of a private group but officially, under the direction of our bishop, and with a mandate from him, then our apostolate reaches its fullness, and we are engaged in what is called Catholic Action.

CHAPTER XII

The Marks and Attributes of the Church

Where Do We Find It?

"None genuine without this trademark!" That is a slogan which manufacturers often feature in their advertising. We may not swallow all the hokum about "quality product" and "discriminating buyers," but most of us, when we go shopping, do insist on getting the particular brand of article for which we ask, and very few of us ever pick up a piece of silverware without turning it over to see if it is stamped "Sterling"; very few of us ever examine a ring without looking inside for the carat mark.

Since His wisdom is the wisdom of God, we would expect that Jesus Christ in establishing His Church would be no less intelligent than modern merchandisers. We would expect Jesus to mark His Church in such a way that all men of good will could easily recognize it. Especially would we expect this in view of the fact that Jesus founded His Church at the cost of His own life. Jesus did not die upon the cross "just for the fun of it." He did not make it a matter of free choice for men to belong to His Church or not to belong, as they might prefer. His Church is the Gate of Heaven through which everyone (at least by implicit desire) must enter.

Having made His Church a prerequisite of our everlasting happiness, our Lord has not failed to stamp it plainly with His "trademark," with the mark of its divine origin. He has marked it so plainly that we can recognize it even on the modern "notions counter" of a thousand differing churches and sects and religions. We might say that the trademark of Christ's Church is a square. He Himself has told us what to look for on each side of that square.

First there is *unity*. "And other sheep I have that are not of this fold. Them also I must bring," Jesus says, "and they shall hear My voice, and there shall be one fold and one Shepherd" (John 10:16). Or again: "Holy Father, keep in Thy name those whom Thou hast given Me, that they may be one even as We are" (John 17:11).

Then there is *holiness*. "Sanctify them in the truth. . . . And for them I sanctify Myself, that they also may be sanctified in truth" (John 17:17, 19). That was our Lord's own prayer for His Church, and St. Paul reminds us that Jesus Christ "gave Himself for us that He might redeem us from all iniquity and cleanse for Himself an acceptable people, pursuing good works" (Titus 2:14).

On the third side of the square there is *catholicity*—with a small "c"—or *universality*. The word "catholic" comes from the Greek; "universal" comes from the Latin. Both mean the same thing, *all*. *All* of Christ's teachings, to *all* men at *all* times in *all* places. Hear our Lord speak: "And this Gospel of the kingdom shall be preached in the whole world, for a witness to all nations" (Matt. 24:14). "Go into the whole world and preach the Gospel to every creature" (Mark 16:15). "You shall be witnesses for Me in Jerusalem and in all Judea and Samaria and even to the very ends of the earth" (Acts 1:8).

The square is then completed with the note of *apos-*

tolicity. The word itself is a bit of a jawbreaker; but it means simply that any Church claiming to be Christ's own must be able to trace its lineage in unbroken continuity back to the Apostles. It must be able to show its legitimate descent from Christ through His Apostles. Again, Jesus Himself speaks: "And I say to thee, thou art Peter, and upon this rock I will build My Church, and the gates of hell shall not prevail against it" (Matt. 16:18). Speaking to all the Apostles: "All power in heaven and on earth has been given to Me. Go, therefore, and make disciples of all nations, baptizing them in the name of the Father, and of the Son, and of the Holy Spirit, teaching them to observe all that I have commanded you; and behold, I am with you all days, even unto the consummation of the world" (Matt. 28:18–20). St. Paul drives home this point of *apostolicity* when he says to the Ephesians, "Therefore, you are now no longer strangers and foreigners, but you are citizens with the saints and members of God's household: you are built upon the foundation of the Apostles and prophets with Christ Jesus Himself as the chief cornerstone" (Eph. 2:19–20).

There we have Christ's own trademark. One, holy, catholic and apostolic. It is a square which He has stamped ineradicably upon His Church, sharp and clear as a goldsmith's die. These are the four marks which must be exhibited by any church which claims to be Christ's own. There are many churches in the world today which claim to be Christian. Let us shorten the labor of our examination by "picking up" our own church, the Catholic Church, for scrutiny. If we find the trademark of Christ there, we shall have no need to look further.

No matter how mistaken you may be about something, it will get your "dander" up if someone tells you flatly that you are wrong. And as they carefully explain to you *why* you are wrong, you get more stubborn by the minute. Maybe not always. Maybe not at all if you are a saint. But in general, human nature is like that. That is why it seldom does any good to argue about religion. We should be ready to *discuss* religion at the drop of a hat, but never to argue. The minute we say to someone, "Your religion is wrong and I'll tell you why," we have slammed the door of the person's mind. Nothing that we say afterwards will get in. On the other hand, if we know our own religion well, and explain it in intelligent and kindly fashion to our neighbor who is not a Catholic, there is a good chance that he may listen to us. If we can show that the Catholic Church is the true Church established by Jesus Christ, we don't have to tell him that his church is not the true Church. He may be stubborn, but he is not stupid. He can be trusted to make his own deductions. Keeping that in mind, then, we proceed to examine the Catholic Church to see whether it bears the trademark of Christ—whether Jesus has unmistakably stamped it as His own.

We look first of all for the *unity* which our Lord said must characterize His flock. We look for this unity in three dimensions: unity of belief, unity of leadership, and unity of worship.

We know that the members of Christ's Church must exhibit unity of belief. The truths which they hold are the truths made known to us by Jesus Christ Himself; they are truths which have come to us directly from God. There are no "truer" truths which the human mind can know and accept than truths revealed by God. God *is* truth. He knows all things and cannot be mistaken. He is infinitely truthful and cannot lie. It is easier to believe that there is no sun in the sky at midday, for example, than to believe that Jesus could be mistaken when He says that there are three Persons in one God.

That is why we think the principle of "private judgment" to be so very illogical. There are many people who maintain the right to private judgment in religious matters. They admit that God has made certain truths known to us, but they say that each man should interpret those truths to suit himself. Let every man read his own Bible; and whatever he thinks the Bible means, that is what it *does* mean for him. Our answer is that whatever God has said is so, and is so for always and for everybody. It is not for us to pick and choose and to adjust God's revelation to our own preferences and our own convenience.

This theory of "private judgment" has led quite naturally one step further: to the denial of *all* absolute truth. There are many men today who claim that truth and goodness are *relative* terms. Something is "true" as long as the generality of men find it helpful, as long as it seems to work. If it helps you to believe in God, then believe in God but be ready to cast the belief aside if it begins to get in the way of progress. The same thing holds for what we call "good." A thing is good, or an action is good if it contributes to the welfare and happiness of humanity. But if chastity, for example, seems to slow up man's onward march in an ever-changing world, then chastity ceases to be good. In short, that may be called good or true which is here and now useful to the community, to man as a constructive member of society, and it is good or true *only so long* as it continues to be useful. This philosophy is called pragmatism. It is very hard to discuss truth with a pragmatist, because he has cut the ground from under your feet by denying that there is any real, absolute truth. About all that the believing Christian can do is to pray for him—and try to show him by a truly Christian life that Christianity *does* work.

The foregoing has been a bit of a sidetrack to our main theme, which is that no church can claim to be Christ's own unless all its members believe the same truths, since they are God's truths, eternally unchangeable and the same for all people. We know that in the Catholic Church all *do* believe the same truths. Bishops, priests and first-grade children; Americans and Frenchmen and Japanese; white or colored; every Catholic, everywhere, means exactly the same things when he recites the Apostles' Creed.

We are united not only in the things we believe but also

are united under the same spiritual leadership. It was Jesus Christ who made St. Peter the chief shepherd of His flock and provided that Peter's successors until the end of time would be the head of His Church and the guardian of His truths. Loyalty to the Bishop of Rome, whom we lovingly call our Holy Father, will ever be the binding center of our unity—and the test of our membership in Christ's Church. "Where Peter is, there is the Church!"

In worship too we are united, as is no other Church. We have but one altar, upon which Jesus Christ daily renews the offering of Himself upon the cross. The Catholic is the only person who can take a trip around the world and know that wherever he goes—Africa or India, Germany or South America—he will feel religiously at home. Everywhere the same Mass, everywhere the same seven sacraments.

One in faith, one in head, one in worship. Here is that unity for which Christ prayed, the unity which He pointed to as one of the marks which would identify His Church forever. It is a unity which we find only in the Catholic Church.

Holy and Catholic

The strongest arguments against the Catholic Church are the lives of bad Catholics and lax Catholics. If you were to ask a lukewarm Catholic, "Is one church as good as another?" he probably would answer indignantly, "Of course not; there is only one true Church, the Catholic Church." And then he will do his best to prove himself a liar by swapping the same dirty stories with his non-Catholic friends, by getting drunk with them at the same parties, tomcatting with them at the same conventions, exchanging with them the same malicious gossip, buying the same contraceptives—perhaps even exceeding them a bit by the sharpness of his business practices or the dirtiness of his politics.

We know that such men and women are in the minority,

but even one would be too many. We know too that we must expect that there will be unworthy members in Christ's Church. Jesus Himself compared His Church to a fish net in which bad fish are caught along with the good (Matt. 13:47–50); to a field of grain in which weeds grow up with the wheat (Matt. 13:24–30); and to a wedding feast at which one of the guests does not have on a wedding garment (Matt. 22:11–14).

The sinners then are with us to stay. To the end of the road they will be the cross that Christ in His Mystical Body must carry on His shoulder. Yet, Jesus pointed to *holiness* as one of the distinguishing marks of His Church. "By their fruits you will know them," He said. "Do men gather grapes from thorns, or figs from thistles? Even so, every good tree bears good fruit, but the bad tree bears bad fruit." (Cf. Matt. 7:16–17.)

In answering the question, "Why is the Catholic Church holy?" the catechism says, "The Catholic Church is holy because it was founded by Jesus Christ, who is all-holy, and because it teaches, according to the will of Christ, holy doctrines, and provides the means of leading a holy life, thereby giving holy members to every age."

Now that is true, every word of it, but it is not an easy point to get across to a non-Catholic acquaintance, especially if he has spent last night "doing the town" in the company of Joe Doakes, who is a member of the Holy Name Society at St. Pia's parish. *We* know that Jesus Christ founded the Church, and that all other churches were founded by mere men. But the Lutheran probably would pooh-pooh the idea that Martin Luther founded a new church; he would say that Luther merely "purified" the ancient church of its errors and abuses. The Episcopalian doubtless would have a similar answer: Henry VIII and Cranmer did not start a new church; they merely cut loose from the "Roman branch" and established the "English branch" of the original Christian church. The Presbyterian would say the same of

John Knox, and the Methodist of John Wesley, and so on through the long list of Protestant sects. All of them doubtless would claim Christ as their founder.

Much the same thing would happen when we pointed to the fact that the Catholic Church teaches a holy doctrine, as proof of the Church's divine origin. "My church teaches a holy doctrine, too," our non-Catholic acquaintance very likely would answer. "In fact," he might even claim, "my church teaches a *holier* doctrine than yours. We don't believe in card-playing or drinking or gambling as you Catholics do." If we were so rude as to bring up such matters as contraceptives and divorce, he perhaps would brush us off with the charge of being unrealistic, not keeping up with the demands of social progress.

But at least we could point to the saints, couldn't we, as proof of the fact that the holiness of Christ is at work in the Catholic Church? Yes, we could; and it is a pretty tough piece of evidence for anyone to evade. The many thousands of men and women and children who have led lives of supereminent sanctity, and whose names make up the calendar of the saints: these are pretty hard to explain away, and there is nothing like them in any other church. However, if our discussant is glib in the terminology of modern psychology, he may double-talk his way around the saints with such words as "hysteria," "neurosis" and "sublimation of basic drives." In any case, the saints are storybook people to him. You can't *show* him a saint, right here and now.

So what does that leave us? It just leaves us ourselves, you and me. Our interested friend (we suppose that he is) may claim Christ as his founder too, may claim a holy doctrine for his church, too, may bypass the saints as an arguable point. But he can't escape *us;* he cannot be blind and deaf to the testimony of our lives. If every Catholic whom our imaginary inquirer meets is a person of outstanding Christian virtue: kind and patient and unselfish and sympathetic; chaste and charitable and reverent in speech; honest and truthful and a stranger to all double-dealing; generous and pure and temperate in conduct—what kind of impression would *that* make?

Just in our own country alone, if our 31,000,000 Catholics led that kind of life, what a thunder of witness that would be to the holiness of Christ's Church! We have need to remind ourselves time and time again that we *are* our brother's keeper. We may not indulge our petty weaknesses and our self-love and think that all is well when we have dusted ourselves off in confession. It is not only for our sins, but for the souls who may have missed heaven because of us that we shall have to answer one day to Christ. Thirty-one million did I say? Let's forget about the other 30,999,999; let's concentrate right now, you on you and me on me. Then will the mark of holiness in the Catholic Church be vindicated at least in the little area where we live and move.

All the time, all the truths, all the places. That, in capsule form, describes the third of the four marks of the Church. It is the third side of the square which is the "trademark" of Christ, the hallmark which proves the divine origin of the Church. It is the stamp of genuineness which only the Catholic Church bears.

The word "catholic" means "embracing all." It is derived from the Greek language, as we have mentioned before; and it means the same thing as the word "universal," which stems from the Latin tongue.

When we say that the Catholic Church (with a capital "C") is catholic (with a small "c") or universal, we mean first of all that the Church has been in existence at *all times*, from Pentecost Sunday right down to today. The pages of any history book will bear this out—and it doesn't have to be a Catholic history book, either. The Catholic Church has had a continuous existence of nineteen hundred and more years, and it is the *only* church of which this is true.

Whatever other churches may say about being "purifications" of the ancient Church, or "branches" of the one true

Church, the fact remains that for the first eight hundred years of Christian history there was no other church but the Catholic Church. The oldest non-Catholic church is the Greek Orthodox Church. That church had its beginning in the ninth century, when the archbishop of Constantinople refused Holy Communion to the Emperor Bardas, who was living in sin. In anger, the emperor tore Greece away from union with Rome, and the Orthodox Church was born.

The oldest Protestant church, which is the Lutheran Church, came into being in the sixteenth century—almost fifteen hundred years after Christ. It began with the revolt of Martin Luther, a Catholic priest of magnetic personality, and owed its quick success to the support of the German princes who resented the power of the Pope at Rome. Luther's attempt to remedy the abuses in the Church (and there were some real ones) ended in the far greater evil of a divided Christendom. Luther made the first break in the dike. After him came a flood of others. We have mentioned Henry VIII and John Knox and John Wesley. But the original Protestant churches splintered and subdivided (mostly in the Germanic and English-speaking countries) into hundreds of differing sects; and the process still goes on. Not one of them existed, however, before the year 1517, when Luther nailed his famous "95 Theses" to the door of the church in Wittenberg, Germany.

Not only is the Catholic Church the only church whose uninterrupted history goes all the way back to Christ; it also is the only church which teaches *all the truths* taught by Jesus, as He taught them. The sacraments of Penance and Extreme Unction, the Mass and the Real Presence of Jesus in the Eucharist, the spiritual supremacy of Peter and his successors the Popes, the efficacy of grace and man's ability to merit grace and heaven—some or all of these are rejected by the various non-Catholic churches. In fact there are churches today which claim the name of "Christian" which even question whether Jesus Christ is truly God. There is not a single truth revealed by Jesus Christ, however (whether personally or through His Apostles), which the Catholic Church does not still declare and teach.

Besides being universal in time (*all* the years since Pentecost) and universal in doctrine (*all* the truths taught by Christ), the Catholic Church also is universal in *extent*. Mindful of her Founder's commission to make disciples of all nations, the Catholic Church has carried Christ's message of salvation to every latitude and longitude on the face of the globe, wherever there are souls to be reached. The Catholic Church is not a "German" church (Lutheran), or an "English" church (Episcopalian), or a "Scotch" church (Presbyterian), or a "Dutch" church (Reformed), or an "American" church (hundreds of different sects). The Catholic Church is in all these countries and in every other country, besides, where missionaries have been permitted to penetrate. But the Catholic Church belongs to no nation and to no race. It is at home in every land, but is the property of none. This is as Jesus Christ willed it. His Church is for *all* men. It must be world-wide. The Catholic Church is the only church of which this is true; it is the only church which is everywhere, throughout the world.

Catholic or universal—in time and truths and territory; that is the third mark of the true Church of Christ. And the fourth mark, which completes the square, is "apostolicity." This means simply that the church which claims to be Christ's own must be able to prove its legitimate descent from the Apostles, upon whom as a foundation Jesus established His Church.

That the Catholic Church does possess this mark of "apostolicity" is easy enough to demonstrate. We have the list of the Bishops of Rome, going back from the Holy Father of our own day in a continuous line to St. Peter. And the other bishops of the Catholic Church, true successors of the Apostles, are today's latest links in an unbroken chain which stretches back through 1900 years. Since the days when the Apostles laid hands upon Timothy and Titus and Mark and Polycarp, the episcopal power has been passed on, in the sacrament of Holy Orders, from generation to generation; from bishop to bishop to bishop.

And so the square is closed. The trademark of Christ is discerned clearly etched in the Catholic Church: one, holy, catholic and apostolic. We are not so naïve as to suppose that converts will come running, wholesale, when we point out the trademark to them. Human prejudices do not yield that easily to reason. But at least let us be sure that we see the trademark plainly ourselves.

Reason and Faith—and Myself

God has given to man the power of reason, and He expects man to use this gift. There are two ways in which the power of reason may be abused. One way is by not using it. A person who has not learned to use his reason is the person who takes as gospel truth everything he reads in newspapers and periodicals, no matter how "slanted" the news may be. He is the person who will accept without question the most extravagant claims of salesmen and advertisers and is the gullible tool of smart propagandists. He is awed by prestige; if a famous scientist or industrialist says there is no God, then, of course, there is no God. In other words, this non-thinker likes his opinions ready-made. It is not always laziness which makes the non-thinker. Unfortunately sometimes parents and teachers are the cause of this mental apathy when they discourage the natural curiosity of youth and squelch every normal "why" with a "because-I-said-so!"

At the other extreme is the man who makes a veritable god of reason. This is the person who will believe nothing that he cannot see and understand. For him the only facts are those which come out of scientific laboratories. Nothing is true unless it "makes sense" for him, unless it has good practical results right here and now. What works is true;

what is useful is good. This type of thinker is called a pragmatist. He rejects any truth that is based upon authority. He will believe in the authority of an Einstein and will accept the theory of relativity, even though he may not understand it. He will believe in the authority of the nuclear physicists and will accept the fact of nuclear fission, even though he may not understand that. But "authority" is a fighting word to him when it is a question of the authority of the Church.

The pragmatist will respect the pronouncements of human authorities, because he says he has confidence that they know what they are talking about; he trusts in their ability. But the pragmatist will look with impatient pity upon the Catholic who, for this very same reason, respects the pronouncements of the Church, confident that the Church knows what it, in the person of the Pope and bishops, is talking about.

It is true that not all Catholics have an intelligent understanding of their faith. With many, faith *is* a blind acceptance of religious truths on the authority of the Church. This unreasoning acceptance may be due to lack of opportunity to study, or to lack of education, or even (unfortunately) to mental laziness. This is not to say that a blind faith is necessarily to be condemned. For children and for the untutored, religious belief has to be an unproved belief, just as their belief in the need for certain foods and the poisonousness of certain substances also must be an unproved belief. The pragmatist who may say, "I'll string along with Einstein; he ought to know what he's talking about," hardly can find fault with the child who says, "I believe it because Daddy says it's so"; and later, "I believe it because the priest (or Sister) says it's so." Nor can he find fault with the unlettered adult who says, "What the Pope says is good enough for me."

For the thinking Catholic, however, the acceptance of religious truths is a *reasoned* acceptance, an intelligent acceptance. It is true that the virtue of faith itself—the *ability* to believe—is a grace, a gift of God. But adult faith is based on reason; it is not a frustration of reason. The instructed Catholic has satisfied himself from the clear evidence of history that God has spoken; that God has spoken through His Son Jesus Christ; that Jesus Christ has established a Church as His mouthpiece, as the visible manifestation of Himself to mankind; that the Catholic Church *is* that Church established by Jesus Christ; that it is to the bishops of that Church, as the successors of the Apostles (and especially to Peter's successor, the Pope), that Jesus Christ gave the power to teach, to sanctify, and to govern spiritually in His name. This competency of the Church to speak in Christ's name on matters of doctrinal belief or moral action, to administer the sacraments and to exercise spiritual governance, we call the *authority* of the Church. The man who has satisfied himself, by the use of his reason, that the Catholic Church does possess this attribute of authority, is not going against reason—on the contrary he is *following* reason—when he asserts, "I believe all that the Catholic Church teaches."

Equally is the Catholic following reason as well as faith when he subscribes to the doctrine of infallibility. This attribute of infallibility means simply that the Church (either in the person of the Pope, or of all the bishops together under the Pope) cannot make a mistake when she solemnly proclaims that a certain matter of belief or of conduct has been revealed by God and must be held and followed by all. Jesus Christ's promise, "Behold, I am with you all days, even unto the consummation of the world" (Matt. 28:20) would be meaningless if His Church were not infallible. Certainly Jesus would not be with His Church if He allowed His Church to fall into error concerning the essentials of salvation. The Catholic knows that the Pope can sin, like any other human being. The Catholic knows that the Pope's personal opinions enjoy only as much standing as the Pope's human wisdom may give them, but the

Catholic also knows that when the Pope, as the head of Christ's Church, publicly and solemnly proclaims that a certain truth has been revealed by Christ, either personally or through His Apostles, Peter's successor cannot be in error. Jesus would not establish a Church which could lead men astray.

The right to speak in Christ's name and to be heard—that is the attribute (or quality) of the Catholic Church we call "authority." The assurance of freedom from error when solemnly proclaiming the truths of God to the universal Church—that is the attribute we call "infallibility." There is a third quality which characterizes the Catholic Church. Jesus not only said, "He who hears you, hears Me; and he who rejects you, rejects Me" (Luke 10:16)—*authority*. He not only said, "Behold, I am with you all days, even unto the consummation of the world" (Matt. 28:20)—*infallibility*. He also said, "Upon this rock I will build My Church, and the gates of hell shall not prevail against it" (Matt. 16:18). It is in these words that our Lord points to the third quality which is inherent in the Catholic Church—*indefectibility*.

The attribute of indefectibility means simply that the Church, as Jesus Himself founded it, will last until the end of time. It means that the Church is here to stay, that it will continue to exist as long as there are souls to be saved. "Permanence" would be a good synonym for indefectibility, but theologians always seem to love the longer words.

It would be a great mistake for us to let this attribute of indefectibility lull us into a feeling of false security. Jesus said that His Church would last until the end of time. But He did not say that it would last in *this* country or in *that* country until the end of time. With atheistic Communism threatening us in the East and in the West, it would be tragic if we remained smugly indifferent to the threat, telling our-selves that nothing really bad can happen to us because Christ is with His Church. If we neglect our high vocation as Christians—and therefore apostles—Christ's Church may again become (as it once was in the Roman empire) an underground Church of martyrdom-marked souls. It is not so much the bombs and the guns of Communism that we have to fear; it is rather the fervor, the dynamism, the missionary-mindedness of the Communists that is the long-range danger. They have so little to offer, and yet are so zealous in proclaiming it. We have so *much* to share and yet seem so lackadaisical, almost indifferent, in showing the truth to others.

"How many converts have I made?" Or at least, how much thought and effort have I given to the making of converts? That is a question that each of us ought to ask himself, at least once a year. The thought of standing before God in judgment, empty-handed, is a thought to make us tremble. "Where are your fruits, where are your souls?" He rightly will ask—and He will ask it of the layman as well as of the priest or religious. We cannot wholly discharge our obligation by giving money to the missions. That is a necessary part of it, but it is only the beginning. There also is the matter of prayer. Our daily prayers would be woefully incomplete if they did not include prayers for the missionaries, home and foreign, and for the souls among whom they labor. But do we pray every day for the gift of faith for our next-door neighbors, if they are not Catholics? Do we pray for that girl who works at the next desk, that fellow who works at the next machine? How often during the year do we invite a non-Catholic friend to attend Mass with us, providing him in advance with a booklet that will explain what is going on? Do we have a few good books on the Catholic faith, and a supply of interesting pamphlets at home, that we offer to give or lend on the slightest provocation, to anyone who seems the least bit interested? If we do all these things, even offering (when a question seems too big for us) to take an inquirer to meet a priest, then we are doing what we ought; we are fulfilling at least some of our responsibility to Christ for the treasure that He has entrusted to us.

We do not believe, of course, that all non-Catholics go

to hell, any more than we believe that just calling oneself a Catholic will get one to heaven. The dictum that "Outside the Church there is no salvation," means no salvation for those who are outside the Church through their own fault. One who has been a Catholic and who deliberately abandons the Church cannot be saved unless he returns; the grace of faith is not lost except through one's own fault. A non-Catholic who knows the Catholic Church to be the true Church but remains outside through his own fault cannot be saved. A non-Catholic whose ignorance of the Catholic faith is a self-willed ignorance, a deliberate blindness, cannot be saved. Those, however, who are outside the Church through no fault of their own, and who do the best they can according to what they know, making good use of the graces that God surely will give them in view of their good will—these *can* be saved. God does not ask the impossible of anyone. He will reward everyone in the light of what he has done with what he has. This does not mean, however, that we can escape our responsibility by saying, "My neighbor can get to heaven without being a Catholic; so why should I worry?" Nor does it mean, "One church is as good as another."

God still wants all men to belong to the Church which He has established. Jesus Christ still wants one fold and one Shepherd. And we *ought* to want our relatives and friends and neighbors to have the greater certainty of salvation which we ourselves have in Christ's own Church: the greater fullness of truth, the greater security in knowledge of what is right and wrong, the unmatchable helps offered by the Mass and the sacraments. We wear our own faith lightly indeed if we can mix with people day after day without ever asking ourselves, "What can I do to help this man (or woman) to recognize the truth of the Catholic Church, and to become one with me in the Mystical Body of Christ?" The Holy Spirit lives in the Church forever, but so often He must wait upon me to find entrance into the soul of that man beside me.

CHAPTER XIII

The Communion of Saints
and the Forgiveness of Sins

The End of the Road

Most of us probably would wince if someone were to call us a saint. We are too conscious of our imperfections to accept such a title. And yet, in the early Church, all faithful members of the Mystical Body of Christ were classified as saints. It was St. Paul's favorite term for members of the Christian community. He speaks of "the saints who are at Ephesus" (Eph. 1:1) and the "saints that are in the whole of Achaia" (2 Cor. 1:1). The Acts of the Apostles, which is the history of the infant Church, also classifies as saints all who are followers of Christ.

The word "saint" derives from the Latin word "sanctus," which means "holy." Every Christian soul, incorporated with Christ by Baptism, and harboring within himself the Holy Spirit (so long as he remains in the state of sanctifying grace) *is* holy, *is* a saint in the original meaning of the word. Nowadays, of course, the word "saint" is limited generally to those who are in heaven. But it is the original meaning of the word that we are using when we say, in the Apostles' Creed, "I believe . . . in the communion of saints." The word "communion" here means "union with" (again from the Latin), and we are saying that we believe that there exists a union, a fellowship, an intercourse among all souls in whom dwells the Holy Spirit, the Spirit of Christ. This fellowship includes first of all ourselves, members of the Church here upon earth. Our "branch" of the communion of saints is called the Church militant—that is, the Church still struggling, still fighting against sin and error. If we should fall into mortal sin, we do not cease to be members of the communion of saints; but we are cut off from all spiritual interchange with our fellows as long as we continue to exclude the Holy Spirit from our soul.

The souls in purgatory also are members of the communion of saints. They are established in grace forever, even though their minor sins and debts of penance have still to be purged away. They cannot yet see God, but the Holy Spirit is in them and with them, never again to be lost. We often refer to this branch of the Church as the Church suffering.

There is, finally, the Church triumphant, made up of all the souls of the blessed in heaven. This is the everlasting Church. Into it will be absorbed, after the last Judgment, both the Church militant and the Church suffering.

And now, what does the communion of saints mean for us in practice? It means that all of us who are united in Christ—the saints in heaven, the souls in purgatory, and we upon earth—must be mindful of the needs of one another. The saints in heaven are not so rapt in their own bliss as to forget the souls they have left behind. They could not forget if they would. Their perfect love for God must include a love for all the souls whom God has made and adorned with His graces, all the souls in whom God Himself dwells, all the souls for whom Jesus died. In short, the saints *must* love the souls whom God loves. The love that the blessed in heaven have for the souls in purgatory and the souls on earth is not a passive love. We might call it an active, *hungry* love. The saints long to help onward to heaven all souls, whose precious value they now realize as never before. And if the prayer of a good man on earth has power with God, there is no estimating the power of the prayers which the saints offer for us. They are God's heroes, God's intimate friends and familiars.

The saints in heaven pray for the souls in purgatory and for us. We for our part must reverence and honor the saints. Not just because they can and will pray for us; but also because our love for God demands it. An artist is honored when his works are praised. The saints are masterpieces of God's grace; when we honor them, we are honoring their Maker, their Sanctifier and their Redeemer. Honor given to the saints is not honor taken from God. On the contrary, it is honor given to God in a manner which He Himself has indicated and desires. And it is worth remembering that when we honor the saints, we are undoubtedly honoring many of our own loved ones who now are with God in heaven. *Every* soul in heaven is a saint, not just the canonized ones. That is why, in addition to special feast days for certain canonized saints, the Church dedicates one day to the honor of the whole Church triumphant, the Feast of All Saints on November 1.

As members of the communion of saints, we upon earth also pray for the suffering souls in purgatory. They cannot help themselves now; their time for meriting is past. But we can help them by the favor of God. We can relieve their sufferings and speed them on to heaven by our prayers for them, by the Masses we offer and have offered for them, by the indulgences we gain for them. (Almost all indulgences granted by the Church can be applied to the souls in purgatory, if we make that intention.) Whether or not the souls in purgatory can pray for us we do not know, but we do know that once they are numbered among the saints in heaven they surely will remember us who remembered them in their need and will be our special intercessors with God.

It is obvious that we upon earth must also pray for and help one another if we are to be faithful to our obligations as members of the communion of saints. We must have a truly supernatural love for one another, practicing the virtue of fraternal charity in thought and word and deed, especially by performing the spiritual and corporal works of mercy. If we are to assure ourselves of *permanent* membership in the communion of saints, we dare not take lightly our responsibilities here.

CHAPTER XIV

The Resurrection and Life Everlasting

The End of the World

We live and we labor, for a few years or for many—and then we die. This life, as we well know, is a time of testing and of trial; it is eternity's proving ground. The happiness of heaven consists essentially in the fulfillment of love. Unless we enter eternity with love for God in our hearts, we would be absolutely incapable of experiencing the happiness of heaven. Our life upon this earth is the time that God has given us to acquire and to *prove* our love for Him. We must prove that our love for God is greater than any of His created gifts, such as pleasure or wealth or fame or friends. We must prove that our love can withstand the pressure of man-made evils, such as poverty or pain or humiliation or injustice. Whether we are on the heights or in the depths, at every moment we must be able to say, "My God I love You!"—and prove what we say by our actions. For some the road is short, for others long. For some the road is comparatively smooth, for others rough. But for all of us the road ends. We die.

Death is simply the separation of the soul from the body. Through the ravages of time or of disease or of accident, the body becomes damaged to the point where the soul no longer can continue to operate through the body. At this point the soul leaves the body, and we say that the person is dead. The exact instant at which the soul leaves the body can seldom be known. The heart may have stopped beating, breathing may have ceased, but the soul may still be present. This is proved by the fact that sometimes persons apparently dead are revived by artificial respiration or other means. Unless the soul still were present, they could not be revived. That is why the Church permits a priest to give conditional absolution and conditional Extreme Unction for as long as two hours after apparent death, just in case the soul *may* still be present. Once the blood has begun to congeal, however, and *rigor mortis* has set in, we know definitely that the soul has left the body.

What happens then? At the very instant the soul leaves the body, it is judged by almighty God. Even while those about the bedside are crossing the hands upon the breast and gently closing the sightless eyes, the soul already has been judged; the soul already knows what its eternal fate is to be. This judgment of the individual soul immediately after death is called the Particular Judgment. It is a tremendous moment for all of us. It is the moment for which all our years upon earth have been spent, the moment towards which our whole life has been directed. For all of us it will be pay day.

Where will this Particular Judgment take place? Probably right there on the spot where we die, humanly speaking. Beyond this life there is no "space" or "place" in the sense in which we ordinarily understand these words. The soul doesn't have to "go" someplace to be judged. As to the form which this Particular Judgment will take, we can only guess. All that God has revealed to us concerning the Particular Judgment is that it will happen; that is all we need to know. The description of the Particular Judgment as a judicial proceeding, with the soul standing before God seated upon His throne, with the devil on one side as the prosecuting attorney and the guardian angel on the other as the defense attorney—all this, of course, is poetic imagery and nothing more. Theologians speculate that what actually takes place probably is that God illumines the soul so that the soul sees itself as God sees it—sees the state it is in, of grace or of unforgiven sin, of God-loving or God-rejecting —and sees what its fate is to be in accordance with the infinite justice of God. It is a fate which cannot be changed, a sentence which cannot be reversed. The time of preparation and trial is ended. God's mercy has done all that it can. Only God's justice prevails now.

What comes next? Well, let us get the worst over with first. Let us consider the lot of the soul which has chosen self in preference to God, and which has died without turning back to God; in other words, the soul which dies in the state of mortal sin. Having deliberately cut itself off from God during life; having died without that bond of union with God which we call sanctifying grace, it has now no means by which it can establish contact with God. It has lost God forever. It is in hell. For such a soul, death, judgment and hell are simultaneous.

What is hell like? No one knows exactly, because no one has ever come back from hell to describe it to us. We know that in hell there is everlasting fire, because Jesus Himself has said so. We also know that it is not the kind of fire we see in our stoves and furnaces. That fire could not afflict the soul, which is a spirit. All we know is that there is in hell a "pain of sense" (as the theologians term it) of such a nature that it cannot be better described by any other word in our human language than by the word "fire."

But what matters most is not the "pain of sense." What matters most is the "pain of loss." It is the pain of loss, the eternal separation from God that constitutes the worst of

hell's suffering. I suppose that within the framework of revealed truths each person views hell in his own way. To me,
the soul-shuddering thing about the thought of hell is its
awful loneliness. I think of myself as standing nakedly alone
in a vast emptiness that is filled only with hatred, hatred for
God and hatred for myself, wishing that I could die and
knowing that I cannot, knowing too that this is the destiny
which I have freely chosen for myself in exchange for some
mess of pottage, and all the while there is being dinned into
my ears the voice of my own jeering conscience: "This
is forever . . . no rest . . . no surcease . . . forever . . .
forever. . . ." But no picture of hell that words or brush can
paint will ever be as bad as the reality. God spare us all!

Probably few of us are so optimistic as to expect that our
Particular Judgment will find us free from every trace of
sin. That would mean being free not only from all mortal
and venial sin, but also free from all undischarged temporal
punishment—the debt of atonement we owe to God even
after sin itself has been forgiven. We do not *expect* to die
with a soul so spotlessly pure, perhaps, but there is no reason
why we should not hope for it. That is what the sacrament
of Extreme Unction is for; to cleanse the soul from the
"remains of sin." That is what plenary indulgences are for,
especially the plenary indulgence at the moment of death,
which the Church grants to the dying by means of the Last
Blessing.

Supposing that we do so die: fortified by the last sacraments and with a plenary indulgence fully gained at the very
moment of death. Supposing that we do die without the
least trace or spot of sin upon our soul. What then can we
expect? In that case our death, which the instinct of self-
preservation has made to seem so fearsome, will in fact be
our moment of brightest victory. As the body reluctantly
relinquishes its hold upon the spirit which has given the body
its life and its value, the instantaneous sight of God will itself be our judgment.

The "beatific vision" is the cold theological term for the magnificent reality which beggars human imagining or description. That reality is not merely a "vision" in the sense of "seeing" God. It is a union with God; God possessing the soul and the soul possessing God in a unity so ravishingly complete as to be infinitely beyond the ecstasy of the most perfect human marriage. As the soul "enters" heaven, the impact upon it of the Infinite Love that is God would be so shattering as to annihilate the soul, if God Himself did not give to the soul the strength it needs to endure the happiness that is God. If we are able for a moment to tear our thoughts from God, how petty then shall we think the worst of our earthly sufferings and trials to have been; what a ridiculously small price we shall have paid for the searing, tearing, choking, spiraling happiness that is ours. It is a happiness, too, that nothing can take from us. It is a telescoped, concentrated instant of pure bliss that will never end. This is happiness eternal; this is the essential happiness of heaven.

There are other incidental joys also that will be ours. There will be our joy in the company of our glorified Saviour Jesus Christ, and of our Mother Mary, whose sweet love and beauty we so long have admired from a distance. There will be our joy in the companionship of the angels and the saints, including our own family members and friends who precede or follow us to heaven. But these joys will be only the tinkling of little bells compared to the crashing symphony of God's love that beats upon us.

But what if, when we die, the Particular Judgment finds us neither severed from God by mortal sin, nor yet with that perfect purity of soul required for union with the all-holy God? This, indeed, is very likely to be the case, if we have been content to remain upon the level of spiritual mediocrity: parsimonious in prayer, dodging self-denial, making compromise with the world. Our mortal sins, if any, may have been forgiven in the sacrament of Penance (do we not say, in the Creed, "I believe in . . . the forgiveness of sins"?); but if ours has been a "comfortable" religion, it is not likely that we shall be capable, in our last moments, of that perfect and selfless love for God which is required for a plenary indulgence. So here we are in Judgment: neither deserving of hell nor fit for heaven. What becomes of us?

It is here that the doctrine of purgatory manifests its eminent reasonableness. Even had the doctrine of purgatory not come down to us from Christ and His Apostles through the tradition of the Church, reason alone would indicate that there must be some final process of purification to cleanse away whatever lesser imperfections might yet stand between the soul and God. This is the function of that state of temporary suffering which we call purgatory. There is in purgatory, as there is in hell, a "pain of sense," but just as the essential suffering of hell is everlasting separation from God, so also the essential suffering of purgatory lies in the excruciating agony which the soul must suffer at being delayed, even for an instant, from union with God. The soul, let us remember, was *made* for God. Because in this life the body serves (we might say) as an insulator, we do not feel the terrific attraction that God has for the soul. Some of the saints feel that attraction faintly, but most of us feel it hardly at all. However, the moment the soul leaves the body, it is exposed to the full power of God's "pull" upon the soul. Crazed with hunger—with hunger for God—the soul beats itself against the barrier of its own remaining imperfections until finally it is purged by the very agony of its own restraint—and the barrier falls, and God is there!

It is consoling to note that the soul in purgatory suffers joyfully, even though the suffering is of an intensity unknown this side of Judgment. The great difference between the suffering of hell and the suffering of purgatory is the hopelessness of hell's eternal separation against the certainty of purgatory's release. The soul in purgatory would not want to appear before God in its present state, and so there is joy in its agony—joy in the knowledge of the ecstasy to come.

It is evident that no one can know "how long" purgatory lasts for any individual soul. I have put "how long" in quotes because, while there is *duration* beyond the grave, there is no "time" as we know it; no nights and days, no hours and minutes. However, whether we measure purgatory by duration or by intensity (and an instant of twisting torture can be worse than a year of mild discomfort), the fact remains that the soul in purgatory cannot lessen or shorten its own sufferings. But we the living can help that soul, by the mercy of God; and the frequency of our remembrance, and the endurance of our remembrance, whether of an individual soul or of all the faithful departed, will be measured only by our love.

If there is one thing that is certain, it is the fact that we do not know when the world will end. It may be tomorrow, it may be a million years from now. Jesus Himself, as we read in the twenty-fourth chapter of St. Matthew's Gospel, has indicated some of the portents that must precede the world's dissolution. There will be wars and famine and pestilence; there will be the reign of Antichrist; the sun and the moon will be darkened and the stars will fall from the heavens; the cross will appear in the sky. Only when all this has happened shall we "see the Son of Man coming upon the clouds of heaven with great power and majesty" (Matt. 24:30). That, however, tells us very little; there already have been wars and famine and pestilence. The Communist domination very easily could be the rule of Antichrist. The spectacles in the sky could happen at any time, and all the prophecies would be fulfilled. On the other hand, the wars and famines and plagues that the world has witnessed up to now may be as nothing compared to those which actually precede the world's end. We just do not know. We can only be ready.

For centuries the twentieth chapter of St. John's Apocalypse (the Book of Revelation in the Protestant versions of the Bible) has provided a source of fascinating material for Scriptural students. There St. John, describing a prophetic vision, says that the devil will be bound and imprisoned for a thousand years, during which the dead will come to life and reign with Christ; at the end of the thousand years the devil will be released and finally vanquished forever, and then will come the second resurrection. Some, such as the Witnesses of Jehovah, have chosen to interpret this passage literally—always a dangerous way to interpret the figures of speech in which prophecy abounds. Those who do take this passage literally and believe that Jesus will come to reign upon earth for a thousand years before the end of the world are called millenarists—from the Latin word "millennium," which means "a thousand years." This view, however, does not agree with Christ's own prophecies, and millenarianism is rejected by the Catholic Church as a heresy.

Some Catholic scholars believe that the "thousand years" is a figure of speech for a long period of time before the end of the world, when the Church will enjoy great peace and Christ will reign over the souls of men. The more common interpretation of Catholic Biblical experts, however, is that the "thousand years" represents the whole period of time from Christ's birth, when Satan, indeed, was chained. All the just who live during this time have a first resurrection by Baptism and reign with Christ so long as they are in the state of grace; and they have a second resurrection at the end of the world. Paralleling this is the first death by sin, and the second death in hell.

We have entered into this brief discussion of the millennium because it is a point that may arise in religious discussions with non-Catholic friends. Of more practical import to us, however, are the things which we know for *certain* concerning the end of the world. One such certainty is the fact that, when man's history ends, the bodies of all who ever have lived will be raised from the dead and will be united again with their proper souls. Since it is the *whole* man, body as well as soul, that has loved God and served God, even at the cost of pain and sacrifice, it is then but just that the *whole* man, body as well as soul, enjoy that eternal union with God which is the reward of love. And since it is the *whole* man who has rejected God by unrepented mortal sin, it is but just that the body share with the soul in the eternal separation from God which the whole man has chosen for himself. Our risen bodies will, of course, be reconstituted in a way that will free them from the physical limitations which characterize them in this world. They no longer will need food or drink or rest, and will be in some sense "spiritualized." In addition, the bodies of those who are in heaven will be "glorified"; they will possess a perfection and a beauty that will be a participation in the perfection and beauty of the soul which is united with God.

Because the body of a person in whom grace has dwelt has been truly a temple of God, the Church always has insisted upon great reverence being shown to the bodies of the faithful departed. They are committed with loving prayers and ceremony to graves which have been especially blessed to receive them. One human person who escaped the corruption of the grave was the Mother of God. *By the special privilege of her Assumption, the body of the Blessed Virgin Mary, united to her immaculate soul, was glorified and taken into heaven.* Her divine Son, who had taken His flesh from hers, took her unto Himself in heaven—an event which we commemorate on August 15, the Feast of the Assumption.

The world ends, the dead rise again—and then comes the General Judgment. The General Judgment will find Jesus Christ occupying the throne of divine Justice, which has replaced His throne of infinite mercy—the cross. The Last Judgment will hold no surprises for us, as far as our own eternal fate is concerned. We already shall have undergone our own Particular Judgment; our souls already will be in heaven or in hell. The purpose of the Last Judgment is primarily to give glory to God by manifesting to all mankind God's justice, and wisdom, and mercy. The whole of life, which so often has seemed to us like a tangled skein of unrelated events, sometimes harsh and cruel, and even unjust and stupid—all now will be unfolded before us. We shall see how the jigsaw piece of life that we have known, fits into the great magnificent whole of God's plan for man. We shall see how God's wisdom and power, His love and mercy and justice have been at work through it all. "Why does God let this happen?" so often we have complained. "Why doesn't God do thus and so?" so often we have asked. Now at last we shall know all the answers. The sentence which was passed upon us in our Particular Judgment now will be publicly confirmed. All our sins—and our virtues too—will be exposed to public view. The shallow sentimentalist who said, "I don't believe in hell; God is too good to let a soul suffer forever," now will find that God is not, after all, a doting grandmother. God's justice is just as infinite as His mercy. The souls of the damned, in spite of themselves, now will glorify God's justice forever, as the souls of the just will everlastingly glorify His mercy. For the rest, let us turn to the twenty-fifth chapter of St. Matthew's Gospel, and let Jesus Himself (verses 34-46) tell us how to prepare for that last and awful day.

And here the story of man's salvation ends, the story that the third Person of the Blessed Trinity, the Holy Spirit, has written. With the end of the world, and the resurrection of the dead, and the final judgment, the Holy Spirit's work is ended. His work of sanctification began with the creation of Adam's soul. For the Church it began on Pentecost Sunday. For you and me it began on the day of our Baptism. As time ends and only eternity remains, the Holy Spirit's work finds its fruition in the communion of saints, now one single company in everlasting glory.

PART TWO —————————————————

THE

COMMANDMENTS

CHAPTER XV

The Two Great Commandments

Faith Proven by Deeds

"Yes, I believe in our American democracy. I believe that a constitutional government of free citizens is the best government there is." A man who would say that, but who at the same time would not vote or pay taxes or respect the laws of his country, would stand convicted by his own actions as a liar and a fraud.

It is equally plain that anyone who professes to believe the truths revealed by God will be completely insincere if he makes no effort to observe God's law. It is easy to say, "I believe"; but our works are the real proof of the strength of our faith. "Not everyone who says to Me, 'Lord, Lord,' shall enter the kingdom of heaven," warns Jesus; "but he who does the will of My Father in heaven shall enter the kingdom of heaven" (Matt. 7:21). Nothing could be clearer than that. If we believe in God, we must do what God asks, we must keep His law.

And let it be noted that God's law is not composed of arbitrary "do's" and "don't's" set up by God just to make the going hard for us. It is true that God's law does test the strength of our moral fiber, but that is not its primary purpose. God is not a capricious God. He has not set up His commandments as so many hurdles to be cleared in an obstacle race for heaven. He is not sitting back, grimly waiting to pounce upon the first hapless mortal who falls on his face.

On the contrary, God's law is an expression of God's infinite love and infinite wisdom. If we buy a piece of machinery or a home appliance of some kind, we use it according to the manufacturer's directions, if we are sensible people. We take it for granted that the man who made it knows best how it should be used in order to work effectively and give lasting satisfaction. Also, if we are sensible people, we give God credit for knowing what is best for the human nature which He has created, what will contribute most to the good and the happiness of the individual and the race. We might say that God's law is simply the "book of instructions" which accompanies God's noble product, Man. More strictly speaking, we can say that the law of God is the expression of the divine wisdom in directing man to the fulfillment of his end and purpose. God's law does so by regulating man's own use of himself, as well as his relationships with God and with his fellow man.

To make graphic to ourselves the fact that God's law is aimed at man's happiness and well-being, we have only to consider what the world would be like if everyone obeyed God's law. There would be no crimes, and therefore no need for courts or policemen or prisons. There would be no greed or ambition, and therefore no need for armies and navies—no war. There would be no broken homes, no juvenile delinquency, no Alcoholics Anonymous. We know that as a result of Original Sin this kind of happy and beautiful world will never be. But it *can* be for us, individually. Just as the human race as a whole would find its truest happiness, even here upon earth, by identifying its will with God's, so can we. We were made to love God, here and hereafter.

That is the purpose of our existence; *that* is where our highest happiness lies. And Jesus gives us the recipe for happiness very simply: "If you love Me, keep My commandments" (John 14:15).

The law of God which governs human conduct is called the *moral* law, from a Latin word "mores," which means "way of acting." The moral law is distinguished from *physical* laws by which God governs the rest of the universe, such as the laws of astronomy, the laws of physics, the laws of reproduction and growth. Physical laws bind all created nature by necessity. There is no escaping them, there is no freedom of choice. If you step off the edge of a roof, the law of gravity takes over inevitably—unless you substitute another physical law (of air pressure) by using a parachute. The moral law, however, binds us in a different way. It operates within the framework of free will. We *may not* disobey the moral law—but we *can* disobey. So we say that by the divine law we are morally bound but physically free. If we were not physically free, we could not merit. If we were not free, our obedience would not be an act of love.

Moral theologians, in discussing the divine law, distinguish between *natural* law and *positive* law. Conduct, such as the reverence of children towards parents, fidelity in marriage, respect for the person and the property of others, belongs to the very *nature* of man. Such conduct, which man's conscience (judgment guided by right reason) tells him is right, is called the natural law. Such conduct would be right and its opposite evil even if God had not specifically said so. Adultery would be wrong even if there were no sixth commandment. Violations of the natural law are said to be *intrinsically* evil; that is, wrong by their very nature. They have been wrong from the very beginning of the human race, even before God gave Moses the Ten Commandments on Mount Sinai.

Besides the divine natural law, there also is the divine *positive* law. Under this heading are those actions which are good simply because God has commanded them or evil simply because God has forbidden them. They are actions whose goodness is not rooted in the very nature of man, but is imposed by God for the perfecting of man according to God's plan for him. A very simple example of divine positive law is the obligation we are under to receive the Holy Eucharist because of the explicit command of Christ.

Whether we consider divine natural law or divine positive law, it is in obedience to God that our happiness lies. "If thou wilt enter into life," Jesus says, "keep the commandments" (Matt. 19:17).

To love means not to count the cost. A mother would not dream of measuring the sweat and tears she expends upon her children. It would not occur to a husband to gauge his fatigue as he watches at the bedside of his sick wife. Love and sacrifice are almost synonymous terms. That is why obedience to God's law poses no problem to one who loves God. That is why Jesus sums up the whole of God's law in the two great commandments of love.

"And one of them, a doctor of the Law, putting Him [Jesus] to the test, asked Him, 'Master, which is the great commandment in the Law?' Jesus said to him, 'Thou shalt love the Lord thy God with thy whole heart, and with thy whole soul, and with thy whole mind. This is the greatest and the first commandment. And the second is like it, Thou shalt love thy neighbor as thyself. On these two commandments depend the whole Law and the Prophets' " (Matt. 22:35–40).

Really the second is contained in the first. Because if we love God with our whole heart and soul, then we shall love all those who possess, either actually or potentially, a share of God's goodness; and we shall want for them what God wants for them. This means that we shall love ourselves in the right way, wanting for ourselves what God wants for us. That is, we shall want above all else to grow in love for God, which means growth in holiness; and we shall want, more than anything else, to be happy with God in heaven.

Nothing will have any value for us if it in any way comes between us and God. And since our love for ourselves is the standard of our love for our neighbor (which means *every-one* except the devils and the damned souls in hell), we shall want for our neighbor what we want for ourselves. We shall want him to grow in love for God—to grow in holiness. We shall want him, also, to achieve the eternal happiness for which God made him.

This means, in turn, that we shall hate whatever may in any way hold our neighbor back from God. We shall hate the injustices and the man-made evils which may be obstacles to his growth in holiness. We shall hate racial injustice, sub-standard housing, inadequate pay, exploitation of the weak and the ignorant. We shall love and we shall labor for all that will contribute to our neighbor's goodness and happiness and fulfillment.

God has made the task somewhat easier for us by spelling out, in the Ten Commandments, our principal duties to God Himself, to our neighbor and to ourselves. The first three commandments outline for us our duties to God; the other seven indicate our principal duties to our neighbor— and indirectly to ourselves. The Ten Commandments were given by God originally, engraved on two slabs of stone, to Moses on Mount Sinai. They were ratified by our Lord Jesus Christ: "Do not think that I have come to destroy the Law or the Prophets. I have not come to destroy, but to fulfill" (Matt. 5:17). Jesus "fulfilled" the Law in two ways.

First of all by pinpointing for us some specific duties to God and neighbor. These duties, scattered through the Gospels and the Epistles, are summarized for us in the spiritual and the corporal works of mercy. Secondly, Jesus clarified our duties for us, by giving His Church the right and the duty of interpreting and applying, in practical terms, the divine law. This is done in what we commonly call the commandments of the Church. It should be borne in mind that the commandments of the Church are not new and additional burdens placed upon us, over and above God's

commandments. The laws of the Church are simply interpretations and particular applications of God's law. For
example, God commands us to devote some time to His
worship. We say, "Yes, I want to do that. How?" And the
Church answers, "Assist at Mass on all Sundays and holydays of obligation." This fact, the fact that the laws of the
Church are ultimately applications of the laws of God, is
a point worthy of emphasis. There are some, even some
Catholics, who will rationalize sin by distinguishing between a law of God and a law of the Church, as though
God could be set in opposition to Himself.

Here, then, are the divine directives which tell us how we
shall fulfill our nature as human beings and how we shall
achieve our destiny as redeemed souls: the Ten Commandments of God, the seven spiritual and the seven corporal
works of mercy, and the commandments of God's Church.

These, of course, prescribe for us only the minimum of
sanctity—the doing of God's will in matters that are of obligation. But there should be no limit, there *is* no limit, to
growth in holiness. Genuine love for God will look beyond
the letter of the law to the spirit of the law. We shall strive
not merely to do what is good, but shall seek always to do
what is better. For those who are not afraid to raise their
sights high, our Lord Jesus Christ has proposed the observance of the so-called Evangelical Counsels: voluntary poverty, perpetual chastity, and perfect obedience.

Of each of these—the commandments of God and of His
Church, the works of mercy, and the Evangelical Counsels
—we shall speak in turn. And since the positive side is perhaps less familiar than the "Thou shalt not's," we shall begin
with the works of mercy.

Accenting the Positive

It is unfortunate that, to many people, "leading a good
life" means "keeping from sin." Actually, "keeping from sin"

is only one side of the coin of virtue. It is necessary, but it is not enough. Perhaps this negative view of religion as a series of "Thou shalt not's" explains the cheerlessness in the spiritual lives of some well-intentioned souls. To keep from sin is an essential beginning, but love for God and neighbor calls for far more than this.

There are, for example, the corporal works of mercy. They are called "corporal" from the Latin word "corpus," meaning "body," because they pertain to our neighbor's physical and temporal welfare. As gleaned from the Bible, they are seven in number: (1) to feed the hungry; (2) to give drink to the thirsty; (3) to clothe the naked; (4) to visit the imprisoned; (5) to shelter the homeless; (6) to visit the sick; and (7) to bury the dead. In His description of the Last Judgment (Matt. 25:34–40), our Lord Jesus Christ makes our performance of these corporal works of mercy the test of our love for Himself: "Amen I say to you, as long as you did it for one of these, the least of My brethren, you did it for Me."

When we turn to examine the ways in which we can perform the corporal works of mercy, we find that there are three directions in which our efforts can be directed. First of all, there are what we call "organized charities." In our modern cities it is easy for the poor and the unfortunate to be overlooked in the crowd. Moreover, some needs are too big for any single person to care for. And so we have all sorts of social service agencies to which those in need of help can turn. There are hospitals, homes for orphans, homes for the aged, institutions for wayward and for handicapped children, the St. Vincent de Paul Society—to mention a few. When we contribute to these, whether we do so directly or through a Catholic Charities drive or a Community Chest campaign, we are discharging *some* of our obligations to our neighbor-in-need but not all.

Another way in which we practice the corporal works of mercy is by our participation in movements for civic and for social betterment. If we work for better and more adequate housing for low-income families; if we work to ameliorate the injustices suffered by migrant agricultural laborers; if we lend support to every just effort of labor unions to obtain a living wage and economic security; if we give active encouragement to credit unions, consumer co-operatives, maternity guilds, and every other kind of self-help plan that will make life a little less burdensome for our neighbor—then we are practicing the corporal works of mercy. We are ministering to Christ-in-our-neighbor.

But none of this will relieve us, of course, from the obligation to render direct and personal help to our brethren when the opportunity—or, rather let me say, when the *privilege*—of doing so presents itself. I dare not say to the poor man at my door, "I gave to the Community Chest; go and talk to them." Let us note, too, that Christ has many disguises. If we try to be too "prudent" in our giving, scientifically assaying the "worthiness" of a need, inevitably there will come a time when Christ will catch us napping. Jesus spoke often of the poor, but never did He say anything about the "worthy" poor. If it is for love of Christ that we give, then the worthiness or unworthiness of the recipient will not concern us much. We should not encourage idleness by *imprudent* giving; but we have need to remember this: to neglect giving help to a poor family on the plea that they are a shiftless lot, or the father drinks, or the mother is a poor manager (which means that we punish the children for the defects of their parents) is to endanger the salvation of our soul. The truth is as stark as that.

There are other ways, obviously, in which we practice the corporal works of mercy besides providing food and clothing and rent-money to those in dire distress. In today's world it is not so easy to "visit the imprisoned" as it was in our Lord's time. Most prisoners are limited in visitors to members of their own immediate families. But it is possible for us to contact the chaplains of prisons and jails and to ask what we can supply that will be helpful to the prisoners. Rosaries, prayer-books, scapulars? Cigarettes, reading material, games? (It so easily could be you or I behind those bars!) Even better than visiting the imprisoned is work that will *prevent* imprisonment. Whatever we can do to make our neighborhood a more wholesome place, by providing recreation facilities and creative activities for youth, extending a helping hand to a youngster teetering on the edge of delinquency—such works as these will more than qualify with Christ.

"To visit the sick." How fortunate are physicians and nurses, whose entire lives are devoted to the fulfillment of the sixth corporal work of mercy—provided, of course, that it is love for God which animates their work and not merely money or "humanitarian" motives. But the illness of our brethren is a Christian challenge to all of us. Christ goes with us in each call that we pay to one of His suffering members; a call that will comfort and cheer, even if it does not heal. Time spent in reading to a convalescent or a blind person, or in relieving a wife for a few hours from the care of a sick husband or child—there is tremendous merit in any of these. Even a get-well card, sent out of love for Christ, will win His smile.

"To bury the dead." No longer do we make rough-boxes and dig graves for our neighbors here in America. But when we visit a house of mourning (more likely a funeral home nowadays) we are honoring Christ, whose grace sanctified the body which we respect. When we attend a funeral, we are watching with Mary at the tomb. The pallbearer can quite truthfully tell himself that it is Christ (in his neighbor) that he is carrying to the grave.

When we labor, out of love for God, to ease the burdens of our fellow man, we do something very pleasing to God. When we strive, by means of the corporal works of mercy, to lighten our neighbor's load of sickness and poverty and misfortune, heaven indeed does smile upon us. Yet man's *eternal* happiness is of immensely greater importance than his physical and temporal well-being. Consequently, the *spiritual* works of mercy exert an even more pressing claim upon the Christian than do the corporal works.

The spiritual works of mercy are traditionally listed as seven. They are: (1) to admonish the sinner; (2) to instruct the ignorant; (3) to counsel the doubtful; (4) to comfort the sorrowful; (5) to bear wrongs patiently; (6) to forgive all injuries; (7) to pray for the living and the dead.

"To admonish the sinner" is a duty that rests most urgently upon parents and only a little less urgently upon teachers and others who may be charged with the formation of youthful character. The duty is plain; what is *not* always so clearly perceived is that example speaks to youth so much more loudly than precept. If there is intemperance in the home, if there is too great a preoccupation with money and worldly success, if there is uncharitable talk in the presence of the children or constant angry bickering between the parents, if Dad makes, and brags of, petty chiselings and Mom is heard telling polite lies over the telephone—well, may God have mercy on the children whom they are schooling in sin.

It is not only parents and teachers, of course, who have the duty to "admonish the sinner." To all of us belongs the responsibility of leading others to virtue, according to the degree of our influence. It is a duty that must be discharged with intelligence and prudence. Sometimes a sinner will only become more obstinate in his sin when corrected, especially if the correction is administered with any appearance of self-righteousness. ("I am *not* drunk; lea' me alone; Charlie, another double Scotch.") It is essential that our admonitions be made gently and with evident love, with a consciousness of our own faults and weaknesses.

However, prudence must not be pushed to the point of cowardice. If I have certain knowledge that my good friend is using contraceptives or indulging in marital infidelity or contemplating marriage outside the Church or is endangering his salvation in any other way, then love for God *demands* that I do my utmost to dissuade him from spiritual suicide. It is cowardice of the worst sort if I try to excuse myself by saying: "Well, he knows what is right and wrong as well as I do. Let him live his own life. It's not my business to tell him what to do." I certainly would consider it my business if I saw him holding a gun to his head or a knife at his throat, however much he might object to my "interference." Surely his spiritual life ought to mean more to me than his physical life. And let us hear what our own reward will be: "My brethren, if any one of you strays from the truth and someone brings him back, he ought to know that he who causes a sinner to be brought back from his misguided way will save his soul from death, and will cover a multitude of sins" (James 5:19–20).

"To instruct the ignorant." The human intellect is a gift of God which God wants us to use. All truth, both natural and supernatural, has its source in God and reflects God's infinite perfection. Consequently, anyone who contributes to developing the human mind and to imparting the truth is doing a truly Christian work if he be motivated by love of God and neighbor. Here again parents play the primary part, with teachers second only to parents. This includes teachers in public schools, even though they be limited to secular subjects; *all* truth is God's truth. It is not hard to see why teaching is such a noble vocation, one which can be made a real road to sanctity.

It is true, of course, that religious knowledge is the highest knowledge. Those who teach parish Religion Schools and in Catholic schools and colleges are practicing the second spiritual work of mercy in the fullest possible way. Even those of us who help to build and support such schools and catechetical centers, whether at home or in mission lands, share in the merit that comes from instructing the ignorant.

"To counsel the doubtful" may be passed over without much comment. Most of us love to give advice. Just let us be sure, when called upon for counsel, that our advice is one hundred per cent sincere and disinterested and based on the principles of faith. Let us be sure on the one hand that we do not take the easy way out by giving the person the advice we know he wants to hear, regardless of its merits; nor, on the other hand, give advice that is based on our own selfish self-interests. "To comfort the sorrowful" also comes quite naturally to most of us. If we are normal human beings, we feel a natural sympathy with those in trouble. Here, however, it is essential that the comfort we offer be more than a matter of shallow words and sentimental sniffling. If there is anything we can *do* to extend comfort, we shall not fail because it means personal inconvenience or sacrifice. Our comforting words will be fortified a thousand times over by our deeds.

"To bear wrongs patiently" and "To forgive all injuries." Ah, there *is* the rub. All that is human in us, all that is merely natural, cries out against the reckless driver who cut in front of us, the friend who betrayed us, the neighbor who spread lies about us, the clerk who cheated us. It is here that we touch the tenderest nerve of self-love. It is so hard to say, with Christ on His cross, "Father, forgive them, for they do not know what they are doing." Yet, say it we must, or we are not Christ's own. It is in this that our love for God passes its supreme test—it is in this that our love for neighbor proves itself to be genuinely supernatural.

Finally, "To pray for the living and the dead." We all do, of course; if we know what it means to be a member of Christ's Mystical Body and of the Communion of Saints. But even here selfishness would enter if our prayers were limited to our own needs and those of our own family and immediate friends. The circle of our prayers must encompass the world—as does the love of God.

The Greater Good

"If you love Me," God says, "this is what you *must* do" —and He gives us His commandments. "If you love Me a *lot*," God adds, "this is what you *may* do"—and He gives us the Evangelical Counsels, the invitation to practice voluntary poverty, perpetual chastity, and perfect obedience. They are called "Evangelical" Counsels from the Latin word for Gospel, which is "Evangelium"; and it is, of course, in the Gospels that Jesus extends to us His invitation to perfection.

It may be worth while to quote here in its entirety the poignant incident which St. Matthew describes for us in the nineteenth chapter of his Gospel (verses 16–20): "And behold, a certain man came to him and said, 'Good Master, what good work shall I do to have eternal life?' He said to him, 'Why dost thou ask Me about what is good? One there is who is good, and He is God. But if thou wilt enter into life, keep the commandments.' He said to Him, 'Which?' And Jesus said, 'Thou shalt not kill, thou shalt not commit adultery, thou shalt not steal, thou shalt not bear false witness, honor thy father and mother, and, thou shalt love thy neighbor as thyself.'

"The young man said to Him, 'All these I have kept; what is yet wanting to me?' Jesus said to him, 'If thou wilt be perfect, go, sell what thou hast, and give to the poor, and thou shalt have treasure in heaven; and come, follow Me.' But when the young man had heard the saying, he went away sad, for he had great possessions."

We feel a pang of pity for this young man who came so close to being one of our Lord's first disciples, yet lost the glorious opportunity because his courage failed. There can be no doubt that still today Jesus continues to issue His invitation to great numbers of souls. There is so much of His work to be done in the world, and so many helpers are needed. If the number of His helpers is insufficient (and it always is), it is not because Jesus is failing to call them. It can only be because His voice is not being heard; or because many who hear are lacking in the courage to follow, like the young man in the Gospel. That is why it is essential that all of us, parents and young people alike, understand the nature of the Evangelical Counsels, and the nature of a vocation to the religious life.

Of all the directives and advice given us in the Gospels, the Counsels are the most perfect. The observance of them will free us, so far as human nature can be freed, from all obstacles to growth in holiness, to growth in love for God. He who embraces the Counsels renounces those precious but lesser goods, those loves which in fallen human nature so often compete with love for God. In espousing voluntary poverty we manacle covetousness and greed, the twin villains responsible for so many sins against God and neighbor. In dedicating ourselves to perfect chastity we discipline the flesh so that the spirit may rise unfettered and undivided to God. In adhering to perfect obedience we make the hardest renunciation of all; we give up what is more dear to man than pride of possessions or power of procreation; we give up dominion over our own will. Emptied of self as completely as man can be—without property, without family, without self-will—we are as free as man can be for the operation of God's grace; we are on the path to perfection.

The *spirit* of the Evangelical Counsels is necessary for all of us, if we have any desire at all to advance in holiness. For all of us, married or single, in religion or out of religion, it is necessary that we preserve a spirit of detachment from worldly goods, cultivating simplicity in our tastes and our wants, generously sharing of our surplus with others less fortunate, grateful to God for what He has given us, the while we grasp the gift very lightly in case God should want it back from us again.

For everyone, too, chastity according to his state in life is a must. For the single person this means absolute chastity, with or without benefit of vow. And it is, surely, one of the glories of our religion that so many do practice perfect chastity, even while living in a world where seductions abound and easy opportunities for sin are plentiful. There is real heroism in the purity of our youth, who must keep the strong urge of their procreative power in check until age and circumstances make it possible for them to marry. There is a quieter but no less real heroism in the chastity of older single persons whose situation is such that they cannot marry —perhaps not ever. There is a noble heroism in the continency of those who have chosen a single life in the world as their lot, freely, so that they may more fully give themselves to the service of others. There is in these unmarried laity a deep sense of reverence for sex as an awsome gift of God; a gift to be used only for God's purposes and to be preserved untarnished so long as those purposes are not possible. And in marriage, too, there is chastity; the beautiful chastity of truly Christian spouses, to whom physical union is not a plaything or a mere tool for self-gratification but rather a joyous expression of an inner and spiritual unity with each other and with God, for the doing of His will, with no family limitation but that of abstinence when that would seem to better serve the purposes of God.

There is obedience, likewise, in the world—that subjection of will which true love of God and neighbor so often makes mandatory. This means not only the subjection of a youthful will to parents and other persons of authority. It means not only the subjection of will on the part of all of us to the voice of God in His Church and to the will of God in the so-often frustrating circumstances of life. It means the daily subjection of will and the disciplining of desire in all who would live in peace and charity with others—between spouse and spouse, between neighbor and neighbor.

Yes indeed; the spirit of the Counsels—poverty, chastity and obedience—is not limited to the enclosure of convent or monastery walls.

The spirit of poverty, chastity, and obedience is essential to any thoroughly Christian life. And it is to the spirit of the Evangelical Counsels, rather than to their absolute observance, that most Christians are called. The Mystical Body of Christ *is* a body and not merely a soul. Hence there must be Christian parents who will perpetuate the membership of that Body. Moreover, if the spirit of Christ is to permeate the world, there must be exemplars of Christ in all walks of life; there must be Christian men and women in the trades and businesses and professions. For them, the fulfillment of the Counsels must be in a relative degree.

But there can be no "relative" degree unless there exists an absolute degree to which the relative can be compared. I can say that my watch is relatively accurate in keeping time only because there is a Naval Observatory which is absolutely accurate in fixing the time. I can say that this picture is a good reproduction only if there is an original from which it was reproduced.

That is why—one reason why—God in His providence has developed in the Church the state of life known as the religious state. It is in the religious state that the Evangelical Counsels are espoused in their completeness, by the vows of absolute poverty, perpetual chastity, and perfect obedience. The religious life is called the life of perfection. Not because a person automatically becomes perfect by pronouncing the three vows of religion; but because he has set his foot upon the path to perfection by divesting himself of all that might hinder him in his progress towards perfection. How perfect he may actually become, after his brave start, will depend upon the use he makes of his plentiful graces and opportunities.

It is obvious that there are many people living "in the world" who are more saintly than many of the people living "in religion." It is equally obvious that no one should feel that he is condemned to an "imperfect" life because he is not a monk or she a nun. The most perfect life for any individual is the state of life to which God has called that individual. There are saints in the kitchen as well as in the cloister, in the shop as well as in the chapel. But absolutely speaking and on its merits, aside from the particular vocation of any individual, the religious life is the life of perfection. In its beginnings the religious life is as old as the Christian Church. The religious life as we know it today, a beautiful mosaic of many Orders and Congregations, had its origin in the "Virgins" and the "Confessors" of the primitive Church.

Besides the world's need for a living witness to the fact that love for God can supplant every lesser love in the human heart—that is, besides the need for an "absolute" pattern from which the "relative" may derive—there is another reason for God's providential promotion of the religious life. The Precious Blood of Jesus cries out for the souls for whom He died with an urgency that will not be stilled. The number is so great and the work so vast that there is need for a host of selfless and dedicated souls who will give themselves, without any competing distraction, to the spiritual and corporal works of mercy. There is need for powerhouses of prayer whence may flow the graces needed by those too heedless to pray for themselves; and so we have the strictly cloistered Orders of monks and nuns whose whole lives are given to the practice of prayer and penance for Christ's Mystical Body.

There is need for countless hands and hearts to care for the sick and the homeless and the unfortunate, to visit homes and seek out the stray sheep, to teach in schools and colleges where God will be recognized as well as Julius Caesar and William Shakespeare, to teach catechism and preach missions. And so we have the religious Congregations of men and women who perform these works of charity, not for pay or prestige or self-satisfaction, but out of love for God and souls. Only God knows how much of this work would have to go undone otherwise. With God's Providence

abreast of modern needs, we have, too, the recent development of "secular institutes." In secular institutes the members, men or women, bind themselves to the observance of
the Evangelical Counsels but live and dress as laymen or
laywomen. They are able thus to go places and perform
works that would be impossible to the conventual religious.

Those who enter religious life bind themselves by vows
to the practice of poverty, chastity, and obedience. The
vows may be taken for life, or for a specified number of
years. But before *any* vows are made there is a period of
spiritual formation and testing called the "novitiate." This
may last for one or two years and is followed by temporary
vows, which permit a further time of self-trial for three
years or more before final vows may be pronounced.

The religious life is open to any unmarried person past
fifteen years of age who is not hindered by obligations or
impediments which would be incompatible with the religious
life; for example, the obligation to support a sick or disabled
parent. If one has normal physical and mental health, nothing
further is needed except the right intention: the desire to
please God, to save one's soul, to help one's neighbor. Considering the pressing need, it can be held as certain that God
is speaking to many such souls who are not heeding His invitation. Perhaps they are not listening to His voice—He
does speak softly, always. Perhaps they hear but are afraid
of the cost; not realizing that if the call is from God He will
give the needed strength. Perhaps they hear and have the
courage but are deterred by well-meaning parents who
counsel caution and delay—until God's voice is stilled and
the vocation lost. As though we should ever be "cautious"
with God! As though it were not better to have tried and
given up than not to have tried at all. It should be a daily intention in the prayers of all of us that all whom God is calling may hear His voice and answer; and that all who answer
may have the grace to persevere.

CHAPTER XVI

The First Commandment of God

Our First Duty

Man's highest destiny is to give honor and glory to God. It is for this that we were made. Any lesser reason for creating us would have been unworthy of God. It is quite correct to say that God made us for eternal happiness with Himself. But our own happiness is the secondary reason for our existence; it is the consequence of fulfilling the prime purpose for which we were fashioned: to glorify God.

It is not surprising, then, that the first of the Ten Commandments reminds us of this obligation. "*I am the Lord thy God,*" the Lord wrote for Moses on the tablets of stone; "*thou shalt not have strange gods before Me.*" That is the condensed form of the first commandment as we learned it from our Catechism. Actually, as it is given in the Bible in the Book of Exodus (chapter 20, verses 2 to 6) the first commandment is much longer: "I, the Lord, am your God, who brought you out of the land of Egypt, that place of slavery. You shall not have other gods besides Me. You shall not carve idols for yourselves in the shape of anything in the sky above or on the earth below or in the waters beneath the earth; you shall not bow down before them or worship them. For I, the Lord, your God, am a jealous God, inflicting punishment for their fathers' wickedness on the children of those who hate Me, down to the third and fourth generation; but bestowing mercy down to the thousandth generation, on the children of those who love Me and keep My commandments."

That is the first commandment in its entirety. It may be of interest to note here that the commandments, as God gave them, were not neatly numbered from one to ten. The arrangement of the commandments into ten divisions as a memory help is a man-made arrangement. Before the invention of printing tended to standardize things, the commandments were numbered now one way and now another. Quite often the long first commandment was divided into two: "I, the Lord, am your God . . . you shall not have other gods besides Me." That was the first commandment. The second was, "You shall not carve idols for yourselves . . . you shall not bow down before them or worship them." This was the second commandment. Then, to keep the round number of ten, the last two commandments, "You shall not covet your neighbor's house. You shall not covet your neighbor's wife . . . nor anything else that belongs to him," were combined as a single commandment. At the time that Martin Luther started the first Protestant church, this is the system of numbering which he chose. The other system of numbering, so familiar to us, became standardized as the one used by the Catholic Church. That is why our second commandment is, for most Protestants, the third; our third is their fourth, and so on. In a Protestant catechism, it is the seventh rather than the sixth commandment which forbids adultery. In both cases the commandments are the same; it is just a difference in numbering.

We referred to the number ten as a memory help. It is worth remembering that the commandments themselves were intended by God as memory helps, even aside from any system of numbering. On Mount Sinai God did not impose upon humankind any *new* obligations except the setting aside of a specific day for Himself. From the day of Adam the natural law required of man the practice of divine worship, and justice, and truthfulness, and chastity, and the other moral virtues. On the tablets of stone, God simply was putting the natural law which required of man the practice of divine worship, justice, etc. But not even on Mount Sinai did God give an exhaustive treatise on the moral law. He was content to list a few of the graver sins against the greater virtues: idolatry against religion, profanity against reverence, murder and theft against justice, perjury against veracity and charity—and left it to us to use these virtues as headings, under which we can group all duties of a similar nature. We might say that the Ten Commandments are like ten hooks on the wall, upon which we can neatly arrange and hang our moral obligations.

Returning now to a specific consideration of the first commandment, we think it safe to say that few of us are in any danger of committing the sin of idolatry in a literal sense. Figuratively speaking, there may be many people who worship the false god of self. This would apply to anyone who might place money, business or social advancement, worldly pleasure or bodily comfort ahead of his duty to God. These sins of self-worship, however, usually fall under some other commandment than the first.

Assuming, then, that the sin of idolatry is no problem for us, we can direct our attention to the *positive* meaning of the first commandment. It is true of most of the first commandment, as it is true of most of the others, that the negative form, "Thou shalt not," is a literary device which emphasizes, in capsule form, our positive duties. Thus, by the first commandment we are commanded to offer to God alone the supreme worship that is due Him as our Creator and our final destiny. And that positive obligation of giving supreme worship covers a lot more ground than merely abstaining from idolatry.

It cannot too often be repeated that to lead a good life calls for much more than mere abstention from sin. Virtue, like a coin, has two sides to it. To keep oneself from what is positively evil is only one side of the coin. On the other side is the necessity of performing the *good* actions which are the very opposite of the bad ones which we have renounced. And so it is not enough to pass by a heathen idol without tipping our hat. We also must actively offer to the true God the worship that is His due. The Catechism sums up our duties in this respect by saying that "we worship God by acts of faith, hope, and charity, and by adoring Him and praying to Him."

In religion, everything begins with faith. Without faith there is nothing. In examining, then, the Catechism statement, "We worship God by acts of faith, hope, and charity, and by adoring Him and praying to Him," it is to the virtue of faith that we first turn our attention.

The virtue of faith, we know, is infused into our souls, along with sanctifying grace, when we are baptized. But the virtue of faith would lie dormant in our soul if we did not put it to use by making *acts* of faith. We make an act of faith whenever we give conscious assent to the truths which God has revealed; not necessarily because we fully understand the truths; not necessarily because the truths have been scientifically demonstrated to our satisfaction; but primarily because God has revealed the truths. God, being infinitely wise, cannot make a mistake. God, being infinitely truthful, cannot lie. Consequently, when God says that something is so, we can ask for no greater certainty than that. There is more certainty in God's word than in all the test-tubes and all the logical reasoning in the world.

It is easy to see why an act of faith is an act of worship offered to God. When we say, "O my God, I believe these . . . truths because Thou hast revealed them, who canst neither deceive nor be deceived," we are honoring God's infinite wisdom and truthfulness in the most practical way possible; we are taking things on His say-so.

This duty of worshiping God by faith imposes upon us certain definite obligations. God does not do things without a reason. It is evident that, if God makes particular truths known to mankind, it is because those truths will be in some way helpful to man in fulfilling his destiny—which is to give glory to God through knowledge and love and service. It becomes our responsibility, then, to learn what those truths are, according to our capacity and opportunities.

For a person who is not a Catholic, this means that the moment he begins to suspect that he does not possess the true religion revealed by God he immediately is bound to seek it. When he has found it, he is bound to embrace it—to make his act of faith. Perhaps we should not judge, since only God can read the heart. But every priest encounters, in the course of this work, persons who seem to be convinced that the Catholic faith is the true faith and yet remain outside the Church. It seems that they count the cost too great: loss of friends, or of business, or of prestige. Sometimes their motive is fear of giving offense to parents, as though loyalty to human parents should ever come before our higher loyalty to our Father, God.

As for us who already possess the true faith, we must be sure that we do not rest upon our laurels. We must not complacently assume that, because we attended a Catholic school or Catechism class in our youth, we know all that we need to know about our religion. An adult mind needs an adult understanding of God's truths. To listen attentively to sermons and religious instructions, to read Catholic books and periodicals, to take an active part in religious discussion clubs —these are not mere matters of choice, to be indulged in if we feel like it. These are not "pious practices" for "devout souls." *Some* degree of growth in a knowledge of our faith is an essential duty, stemming from the first commandment.

We cannot make an act of faith in a truth or truths which we do not even know. Many of our temptations against faith, if we have any, would disappear if we took the trouble to learn more about our faith.

The first commandment not only obliges us to seek to know the truths of God and to accept them. It requires of us also that we make *acts* of faith, that we worship God by giving explicit assent of our minds to His truths, once we have reached the use of reason. How often *must* I make an act of faith? It goes without saying that I *should* do so often. But I *must* make an act of faith any time that I learn of a revealed truth of God that I did not know before. I *must* make an act of faith any time it is needed in order to resist a temptation against faith or against some other virtue where faith is involved. I *must* make an act of faith frequently during life—that the virtue of faith may not become inactive within me for lack of exercise. The practice of good Catholics generally is to make an act of faith as a part of their daily prayers, morning and night.

Not only must we seek to know the truth. Not only must we give interior assent to the truth. The first commandment requires also that we make outward *profession* of our faith. This obligation becomes operative whenever God's honor or our neighbor's good might otherwise suffer. God's honor suffers any time that failure to profess our faith is equivalent to a denial of our faith. This obligation does not apply only to those extreme cases where an outright demand is made upon one to deny his faith—as in ancient Rome or modern Communist countries. It applies also in the daily lives of all of us. We may fear to profess our faith because it will mean a loss of business, or because it will make us "conspicuous," or because we fear raised eyebrows or ridicule. The Catholic man attending a convention, the Catholic student attending a secular university, a Catholic woman attending her card club—in these and a hundred similar instances, there easily can arise circumstances when to hide one's faith will be equivalent to denial—and God's honor will suffer.

And so often when we fail, through cowardice, to profess our faith, our neighbor suffers too. So often a weaker brother (or sister) is just waiting to see what we do before making his own decision. Indeed, there may be times when there is no particular need for us to make open profession of our faith except the need of someone else for the strength and courage our example will give.

Sins Against Faith

The first commandment obliges us to find out what God has revealed, to believe firmly what God has revealed. This is what it means to practice the virtue of faith. Any time we deliberately fail in one of these three directions we are guilty of a sin against faith.

But there are certain specific and grievous sins against faith which merit special mention. There is first of all the sin of apostasy. The word "apostate" may look something like the word "apostle"; in meaning, however, the two words are almost opposites. An apostle is one who spreads the faith. An apostate is one who completely abandons the faith. Apostates are to be found in almost every parish: people who will tell you that they once were Catholics but that they don't believe in any of it any more. Very often apostasy is the end-result of a bad marriage. First a Catholic excommunicates himself by marrying out of the Church before a non-Catholic clergyman, perhaps to a divorced person or to a partner who refuses to be married by a priest. Cut off from the flow of God's grace, the excommunicated Catholic's faith withers and dies, and he ends up with no faith at all.

Apostasy is not the same thing as laxity. There may be a lax Catholic who hasn't attended Mass or received Holy Communion for ten years. Usually sheer laziness is at the root of such neglect. "I work hard all week; I need my rest on Sunday morning," he may say. If you ask this man what his religion is, he will answer, "Why, I'm a Catholic,

of course." Usually he will go on to defend himself by saying that he is a better Catholic than "lots of people who go
to church every Sunday." That is an overworked piece of
rationalization that every priest has to listen to time and time
again.

The point is, however, that this lax Catholic is not yet an
apostate. In a vague sort of way he does intend, at some
time in the formless future, to get back to the practice of
his religion. If he dies before doing so, he will not necessarily be denied Christian burial—not if the pastor can find any
evidence at all that the man did still retain his faith and was
repentant at the hour of death. It is a mistaken notion that
the Church denies Christian burial to everyone who missed
his so-called "Easter duty." It is true the Church does take
Easter-time Communion as plain evidence that a person does
profess the true faith. If that evidence is at hand, then no
further questions need be asked. But the Church is still the
loving Mother even of her wayward children. She will lean
over backwards to give Christian burial if there is any evidence at all that the dead person still professed the true faith
and was sorry for his sins—provided the person did not die
excommunicated or manifestly unrepentant. Christian burial
by no means guarantees that the soul will go to heaven; but
the Church does not want to compound the sorrow of the
survivors by denying Christian burial if any valid excuse for
it can be established.

A lax Catholic, then, is not necessarily an apostate Catholic. Very often however, laxity does lead to apostasy. A
person cannot go on living with his back turned upon God
month after month and year after year; a person cannot go
on indefinitely living in mortal sin, continually rejecting
God's grace, without in the end finding that his faith is
gone. Faith is a gift of God. There must come a time when
God, who is infinitely just as well as infinitely merciful, will
no longer allow His gift to be abused, His love flouted. With
God's supporting hand withdrawn, faith dies.

Besides laxity, another cause of apostasy is intellectual pride. This is a danger to which a person exposes himself when he wades beyond his intellectual and spiritual depth. There is, for example, the young man or young woman who attends a secular university and grows careless in the matter of prayer and Mass and the sacraments. At the same time his or her spiritual life is neglected the young person becomes dazzled by the lofty superiority of some professor who has a patronizing disdain for "outmoded superstitions" such as religion. Instead of accepting the challenge of the shallow irreligion that is thrown at him in the classroom and looking up the answers, the young student abandons the authority of God and God's Church for the authority of the instructor. This is not to say that all teachers in secular universities are atheists; far from it. But all too often there are some who, in their own insecurity, seek to bolster their ego by belittling greater minds than their own. Even one man like this can do irreparable harm to impressionable youngsters and can spread the contagion of his own intellectual pride.

Unwise reading can be another threat to faith. A person who himself is suffering from intellectual poverty may easily get caught in the quicksands of smart and sophisticated authors whose attitude towards religion is one of gentle amusement or lofty scorn. Reading such authors, the superficial mind is likely to begin questioning his own religious beliefs. Not having learned to weigh evidence and to think for himself—forgetting that "a fool can ask more questions in an hour than a wise man can answer in a year" —the unwary reader surrenders his faith to the sparkling sophistries and the profound absurdities which he reads.

Finally, apostasy may result from habitual sin. A person cannot continually live in conflict with himself. If his actions are at war with his beliefs, something has to give. If grace is neglected, it is likely to be faith rather than sin which goes out the window. Many who explain their loss of faith as due to intellectual difficulties are really trying to cover up a more basic and less noble conflict with their passions.

Besides the complete rejection of the Catholic faith, which is the sin of apostasy, there also can be a partial rejection of one's faith, and this is the sin of heresy. One who commits the sin of heresy is called a heretic. A heretic is a baptized person who refuses to believe one or more of the truths revealed by God and taught by the Catholic Church. A truth revealed by God, and solemnly proclaimed as such by the Church, is termed a *dogma* of faith. The virgin conception of Jesus—the fact that He did not have a human father—is an example of a dogma of faith. The fact that the Holy Father, St. Peter's successor, is infallible when he officially teaches a doctrine of faith or morals to all Christendom also is a dogma. Another example is the fact that God created Mary's soul free from original sin—the dogma of the Immaculate Conception.

These are but a few of the dogmas which, interwoven with each other, make up the fabric of Christian faith. To reject one is, in substance, to reject all. If God, speaking through His Church, could be wrong on one point, there is no particular reason for believing God on any point. There is no such thing as being "slightly heretical" any more than there is any such thing as being "slightly dead." We sometimes feel that the members of the High Episcopalian church (or Anglo-Catholics) are very close to the Catholic Church because they believe almost everything which we believe and have ceremonies like our ceremonies of the Mass, have confessionals in their churches, and wear vestments and use incense. But in truth the phrase "almost a Catholic" is as meaningless as the phrase "almost alive."

It should be noted that in the sin of heresy, as in every sin, we have to distinguish between *material* sin and *formal* sin. If a person does something which is wrong, objectively —but a wrong of which the person, through no fault of his own, is unaware—then we say that the person has sinned materially but not formally. In his wrong action there is no personal guilt. A Catholic who would reject a truth of faith, who would decide, for example, that he didn't want to believe in hell, would be guilty of the sin of heresy, both materially and formally. A Protestant, however, sincerely believing the teachings of the church in which he was raised and with no opportunity for knowing otherwise, would be a material heretic only; he would not be *formally* guilty of the sin of heresy.

There is one form of heresy that is especially prevalent and especially dangerous. That is the error of *indifferentism*. Indifferentism holds that all religions are equally pleasing to God; one religion is as good as another, and it is just a matter of personal preference which religion you profess or whether you profess any religion at all. The basic error in indifferentism is the supposition that truth and error are equally pleasing to God; or else the error of assuming that there is no such thing as absolute truth; that truth is whatever you want to make it. If we suppose that one religion is as good as another, the next logical step is to conclude that no religion is really worth bothering about, since no religion can be divinely established and approved.

The heresy of indifferentism is particularly widespread in America, where we like to pride ourselves on our "broadmindedness." So many people are fuzzy in their understanding of what democracy means. Democracy demands—indeed Christian charity demands—that we respect our neighbor's conscience and sincere convictions even when we know that he is wrong. But democracy does *not* demand that we pretend that the wrongness doesn't matter. Democracy does not demand that we put error on the same pedestal as truth. In short, the Catholic who bows his head in agreement when someone says, "It doesn't matter what you believe; it's what you do that counts," is guilty of a sin against faith.

Indifferentism can be preached by actions as well as by

words. That is why it is wrong for a Catholic to attend non-Catholic religious services, even though he may take no active part in such services. It is obvious that to participate *actively* in a non-Catholic religious service would be a grievous sin against the virtue of faith. We *know* how God wants to be worshiped and therefore it is gravely sinful for us to worship Him in ways that are fashioned by men rather than dictated by God.

But even though we take no active part, it still is wrong for us to attend non-Catholic religious services. By our very presence there we are silently proclaiming our acceptance of the heresy that one religion is as good as another; we are giving scandal to all who recognize us as Catholics. The only time that we may attend non-Catholic religious services without sin (provided we take no active part) is when there is a sufficiently grave reason. Charity, for example, would justify our attendance at the funeral or wedding of a non-Catholic relative or close friend or business associate. In such cases everyone knows why we are there and there is no danger of giving scandal.

Sometimes our fellow citizens find it hard to understand this firm attitude which we Catholics take in the matter of non-participation. Several Protestant ministers may join together for an interdenominational service on some special occasion; and they are likely to consider the local Catholic priest as unduly narrow-minded because he will take no part in it. A non-Catholic neighbor may say, "I went to midnight Mass with you on Christmas; why can't you come to our Harvest Service with me?"—and will be rather resentful of the Catholic's "intolerance." It is not easy to explain our position to such critics, to make them see how supremely logical is our attitude. If one possesses religious truth, he may not in conscience compromise with religious fallacy. Tolerance is something which we show towards *persons*, not towards the person's errors, however honestly those errors may be held.

Hope and Love

"My Daddy will fix it. He can do anything." "I'll ask my Daddy; he knows everything." Every parent finds himself, or herself, deeply touched at times by the child's absolute confidence in the limitless power and knowledge of Daddy and Mommy. Indeed, it is a confidence that sometimes can prove embarrassing when Daddy or Mommy finds it hard to deliver according to expectations. But it would be a strange sort of parent who would not feel an inner thrill of pleasure at such manifest acts of unquestioning trust on the part of his children.

It is easy to see, then, why an act of hope in God is also an act of worship. An act of hope is an expression of our complete trust in God as an all-wise, all-powerful, and all-loving Father. Whether our act of hope be an interior one, limited to a movement of the heart and mind, or whether it be externalized in the form of verbal prayer, in either case we are praising the infinite power and fidelity and mercy of God. We are performing an act of true worship. We are fulfilling one of our duties under the first commandment.

When we make an act of hope we are asserting our conviction in the fact that God loves us so much that He has bound Himself by solemn covenant to bring us safely to heaven (". . . relying on Thy almighty power and infinite mercy and promises"). We are asserting, too, our conviction of the fact that God's mercy is so boundless that it will even outwit our human weakness and waywardness ("I hope to obtain pardon of my sins, the help of Thy grace, and life everlasting"). There is just one condition to all this. It is a condition presupposed and taken for granted, even though not expressed vocally in a formal act of faith: "provided that I, for my part, do my reasonable best." Not my *absolute* best, necessarily. Few, if any, ever do their *absolute* best. But at least my reasonable best.

In other words, when I make an act of hope, I am reminding myself and acknowledging to God that I shall not lose heaven except through my own fault. If I go to hell it will not be because of any "bad breaks"; it will not be by accident; it will not be through any failure of God's. If I lose my soul, it will be because I have chosen to go my way rather than God's way. If I find myself separated from God for all eternity, it will be because I have deliberately separated myself from God here and now, with my eyes wide open.

With this understanding of the act of hope, it is easy for us to detect what the sins against hope will be. We may sin against hope by forgetting the "silent clause" in the act of hope: by expecting God to do *everything*, instead of *almost* everything. God will give to every one of us all the grace we need to get to heaven, but He expects us to co-operate with His grace. Just as a loving parent will provide his children with food and clothing and shelter and medical care, and yet will expect the children at least to fork the food into their own mouths and to swallow, to put on the clothes provided, to come into the house out of the rain, and to stay away from dangerous places like deep ditches and blazing fires; so also does God expect us to use each grace which He gives and to stay away from unnecessary danger.

If we do *not* do our part, if we blandly assume that because God wants us in heaven then it is up to Him to get us there regardless of what we may do, then we are guilty of the sin of *presumption*, one of the two sins against the virtue of hope.

Here are some simple illustrations of the sin of presumption. A man knows that every time he stops at a certain bar he ends up by getting drunk; the place is an occasion of sin to him, and he knows that he should stay away. But passing by the bar, he says to himself, "I'll just drop in to chin with the boys for a few minutes and maybe have one drink. I'll not get drunk this time." But by the very fact that he willingly returns to this unnecessary occasion of sin, he is trying to extort from God grace to which he has no right. He is not doing his part. Even though it may happen that this time he *doesn't* get drunk, he still has been guilty of the sin of presumption by exposing himself needlessly to danger. Another example would be that of a girl who knows that almost every time she goes out with a certain boy, she commits sin. But she says, "Well, I'll go out with him again tonight, but this time I'll make him behave himself." Again, unnecessary danger; again, the sin of presumption. A final example might be the person who, troubled by strong temptations, knows that he should pray more and should receive the sacraments more frequently, since these are precisely the helps God offers us for the conquest of temptation. But the person sinfully neglects his prayers and is very irregular in receiving the sacraments. Again it is the sin of presumption—we might call it presumption by default.

Besides presumption, there is another sin against the virtue of hope: the sin of despair. It is the very opposite of presumption. Where presumption expects too much of God, despair expects too little. The classic example of the sin of despair is the man who says: "I've been too big a sinner all my life to expect God to forgive me now. God couldn't forgive the likes of me. It's no use asking Him." The gravity of the sin of despair lies in the insult which it offers to the infinite mercy and inexhaustible love of God. Judas Iscariot, swinging at the end of a rope, is the perfect type of the despairing sinner: the man with remorse but without contrition.

For most of us, genuine despair is a remote danger. We are more likely to sin by presumption than by despair. But every time we commit a sin to avoid some real or fancied danger—whether it is telling a lie to avoid embarrassment or using contraceptives to avoid having a child—there is some degree of lack of hope involved. We aren't quite fully convinced that, if we do what is right, we can trust God to take care of the consequences.

We honor God by our faith in Him. We honor God by our hope in Him. But most of all do we worship God by our love for Him. We make an act of love every time that we give expression—either internally in mind and heart, or externally by words or actions—to the fact that we do love God above everybody and everything else for His own sake.

"For His own sake" are key words. True charity, or love for God, is not motivated by what God has done for us, nor by what God is going to do for us. In true charity we love God solely—or at least mainly—because He is so good and so infinitely lovable in Himself. Genuine love for God is not a mercenary, self-seeking love, no more than is the love of a child for his parents.

It is true that a child owes much to his parents and hopes for much from his parents. But true filial love goes far beyond these selfish motives. A normal child still will love his parents even if they have lost all their possessions and can do nothing, materially speaking, for the child. So too does our love for God rise above His benefits and His mercies (although these may be a starting point) and fasten upon the infinite lovableness of God Himself.

It bears noting that love for God resides primarily in the will and not in the emotions. Quite conceivably a person might feel perfectly cold towards God on a purely emotional level and yet might have a very strong love for God. It is the fixing of the *will* upon God that constitutes true love for Him. If habitually we have the desire to do all that God wants us to do (simply because He wants it) and the determination to avoid all that He does not want us to do (simply because He does not want it), then we have love for God, regardless of how we *feel*.

If we love God rightly and truly, it follows, of course, that we love all those whom He loves. That means we love every soul whom God has created and for whom Christ has died, barring only the souls in hell.

Since we love our neighbor (meaning everyone) for the sake of God, it does not particularly matter to us whether our neighbor is *naturally* lovable or not. It helps a lot, of course, if our neighbor is naturally lovable; but then there is less merit in our love. However, whether he be handsome or ugly, mean or kind, pleasant or repulsive—our love for God makes us want to see *everyone* get to heaven, since that is what God wants. And we'll do all that we reasonably can to help our neighbor get there.

It plainly can be seen that supernatural love for our neighbor does not reside in the emotions, any more than does love for God. On a natural level we might feel quite a strong distaste for some particular person and yet have a truly supernatural love for him. Our supernatural love, or charity, would be evidenced by our desire for his welfare, by our desire especially for his eternal salvation, by our willingness to pray for him, by our forgiveness of any injuries he may have inflicted upon us, by our refusal to entertain bitter and vengeful thoughts concerning him.

No one likes to be cheated or double-crossed or lied about, and God does not expect us to enjoy being abused. But God does expect us to follow His own example and to will the salvation of the sinner, even while we are smarting from the impact of his sins.

What, then, are the principal sins against charity? One sin would be to fail to make an *act* of charity, knowingly, when it is our duty to do so. Our duty to make an act of charity arises, in the first instance, when we become aware of our obligation to love God for His own sake, and our neighbor for love of God. We also have the duty to make an act of charity in those temptations which can be overcome only by an act of charity—for example, in a temptation to hatred. We are obliged, too, to make an act of love often during life (this is part of our duty to worship God) and above all in the hour of our death, as we prepare to meet God face to face.

Turning to some specific sins against charity, we shall consider first of all the sin of hatred. Hatred, as we have seen, is not the same thing as personal dislike. It is not the same thing as feeling pain because we have been betrayed or otherwise injured. Hatred is a spirit of bitterness, of unforgiveness. Hatred is a desire to see harm befall another. Hatred is a feeling of joy at another's misfortune.

The worst kind of hatred is, obviously, hatred of God: a desire (absurd, of course) to see God come to harm, an eagerness to see God's will flouted, an unholy glee in seeing sins committed because they are an insult to God. The devils and the souls in hell hate God, but it is not a sin that men on earth commonly commit; fortunately so, since hatred of God is the worst sin that can be committed against Him. It is to be suspected, however, that some professed atheists are really haters of God rather than disbelievers in Him.

Hatred of neighbor is a far more common sin. This is the desire to see harm come to another and a feeling of pleasure at whatever harm may befall him. If we were to wish our neighbor *serious* harm, such as sickness or loss of job, then our sin would be a mortal sin. To wish him a slight evil, such as that he may miss his bus or get a tongue-lashing from his wife, would be a venial sin. It is not a sin, however, to wish a lesser evil for the sake of a greater good. We might rightly wish our drunken neighbor to have a bad hangover so that he may stop drinking. We might wish the lawbreaker to be caught so that he may stop his crimes. We might wish the tyrant to die so that his people may know peace. Always provided, however, that we still desire the person's spiritual good and eternal salvation.

Envy is another sin against charity. This consists of resentment of our neighbor's good fortune, as though it were in some way a robbery of ourselves. Even more serious is the sin of scandal, whereby we, by our word or example, give occasion to another person to commit sin or put him in danger of sinning, even if no sin actually follows. This is sin that parents, as patterns for their children, must especially guard against.

Finally, there is the sin of sloth, a sin against the supernatural love we owe ourselves. Sloth is a spiritual laziness by which we disesteem spiritual things (such as prayer and the sacraments) because of the effort involved.

Sacrilege and Superstition

Faith is not easily lost. If we cherish and cultivate the gift of faith which God has given us, we shall not become apostates or heretics. To cherish and to cultivate it means, among other things, to make frequent acts of faith; an act of faith being simply a grateful avowal to God of the fact that we do believe in Him and in all that He has revealed. An act of faith should be one of our daily prayers.

To cherish and cultivate our faith also means that we never stop trying to learn more about our faith. So that we may have a better understanding of what it is that we believe, we shall be attentive to sermons and instructions and read Catholic periodicals and books that will enlarge our knowledge of the faith. When opportunity offers, we shall take part in religious discussion clubs.

To cherish and cultivate our faith means above all that we shall *live* our faith, that we shall lead a good life in accord with the principles which we profess. An act of faith becomes a jumble of meaningless words on the lips of one whose daily actions shout: "There is no God; or, if there is, I don't care what He wants."

And of course, on the negative side, the cherishing and cultivating of our faith requires that we avoid the company of persons who might pose a threat to our faith. It is not so much the outright anti-Catholic whom we have to fear here, with his bitter attacks upon the faith. It is rather the polished and urbane unbeliever, with his friendly condescension for our "naïve" beliefs and his smiling innuendoes, who is our greater danger. We do so hate to be thought unmodern, we do shrink from being laughed at.

Our concern for our faith also will steer us away from any type of literature which might imperil our faith. However highly praised by the critics a book may be, however sophisticated a magazine may seem—if they are opposed to what we as Catholics believe, then they are not for us. And it will be not only the Index of Prohibited Books which will guide us in our reading. Our own well-formed conscience will warn us away from many publications which may never reach the eyes of the Church's official censors.

Some so-called intellectuals resent this restriction which we Catholics place upon our reading. "What are you afraid of?" they will ask. "Are you afraid you'll find out that you're wrong? You shouldn't be so narrow-minded. You should be willing to listen to both sides of the question. If your faith is any good, you should be able to read anything without coming to harm."

Our answer is that, quite honestly, we *are* afraid. We are afraid not of finding out that we are wrong but of finding out, too late, that we are weak. Original sin has dimmed our reason and weakened our will. Faith requires no small degree of sacrifice. What God wants is so often not what we want, humanly speaking. The little devil of self-love tells us that life could be so much easier if we didn't believe. Yes, quite honestly we *are* afraid that some clever writer may succeed in inflating our ego to the point where, like Adam, we shall decide to be our own god. And, whether the censorship be that of the Church or that of our own conscience, we do not deem it a denial of our liberty. The refusal of poison to the mind is no more a frustration of liberty than is denial of poison to the stomach. We do not have to drink carbolic acid in order to prove that we have a good digestion.

Assuming, then, that our faith is a strong, living, and well cared-for faith, there is not much danger that we shall fall into another sin against the first commandment stemming from lack of faith: the sin of sacrilege. A person sins by sacrilege when he mistreats sacred persons, places, or things. In its slighter manifestations, sacrilege is due to a lack of reverence for that which belongs to God. At its worst, sacrilege is due to hatred for God and for all that belongs to God. In our own day the Communists give us heartbreaking examples of sacrilege at its worst, as they stable horses in churches, imprison and torture priests and nuns, and trample the Holy Eucharist underfoot. These examples, incidentally, typify the three classes of sacrilege which theologians distinguish. The mistreatment of a *person* consecrated to God in the clerical or the religious state is called a *personal* sacrilege. To profane or defile a *place* of divine worship which has been publicly dedicated to God by the Church is called a *local* sacrilege—from the Latin word "locus," meaning "place." To misuse sacred *things,* such as the sacraments, the Bible, the vessels of the altar—anything, in short, which has been blessed or consecrated for use in divine worship or for religious devotion—would be a *real* sacrilege: from the Latin word "realis," meaning "pertaining to things."

An act of sacrilege, if it were fully deliberate and involved a serious matter, such as receiving a sacrament unworthily, would be a mortal sin. For example, making a bad confession or receiving Holy Communion in the state of mortal sin would be a sacrilege of a grievous nature. Such a sacrilege might, however, be a venial sin if it were committed without full realization or without full consent of the will. A sacrilege might also be a venial sin because of the slightness of the irreverence involved, as in the case of a layman picking up a consecrated chalice out of curiosity.

However, if ours is a healthy faith, there is little likelihood that the sin of sacrilege will be any problem for us. For the majority of us, the most pertinent point will be the need to show due reverence for religious articles and holy things which we personally use. There is the matter of keeping the holy water in a clean container and in a decent place; handling the Bible with reverence and giving it a position of honor in the home; burning our soiled scapulars and broken rosaries, rather than throwing them in the trash; overlooking the human infirmities of priests or religious whom we may dislike and speaking of them with respect because of the God-ownership that we see in them; conducting ourselves with reverence in church, particularly at baptisms and weddings, when hilarity may tend to make us forgetful. Reverence such as this is the outer garment of our faith.

Do you carry a "lucky piece" in your pocket or pocketbook? Are you tempted to knock on wood if you tell someone how healthy you have been or how good your business has been doing? Do you feel a little uneasy if you have to sit at table with twelve other persons? If a black cat runs across the street in front of your car, do you drive a little more carefully afterwards? If you can answer "no" to all these questions and have never succumbed to any other popular superstition, then indeed you are a well-balanced person—your faith and your reason are in firm control of your emotions.

Superstition is a sin against the first commandment. It is a sin against the first commandment because it gives credit to some created thing or to a human person for powers that belong only to God. Honor that should go to God goes instead to one of God's creatures.

For example, everything good that comes to us comes from God; it does not come from a rabbit's foot or a horseshoe. And nothing bad happens to us unless God permits it to happen, and God does not permit it to happen unless in some way it will work to our ultimate good; no spilled salt or broken mirror or number thirteen is going to bring trouble upon our heads. God does not fall asleep and let the devil have a field day with us.

Similarly, no one but God knows the contingent future absolutely, with no ifs or buts. We all can make educated guesses about the future. We know what time we are going to get up tomorrow (if we don't forget to set the alarm); we know what we are going to do next Sunday (if nothing unforeseen occurs); astronomers can tell us what time the sun will rise and set on February 15, 1987 (if the world has not yet ended). But only God can know the future with absolute certainty—both those events which depend upon His own eternal decrees and those which depend upon the free choice of other human wills.

That is why it is a sin against the first commandment—a dishonoring of God—to believe in fortunetellers or spiritist mediums. Fortunetellers, combining psychology with the law of averages—and perhaps a bit of chicanery, can mislead some very smart people. Spiritist mediums, combining their own abnormality (self-induced hysteria) with human suggestibility and very often with outright fraud, can stage séances that will thrill even the supposedly sophisticated. The question as to whether some fortunetellers and some mediums may not be in league with the devil is a disputed point that never has been satisfactorily settled. The great Houdini claimed that there was no séance that he could not reproduce by natural means—by trickery—and he proved his claim in a score of cases.

Superstition is, by its nature, a mortal sin. In practice, however, many sins of superstition are venial, because the act is not fully deliberate. This holds true particularly of the many popular superstitions with which our materialistic culture abounds: unlucky days and lucky numbers and knocking on wood and all the rest. It definitely is a grievous matter, however, and a mortal sin to believe in the supernatural powers of fortunetellers or mediums. Even if we do not believe in them, it is a sin to consult such people professionally. Even though we do so only out of curiosity, we are giving bad example and co-operating in their sin. Telling one another's fortunes with cards or tea leaves at a

party, where everyone knows that it is a game for amusement only and not to be taken seriously, would not be a sin.
This is quite a different matter from consulting professional
fortunetellers.

Sometimes our non-Catholic friends suspect us of sinning
against the first commandment because of the honor we pay
to the saints. This accusation would be true if we paid to
the saints the divine worship that is due to God alone. But
we do not, not if we are in our right minds. Even the honor
which we pay to Mary, the Blessed Mother of God, surpassing though it does the reverence we pay to the angels and
the other canonized saints, is still of an entirely different
nature from the adoration which we give, and *may* give,
only to God.

When we pray to our Blessed Mother and to the saints in
heaven (as we should) and beg their help, we know that
whatever they may do for us will not be done of their own
power, as though they were divine. Whatever they may do
for us will be done for us by God, through their intercession. If we value the prayers of our friends here upon earth
and feel that their prayers will help us, then surely we have
the right to feel that the prayers of our friends in heaven
will be even more powerful. The saints are God's chosen
friends, heroes in the spiritual combat. It pleases God to encourage our imitation of them and to show His own love
for them by dispensing His graces through their hands. Nor
does the honor we show to the saints detract one whit from
the honor that is due to God. The saints are God's masterpieces of grace. When we praise them, it is God—who made
them what they are—whom we honor most. The highest
honor that can be paid to an artist is to praise the work of
his hands.

We honor the statues and the pictures of the saints, yes;
and we venerate their relics. But we are not *adoring* these
representations and relics. No more so than a hardheaded
business man is adoring the picture of his sainted mother

before which he places a fresh flower every morning, or the lock of whose hair he carries reverently in his wallet. And when we pray before the crucifix or the image of a saint, in order to better fix our mind upon what we are doing, we are not so stupid (let us hope) as to suppose that the plaster or wooden image has in itself any power to help us. That *would* be a sin against the first commandment, which forbids the making of images in order to adore them. But we do not, of course, adore them.

CHAPTER XVII

The Second and Third Commandments of God

Holy Is His Name

"What's in a name? That which we call a rose by any other name would smell as sweet." These famous words of Shakespeare are only half true. A name, whether it be of a person or of a thing, gathers many emotional overtones by constant use. A name ceases to be just a group of letters taken from the alphabet; a name comes to represent the person or thing which bears the name. The emotions aroused in us by the word "rose" are quite different from those evoked by the name "skunk cabbage." A young man in love only has to hear his sweetheart's name mentioned, even casually by a stranger, to make his pulse rate rise. A man who has suffered great injury at the hands of someone named George will forever have a distaste for the name "George." Men have killed—and been killed—"in defense of their good name." Whole families have been grieved because some member of the family "brought disgrace on the family name." In short, a name stands for the one who bears the name—and our attitude towards a name reflects our attitude towards the person whose name it is.

All this is obvious, of course. But it serves to recall to mind why it is a sin to misuse God's name—to use it carelessly or irreverently. If we love God we shall love His name and never speak it except with reverence and respect. We shall never use it as an expletive, as an expression of anger or impatience or surprise; we shall do nothing to bring infamy upon His name. Indeed, our love for God's name will extend to those of Mary, His Mother, and to His friends the saints, and to all holy things which belong to God. Their names, too, will pass our lips only with thoughtful reverence. That we may never forget this aspect of our love for God, He has given us the second commandment: *"Thou shalt not take the name of the Lord thy God in vain."*

There are many ways in which we may fail in this duty of reverence for God's name. The most common failure is the sin of simple profanity—the use of the Holy Name simply to relieve our feelings. "My God, no!"; By Jesus Christ, I'll show him!"; "For Christ's sake, stop making that noise!" Seldom a day passes, as we go about our activities, that we do not hear these and similar phrases. Sometimes, indeed, there is not even the excuse of emotion; we encounter persons who scatter God's name throughout their conversation as casually as you or I might mention apples or onions. Always, of course, they testify to a lack or shallowness in their love for God.

Usually this type of "simple profanity" is a venial sin, because there is no deliberate intent to dishonor God or to show contempt for His name. Such an intent would make the sin a grievous one—but ordinarily such language is the result of thoughtlessness and carelessness rather than malice. This type of profanity might become a mortal sin, however, if it were the occasion of grave scandal: for example, if a parent by his profanity weakened respect for God's name in his children.

The profanity of which we have been speaking is what many people—mistakenly—call "swearing." Actually swearing is something quite different. It would be an error for a person to say in confession "I swore," when what he really means is that he used profanity.

To swear means to take an oath, to call upon God to be the witness that what we say is true. If I say "For Christ's sake!," I am using profanity; if I say "I am telling the truth, so help me God!," I am swearing. It is quite evident that swearing is not necessarily a sin at all. On the contrary, an oath reverently taken is an act of worship pleasing to God, provided three conditions are fulfilled.

First of all, there must be a good reason for taking an oath. God is not to be invoked lightly as our witness. Sometimes it is necessary for us to take an oath; for example, if we are a witness in a court of law or are being inducted into an office where we must swear to uphold the constitution. Sometimes, too, the Church calls upon us to take an oath, as when godparents swear to the baptism of a person whose baptismal record cannot be found. At other times we may not *have* to take an oath, but some good purpose may be served by guaranteeing, with an oath, the truth of what we say—as when God's honor or our neighbor's welfare or our own may be at stake. To take an oath when there is no need or reason for it, to interlard our conversation with such phrases as, "May God strike me dead if it isn't true," "As God sees me, I swear it is true," and similar phrases, is a sin. Usually the sin is venial if we are speaking the truth because, as with profanity, it is done in thoughtlessness rather than in malice.

It could be a mortal sin, however, if what we say is not true and we know it is not true. This is the second requirement for a lawful oath: that, having taken an oath, we be scrupulous in speaking the truth as we know it. It is a serious dishonor that we do to God if we make Him the witness to a lie. This is the sin of perjury, and deliberate perjury always is a mortal sin.

For an oath to be good and meritorious and an act of honor to God, there is a third requirement when the oath is what we call a *promissory* oath. If we bind ourselves by oath to do something, we must be sure that the action we promise is a good and useful thing and possible to do. If a man were to take an oath, for example, to get even with his neighbor, it is plain that such an oath would be wrong to take and wrong to keep. One is obliged *not* to keep an oath like that. But if my promissory oath is a good one, then I must be sure to intend sincerely to do what I have sworn to do. Circumstances might arise, admittedly, which would end the binding power of the oath. For example, an older son who swore to his dying parent to look after his younger brother would be released from his oath if the parent recovered (the reason for making the oath ceases to exist); or if the older brother himself became ill and needy (the condition under which the oath was given, the older brother's ability, ceases); or the younger brother grows up and becomes self-supporting (the object of the promise changes substantially). Other factors which might cause a promissory oath to lose its binding force would be release from the obligation by the one to whom the promise was made; the discovery that the object of the oath (the thing to be done) would be useless or even sinful; or the annulment of the oath (or dispensation from it) by competent authority, such as one's confessor.

What is the difference between an oath and a vow? When we take an oath, we call upon God to be witness to the fact that we are speaking the truth as we know it. If we are swearing to a simple statement of fact, we call that an assertory oath. If we are swearing that we shall do something for someone in the future, we call that a *promissory* oath. In either case, we simply ask God, the Lord of Truth, to be witness to our truthfulness and our purpose of fidelity. We are not promising God anything, for Himself.

If we take a vow, however, we do promise God some-thing. We promise God, with the intention of binding ourselves under pain of sin, to do something especially pleasing to God. In this case God is not merely our witness; He also is the recipient of whatever it is we intend to do.

A vow may be either a *private* vow or a *public* vow. For example, a person might privately make a vow to visit the shrine of St. Anne in Quebec in gratitude for recovery from an illness; a single person living in the world might privately make a vow of chastity. In reference to private vows, it should be pointed out that such a vow should not be made lightly. A vow binds under pain of sin, or it is not a vow at all. Whether the violation of the vow would be a mortal sin or a venial sin depends, in a private vow, on the intention of the one who makes it and on the importance of the matter involved. (One cannot bind himself to something of slight importance under penalty of grave sin.) But even if a person intended to bind himself only under pain of venial sin, the obligation is too serious to be entered into lightly. No one should take a private vow without first consulting his confessor.

A public vow is one which is made to an official representative of the Church, such as a bishop or a religious superior, and is accepted by the superior in the name of the Church. The public vows most familiar to us are those which bind a person to the complete observance of the Evangelical Counsels of poverty, chastity, and obedience in a religious community. Any person who makes these three vows publicly is said to have "entered religion," to have embraced the religious state. If the person is a woman, she has become a Sister. If the person is a man, he has become a Brother; or, if he receives the sacrament of Holy Orders in addition to making the three vows, he is called a religious priest.

This is a point on which not even Catholics are always clear—the difference between a Brother and a priest. There are many splendid young men who feel the generous desire to devote their lives to the service of God and of souls and yet do not feel that they are called to the priesthood. Such young men may do one of two things; they may enter one of the religious Orders or Societies which is made up of both Brothers and priests—such as the Franciscans, the Passionists, the Jesuits. Here the young man in question would make his religious novitiate and take the three vows of religion; but he would not study theology, he would not receive Holy Orders. He would spend his life in devoted service as a helper to the priests; perhaps as a secretary, or a cook, or a librarian. He would be what is called an auxiliary Brother. Every religious Order that I know of is in urgent need of such Brothers; every auxiliary Brother releases another priest for work that only a priest can do.

Or the young man who feels called to the religious life but not to the priesthood might prefer to join one of the religious Societies which is made up entirely of Brothers—such as the Christian Brothers, the Xaverian Brothers, the Alexian Brothers. These Societies of dedicated religious men conduct schools, colleges, hospitals—any number of works of mercy. The members make a religious novitiate, they profess the three vows of poverty, chastity, and obedience; but they do not attend a theological seminary, they do not receive the sacrament of Holy Orders. They are Brothers, not priests. And there are never enough of them; never enough hands for the work that needs doing.

Another distinction that sometimes is confusing to people is that between religious priests and secular priests. It hardly needs remarking that this does *not* mean that some priests are religious and others are irreligious. It means that some men have felt themselves called not only to the religious life but also to the priesthood. They have entered a religious Order, such as the Benedictines, the Dominicans, the Redemptorists; they have made a religious novitiate and have pronounced the three vows of poverty, chastity, and obedience. Then, after becoming religious, they have gone on to study theology and have received the sacrament of Holy Orders. They are called *religious* priests because they have embraced the religious life and live as members of a religious Order.

Some young men, on the other hand, feel themselves called by God to the priesthood but not to the religious life, not to life in a religious Order. Such a young man states his desire to the bishop of his diocese. If the young man has the necessary qualifications, the bishop sends him to the seminary; first, a college course, then theology. In due time, if the young man perseveres and gives proof of his fitness, he receives the sacrament of Holy Orders; he is a priest. He is called a *secular* priest (from the Latin word "saeculum," meaning "world") because he lives not in a religious community but in the world, in the midst of the people to whom he ministers. He also is called a *diocesan* priest because he belongs to a diocese, not to a religious Order. His "boss" is the bishop of the diocese, not the superior of a religious community. At the time of his ordination, he promised obedience to his bishop. Normally, so long as he lives, his work will be within the limits of his own diocese. And he has but one vow, the vow of perpetual chastity, which he made when he was ordained a subdeacon—his first major step towards the altar.

"Bless and Do Not Curse"

"Bless those who persecute you; bless and do not curse," says St. Paul in his epistle to the Romans (12:14). To curse means to wish evil upon some person or place or thing. A form of curse that frequently is heard upon the lips of those who have little regard for the honor of God's name is "God damn you!" The meaning of these words is "May God send you to hell!" It is easy to see why such a curse would be a mortal sin, if a person spoke the words deliberately and really meant what he said. To ask God to send to hell a soul whom He has created, a soul for whom He died, is a most serious act of dishonor towards our infinitely merciful

CHAPTER XX

The Seventh and Tenth Commandments of God

Mine and Thine

Is it a sin for a starving man to seize a loaf of bread even if he has to break the bakery window to get it? Is it a sin for a man to steal tools from the shop where he works if everyone else is doing it? If a woman finds a diamond ring and no one comes around to claim it, may she keep it? Is it wrong to buy tires at a bargain price if you suspect that they were stolen? The seventh commandment of God says, *"Thou shalt not steal,"* and it sounds very simple on the face of it; until the ifs and the ands begin to come rolling in.

Before proceeding to an examination of the seventh commandment, we might do well to dispose very briefly of the tenth commandment: *"Thou shalt not covet thy neighbor's goods."* The tenth commandment is the companion of the seventh, just as the ninth commandment is the companion of the sixth. In both cases we are forbidden to do in our thoughts what it would be sinful to do in our actions. It is therefore not only a sin to steal, it also is a sin to *want* to steal; to wish that we might get and keep for ourselves something that belongs to another. Whatever we may say as to the nature and gravity of dishonest actions would apply also to dishonest thoughts—except that there is no "paying back" to do when dishonesty is confined to thought. This is a point to keep in mind concerning all the commandments: the fact that sin is committed the moment that a person deliberately desires or decides to commit a sin. The actual deed aggravates the guilt, but the sin really is committed the moment the decision is made or the desire is consented to. For example, if I were to decide to steal a certain article if I got the chance but then something happened which made it impossible to carry out my plan, I still would have the sin of intended theft upon my conscience.

Now, to what does the seventh commandment oblige us? It demands of us that we practice the virtue of justice, which is defined as the moral virtue which impels a person to give to everyone his due, that which is his by right. There are many ways in which the virtue of justice may be violated. There is first of all the sin of stealing—stealing by stealth, which we call theft, or stealing by violence, which we commonly call robbery. Stealing is the voluntary taking or keeping of something that belongs to another, against the owner's reasonable will. "Against the owner's reasonable will" is an important clause. Life is more important than property. It would be unreasonable to refuse to give to another what that other person needs to save his life. Thus the starving man who takes the loaf of bread is not stealing. The refugee who takes a car or a boat to escape the pursuers who threaten his life or liberty is not stealing.

"Against the owner's reasonable will" also distinguishes stealing from borrowing. If my neighbor is not at home and I take the mower out of his garage to cut my lawn, knowing that he would not object, then it is plain that I am not stealing. It is equally plain that it is not lawful borrowing to take something secretly if I know that the owner *would* object. The employee who borrows from the till, even though he

This is the virtue which God demands of us in the sixth and ninth commandments: *"Thou shalt not commit adultery"* and *"Thou shalt not covet thy neighbor's wife."* We recall that the commandments as we have them are intended to be memory helps: pigeonholes in which we can classify our various duties to God. Each commandment mentions specifically one of the most serious sins against the virtue to be practiced ("Thou shalt not kill," "Thou shalt not steal") and under that one heading are grouped all the duties and all the sins of an allied nature. Thus, not only is it a sin to kill, it is also a sin to fight and to hate; not only is it a sin to steal, it is also a sin to damage property or to defraud. Similarly, not only is it a sin to commit adultery—carnal intercourse when one (or both) of the participants is married to someone else; it is also a sin to commit fornication —sexual intercourse between two unmarried persons; it is also a sin to indulge in *any* deliberate actions, such as touches with oneself alone or with another, for the purpose of arousing the sexual appetite outside of marriage. Not only is it a sin to covet a neighbor's wife; it is also a sin to willingly entertain unchaste thoughts or desires concerning *any* person.

Chastity—or purity—is defined as the moral virtue which rightly regulates all voluntary expressions of sexual pleasure in marriage and excludes it altogether outside the married state. Sins against the virtue of chastity differ from sins against most other virtues in one notable point: a thought, word, or action against the virtue of chastity, if fully deliberate, is *always* a mortal sin. One may violate other virtues, even deliberately, and yet sin venially because of the slightness of the matter. A person may be slightly intemperate, slightly dishonest, slightly untruthful. But no one can be "slightly" unchaste if his violation of purity is fully voluntary. Whether in thought or word or deed, there is no "small matter" touching this virtue.

The reason should be quite plain. The procreative power

is the most sacred of all man's physical gifts, the one which involves God most directly. Its very sacredness makes its defilement the more malicious. Add to this the fact that sex (to use the common term) is the very wellspring of human life. Poison the spring, and you have poisoned humanity. That is why God has erected a high, tight fence around the spring and has posted signs for all to see: No TRESPASSING! God is adamant that His plan for the creation of new human life shall not be twisted from His hand and distorted into an instrument to satisfy a perverse greed for pleasure and excitement. The only time that a sin against chastity can be a venial sin is when there is a lack of full realization or a lack of full consent.

The matter is somewhat different with respect to the virtue of modesty. Modesty is a virtue distinct from chastity, although it is chastity's guardian, the keeper of the approaches to the citadel. Modesty is the virtue which moves a person to abstain from any actions, words, or looks which are likely to arouse unlawfully the sexual appetite— in oneself or in others. Such actions might be indiscreet kissing, embracing, caressing; might be extreme forms of dress, such as Bikini bathing suits or plunging necklines; might be the hot-eyed reading of an obscene "modern" novel. Such words might be the telling or listening to suggestive or off-color stories, singing or enjoying lewd songs and double-meaning talk. Such looks might be a roving eye on a bathing beach or a windy corner, a drooling contemplation of so-called "leg art" on calendars and in magazines. It is true that "to the pure all things are pure"; but it also is true that to the pure all things are offensive which threaten purity.

Unlike chastity, sins against modesty may sometimes be venial. Failures in modesty which are directly aimed at unlawfully arousing the sexual appetite always are mortal sins. Barring that, the gravity of sins against modesty will depend upon the intention of the sinner, the degree to which the immodesty does excite sexual stirrings, and the amount of scandal that may be given. One facet of the matter that should be remembered by the ladies is the fact that God, in providing for the perpetuation of the human race, has made man the active principle in the act of procreation. For this reason a man's desires, normally, are much more easily aroused than a woman's. It can happen that a girl, in all innocence, will indulge in a bit of affectionate interplay which to her is no more than a romantic moment under the moonlight; and yet to the boy involved it may have been the occasion of a mortal sin. In the same sort of ignorant innocence a woman may offend against modesty in dress unintentionally, simply because she judges the strength of a man's sexual drives by her own.

In our contemporary American culture, there are two "soft" spots that have need of special emphasis in a discussion of the virtue of chastity. One is the widespread practice of steady company-keeping on the part of adolescents. As early as the eighth and ninth grades boys and girls are pairing off, "going steady," exchanging rings and pins, spending two and three nights a week in one another's company. Such steady company-keeping (going always and frequently with the same person of the opposite sex for a long period of time) is always a danger to purity. For those old enough to get married and able to get married should they so wish, the danger is justified; a reasonable courtship is necessary in order to find a suitable partner for marriage. But for young adolescents who are in no position to be married for several years, *steady company-keeping is a sin* because it is an unjustified occasion of sin, one which foolish parents all too often encourage because they think it is "cute."

Another form of company-keeping that is sinful, and sinful by its very nature, is the dating of divorced persons. In this instance the company-keeping does not have to be steady, either. One date with a divorced man (or woman) may be enough to get the other person's heart involved—

and the end result so easily becomes sins of adultery or life-long adultery in a marriage outside the Church.

Sometimes, in moments of severe temptation, we may feel that this wonderful power of procreation which God has given us is a questionable blessing. At such times we have only to remind ourselves of two things. Of the fact, first of all, that there is no real virtue, or proven goodness, without effort. A person who never has any temptations may be said to be innocent, but he cannot be said to be *virtuous* in the ordinary (not the theological) meaning of the word. God, of course, can impart surpassing virtue without the test of temptation, as He did in the case of our Blessed Mother. But normally it is precisely in the conquest of strong temptations that a person becomes virtuous and acquires merit in heaven.

We need to remind ourselves, too, that the bigger the temptation, the more grace God will give us—if we want it, if we will use it, if we will do our part. God will never let us be tempted beyond our ability (with the help of His grace) to resist. No one can ever say, "I sinned because I couldn't help it." Our part, of course, is to avoid unnecessary danger; to be faithful to prayer, especially in time of weakness; to be frequently at confession and Holy Communion and Holy Mass; to have a very real and personal devotion to Mary, our Mother Most Chaste.

Father. It also would be a grievous sin against charity. Charity binds us to wish for, and to pray for the *salvation* of all souls—not for their eternal condemnation.

Usually such a curse is uttered in anger or impatience rather than with cold-blooded intent; the person does not really mean what he says. In such a case the curse would not be a mortal sin—although the anger might be. This is a point to bear in mind with regard to other misuses of God's name, also: the fact that very often it is the hatred, or the anger, or the impatience which is the real sin, rather than what we say. In going to confession, it would be more correct to say, "I was angry, and in my anger I cursed another," or "in my anger I used profanity,"—rather than to confess simply, "I cursed" or "I used profane language."

There are, of course, other forms of cursing besides the common one mentioned above. *Any time* I wish evil to another, I am guilty of cursing. "I hope that he breaks his neck." "If he never gets well, it will be too soon to suit me." "May the devil take him and the likes of him." In these and similar phrases (usually uttered without full deliberation) charity is wounded and God is dishonored.

The general principle is that if the harm we wish another is a grave harm, and we mean what we say, and the evil we wish is great, then the curse is a mortal sin. If it is only a small evil that we wish ("I hope his golf ball goes in the sand trap"; "I hope she gets caught in the rain with her new hair-do"), then the sin is venial. And, as already mentioned, even a grave evil wished upon someone might be a venial sin because of the thoughtlessness with which it was voiced.

Remembering that *everything* that God has made is dear to God, we can understand that it dishonors God to curse *any* of His creatures, not only human beings. However, animals and inanimate things are of incomparably less value than an immortal soul. Thus, the race-fan who says, "I hope that horse drops dead," and the "do-it-yourselfer" who says, "God damn that leaky faucet," are not guilty of mortal sin.

It might be useful, at this point, to remind parents of the importance of forming right consciences in their children in the matter of bad language as well as in other matters. Not all so-called bad language is a sin, and children should not be told that it is a sin if it is not. For example, the words "hell" and "damn" are not in themselves sinful words. The man who says, "Dammit, I forgot to mail that letter," the woman who says, "Oh, hell, another cup broken," may be using language that is ungentlemanly or unladylike—but not language that is sinful.

This is true also of the four-letter Anglo-Saxon words which frequently are used (instead of the more respectable Latin derivatives) to describe bodily parts and processes. The four-letter words for urine and for excrement, for example, are coarse words, vulgar words, but they are not sinful words.

When a child comes in from play with a newly learned word such as these upon his lips, parents would make a great mistake to appear profoundly shocked and to tell the child that such language "is a big sin, and God won't love you any more." To tell a child that is to give him a distorted idea of God and a tangled conscience that perhaps never will quite get straightened out. Sin is too awful an evil to be used as a bogeyman to teach a child good manners. It should be enough to tell a child quietly: "That isn't a nice word, Joey; it isn't a *sinful* word, but it's what we call a *vulgar* word, and Mother (or Daddy) wishes you wouldn't use it." For most youngsters, a request such as this will be enough. If a child's lapses are too frequent, it may be necessary to explain to him that there is a sin of disobedience involved. But always, in the moral education of children, there should be adherence to the truth.

Blasphemy is the sin which is most directly opposed to the second commandment. One who uses profanity dishonors God by using His name carelessly, thoughtlessly, disrespectfully as does he, also, who takes an oath when there is no

need to take an oath. The perjurer, the one who takes an oath to tell the truth and then proceeds to tell a lie, dishonors God by making Him the unwilling witness to an untruth. One who curses dishonors God by asking God to work evil upon one of His own creatures. But the blasphemer dishonors God, not indirectly as do these others, but in the most direct way possible: by speaking insultingly of God or of what is dear to God.

He is guilty of blasphemy who speaks of God (or of the saints or of holy things) in a spirit of contempt or ridicule, or in any other vicious spirit. There are varying degrees of blasphemy. Sometimes it is a thoughtless reaction to emotional strain, such as impatience or pique or pain: "If God is good, why does He let such things happen?" "God can't love me, or He'd never let me suffer like this." Sometimes blasphemy has a smart-alecky origin: "That cranky old Man upstairs won't let me do it." "If that guy goes to heaven, then I want to go to hell." Sometimes blasphemy is outright irreligious and even God-hating: "The Bible is just a bunch of fairy stories." "The Mass is a lot of hocus-pocus." Or even, "God is a fable and a myth."

In such blasphemies as these latter ones, there is, of course, the sin of heresy or infidelity as well as the sin of blasphemy. Any time that a blasphemous utterance contains a denial of a particular truth of faith—a denial of God's goodness or justice, for example, or a denial of the Blessed Mother's virginity, or of the power of prayer—then the sin of heresy is joined to the sin of blasphemy. (A denial of the faith in general would be the grave sin of infidelity.)

By its nature, blasphemy always is a mortal sin, because always it involves a *grievous* dishonoring of God. The only time blasphemy might be a venial sin would be when sufficient reflection or consent was lacking. Such an instance might be a blasphemy uttered under stress of great pain or anguish.

With the sin of blasphemy we round out the catalogue of

offenses against the second commandment: profanity, unnecessary or false swearing, vows rashly made or vows broken, cursing, and blasphemy. In a discussion of the commandments it is necessary to examine the negative side, in order that we may have a rightly formed conscience. However, it is true of the second commandment, as it is true of all the commandments, that abstaining from outright sin is only half the picture. We must not only avoid what is displeasing to God; we also must *do* what is pleasing to Him. Otherwise our religion would be as one-sided as a man whose right arm and leg are missing.

On the positive side, then, we honor God's name when we reverently take an oath at a time when an oath is necessary. Under such circumstances an oath is an act of divine worship, meritorious and pleasing to God. The same holds true of a vow; a person who prudently binds himself under pain of sin to do something pleasing to God, is performing an act of divine worship, an act of the virtue of religion. And every subsequent action which pertains to the vow is likewise an act of religion.

Our opportunities for honoring God's name are not, obviously, limited to oaths and vows. There is, for example, the quite common and very praiseworthy practice of bowing the head or tipping the hat at the name of Jesus, whether pronounced by ourselves or by someone else in our hearing. When we hear the name of God or of Jesus misused by another, there is the admirable habit of making instant reparation by saying silently, "Blessed be God" or "Blessed be the name of Jesus." There also is the public reparation which we make for blasphemy and profanity each time that we join in reciting the Divine Praises after Mass or Benediction.

God's holy name also is publicly honored by the rallies, processions, and other group demonstrations which are held on special occasions, testimonials in which we should be eager to take part. Whether the divinity of Christ or the glory of His Mother is the proximate reason for such public

manifestations, God and His holy name are being honored and God will bless us for our participation.

The important thing to remember is that if we love God truly we shall also love His name. It will be only with love that we shall speak it—with love and reverence and respect. If we have the unfortunate habit of profanity, we shall pray for the love we need; a love for God that will make the irreverent use of His name as bitter as quinine upon our lips.

Our reverence for God's name will lead us, too, to find a special joy in those prayers which are primarily prayers of praise—such as the "Glory be to the Father," which we recite so often, and the "Gloria" and the "Sanctus" of the Mass. We may even be moved to make use of the Book of Psalms as our occasional prayerbook, those beautiful hymns of David in which praise of God is sung and sung again—as in the 112th Psalm, which begins:

> "Praise you servants of the LORD,
>   praise the name of the LORD.
> Blessed be the name of the LORD
>   both now and forever.
> From the rising to the setting of the sun
>   is the name of the LORD to be praised."

Why Sunday Mass?

A song which was quite popular during World War I has a line something like this: "Oh, it's nice to get up in the morning, but it's nicer to stay in bed." It is a rare Catholic who has not, at one time or another, voiced a similar sentiment as he rolled out of the sheets on a Sunday morning, feeling quite heroic as he arose in obedience to the third commandment of God: *"Remember thou keep holy the Lord's day."*

The fact that there *is* a Lord's day is something which follows quite logically from the natural law. The natural law

(that is, man's obligation to be true to his nature as a creature of God) demands that we adore God. It demands that we acknowledge our complete dependence upon God and that we thank Him for His goodness to us. In practice we know that it would be impossible for the average human to maintain, all the time, a conscious state of adoration. And so it is to be expected that a definite time, or times, be set aside for the discharge of this absolutely necessary duty. It is in accordance with this need that one day out of seven has been set aside on which all men, everywhere, must consciously and deliberately give to God the homage which is His by right.

We know that in Old Testament times it was the seventh day of the week—the Sabbath day—which was observed as the Lord's day. That was the law as God gave it to Moses on Mount Sinai: "Remember to keep holy the Sabbath day" (Exodus 20:8). However, with the establishment of the New Law by Christ, the positive Liturgical Law passed away. The early Christian Church determined as the Lord's day the first day of the week, our Sunday. That the Church had the right to make such a law is evident from the many passages in the Gospels in which Jesus confers upon His Church the power to make laws in His name. For example, "He who hears you, hears me" (Luke 10:16) and "Whatever thou shalt bind on earth shall be bound in heaven" (Matthew 16:19).

The reason for changing the Lord's day from Saturday to Sunday lies in the fact that to the Christian Church the first day of the week had been made doubly holy. It is the day on which Jesus conquered sin and death by His resurrection from the dead, to give assurance of our future glory. It is the day, too, which Jesus chose for the sending down of the Holy Spirit—the birthday of the Church. It is very likely, also, that the Church changed the Lord's day for a psychological reason: to emphasize the fact that the Old Testament worship of the Hebrews, which had been a

preparation for the coming of the Messias, was now at an end. The Christian religion was not a mere "revision" of the worship of the Synagogue; the Christian religion was God's final plan for the salvation of the world. The curtain of completion was drawn across the Sabbath. Christians would not be merely another "sect" among the Jews; they would be a new people with a new Law and a new Sacrifice.

Nothing is said in the Bible about the change of the Lord's day from Saturday to Sunday. We know of the change only from the tradition of the Church—a fact handed down to us from earliest times by the living voice of the Church. That is why we find so illogical the attitude of many non-Catholics, who say that they will believe nothing unless they can find it in the Bible and yet will continue to keep Sunday as the Lord's day on the say-so of the Catholic Church.

"Remember thou keep holy the Lord's day." "Yes," we say, "but *how* must I keep it holy?" In her role of divinely established legislator, the Church answers our question by telling us that first and above all we must keep the Lord's day holy by assisting at the holy Sacrifice of the Mass. The Mass is the *perfect* act of worship, given to us by Jesus so that we might, with Him, offer adequate honor to God.

Sacrifice, in the religious sense, is the offering of a gift to God, accompanied by some manner of destruction of the gift on behalf of a group, by someone who has the right to represent the group. From humankind's very beginnings and among all peoples, sacrifice has been man's natural way of worshiping God. The group might be a family, a tribe, or a nation. The priest might be the father or the patriarch or the king; or, as designated by God for the Hebrews, the sons of Aaron. The victim (the gift offered) might be bread and wine or grain or fruit or animals. But in all these sacrifices there was one great defect: none of the gifts were really worthy of God; He Himself had made them all in the first place.

But now, in the Sacrifice of the Mass, Jesus has provided a gift that really is worthy of God, a perfect gift whose value is proportionate to God—the gift of God's own Son, co-equal with the Father. Jesus, the great High Priest, made that offering of Himself as Victim, once and for all on Calvary, where He was slain by the executioners. However, you and I could not be there on Calvary to unite ourselves with Jesus in the offering of this Gift to God. So Jesus has given us the Sacrifice of the Mass in which, through the change of the bread and wine into His own body and blood that were separated at His death on Calvary, He endlessly renews the offering of Himself to the Father *and gives us a chance to unite ourselves with Him in the offering,* gives us a chance to unite our love with His, to make ourselves a part of the Gift that is being offered. There could surely be no better way than this to keep the Lord's day holy and to sanctify the week that lies ahead.

All our time belongs to God—as we ourselves belong to God. But God and His Church are very generous with us. They give us for our own use six days out of every seven—a total of 144 hours in which to work and recreate and sleep. Even with the one day which the Church reserves for God, the Church is very generous. As God's absolute own the Church takes only the one hour (perhaps a little more or a little less) which is required for our attendance at the holy Sacrifice of the Mass. The other twenty-three hours God surrenders back to us again for our own use and enjoyment. God will be grateful if we use some of this extra time for Him and His work—but the Mass is all that is strictly of obligation in the matter of worship. In practice, then, we are obliged to reserve for God's very own only one hour out of the weekly 168 hours which He has given us.

Recalling this, we can understand why it is a mortal sin to miss Mass deliberately on Sunday. We can understand the depth of ingratitude displayed by the person who is "too busy" or "too tired" to go to Mass, to give God the

one hour that He asks for Himself; the person who, not content with the 167 hours he already has, steals from God the extra sixty minutes that are His. We can recognize the total lack of love—indeed, the lack of common decency—in the heart of him who will not, for one hour once a week, unite himself with Christ in order to adore adequately God the Most Blessed Trinity; to thank God for His blessings of the week that is past; and to beg His help in the week that is beginning.

Not only are we bound to assist at Mass; we are bound to assist at an *entire* Mass. If we were to miss an essential part of the Mass—the Consecration or the priest's Communion—it would be almost equivalent to missing Mass entirely; and the sin would be a mortal sin, if our failure to be present were deliberate. To miss a small part of the Mass—coming in, for example, at the Epistle or leaving at the Last Blessing —would be a venial sin. This is something to remember, if we are inclined to dawdle in getting ready for Sunday Mass or if we are tempted to slip out early in order to "beat the traffic." The Mass is our weekly gift to God; it should not be an incomplete gift or a damaged gift. We would not dream of giving tarnished silver or shopworn linen as a wedding present; we should have at least an equal respect for God.

To fulfill our obligation, we must be physically present at Mass, we must be a part of the congregation. We cannot discharge our Sunday duty by watching Mass on television or by watching Mass from across the street through open church doors when there is room inside. It may sometimes happen (as in small churches in resort areas) that the congregation overflows onto the street outside the church. In such a case we *are* assisting at Mass because we *are* a part of the congregation, we are actually physically present, as close as we can get.

Not only must we be physically present; we also must be *mentally* present at Mass. This means that we must have

the intention, at least implicit, of assisting at Mass; and we must have some idea of what is going on. A person who would deliberately settle himself to sleep through the Mass, or who would deliberately pay no attention even to the principal parts of the Mass, would be guilty of a mortal sin. Lesser distractions and inattentiveness, if deliberate, would be venially sinful. Indeliberate distractions are not sinful.

However, our love for God surely will raise our appreciation of the Mass above the level of the measuring stick of sin. We shall be in our place before Mass begins and will remain until the priest has left the sanctuary. We shall unite ourselves with Christ in the offering of the Sacrifice and will follow the Mass attentively in prayer book or missal. If we do miss Mass, it will be only because a grave reason prevents our attendance: sickness, whether our own or of someone for whom we must care; distance and lack of transportation; or some unforeseen emergency that must be dealt with even at the cost of Mass.

Besides obliging us to assist at Sunday Mass, the third commandment also requires that we abstain from unnecessary servile work on Sundays; servile work being defined as that which requires the use of the body rather than of the mind. Primarily, it is to preserve the sanctity of Sunday and to guarantee time for men to worship and to pray that the Church has made the Lord's day a day of rest. But it also is because none knows better than she the limitations of the children whom God has created, their need for respite from daily drudgery, for time in which to enjoy the world of fellowship, of beauty, of knowledge, of creative activity which God has provided.

To engage in unnecessary servile work on Sunday is a sin, mortal or venial depending on whether the amount of time given to the work is slight or considerable. To work unnecessarily two and a half or three hours would be a mortal sin. In determining whether or not a particular work is permissible on Sunday, we have to ask ourselves two

questions: is the work more mental than physical, as are typing, drawing, embroidering? If not, then is the work genuinely necessary, something that could not have been done on Saturday and cannot be put off until Monday, such as a farmer's feeding of his stock, a housewife making the beds and doing the dishes? It takes only honesty, not a lawyer, to answer such questions; and, if the answer to either is "yes," then the work is permissible on Sunday.

CHAPTER XVIII

The Fourth and Fifth Commandments of God

Parents, Children and Citizens

Parents as well as children have need to examine themselves periodically on their fidelity to the fourth commandment of God. Explicitly God speaks to the children: "*Honor thy father and thy mother,*" commanding them to love and respect their parents to obey them in all that is not sinful, and to help them when they are in need. However, even while He is speaking to the children, God is looking over their shoulders at the parents, implicitly commanding them to be *worthy* of the love and respect which the children are required to give.

In this matter of the fourth commandment, the obligations of parents and children alike stem from the fact that all rightful authority comes from God. Whether it be a parent or a civil ruler or a religious superior, their authority is ultimately God's own authority which He has chosen to share with them. Obedience given to them in their lawful capacity is obedience given to God and will be so regarded. It follows also that those who are superiors have a grave

obligation, as agents and partners of God, to be faithful to the trust that God has placed in them. For parents in particular it should be a sobering thought to contemplate the strict accounting that they will have to render one day to God for the souls of their children.

This is a point that needs recalling by the money-short mother who is tempted to take a job outside the home; by the "go-getter" husband who brings home his bottled-up nervous tensions to discharge upon his family. It is a point that needs remembering by parents who leave their children with babysitters three and four nights a week; by parents who stage heavy-drinking and loose-talking parties in their home; by quarrelling parents who continually bicker in front of the children. In fact this is a point to be emphasized for *any* parents who fail to see that raising their children in a peaceful, happy, and Christ-directed home is the main business of their lives.

What, in detail, are the principal duties of parents towards their children? There are, first of all, the obvious ones of physical care: food, clothing, housing, medical care as needed. Then there is the duty of raising a child to be a good citizen: a useful, self-supporting, well-informed, intelligently patriotic individual. There is the duty, also, of providing for the child's intellectual development to the degree that his own talents and family finances will permit. Since there can be no complete intellectual development without a knowledge (growing as the child grows) of the truths of faith, this means sending the child to a Catholic school, if at all possible—high school as well as grade school; college also, if he attends one. This, be it noted, is a duty which binds in conscience.

Here we have passed from the natural needs of a child—physical, civic, and intellectual—to his spiritual and supernatural needs. Obviously, since the child is made for eternal life, the fulfillment of these needs is the most important of all parental duties. There is, first of all, the obligation to

have the child baptized as soon as possible after birth, normally within two weeks, or a month at the very most. Then, as the child's mind begins to unfold, comes the duty of teaching the child about God,[1] especially about His goodness and the loving care and the obedience we owe to God. As the child begins to talk, he also will be taught to pray, long before he goes to school.

If, unfortunately, a Catholic schooling is not possible, the child will be sent regularly to religious instruction classes for as many years as he remains in school. What he learns from instructions will be triply reinforced by what he sees at home. It is in this, especially, that Catholic parents will do their most fruitful work, because a child absorbs so much more fully what he *sees* than what he is told. That is why the best Catholic school in the world cannot make up for a lax Catholic home.

As the child grows, parents will keep an unobtrusive but watchful eye on his companions, his reading, his recreations, offering counsel and even firm insistence when any of these become questionable. The child will learn to love Sunday Mass and frequent confession and Communion, not by being "sent" but by proudly accompanying his parents in the fulfillment of these duties.

It all adds up to rather a large order; but fortunately God gives to good parents the wisdom they need for their job. And being good parents begins, strangely enough, not with the child but with a genuine love between husband and wife. Psychologists point out that parents who depend upon their children for their own emotional satisfaction rather than upon each other, can never be fully successful in rearing children. In such a case, love for the child is likely to be an over-possessive and jealous love that seeks satisfaction of

---

[1] See *Suggestions for the Parent-Educators*—No. 5D (Confraternity Publications, Paterson 3, N. J.), for information about the Confraternity of Christian Doctrine's program to help parents teach religion in the home to pre-school children.

self rather than the child's own best interests. Out of such a love rise spoiled children.

However, parents who truly love each other in God, and their children as gifts of God, may be comforted to know that not much else is needed, even if they never read a single book on child psychology (although such reading is surely advisable if the books read are sound).

They can make a lot of mistakes without doing the child any lasting harm. Because in such a home the child will feel loved, and *wanted*, and secure; he will grow up to be emotionally stable and spiritually strong.

All of us, without exception, have duties to our parents. If our parents are dead, then our duties are quite simple: we remember them in all our prayers and Masses and occasionally have a Mass offered for the repose of their souls. If our parents are still living, then our duties will depend upon our age and our status and theirs. Or perhaps it would be more correct to say that the way of *fulfilling* our duties will vary according to age and status. Because, of course, *all* children, even though they themselves be married with families of their own, share the basic duties of love and respect for their parents.

Usually the debt of love is not a hard one to pay, mothers and fathers being what they are. But the duty of love does not cease in those cases, fortunately rare, where a parent proves to be unlovable on the natural level—a brutal father, for example, or a deserting mother. Then the child must love with the supernatural love that Christ commands us to have towards all unlovable people, even towards our enemies. We must wish them well, desire their eternal salvation, and pray for them. No matter what they may have done to us, we must be willing to extend them a helping hand, if and when we can.

With the progressive increase in life expectancy, married children are more and more often faced with the problem of an aged and dependent parent. What does filial love dic-

tate in such circumstances? Is it a strict duty to take the parent into one's own home, even though the home already is crowded with children and the wife already has more than she can do? That is not a question that can be answered with a yes or no. No two cases are alike, and the son or daughter faced with such a dilemma should talk it over with the pastor or confessor or Catholic marriage counselor. Here we must be content to observe that the whole history of man testifies to the fact that God does bless, with a very special blessing, those sons and daughters whose filial love is an unselfish love which proves itself by self-sacrifice. The duty of children to support indigent or disabled parents is plain enough; it is a duty that binds in conscience. But whether the duty must be fulfilled in the offspring's own home or in a home for the aged or other facility is a matter for individual counseling. It will be the genuineness of the love that is behind what is done that will count the most.

The respect which we owe to our parents comes almost as naturally as love in a truly Christian home: treating them with reverence, deferring to their wishes, accepting their corrections without insolence, seeking their advice regarding important decisions—such as the choice of a state of life, or the suitability of a prospective partner in marriage. In matters which pertain to a child's natural rights, parents may advise but they must not command. For example, parents may not command a child to get married, should the son or daughter prefer to remain single; they may not command their child to marry a certain person; they may not forbid their child to enter the priesthood or to embrace the religious life.

Concerning the duty of respect for parents, the most difficult period of a child's life is the period of adolescence. These are the "growing-up" years when the child is torn between the need for dependence on his parents and the emerging urge for adult independence. It is a stormy time for almost every youngster. Wise parents will try to temper their firmness with understanding and patience.

It hardly seems necessary to observe that hating one's parents, striking them, threatening them, seriously ridiculing or insulting them, cursing them, refusing them help when they are in grave need, or doing anything else to cause them grave sorrow or great anger, would be mortally sinful. These things would be sinful if done to a stranger; towards parents it would be evil twice compounded. Generally, however, a child's disobedience is a venial sin (or perhaps no sin at all) unless there is a serious matter involved (such as avoiding bad companions) or unless the disobedience springs from contempt for parental authority. Most childish disobedience is due to thoughtlessness or forgetfulness or carelessness and is lacking in the advertence and deliberateness necessary for sin, or at least grave sin.

We cannot end our discussion of the fourth commandment without referring to the obligation it imposes upon all of us to love our nation (our family on a larger scale); to be sincerely interested in its welfare, to respect and obey its lawful authority. Perhaps we should emphasize the word "lawful." Because citizens do of course have the right to defend themselves against tyranny (as in Communist lands) when their fundamental human rights are threatened. No government may interfere with an individual's (or a family's) right to worship God and to love according to His laws, to receive religious instructions and the ministrations of the Church. A government has not the right, any more than a parent, to command what God forbids or to forbid what God commands.

But, such cases excepted, the good Catholic will of necessity be a good citizen. Knowing that right reason requires that he work for the welfare of his country, he will exercise regularly his right to vote and will vote for the candidates (putting prejudices aside) whom he feels to be best qualified for public office. He will obey his country's laws and will pay his taxes as his just contribution to the expenses of good government. He will help to defend his country in the event of a just war (as he would defend his own family

against unjust attack), bearing arms if called upon to do so, judging his nation's cause to be just unless there is adequate and unquestionable evidence to the contrary. He will do all this, not solely from motives of natural patriotism but because his Catholic conscience tells him that respect for and obedience to the lawful authority of his government is service given to God, from whom all authority flows.

Life Belongs To God

It is only by God that human life is given; it is only by God that human life may be taken away. Every human soul is individually and personally created by God. God alone has the right to decide when that soul's time upon earth is finished.

It is only to human life that the fifth commandment, "Thou shalt not kill," refers. Animals have been given by God to mankind for man's use and convenience. It is no sin to kill animals for any reasonable cause, such as the elimination of pests, the providing of food, the performance of scientific experiments. It would be a sin to injure or kill animals without reason; but the sin would lie in the abuse of God's gifts. It would not be a sin against the fifth commandment.

The fact that human life belongs to God is so obvious that the gravity of the sin of murder—the unjust taking of another's life—is recognized even through the light of reason by all men of good will. The gravity of the sin of suicide—the deliberate taking of one's own life—is equally apparent. Since the person who deliberately takes his own life dies in the very act of committing a mortal sin, he cannot be given Christian burial. In practice, however, it is very seldom that a Catholic in his right mind will take his own life; and Christian burial is never denied when suicide seems to be the result of mental derangement, even temporary.

Is it ever lawful to take the life of another person? Yes,

in self-defense. If my own life or the life of my neighbor is being threatened by an unjust aggressor and there is no way to stop the aggressor-murderer except by killing him, then I may do so. In fact it is permissible to kill in defense of property as well as in defense of life if it is a large amount of property that the criminal is threatening to take or destroy and there is no other way to stop him. It follows, then, that law-enforcement officers are not violating the fifth commandment when, given no other way to stop or apprehend a dangerous criminal, they take his life.

A duel, however, does not qualify as self-defense. A duel is a prearranged combat between two persons, with deadly weapons, usually "for the defense of honor," real or imaginary. Dueling is a sin more common in continental Europe than in the United States. In an effort to stamp out this evil, the Church has imposed excommunication on all who take part in a duel, not only the actual combatants but also the seconds and any other willing spectators who do not try their best to prevent or stop the duel.

It should be noted that the principle of self-defense applies only when we are the victim of an *unjust* attack. It never is permissible directly to take the life of an innocent person in order to save one's own. If I am shipwrecked with another person and there is only food enough for one, I may not kill the other person in order to save my own life. Neither may an unborn infant be directly killed in order to save the life of the mother. The unborn child is *not* an unjust aggressor against the mother and has a right to life as long as God permits him to live. To destroy the life of an unborn child directly and deliberately is a most grave sin; murder made more vicious by sending into eternity a soul with no opportunity for baptism. This is another sin which the Church has tried to check by imposing excommunication on all who have any willing part in it: not only the mother but also the co-operating father and any doctor or nurse involved.

What about capital punishment? Basically, capital punishment is an extension of the principle of self-defense. One of the duties of government is to protect citizens against unjust attack. Therefore a lawfully constituted government has the right, for the common good of its citizens, to take the life of a person who, in a fair trial, has been convicted of a grave crime. And the executioner who is delegated by the government to carry out such a sentence of death commits no sin. This does not mean that the Church favors or *advocates* capital punishment. The Church says that it is permitted but leaves it to governments to incorporate it in their laws as they may judge it expedient. There *is* sin involved, however, if private citizens take into their own hands the execution of a real or a supposed criminal. "Lynch law" has no place in God's law. All who take part in a lynching, even if only by their approving presence, are guilty of the sin of murder.

The principle of self-defense extends to nations as well as to individuals. Consequently a soldier who is fighting for his country in a just war does not sin if he must kill in the line of duty. A war is considered to be just (a) if it becomes necessary for a nation to defend its rights in a grave matter; (b) if war is undertaken only as a last resort after all other possible methods of settling the dispute have been tried; (c) if the war is waged in accordance with the dictates of the natural law and international law; and (d) if the war is stopped as soon as due satisfaction has been given or offered by the unjust aggressor nation. In practice it may sometimes be difficult for the average citizen to decide whether or not a war upon which his nation embarks is a just war. It is seldom that the common man knows all the ins and outs of the international situation. But, just as children in doubtful matters must give their parents the benefit of the doubt, so also, in doubt as to the justice of a war, the citizen must give his government the benefit of the doubt. Even in a just war, however, it is possible to sin by the use of unjust

means, such as the direct and indiscriminate bombing of non-combatants when there is no military target as objective.

Our life is not our own. It is a gift from God, and we are His stewards in the care of it. That is why we must do all that we reasonably can to safeguard our own life and the life of our neighbor. It is plain enough that we become guilty of sin if we deliberately do physical harm to another; guilty of a mortal sin if the injury we do is a serious one. That is why fighting is a sin against the fifth commandment, as well as a sin against the virtue of charity. And because anger, hatred, and revenge can so easily lead to doing physical injury to others, they also are sins against the fifth commandment in addition to being sins against charity. If a fort is to be defended (in this case, life), the approaches to the fort must also be defended. Consequently the fifth commandment proscribes *all* that might result in the unjust taking of life or unjust physical injury.

Some practical applications flow from this. It is evident that one who deliberately drives a car in a reckless manner is guilty of grave sin, since he exposes his own life and the lives of others to unnecessary danger. This would be true also of one who drives a car knowing that his faculties have been deadened by alcohol. The drunk driver is a sinner as well as a criminal. In fact, drunkenness itself is a sin against the fifth commandment, even when the sin is not aggravated by car-driving. Excessive drinking, as well as excessive eating, are sinful in the first place because they injure the health of the over-indulger. Excessive drinking much more easily becomes a mortal sin than excessive eating, because intemperance in drink can lead to many other evil effects. Drunkenness becomes a mortal sin when it so befuddles a person that he no longer knows what he is doing. But even a lesser degree of deliberate excess in drinking may be a mortal sin because of harmful consequences: damage to health, or scandal given, or duties to family or God neglected. The habitual and heavy drinker who judges himself free from

serious sin simply because he always knows the time of day usually is deceiving himself; it is very seldom that grave harm is not being done to himself or others by his constant drinking.

Our responsibility to God for the life He has given us requires that we take reasonable care of our health. To expose our health to danger, deliberately and unnecessarily, or to neglect seeking medical help when we know or suspect that we have an illness which could be cured would be to fail in our duty as God's stewards. There are, of course, people who become *too* preoccupied with their health, never happy unless they are taking medicine. We call them hypochondriacs. Their trouble is in their minds rather than in their bodies. They are to be pitied because their sufferings are very real to themselves.

The life of the *whole* body is more important than any of its parts; consequently, it is permissible to have an organ or a member removed in order to preserve life. Obviously, the amputation of a gangrenous leg or the excision of a tumored ovary is morally right. It is sinful, however, to mutilate the human body unnecessarily; mortally sinful if the mutilation is serious either in itself or in its effects. A man or a woman who would have an operation performed directly to cause sterility would be guilty of grave sin; as would also be the surgeon who performs such an operation. Some states have laws providing for the sterilization of the insane and feeble-minded. Such laws are contrary to God's law, since not even the government has the right to mutilate an innocent person. Much less has the government the right to kill or to permit the killing of an innocent person. So-called "euthanasia"—putting an incurable sufferer to death in order to end his misery—is a grave sin, even if the sufferer asks for it. *Life belongs to God.* If incurable suffering is part of God's plan for me, then neither I nor any human authority has the right to circumvent God's will.

Moving now from the realm of action to the realm of

thought, we note that hatred (bitter unforgivingness which wishes harm to another or rejoices in his misfortune) and vengefulness (which seeks ways to "get even" with another) almost always will be mortal sins. Theoretically it might be possible to hate "just a little" or to seek "just a little" revenge. But in practice the "just a little" is not so easily controlled.

The gravity of the sin of anger is not so simple to assess. Anger which is directed at an evil deed and not at a person (and which is not excessive) is no sin at all. This is what we call righteous anger. A good example is the anger of a parent (remember, not excessive!) at the misconduct of a child. The parent still loves the *child* but is angry at the child's wrong *conduct*. Anger, however, which is directed at persons—usually at someone who has hurt our pride or interfered with our convenience—and not at their evil deeds, is sinful anger. We may say, in general, that whenever we are angry because of what has been done to ourselves rather than because of what has been done to God, ours is the wrong kind of anger. Most such anger is of the unthinking and "flare-up" sort and is not grievously sinful. However, if we realize that we are sinfully angry at someone and we deliberately continue to feed and fan our anger, our sin does become grave. Or, if we have a hot temper by nature and we know we have a hot temper yet make no attempt to control it, then also we could easily become guilty of mortal sin.

There is one final way in which we may fail in our observance of the fifth commandment: by giving bad example. If it is a sin to kill or injure the body of our neighbor, it is even more serious to kill or to injure his soul. Any time that wrong words or actions of my own are such as to encourage sin in another, I myself become guilty of the sin of scandal, the sin of bad example; a mortal sin, if the possible harm I do is serious. Spiritually as well as physically, I *am* my brother's keeper.

CHAPTER XIX

The Sixth and Ninth Commandments of God

Commandments Six and Nine

There are two mistaken attitudes towards sex, both of them fairly common. One is the attitude of the modern hedonist—a hedonist being a person whose highest aim in life is pleasure. A hedonist looks upon the sexual power as a personal possession whose use is no one else's business except his own. To him (or her) the purpose of the genital organs is for self-gratification and physical thrills, nothing more. This is the attitude of the man-about-town and the bachelor girl of easy virtue, who dally often but never love. It is the attitude, too, of the men and women who appear often in the divorce courts, always seeking new worlds to conquer.

Then there is the other mistaken attitude, that of the prude, which looks upon sex as something nasty and degrading; as a necessary evil with which the human race has been saddled. The procreative faculty must be used, of course, for the propagation of the human race, but the act of physical union between husband and wife remains a defiling

sort of thing which hardly bears thinking of. This unfortunate pattern of thought usually is acquired in childhood through the misguided training methods of parents or teachers. In their efforts to train the child to purity, adults sometimes give a child the impression that the private parts of his body are bad and essentially shameful rather than special gifts from God to be reverenced and cherished. The child gathers that sex is something that "nice people don't talk about," not even in their own home or to their own parents. The worst feature of this state of mind is that it tends to be self-perpetuating; the child trained in such a tradition passes it on in turn to *his* children. It is a mistaken concept of sex that mars many an otherwise happy marriage.

The truth is that the procreative power is a wonderful gift with which God has endowed humanity. God didn't have to make the human race male and female. He could have made human beings a non-sexed type of being, Himself creating each body (as He does create each soul) by a direct act of His own. Instead, God in His goodness chose to share His creative power with mankind so that the beautiful institutions of marriage and parenthood might come into being. So that, too, through human fatherhood we might better understand the paternity of God, His justice and His providence; and through human motherhood, might better understand God's maternal tenderness, His mercy and compassion. So that the way might be paved, also, for the holy maternity of Mary, and so that in future time we might better understand the union between Christ and His Spouse the Church.

For all these reasons, and doubtless for other reasons buried in the depths of Divine Wisdom, God made man male and female. With Himself at the apex, God established a creative trinity—husband, wife, and Himself; husband and wife acting as God's instruments in the formation of a new human body, God in a sense standing by at their

beck and call, ready to create an immortal soul for the tiny body that, under God, their love has fashioned.

This is sex, *this* is marriage. Because it is the handiwork of God, sex is by its nature something good, something sacred and holy. It is not an evil thing, it is not a sordid and a tawdry affair. It is only when sex is torn from its holy framework of marriage and potential parenthood that evil and tawdriness enters in. It is not to the procreative power nor to the genital organs that the stigma of evil is attached; it is solely to the perverse human will that turns sex from its true purpose and seeks to use it as a mere tool for pleasure and self-gratification—like a drunk swilling beer from an altar-chalice.

Not that it is any sin for husband and wife (to whom, and *solely* to whom the exercise of the procreative faculty belongs)—not that it is a sin for husband and wife to seek and enjoy pleasure in their marital embrace. On the contrary, God has attached a keen physical pleasure to that act in order to ensure the perpetuation of the human race. With no impulsion from physical desire and no reward of immediate pleasure, spouses might be reluctant to use their God-given power in the face of the burdens of prospective parenthood. God's command to increase and multiply might be frustrated. Since God has *given* the pleasure, it is not a sin for husband and wife to enjoy the pleasure, so long as God's purpose is not positively excluded.

But for many people—and at one time or another probably for most people—that God-given pleasure poses a danger and a stumbling block. As a result of original sin, the perfect control which reason should exert over the body and its desires has been gravely weakened. Under the urgent proddings of rebellious flesh, there is a hunger for the pleasure of sex, regardless of God's purposes and regardless of the strict limitation (within Christian marriage) which God placed upon the use of sex. In other words, we are afflicted with temptations against the virtue of chastity.

intends someday to pay back what he "borrows," still is guilty of a sin.

Following the principle that anything which deprives another against his will of what is his is a sin if deliberate, we can see that there are many other ways besides stealing in which the seventh commandment may be violated. To break a lawful contract or business agreement with another would be such a sin if it causes a loss to the other party. It also would be a sin for a person to incur debts which he knows he cannot pay—a not uncommon sin in this age of living beyond one's means. It likewise would be a sin to damage or destroy another's property deliberately.

Then there is the sin of cheating: depriving another of what is his, by deceit, by fraud. To this category belong such practices as short-weight, short-measure, short-change, cheapening a product without cheapening the price, misrepresenting merchandise (used-car salesmen—in fact, salesmen in general—need to be on their guard against this) and selling at exorbitant profits, passing counterfeit money, selling worthless stock, and all the swindles and get-rich-quick schemes so prolific in American life. It is a form of cheating, too, for an employer to underpay his help, refusing them a living wage simply because a plentiful labor market makes it possible for him to be able to say, "If you don't like it here, then get out." And workmen who *do* receive a just wage become guilty of sin if they deliberately waste an employer's time or materials and fail to give a fair day's work for a fair day's wage.

Public officials are another class of persons who need to be especially mindful of the seventh commandment. Public officials are chosen by (and paid by) the citizens for the purpose of executing the laws and administering public affairs in an impartial and conscientious manner, for the greatest good of all. An official who accepts bribes—however sweetly the bribes may be disguised—in exchange for political favors is betraying the trust of those who have elected or appointed him. He sins against the seventh commandment; as he also would sin who would demand a "kick-back" from the salaries of lesser office-holders.

Two other failures in justice will complete the major offenses against the seventh commandment. One is the receiving of goods which we know to be stolen, whether the stolen goods are given to us freely or whether we pay for them; and strong suspicion is equivalent to knowledge in this respect. In the eyes of God, the receiver of stolen goods becomes equally guilty with the thief. It is a sin also to keep *found* articles for ourselves without making a reasonable effort to find the owner. The extent of such an effort (inquiry and advertisement) will, of course, depend upon the value of the article; and the owner, if discovered, is bound to reimburse the finder for whatever expenses his inquiries have entailed.

We cannot measure moral evil with a yardstick—nor compute it on an adding machine. So when someone asks, "How much of a theft does it take to make a mortal sin?" there is no quick and ready answer. We cannot say, "Anything up to $49.99 will be venial sin; from $50.00 up will be a mortal sin." We can only say in general that the theft of something of small value will be venially sinful; the theft of something of great worth (whether the great worth is *relative* or *absolute*) will be a mortal sin. This, of course, will be true not only of actual theft but of all other sins against property rights: deliberate damage to another's property, cheating, receiving stolen goods, and so on.

When we speak of the *relative* worth of something, we are referring to the value which it has considering the circumstances. For an ordinary workingman with a family to support, the loss of a day's wages would normally be a serious loss. To rob or cheat him of the equivalent of a day's pay could easily be a mortal sin. The gravity of the sin of dishonesty, then, is measured by the harm it does to the one who is deprived, as well as by the actual value involved.

But, in judging the worth of a thing (or of an amount of money), we reach a point where all reasonable persons will agree that the value is considerable—whether it is a rich man or a poor man who suffers the loss. This is what we term the *absolute* value, the value regardless of circumstances. It is here that the shading between mortal sin and venial sin becomes a matter known only to God. We can say with certainty that it is a venial sin to steal a nickel and that it is a mortal sin to steal a hundred dollars—even from the General Motors Corporation; where exactly to put the dividing line no man can say. Ten years ago, theologians were agreed that fifty dollars or more would be absolutely grave matter; injustice at that point and beyond would be a mortal sin. However, a dollar today is worth much less than it was ten years ago, and theology books cannot be revised on a monthly "cost-of-living" index. The obvious conclusion is that, if we are scrupulously honest in all our dealings with our fellowman, we shall never need to ask, "Was it a mortal or a venial sin?" For him who *has* sinned against justice, another obvious conclusion is to be sorry for the sin, confess it, make good the injustice, and not do it again.

Which brings us to the question of restitution—the paying back of what we have gotten dishonestly or damaged unjustly. True sorrow for sins against the seventh commandment must always include the intention to pay back as soon as possible (right *now* if we can) the fruits of our dishonesty. Without that sincere intention on the part of the penitent, the sacrament of Penance is powerless to forgive a sin of injustice. If the sin has been a mortal sin and the thief or the cheater dies without having made any attempt at restitution even when he could have done so, then he dies in the state of mortal sin. He has bartered away his eternal happiness in exchange for his dishonest gains.

Even a venial sin of injustice cannot be forgiven unless restitution is made or sincerely intended. The person who dies with petty thefts or frauds unatoned for will find that the price he has to pay in Purgatory for his chicanery is far beyond whatever illicit profits he may have realized during life. Concerning venial sins against the seventh commandment, we might point out in passing that even small thefts can become mortally sinful if there is a continuous series of such thefts within a brief period of time, which, in the aggregate, amount to a large total. A person who dishonestly acquired the value of a dollar or two a day over a period of several weeks would be guilty of mortal sin if the total value reached the amount of gravely sinful matter.

There are certain fundamental principles governing the matter of restitution. First is the principle that restitution must be made *to the person who suffered the loss*—or to his heirs if he is dead. But suppose that the person cannot now be found, even by diligent inquiry, or his heirs are unknown. Then another principle comes into play: a person may not profit by his own dishonesty. If the true owner is unknown or cannot be found, then restitution must be made by giving the illicit gains to charity—for example, by donating the amount to the St. Vincent de Paul Society. It is not required that the person making restitution expose his dishonesty or ruin his reputation to do so; he can make restitution anonymously, by mail or through a third party or in any other way that will protect his good name. Nor is it required that a person deprive himself or his family of the ordinary necessities of life in order to make restitution. It would be very wrong to spend money on superfluities or luxuries until restitution has been made; on fur coats or new cars. But this does not mean living on canned beans and sleeping on park benches.

Another principle is that the article itself which was stolen (if it was an article) must be restored to the owner, together with any natural profit which resulted from the article; the calves, for example, from a stolen cow. It is only when the article itself is no longer in existence or damaged beyond use that restitution may be made in cash value instead.

Perhaps enough has been said to indicate how complicated questions sometimes can be which pertain to matters of justice and rights. In practice, in particular cases, it is best to consult a priest. And we should not be surprised, in matters that are involved, if even the priest has to consult his theology books.

CHAPTER XXI

The Eighth Commandment of God

Nothing But the Truth

The fifth commandment forbids many other things besides outright murder. The sixth commandment applies to many other sins besides marital infidelity. The seventh commandment extends to many dishonest actions besides simple theft. The commandments, as we know, are intended as memory helps. Each commandment mentions one specific sin against the virtue to which the commandment applies; and we are expected to use the commandment as a sort of shelf upon which we can gather together all other sins against the same virtue.

We would expect the eighth commandment to be of the same nature—and it is. *"Thou shalt not bear false witness against thy neighbor"* explicitly forbids the sin of slander or calumny—the damaging of our neighbor's reputation by lying about him. However, there are many other ways besides slander in which we can sin against the virtue of truthfulness and against charity in speech and action.

Calumny is one of the worst sins against the eighth commandment, because it combines a sin against truthfulness (lying) with a sin against justice (damaging another's good name) and a sin against charity (failure in love of neighbor). Calumny hurts our neighbor where the pain is keenest—in his reputation. If we steal a man's money, he may be angry and he may be sad, but normally he can go out and earn some money. When we cast a shadow on a man's good name, we have robbed him of something that all the sweat in the world may not be able to restore. As we can readily perceive, the sin of calumny is a mortal sin if by our slander we *seriously* hurt our neighbor in the esteem of only one other person. It is true even if our neighbor himself is unaware of what we have done.

In fact it is true even if we seriously hurt our neighbor's reputation deliberately and unjustly, only in our own mind. This is the sin of rash judgment, a sin concerning which many people, it is to be feared, neglect to examine themselves when preparing for confession. If someone does an unexpected kind deed and I think to myself, "I wonder whom he's trying to hook now?" I have been guilty of rash judgment. If someone performs an act of generosity and I say to myself, "There he goes, trying to act like a big shot," I have sinned against the eighth commandment. Not mortally, perhaps; although it easily can be a mortal sin if another's reputation suffers *seriously* in my own mind because of my unjust judgments.

Detraction is another sin against the eighth commandment. Detraction consists of hurting our neighbor's reputation by unnecessarily telling something discreditable about him which is *true* but which is not commonly known. For example, I tell my friends or neighbors about the awful quarrels which the couple next door are always having and how the husband always comes home drunk on Saturday nights. There may be times when, for purposes of correction or prevention, it is necessary to reveal the faults of others. It may be necessary to tell a father about the bad company his son has been keeping. It may be necessary to tell the police about a certain person who was seen sneaking out of the burglarized store. It may be necessary to warn neighborhood parents that the newcomer on the street has a court record for molesting children. But, often, when we begin by saying, "I think I ought to tell you this . . . ," what we really mean is, "I'm dying to tell you this—but I can't admit even to myself that I love to gossip." Even though a person may have hurt his own reputation, so to speak, by doing something disgraceful, it still is a sin for me to spread knowledge of his fault without necessity—somewhat as it would still be a sin for me to steal, even though I stole from a thief. It is not, of course, a sin of detraction to discuss matters which are common knowledge to everyone, such as the crime of a person who has been convicted in court of wrongdoing. Even in such cases, however, charity directs us to condemn the sin rather than the sinner and to pray for the wrongdoer.

There are sins of the ear, as well as sins of the mouth and mind, against the eighth commandment. We become guilty of sin if we listen with pleasure to slander and detraction even though we say nothing ourselves. Our very silence is an encouragement to the spreader of malicious gossip. If our pleasure in listening springs merely from curiosity, the sin would be a venial one. If our eager attention were motivated by hatred for the person being defamed, the sin would be mortal. Our duty, when someone's character is attacked in our presence, is to try to change the subject or otherwise show that we are not interested in listening.

Personal insult also is a sin against the eighth commandment. (Theologians prefer the term "contumely.") This sin against our neighbor is committed in his presence and has many forms. In speech or in action we may refuse him the marks of decent respect or friendship that are due him, as by "cutting him dead" or ignoring his outstretched hand, by speaking to him rudely or abusively, by calling him opprobrious names. A similar sin of lesser degree is spiteful criticism and faultfinding, a sin which in some persons seems to become an established habit.

Talebearing is still another sin against the eighth commandment. This is the sin of the trouble-loving busybody who tells Joe what Jack said about him. Here again the talebearing usually is prefaced with, "I think you ought to know . . . ," when actually it would be much better for Joe if he *didn't* know the nasty crack that Jack made about him, a crack that probably was tossed off thoughtlessly in a moment of irritation. "Blessed are the peacemakers, for they shall be called children of God" is a good quotation to remember here.

A *simple* lie—a lie which does no harm and is not told under oath—is a venial sin. Simple lies are the kind that braggarts tell about themselves (and sometimes fishermen tell). They are the lies which people tell to save embarrassment to themselves or to someone else. They are the lies of which practical jokers are fond. Whatever may be the reason for departing from the truth, a lie is always a sin. God gave us the gift of communicating our thoughts to others in order that we might communicate truth. Any time we use speech or actions to comunicate falsehood we are abusing one of God's gifts; we sin.

It follows that there is no such thing as "a little white lie." Moral evil, even the moral evil of a venial sin, is greater than any possible physical evil. It would not be permissible for me to commit even a venial sin in order to save the whole world from destruction. However, it should be mentioned that I may, without sin, give a false answer to someone who is *unjustly* trying to get the truth from me. What I say in this instance may be false, but it is not a lie. It is a lawful means of self-defense when there is no other alternative.

Neither am I obliged always to tell *all* of the truth. Unfortunately, there are many nosy people in the world who ask questions which they have no right to ask. To such persons it is quite legitimate to give an evasive answer. If some-one asks me how much money I've got (I suspect he wants to make a touch) and I tell him that I've got five dollars when actually I have fifty, I tell no lie. I *have* got five dollars; I just don't tell him about the other forty-five. Obviously, however, it would be a lie to say that I have fifty when I have only five.

There are certain conventional phrases, too, which on the face of them might appear to be lies but which are not lies because all intelligent people understand what they mean. "I don't know" is an example of such a phrase. An intelligent person understands that "I don't know" may mean either of two things: I *really* don't know or I am not at liberty to tell. This is the answer that a priest—or a doctor or lawyer or parent—might give to someone seeking information which is confidential. A similar phrase is "Not at home." To be "not at home" may mean that the person really is away or that he is not seeing visitors. It is not a sin if Mary tells the caller at the door that mother is not at home; Mary doesn't have to tell the caller that mother is in the bathtub or in the basement washing clothes. A person who is deceived by phrases such as these (and there are others, universally understood) is not *being* deceived; he deceives himself.

The same principle would apply to a person who accepts as true a story which is told as a joke and which so obviously is a joke that any intelligent person should recognize it as such. For example, if I say that back home on the farm our corn grew so high that we had to harvest with helicopters, anyone who accepts that as a fact is plainly deceiving himself. However, joking lies can be real lies—and sinful—if it is not plain to the listener that I am joking.

Another possible sin against the eighth commandment is the revealing of a secret which has been entrusted to me. My obligation to secrecy may arise from a promise made, or from my profession (doctor, lawyer, newsman, etc.), or simply because charity forbids that I make known what would offend or hurt another. The only times I might reveal such a secret without sin would be when it was necessary in order to prevent grave harm—to the community, to an innocent third party, or to the holder of the secret himself. Akin to this sin is the sin of reading another's mail without his permission and the sin of deliberately listening-in on a private conversation. In all these instances, the gravity of the sin will be proportionate to the harm done or the offense given.

Before we close the book on the eighth commandment, we must recall that this commandment, like the seventh, *obliges us to restitution*. If I have hurt another, whether by slander, detraction, insult, or revealing his secret, my sin cannot be forgiven unless I intend to make good the harm I have done, to the best of my ability. This holds true even though, in making restitution, I must suffer humiliation or other harm myself. If I have slandered, I must broadcast the fact that I was grossly mistaken. If I have detracted, I must, by honest praise and pleas for charity, try to outbalance the effects of my detraction. If I have insulted, I must apologize; publicly, if the insult was a public one. If I have violated a secret, I must repair the harm in whatever way I can and as far as I can.

All of which should lead us to renewed determination in two resolutions which we have no doubt long ago made: never to open our mouths except to say what we honestly believe to be true; and never to speak about our neighbor, even the *truth* about him, unless what we say is to his credit; or, if it is detrimental to his character, is called for because of some grave reason.

CHAPTER XXII

The Commandments of the Church

Laws of the Church

Occasionally we meet persons who seem to think that the laws of the Church are less binding upon us than are the laws of God. "It is only a law of the Church," such a one is likely to say. "Only a law of the Church" is a nonsense phrase. The laws of the Church are practically the same as the laws of God, because they are applications of these laws. One of the reasons Jesus established His Church was precisely this: to make whatever laws would be necessary to implement His teachings—whatever laws would be necessary for the good of souls. As a reminder of this we have only to recall Christ's words, "He who hears you, hears Me; and he who rejects you, rejects Me" (Luke 10:16). It was to His Church, in the person of the apostles, that Christ was speaking. The laws of the Church, then, have all the authority of our Lord behind them. To break a law of the Church deliberately is just as truly a sin as to break one of the Ten Commandments.

How many laws of the Church are there? Most people

probably would answer "six," since that is the number listed in the Catechism. Actually, there are 2,214 laws of the Church. They are contained in an official book called the Code of Canon Law. These laws cover many phases of Catholic life—when, how, and by whom the various sacraments may be received, vows may be taken, convents and monasteries may be established and governed, and hundreds of other matters pertaining to right order within Christ's Church. Many of these laws we learn in connection with our study of the Mass and the sacraments. Many others have no particular bearing on the life of the layman. But compilers of the Catechism have singled out six of these laws for our special attention—the ones which we commonly call the six commandments of the Church. They are: (1) to assist at Mass on all Sundays and holydays of obligation; (2) to fast and to abstain on the days appointed; (3) to confess our sins at least once a year; (4) to receive Holy Communion during the Easter time; (5) to contribute to the support of the Church; and (6) to observe the laws of the Church concerning marriage.

The obligation to assist at Mass on Sundays—an obligation which begins for every Catholic at the age of seven—has been discussed under the third commandment of the decalogue: "Remember thou keep holy the Lord's day." There is no need to repeat that discussion here, but it may be useful to say a word or two concerning the holydays of obligation.

In her role of spiritual guide, it is the duty of the Church to make our faith a *living* faith; to make real and vital the persons and events which have gone into the making of Christ's Mystical Body. For this reason the Church sets aside a certain few days of the year to be observed as sacred days. On these days the Church recalls to our minds certain great events in the lives of Jesus Himself, or of His Blessed Mother, or of the saints. The Church underlines the need for such periodic recollection by making these days of equal dignity with the Lord's day—commanding us, under pain of mortal sin, to assist at Mass, and to abstain, if possible, from our everyday work.

In the calendar of the Church there are ten such days, and in most Catholic countries all ten are observed. In our own country, however, the Church has eased the burden of the American workingman (whose employer will take no cognizance of holydays) and has reduced the number of holydays of obligation to six: Christmas (December 25), when we celebrate the birth of our Lord; the Circumcision (January 1), when we commemorate the official bestowal on Jesus of His Holy Name; Ascension Thursday (forty days after Easter), when we mark our Lord's glorious return to heaven; the Assumption (August 15), when we rejoice at our Blessed Mother's bodily entrance into heaven; All Saints' Day (November 1), when we honor *all* the saints in heaven, including our own loved ones there; and the Immaculate Conception (December 8), when we commemorate the fact that God created Mary's soul free from original sin—the first step in our redemption.

Besides holydays there are other days of special significance to Catholics. These are the fast days and the days of abstinence. In reading the Gospels we must have noticed how, time and again, our Lord commands us to do penance for our sins. We ask: "Yes, but *how* shall we do penance?" The Church, fulfilling her duty as our guide and teacher, establishes a minimum of penance that all of us, within certain set limits, must perform. She does so by setting aside certain days as days of abstinence (when we may eat no meat); other days as days of fast (when we may eat only one full meal); and still other days as days of both fast and abstinence.

Since Friday is the day on which our Saviour died, the Church has chosen Friday as our weekly day of abstinence. Deliberately to eat meat (or meat products, such as gravy or soup made with meat) on a day of abstinence is a mortal sin if the amount taken is a significant one. But even a small amount—a few spoonfuls of meat soup, for example—would be a venial sin if taken deliberately.

The days which are *fast* days (but not days of abstinence) are the weekdays of Lent (except Fridays—which are days of fast *and* abstinence). On these days we are limited to one full meal, at which we may eat meat. If we are exempted from fasting, we may eat meat as often as we wish. On a fast day, besides the main meal, those obliged to fast may have two other light meals without meat—which together should amount to less than the main meal. In the United States, the Wednesdays and Saturdays of Ember weeks and the vigil of Pentecost are days of fast and *partial* abstinence. On these days meat is allowed only at the main meal, even for those who may be exempted from fasting.

Finally there are the days of fast and *complete* abstinence. The Fridays of Lent and of Ember weeks are such, obviously. In addition, Ash Wednesday, Holy Saturday,[1] and the vigils of Assumption and Christmas are days of both fast and complete abstinence. On these days even our full meal must be a meatless one.

Sick persons who need the nourishment, those engaged in exteremely hard work, and those who have to eat what they can get (the poor, for example) are excused from the laws of fasting and abstinence. Others, for whom fasting or abstaining would present a serious problem, may obtain a dispensation from their pastor or confessor. The obligation to abstain begins at the age of seven and continues for life; the obligation to fast begins at the age of twenty-one and ends at the age of fifty-nine.

The law pertaining to yearly confession means this: anyone who is obliged to confess a mortal sin explicitly, becomes guilty of a new mortal sin if he lets more than a year elapse without again receiving the sacrament of Penance. Plainly the Church does not intend to say that yearly con-

[1] Sometimes a Bishop will dispense to the extent of making Holy Saturday a day of fast only—or a day of fast and partial abstinence.

fession is sufficient for practicing Catholics. The sacrament of Penance builds up in us a resistance to temptation and enables us to grow in virtue if we receive it often. It is a sacrament for saints as well as for sinners.

However, the Church does want to make sure that no one goes on indefinitely living in the state of mortal sin at a constant peril to his eternal salvation. Hence the Church requires that anyone conscious of having a mortal sin to be confessed explicitly (even though the sin may already have been remitted by perfect contrition) must receive the sacrament of Penance within a year. Similarly, in her concern for souls, the Church establishes an absolute minimum of once a year for the receiving of Holy Communion. Jesus Himself said, "Unless you eat the flesh of the Son of Man, and drink His blood, you shall not have life in you" (John 6:54). There are no ifs or ands there. Either members of Christ's Mystical Body receive Holy Communion or they do not go to heaven. We naturally ask, "How often should I receive Holy Communion?" Christ through His Church then answers us: "As often as you can; weekly, even daily, if possible. But as an absolute minimum you *must* receive Holy Communion at least once a year—and that during the Easter time; in the United States between the first Sunday of Lent and Trinity Sunday." If we fail to give Jesus this minimum of love, then we become guilty of a mortal sin.

Another of our obligations—to contribute to the support of the Church—flows from the very nature of our membership in Christ's Mystical Body. In Baptism and again in Confirmation, Jesus has made us sharers in His mission of saving souls. We are not truly Christ's own unless we are willing to help Him, with material means as well as with labors and prayers, to carry on His work. Normally, we discharge the obligation of material support by giving, as generously as our means allow, to the various collections taken up in our own parish church and in our own diocese. These will include not only offerings for the church and school of our own parish but also contributions to the Holy

Father and his world-wide needs, as well as collections for the foreign missions, for the sick and the poor and the homeless. If we ask, "How much should I give?" there is no answer except the reminder that God will never let us outdo Him in generosity.

That He might be with us always with the power of His grace, Jesus fashioned for us the seven sacraments. He confided the sacraments into the keeping of His Church. He gave to His Church the authority and the duty to make the necessary laws which would govern the giving of the sacraments and the receiving of them. Matrimony is one of these sacraments. It is important for us to realize that the Church laws regulating the reception of the sacrament of Matrimony are not mere man-made rules. They are Christ's own directives, given through His Church.

The basic law governing the sacrament of Matrimony is that it must be received in the presence of an authorized priest and two other witnesses. By "authorized" priest is meant the pastor of the parish where the marriage takes place, or a priest delegated by such pastor or by the bishop of the diocese. Just "any priest" may not officiate at a Catholic wedding. Marriage is too serious a commitment to be entered into by the mere ringing of any rectory doorbell. Normally, the sacrament of Matrimony is followed by a Nuptial Mass and the Nuptial blessing. The Nuptial Mass and blessing are not permitted, however, during the penitential seasons of Lent and Advent. The sacrament of Matrimony can be received during those times, but most Catholics are anxious to begin married life with all the grace possible. Hence it is rare that Catholics seek to receive the sacrament of Matrimony during Lent or Advent.

To receive Matrimony validly, the male spouse must be at least sixteen years of age, the feminine partner at least fourteen. However, if the civil law sets a higher age, the Church will respect that law though not be strictly bound to obey it. The preparedness of a boy and girl to take on the responsibility of a family is of civil as well as spiritual importance.

In the matter of marriage, when the civil effects are in question, the Church recognizes the right of the government to make necessary regulations.

Besides being of the necessary age, the prospective spouses must not be related by blood more closely than third cousins. However, the Church will for serious reasons grant a dispensation for first or second cousins to marry. The Church also will dispense, with reason, if the couple are related by Baptism (one the godparent of the other) or by marriage (as a widower and his sister-in-law), both of which relationships are impediments to marriage.

The laws of marriage also require that a Catholic marry a Catholic. The Church does grant, for a grave reason, a dispensation for a Catholic to marry one who is not a Catholic. In such an instance, the non-Catholic partner must give a written guarantee not to interfere with the religious faith and practice of the Catholic spouse. Both partners must give written assurance that all their children will be raised Catholics. The Catholic party must promise to work, by prayer and good example, for the conversion of the non-Catholic. Even with such safeguards, the result of a mixed marriage often is the weakening or loss of faith on the part of the Catholic spouse; or loss of faith on the part of children who see their parents divided on the matter of religion; or lack of complete happiness in the marriage because a basic ingredient, unity of faith, is lacking. It is with the reluctance of a Mother who has nineteen hundred years of sad experience behind her that the Church grants a dispensation for a mixed marriage.

The most essential thing to remember is that there just is no true marriage for a Catholic except "marriage by the priest," as we commonly say. A Catholic married by the judge or minister is not really married at all—not in the eyes of God, who is the One who counts. A Catholic living in such a union is living in the state of habitual sin, regardless of the outward respectability which the civil law may accord.

PART THREE _____

THE

SACRAMENTS

AND PRAYER

CHAPTER XXIII

The Sacraments

We Begin the Sacraments

Theology, the science which treats of God and man's relationship to God, covers three broad fields. There are first of all *the truths we must believe*. These are the truths revealed by God through His prophets, and especially through His Son, our Lord Jesus Christ, and His Apostles, and taught to us by Christ through His Church. These are the truths summarized for us in the Apostles' Creed.

But it is not enough to believe with a merely passive faith. If our faith has real meaning for us, it will move us to action. The second broad field of theology, therefore, concerns itself with *what we must do* in the light of what we believe. It examines our duties to God, to ourselves, and to our neighbor—duties imposed by God Himself in His commandments—and His further directives given through His Church.

Having progressed that far in our investigation of religion, we might be tempted to discouragement. The loftiness of divine truths so taxes our limited human intelligence; the moral code, particularly the Great Law of Love, is so opposed to weak human nature's self-attachment. But our discouragement dies a-borning as we enter the third broad field of theology and discover *the helps which God gives us* to enable us to believe and to do. It is here that we learn what God has done, through His sacraments, to provide us with His grace. It is here that we learn what we ourselves may do, through prayer and penance and almsgiving, to augment that grace. This is the field of theology that deals with the sacraments and prayer.

We know that God, having made us with free wills, continues to respect our free will to the end. When Jesus died upon the Cross to redeem us from our sins, it did not mean that from then on everyone would *have* to go to Heaven whether he wanted to or not. It did not mean that God took back our physical freedom, so that we would *have* to be good—in spite of ourselves if necessary. What it did mean, when Jesus died upon the Cross, was that infinite atonement had been made for the infinite evil of man's rebellion against God; and that an infinite price had been paid for an inexhaustible flow of grace which would enable each man to turn back to God and to remain united with God through this life and through eternity.

That brings us to the question of means to be used. How would Jesus provide for this flow of grace to individual souls —this grace which would both reconcile us to God and maintain us in union with God despite human weakness? Would the whole thing be invisible? Would God, in view of the merits of His divine Son, simply give to each person of good will a silent inner conviction of being saved? And each time that we felt the need of divine help, would we simply ask for it and immediately feel welling up within us a great surge of spiritual strength?

God could have done it that way, of course; no one can put limits upon God's power. But God chose to be consistent. He chose to deal with man, in this matter of grace, in the same manner in which He had made man—through a union of the material and the spiritual, of body and of soul. We are citizens of two worlds, living now in the world of visible things from which our knowledge comes to us, even our knowledge of God; yet citizens, too, of an invisible world which is to be our permanent abode. It is in accordance with this duality of nature that Jesus provided for the dispensing of His grace. The grace itself would be invisible, as by its nature it must be; but it would be through the visible things with which we deal daily that the grace would come to us.

There is another reason—in fact there are two reasons—why God in His wisdom chose to bestow His grace in a visible way. By doing so He would protect us against self-deception on the one hand, so that we might not assume that we had received grace when really we hadn't; and on the other hand He would give us the quieting certainty that we *had* received grace when He did give it. We know what torture it would be for most of us if we had to flounder through life tormented by doubt as to our status with God and our prospects for eternity.

And so God took the common things from the world about us—objects which we could taste and touch and feel, words that we could hear and gestures that we could understand—and made these the carriers of His grace. He even proportioned the sign to the purpose for which the grace was given: water for the grace which cleanses, the appearances of bread and wine for the grace which nourishes and gives growth, oil for the grace which strengthens. To this combination of outward sign and inner grace, welded together by Christ, the Church gives the Latin name of "sacramentum"—a holy thing. With this background, we embark upon our excursion into the realm of sacramental theology.

Sometimes we can get a better understanding of a thing by taking it apart and examining it piece by piece. It is not a very wise procedure with watches or automobiles unless we are expert mechanics; but with a sacrament we can be quite sure of getting the pieces back together again.

The exact definition of a sacrament is that it is "an outward sign instituted by Christ to give grace." We readily can see that there are three distinct ideas contained in that short definition. "Outward sign" is the first one; "instituted by Christ" is the second; and "to give grace" is the third. Taking them one by one, we can begin by asking, "Is there anything special to be known about the outward signs?"

The outward signs, we recall, are God's way of treating us like the human beings we are: conveying His unseen grace into our spiritual souls through material symbols which our physical bodies can perceive—things and words and gestures. In the signs which constitute the physical part of a sacrament, theologians distinguish two elements. There is the "thing" itself which is used, and this is called the "matter" of the sacrament; for example, the application of water to a person being baptized. We can see that this action in itself is meaningless unless its purpose is in some way specified. We might simply be giving the person a shower bath, or wetting down his hair preparatory to combing it, or playing a practical joke. There has to be some word or gesture that will give *meaning* to what we do. This second element in the sign of a sacrament—the words or gestures which give significance to what is being done—is called the "form" of the sacrament. In Baptism the application of the water is the *matter* of the sacrament; the words, "I baptize thee in the name of the Father and of the Son and of the Holy Ghost," are the *form* of the sacrament. The two together make up the "outward sign."

We know that no human power, not even the divinely guided but humanly applied power of the Church, could attach an inward grace to an outward sign. This is something that only God can do; which brings us to the second element in the definition of a sacrament: "instituted by Christ." Between the time He began His public life and the time He ascended into heaven, Jesus fashioned the seven sacraments. When He ascended into heaven, that put a period to the making of sacraments. The Church cannot institute new sacraments. There never can be more or less than seven, the seven Jesus has given us: Baptism, Confirmation, Holy Eucharist, Penance, Extreme Unction, Holy Orders, and Matrimony.

Although Jesus did completely specify the matter and form of some of the sacraments—notably Baptism and the Holy Eucharist—this does not mean that He necessarily fixed the matter and form of all the sacraments down to the last detail. Concerning some of the sacraments (Confirmation, for example) He probably left it to His Church, the keeper and the giver of His sacraments, to specify in detail the broad matter and form assigned by Christ.

Coming now to the third element in the definition of a sacrament, we have its essential purpose: "to give grace." Unless it gives grace of itself, as a chosen instrument of divine power, an outward sign is not a sacrament, even though it were instituted by Jesus Himself. We have an example of this in the so-called "mandatum"—the washing of feet on Holy Thursday. This is a ceremony which was instituted by Christ Himself at the Last Supper, but it does not of itself give grace and so remains a sacramental rather than a sacrament.

What kind of grace do the sacraments give? First and most important of all, they give *sanctifying grace*. Sanctifying grace, we will remember, is that marvelous supernatural life, that sharing-in-God's-own-life that is the result of God's Love, the Holy Spirit, indwelling in the soul. To the soul cut off from God by original sin Baptism brings sanctifying grace for the first time. Baptism opens the soul to the flow of God's love, and establishes union between the soul and God. To the soul cut off from God by its own sin, by mortal sin, the sacrament of Penance restores the sanctifying grace that has been lost. Penance removes the barrier that has kept the Holy Spirit outside and once again gives entrance to God's life-giving love. Because these two sacraments can be received when the soul is spiritually without life, they sometimes are called "the sacraments of the dead."

The other five sacraments—Confirmation, Holy Eucharist, Extreme Unction, Holy Orders, and Matrimony—give an *increase* in sanctifying grace. These five (and Penance, too, if the soul already is free from mortal sin) deepen and intensify the spiritual life of sanctifying grace which already pulsates through the soul. As each additional sacrament is received (and repeated, when it can be) the level of spiritual vitality rises in the soul—somewhat as the brightness of a light increases with each turn of the rheostat. God's *love* does not increase; it is infinite to begin with. But the soul's capacity to absorb His love increases as a child's capacity for life increases with each meal that he eats. These five sacraments, since they can be received worthily and fruitfully only by a soul already in the state of sanctifying grace, often are termed "sacraments of the living."

Why Seven Sacraments?

If each sacrament gives (or increases) sanctifying grace in the soul, then why did Jesus institute *seven* sacraments? Wouldn't just one sacrament have been enough, to be received as needed?

Yes, one sacrament would have been enough, if sanctifying grace were the only kind of grace God wanted to give us. If the spiritual aliveness which constitutes sanctifying grace had been the only help God intended us to have, then one sacrament would have been sufficient. But God, from Whom all parenthood takes its meaning, did not choose simply to give us spiritual life and then let us shift for ourselves. Parents do not say to the newborn baby; "We have given you life; from now on it's up to you. There'll be no food when you're hungry; no medicine when you are sick; no supporting hand when you are weak. Just go ahead and live as long as you can."

God gives us the spiritual life which is sanctifying grace and then does all that He can (short of taking away our free will) to make that life operative within us; all that He can to expand that life and intensify it; all that He can to preserve and protect it. Consequently, in addition to the sanctifying grace which is common to all the sacraments, there are other special helps which God wills to give us, helps keyed to our particular spiritual needs and our particular state in life. The specific kind of help which each sacrament gives is called the "sacramental grace" of that particular sacrament.

At this point it might be interesting to pause and to ask ourselves, "Now, if God had left it up to me to decide how many sacraments there ought to be, how many sacraments would *I* have designed?" We might, of course, decide on three or five or ten or some other number; but, thinking of our spiritual needs in terms of our human needs, it is very possible that we, too, might come up with a total of seven, even as did God.

The first thing that happens to us, in the natural order, is that we are born. In birth, we not only receive life but also the power to *renew* life—the regenerative power by which bodily cells are continuously replaced and repaired and life is continued. It would seem to us very apposite, then, that there should be a sacrament which not only would give us spiritual life (sanctifying grace) but also would confer upon us the power (sacramental grace) to preserve and ceaselessly to renew that life. It is no surprise to discover that God has given us such a sacrament—Baptism—in which we not only receive sanctifying grace but also a continuing chain of graces enabling us to preserve and extend that grace by the practice of the virtues of faith, hope, and charity.

After birth, the next great thing that happens to us in the physical order is that we grow up, we mature. Should we not then have a sacrament which confers spiritual maturity, freeing us from childhood fears and weaknesses, making us strong and fearless and apostolic in the profession and practice of our faith? It is quite in line with our own reasoning to find that we have such a sacrament—Confirmation—which not only increases our basic vitality (sanctifying grace) but also establishes a permanent fund of actual graces (sacramental grace) upon which we may draw in order to be strong and active and *productive* exemplars of Christian living.

After birth and maturity the third great phenomenon of our physical being is death: we are born, we grow up, we die. To prepare us to meet with confidence that dreaded moment of physical dissolution, we have the sacrament of Extreme Unction, with its own special sacramental grace which comforts us in our sufferings and, by supporting us in any final temptations that may assail us, enables us to face eternity unafraid.

Besides the three great epochs of life, there are the two great needs of life: the need for food so that we may grow and be healthy, and the need for medicine, that we may be cured of sickness and inoculated against disease. Behold, we do have two sacraments which do for us spiritually what food and medicine do for us physically: the sacrament of the Holy Eucharist, whose special sacramental grace is growth in supernatural charity (love for God and neighbor); and the sacrament of Penance—inoculation against sin—whose special sacramental grace is to cure us of the spiritual illness of sin and to help us resist temptation.

Besides the three great stages in life and the two crucial needs of life, there are the two great *states* in life which impose upon us grave responsibility for the souls of others: the priesthood and marriage. And so we are quite prepared to discover that there are two sacraments, Holy Orders and Matrimony, which give to their recipients each its own sacramental grace, which will enable priests and spouses to discharge, creditably before God, the sometimes heavy burdens of their state in life.

As we can see, the "sacramental grace" of a sacrament is not something that we receive all at once. It is, rather, a moral claim upon God (something like a membership card in an auto club) for whatever help we need, *as and when we need it,* to fulfill the particular purpose of that particular sacrament. It gives us a right to a *chain* of actual graces. That chain of grace will be long or short, depending on whether the sacrament is one which can be received only once (or seldom) or very often.

If you dip your finger in holy water and make the sign of the cross, you will receive grace; actual grace always if you do not resist it, and also an increase in sanctifying grace if you already are free from mortal sin and you perform the action devoutly. Holy water is a sacramental, and the sacramentals get their power, their efficacy, mainly from the prayers which the Church offers (for example, in the ceremony for the blessing of the holy water) for those who use the sacramental. It is the prayer of the Church which makes a sacramental a means of grace. The outward sign of the sacramental—in this case the water—of and by itself has no power to give grace.

With a sacrament the story is different. A sacrament gives grace *of and by itself, by its own power;* this is because Jesus attached grace to the outward sign, so to speak, so that that outward sign and grace always go together. This does not mean that our own attitude does not matter. We can, of course, by a positive act of the will prevent the grace of the sacrament from entering our soul; for example, by positively not wanting to receive it or by not being truly repentant for mortal sin. But, unless we interpose an outright barrier, when we receive a sacrament we receive grace; the sacrament itself *gives* grace.

Our interior dispositions will, however, have an effect on the *amount* of grace we receive. The more perfect is our sorrow in the sacrament of Penance, the more ardent our love in receiving the Holy Eucharist, the more lively our faith in receiving Confirmation—then the greater will be the grace we receive. Our dispositions do not cause the grace; they simply remove the obstacles to the freer flow of grace and, in a sense, make more room for grace. We might illustrate this by saying that the more sand we empty out of the pail, the more water the pail will hold.

The dispositions of the one who administers the sacrament do not influence the effect of a sacrament. It would be very wrong for a priest to administer a sacrament if he had mortal sin on his soul, but it wouldn't one whit diminish the grace the sacrament gave. The person receiving the sacrament would receive the same amount of grace, regardless of whether the priest was a saint or a sinner. All that is required of the one who administers a sacrament is that he have the *power* to give it—this means the power of the priesthood (except for Baptism and Matrimony)—that he have the *intention* of administering the sacrament (the intention of doing what the Catholic Church intends); that he perform the essential ceremonies of the sacrament (such as the pouring of the water and the saying of the words in Baptism). If you assume a receiver who does not put any obstacles to grace and a giver who is qualified to administer the sacrament—then always and infallibly a sacrament will confer grace.

Besides the bestowal of grace (sanctifying and sacramental) there should be mentioned another effect peculiar to three of the sacraments. This is the *character* imprinted on the soul by the sacraments of Baptism, Confirmation, and Holy Orders. Although in teaching catechism to children we sometimes say that in these sacraments God puts a "mark" on the soul, we know that the soul is a spirit and cannot be marked as you might rubber-stamp a piece of paper or cloth. The individual mark imparted by Baptism, Confirmation, and Holy Orders is defined by theologians as a "quality" which imparts to the soul powers which it did not previously possess. It is a *permanent* quality of the soul, an alteration in the soul which forever will be visible to God, the angels, and the saints.

"Quality" is a rather vague word—easier to understand than to define. If we say, "There is a difference in the quality of sunlight and electric light," everyone understands what we mean. But if someone then asks us, "What do you mean by *quality?*" we are stumped. We can only stammer, "well, somehow they are different."

It may be helpful to compare the characters of the three once-in-a-lifetime (because their effect is permanent they can be received only once) sacraments to talents. Here, for example, is a person who has a talent for art. He can paint beautiful pictures. He doesn't spend all his time painting pictures, but the talent is there all the time. Even if he loses his hands in an accident and can no longer paint, the talent itself still is there. He definitely has got something which we haven't got, a *quality* which is real, and permanent, and which gives him a power not possessed by one who hasn't that particular quality.

The character of Baptism, then, is a supernatural "talent" which gives us the power to absorb the grace of the other six sacraments and to participate in the Mass. The character of Confirmation gives us the power to profess the faith fearlessly and to spread the faith. The character of Holy Orders gives the priest the power to celebrate Mass and to administer the other sacraments.

CHAPTER XXIV

Baptism

The Beginning of Life

The newborn baby comes into the world with a soul which is supernaturally dead. The infant has the fullness of *natural* life. He has all the capacities and powers (some of them still undeveloped) which by strict right belong to the nature of a human being. He has the ability to see and hear and feel. He has the latent power to think and to remember and to love. He has all that is due to a human nature—and nothing more.

The reason that he has "nothing more" is because his forefather Adam failed to earn for him the "something more" that God wanted to give. In creating Adam, God imparted to him a *supernatural* life in addition to his natural life. God Himself dwelt in Adam's soul, sharing His own divine life with Adam somewhat as the mother shares her own life with the child in her womb. All of Adam's actions had a supernatural as well as a natural value; in whatever he did, God was acting in and with him. When Adam's life in this world was finished, not merely would he enter the unending life of natural happiness in limbo—he would pass from union with God unseen to union with God seen. He would share the indescribable ecstasy of God's own happiness forever.

This supernatural life which Adam enjoyed—a spiritual aliveness imparted by the indwelling God—has been named "sanctifying grace" by theologians. According to God's plan, sanctifying grace was a heritage that Adam would transmit to his posterity. For Adam to make sanctifying grace secure for himself and his descendents only one thing was necessary: he must obey God's command not to eat of the fruit of a certain tree in the Garden of Paradise.

The sequel is familiar to us. Adam refused God that act of obedience. He chose self in preference to God. He committed the first human sin, the *original sin*. In rejecting God, Adam cut himself off from union with God. He extinguished in his soul the supernatural life with which God had endowed him. He lost sanctifying grace. He lost it not only for himself but for his posterity forever. Because at the time of his sin Adam *was* the human race; in him all mankind was potentially present. And sanctifying grace, be it remembered, was not something to which man was by his nature entitled. It was (and is) a totally undeserved gift, a tremendous "bonus" offered by God to humankind through Adam, a "bonus" which Adam struck from God's proffering hand.

In His depthless love, God then chose to give each individual a chance to gain for himself the gift which Adam had failed to gain for the human race as a group. God Himself, in the Person of Jesus Christ, made infinite atonement for the infinite malice of Adam's ingratitude. Being both God and Man, Jesus bridged the abyss between humanity and divinity. He (as only God could) made adequate satisfaction for man's unpayable debt; He atoned for original sin. (We are reminded here of a loving father who takes money out of his own bank account to pay the bank for a debt owed to it by a wayward son.)

Returning now to our newborn infant, we can understand

why it is that he comes into the world with only the *natural* endowments of human nature. The supernatural life which is the result of God's personal and intimate indwelling, is absent from his soul. We say that the child is "in the state of original sin." Original sin is not, in the strict sense, a "blot" upon the soul. Indeed, original sin is not a "something" at all. It is the *absence* of something that should be there. It is a darkness where there ought to be light.

In order to restore to the soul of this child—the work of His Father's hands and the object of His Father's love—his lost heritage, Jesus instituted the sacrament of Baptism. Baptism is the means devised by Jesus to apply to each individual soul the atonement which He made on the Cross for original sin. Jesus will not force His gift upon us, the gift of supernatural life for which He paid. He holds the gift out to us hopefully, but each of us must freely accept it. We make that acceptance by receiving the sacrament of Baptism.

With those of us who are "born in the Faith" and baptized as infants, our acceptance is a passive one. We might say that God, in His anxiety to dwell in our soul, presumes our acceptance; although, when godparents are available, they do make formal acceptance of the supernatural life in the name of the child. But, whether it be the passive acceptance of the infant or the explicit acceptance of the adult, when the sacrament of Baptism is administered the spiritual vacuum which we call original sin disappears as God becomes present in the soul, and the soul is caught up into that sharing of God's own life which we call sanctifying grace.

It often happens that a couple who find that they cannot have children of their own adopt one or more children. When the adoption papers have been signed by the judge, the adopted child becomes—really and truly as far as the law is concerned—the son or daughter of the adopting parents. Usually such parents love their adopted children just as much as though the children were their own flesh and blood.

In fact, if they could, they gladly would give their own flesh and blood to each adopted child. If there were any way to do it, they would share their own nature with the child so that he might truly be the image of themselves.

But of course they cannot do so. No matter how tiny the adopted baby may be, he cannot be placed in his new mother's womb, there to absorb her physical characteristics and those of the father. Neither has medical science discovered any way in which the genes of the adopting parents can be injected into the child's veins in order to fashion him, physically and mentally, in the pattern of his foster parents.

However, what parents cannot do physically for their adopted children, God can and does do spiritually for His adopted children. The sacrament of Baptism, as we may remember from our school days, is defined as, "the sacrament that gives our souls the new life of sanctifying grace by which we become children of God and heirs of heaven." With the coming of God into the soul at Baptism, the new kind of life (called sanctifying grace) which God imparts to the soul is *really and truly* a sharing in God's own life. Now as never before can we say of the newly baptized soul: "It is made in the image and likeness of God." Now as never before can God love this soul, because the soul for the first time presents an aspect genuinely worthy of God's love: the reflection, as in a mirror, of God Himself.

There is a difference, also, in the inheritance rights of God's adopted children and the children of human adoption. Legally, an adopted child becomes the heir of his foster parents. Unless they specifically cut him off by an unfavorable will, the adopted child will inherit the property of his foster parents when they die—but *not until they die*. The child of God, however, receives his inheritance at the very moment of his adoption, at the very moment of Baptism. His inheritance is eternal union with God, and he has that inheritance *now*. Nobody can take it away from him; not even God, Who has bound Himself by irrevocable promise never to take back what He has given. The heir himself can re-nounce his rights—as he will do if he commits mortal sin—but no one else can deprive him of his heritage.

The nature of this heirship might be illustrated by the example of foster parents who would make over all their property to their adopted child at the very time of his adoption. Even though he might not enter into the full enjoyment of his property until he was twenty-one, or perhaps not until his foster parents died, nevertheless in the meantime the property would be his and would be accumulating dividends and profits.

Similarly, when we are baptized we enter into possession of our inheritance immediately. Heaven already is ours because we already are united with God. The full enjoyment of our inheritance—the face-to-face vision of God—must await our physical death. In the meantime, all the graces we receive and all the merits we acquire are as so many dividends which will add to the eventual richness of our inheritance. The point to be emphasized, and never to be forgotten, is that we are potentially in heaven the moment we are baptized.

The point needs to be emphasized because to so many people Baptism is a negative thing: "It takes away original sin." Baptism does take away original sin, of course. Also, in the case of an adult, it takes away all mortal and venial sins if the person baptized has committed any and is truly sorry for them. It takes away also the debt of punishment due to sin, the eternal punishment due to unforgiven mortal sin, and the temporal punishment (whether here upon earth or in purgatory) which, because of the imperfection of our sorrow, is due to most of us even after our sins are forgiven. Even the temporal punishment due to venial sin is wiped away, if the baptized person has been guilty of any.

Baptism makes a clean sweep of everything. But the "taking away" is not a negative removal, like the emptying of a trash can by the garbage collector. Sin and its consequences disappear when God comes into the soul, just as darkness disappears when the light is turned on. Sin is a spiritual emptiness which is obliterated by the coming of grace.

Baptism does not restore the *preternatural* gifts which were lost for us by Adam: freedom from suffering and death, from ignorance, and inordinate inclinations of passion. But who cares? These are insignificant compared to the *supernatural* gifts which are restored. Here is a newly baptized soul, beautiful with a beauty which even the most wild-eyed artist could not imagine, splendid with a splendor which ravishes the onlooking angels and saints. Here is a soul that already is in heaven except for the formality of a few (even though they be numbered a hundred) quickly passing years. *That* is what matters!

The Mark of a Christian

Two big things happen to us when we are baptized. We receive the supernatural life, called sanctifying grace, which dissipates the spiritual emptiness of original sin. And there is imparted to the soul a permanent and distinctive quality which we call the *character* or the *mark* of Baptism. If we commit mortal sin after Baptism, then we cut ourselves off from God and from the flow of His divine life, as a severed artery would cause an organ to be cut off from the flow of the heart's blood. We lose sanctifying grace. But we do *not* lose the baptismal character, by which the soul has been forever transformed.

Precisely because we possess the baptismal character, it is easy for us to regain the grace that we have lost. Because of the character, we have the right to receive the sacrament of Penance and to restore our soul to spiritual life. If our soul did not have that character, then we could go to confession a dozen times or a hundred times and nothing would happen. The mortal sin would remain unforgiven; the soul would remain spiritually dead. The mortal sin could be forgiven by perfect contrition, but that is another story. As far as the sacrament of Penance was concerned, it would be just as though we didn't even exist, just as though we weren't even present when the words of absolution were pronounced. That is true, also, of the other five sacraments. None of them can mean a thing to us until first the *capacity* for receiving the other sacraments has been established in the soul by the character of Baptism.

Let us suppose that someone who cannot at present be baptized (a prospective convert, perhaps, who still is receiving instructions) makes an act of perfect love for God. His sins are immediately forgiven, including original sin. We call this "Baptism of desire." However, such a person still could not receive any other sacrament. If he committed a mortal sin, confession couldn't help him. If he received the Holy Eucharist, no grace would flow from his Communion. The qualifying and enabling change in his soul, which only the actual sacrament of Baptism can effect and which we call the *character* of Baptism, has not yet been wrought in his soul. Without the baptismal character a person is as impervious to the direct graces of the sacraments as a person wrapped in pliofilm is impervious to the rain.

The same thing would be true of his assistance at the Sacrifice of the Mass. We do not mean to say that this person's prayers would not be pleasing to God and that the faith with which he worshiped would not bring grace from God. Nor do we mean to say that the Mass, which is offered for the whole world, would not profit him at all. But the point is that whatever grace he received would not flow from his personal participation in the Mass itself.

This is because it is by the character of actual Baptism that we "put on Christ," in the words of St. Paul. It is the character of Baptism, according to St. Thomas, that "configures" us to Christ and makes us participants in His eternal priesthood. By Baptism we are given the power—and the obligation—to share with Christ in those things which pertain to divine worship—the Mass and the sacraments. We become co-offerers of the Holy Sacrifice with Christ. Not, of course, in the same way in which a man who has received Holy Orders—the power of the priesthood—offers Mass. Only the ordained priest can *celebrate* Mass, can consecrate. However, as members of Christ's Mystical Body and sharers in His priesthood, we do share in the offering of the Mass; we do "put something into" the Mass in a way impossible to one who is unbaptized. And we share in a special way in the graces of every Mass that is offered, even the Masses at which we are not personally present.

This is only a little of what it means to bear within our soul the "mark" of Baptism. Besides the "configurative" aspect of the baptismal character which we have discussed above, theologians also point to its *distinguishing* effect, by which it differentiates between those who are members of the Church, Christ's Mystical Body, and those who are not. Indeed, it is the impression of the baptismal character upon the soul that *makes* us members of the Church. In addition to being a configurative and a distinguishing sign, the baptismal character also is classified as an *obligative* sign; that is, it imposes upon us the obligation to discharge the duties that go with our Christlikeness, our membership in Christ's Church. This means to lead a life according to the pattern that Christ has given us, and to give obedience to Christ's representatives, our bishops and especially our Holy Father the Pope. It might be observed here that every baptized person is a *member* of Christ's Church as long as the bond of union is not broken by heresy, schism, or the most severe form of excommunication. But even these latter—baptized persons who are severed from actual membership in the Church—still are *subject* (as are all men) to Christ and subject to His Church (as are all baptized persons). Unless specifically exempted (as the Church does exempt baptized non-Catholics in regard to certain laws), they still are subject to the laws of the Church. It still would be mortal sin, for example, for an excommunicated Catholic to eat meat on Friday.

If someone were to ask you, "What is the most important thing in life for everybody without exception?," I wonder whether you would come up with the right answer, instantly and without hesitation. You would, if your Catholic training has been adequate. You would whip back the answer, "Baptism!" without a second thought.

We know that if a person were deprived of food or drink or oxygen for any length of time that person would die physically. But if he had been baptized, he would enter into eternal life. Physical death is an evil mainly for the people who are left behind. So far as the person who dies is concerned, it simply means that he gets to heaven that much sooner—always supposing that he has not committed spiritual suicide by unrepented mortal sin.

On the other hand, a person might live to be a hundred, with a whole century of health and wealth and "successful living" behind him. And if he dies without Baptism, his have been a hundred wasted years. What does anything matter now if this person has missed out on the one thing for which he was made—eternal union with God?

There is no escaping the absolute necessity of Baptism. ". . . Unless a man be born again of water and the Spirit, he cannot enter into the kingdom of God," Jesus told Nicodemus (John 3:5). And His command to the Apostles was: "Go into the whole world and preach the Gospel to every creature. He who believes and is baptized shall be saved, but he who does not believe" (and, by inference, is not baptized) "shall be condemned" (Mark 16:15-16). There is no "if" or "maybe" about those two statements; no way around them.

We can understand, then, why it is that the Church insists that babies be baptized as soon as possible after birth—as soon as the infant can safely be carried to church—which in practice means when the baby is ten to fourteen days old. It is an article of faith that anyone who dies in the state of original sin is excluded from heaven, from the vision of God. However, the Church has never officially taught that the souls of infants who die without Baptism do not see God; it may be that God has some way of compensating in such souls for their lack of Baptism. But if so, God has not revealed it to us. Most theologians are of the opinion that the souls of unbaptized infants enjoy a high degree of *natural* happiness (to which they give the name of "limbo") but not the supernatural and supreme happiness of the beatific vision. In any event, our obligation is to follow the safer course: *never* through our fault to let a soul enter eternity without Baptism.

For parents, this means that they should not unduly delay the Baptism of their newborn child. The infant's hold on life is too frail, the danger of sudden sickness and death too great, to risk any unnecessary postponement of Baptism.

Parents who unnecessarily delay or neglect the Baptism of their child for a long time become guilty of grave sin—and theologians establish one month or more as "a long time" in this connection. It would be very wrong, for example, for parents to put off Baptism simply because Uncle George is coming to town next month, and they want Uncle George to be godfather of the baby. Right now, the baby needs Baptism more than he needs Uncle George—and Uncle George still can be godfather by proxy. It would be still worse to postpone Baptism "until payday after next, so we can have a big party." The baby's big party is with God and the angels and saints at the baptismal font; none of them are interested in a keg of beer.

Can a baby be baptized if his parents are "married out of the Church"—perhaps because one of them was previously married and divorced? The answer is yes. The Church does not punish the child for the sin of his parents. *Any* baby can be baptized in the Catholic Church under one condition: the priest must have reasonable assurance that the child will be reared a Catholic. Since this is a matter of judgment, it is up to each pastor to settle each such case on its particular merits. If the invalid marriage is one that could be rectified easily, the pastor is likely to insist on this being done before he will agree to baptize the baby. The reason is that the chances of the baby being reared a Catholic are very slim if the faith of the parents is so weak that they *deliberately* continue in an invalid marriage without any shadow of excuse. If the invalid marriage is one that cannot be rectified because of a previous marriage, but the parents (or at least one of them) still attend Mass and give evidence of retaining the Catholic faith, then their child can be baptized. Always the one question that each pastor must answer to his own satisfaction is: "Is it likely that this child will be reared a Catholic? That is, is it likely that he will be sent to a Catholic school or at least to Catholic instructions? Will he be given the opportunity to make his First Holy Communion and to be confirmed? Will he be trained in the habit of Sunday Mass? Will there be anyone in the family who can give him some kind of example of Christian living?" If the answer is yes—even a somewhat dubious yes—then the baby will be baptized.

Getting Baby Baptized

When a person is baptized in the Catholic Church, he becomes a historical character. His name and other pertinent data are inscribed in the baptismal register of the parish church and will be carefully preserved. Barring such catastrophes as destructive fire or flood or bombing, that record will remain in existence until the end of the world. As an instance, St. Anne's parish in Detroit, founded in 1701, still preserves in its archives the baptismal records stretching back through more than two hundred and fifty years.

Perhaps you are not interested in your child becoming a historical figure, but you *are* interested in the future development of his Catholic life. For this, his baptismal record will be essential. Since no other sacrament is valid unless first a person is baptized, a Catholic must give proof of his Baptism at every step of his spiritual progress. When your child comes to make his First Holy Communion, he will be required to present a copy of his baptismal certificate. Before he can be confirmed he again must present a copy of his baptismal certificate. When he and his betrothed go to see the pastor to arrange their marriage, both will have to supply copies of their baptismal certificates. Or if, instead, the young man goes to the seminary and the young lady to the convent, each will have to provide a baptismal certificate. Baptism is of such supreme importance that the Church checks and double checks at every point along the line, to make sure there has been no slip-up in the matter of Baptism.

An official copy of one's baptismal record can be had for the asking at the parish of Baptism. There is no charge for such a transcript when it is needed for a church purpose such as First Holy Communion. There may be a small charge if it is for some other purpose, such as proving citizenship or to qualify for an old-age pension. Incidentally, parents should make sure that a child, when he is old enough to understand, knows the church of his Baptism. It doesn't happen often, but it does happen sometimes, that a person comes to arrange for his marriage and does not know where to go or where to write for his baptismal certificate; the family moved while he was a child, and his parents both have died. It can be very difficult in such cases to establish the fact of Baptism.

All of which is by way of indicating the first step to be taken in planning for the Baptism of a newborn baby. As soon as possible after the baby's arrival, the father (or some adult member of the family) should stop in at the parish rectory to arrange for the date of the Baptism and to give the necessary information for the baptismal record. The priest will want to know the baby's full name, the name of the father and the maiden name of the mother, the date of the baby's birth, and the names of the godparents. This is the data that will go down in the permanent baptismal record.

The parish at which this is done will, of course, be the parish within whose limits the parents reside. Except in an emergency, no other priest except the pastor of the parents has the right to administer the sacrament of Baptism to a child. This is for the sake of good order in the Church—so that the shepherd may have a chance to know his own flock. Ordinarily, no other priest may baptize the child, unless the parents' own pastor gives his permission for Baptism elsewhere.

Christian parents will quite naturally want to give a Christian name to their child. In fact, the choice of a name probably has been a topic of discussion between the parents for several months before the baby's birth. At least one of the child's names must be a saint's name, so that the child may have a patron in heaven whose virtues he may imitate and to whom he may look for protection and help. Beyond that, it is quite permissible to add non-saint names, such as family names, if the parents wish. There are books and pamphlets available at Catholic bookstores and libraries which contain lists of saints' names to help parents with their choice. One such booklet is entitled, *Is It a Saint's Name?** and contains the names and feast days of more than three thousand saints. It is surprising to see there some fancy names that *are* Christian names, such as Ivetta and Kenwyn and Yolanthe for girls, and Dion and Forde and Thurstan for boys.

It might be mentioned here that it is not necessary to give any money to the priest when making arrangements for a Baptism. It is customary at the time of the Baptism for the godfather to make an offering to the priest who baptizes. The amount may vary by custom in different places. The

* Published by Integrity Supply, P. O. Box 6508, Chicago, Ill., 25c.

gesture of the offering is much more graceful if the offering is handed to the priest in an envelope prepared beforehand. To instructed Catholics it needs no pointing out, of course, that no stipend will be *demanded*. The baby will be baptized just as willingly and just as holily, whether or not an offering is made.

It is a great honor to be asked to be a godparent. When the parents of a new baby ask a friend or relative to be godfather or godmother at the baby's Baptism, they are saying in effect, "If anything should happen to us, there is no one in the whole wide world to whom we would rather entrust our child than to you." At least, that is what the parents should be thinking as they choose the sponsors for the new baby. The duties of godparents do not end when they carry their godchild out of church after the Baptism. The godparents have taken on a lifelong responsibility for the spiritual welfare of the child.

In most instances, this responsibility will be fulfilled by remembering to pray for their godchild in their daily prayers and by setting him (or her) a good example of Christian living. But if anything should happen to the parents (and hardly a week passes without one's reading of a traffic accident in which a couple who are parents have lost their lives), then it devolves upon the godparents to see to it that the child is raised a good Catholic.

Or, if the parents should neglect the Catholic upbringing of their child, then it becomes the duty of the godparents to do what they can to offset the parents' laxity. This can be a delicate situation, one calling for considerable tact on the part of the godparents; otherwise the parents might be angry and dismiss the godparents as busybodies. But if, when little Mary is seven years old, there is no sign of her making her First Holy Communion, then her godmother Aunt Jane might say to Mary's mother: "I know you are awfully busy, dear; I wonder if you would mind if I stopped by on Saturday mornings and took Mary to catechism class while I do my shopping?"

It is evident that the first consideration in choosing godparents is that they themselves be good Catholics. It is an old axiom that no one can give what he hasn't got, and that includes religion. It may be a temptation to ask rich Uncle Gus to be godfather. He goes to church only at Christmas and Easter, but perhaps he will remember baby in his will. However, all Uncle Gus's money can't buy baby's way into heaven. His name should be scratched from the list of possibles.

Non-Catholics, of course, cannot be godparents. This may pose a problem in a mixed marriage. The non-Catholic grandparents may feel slighted at not being asked to be sponsors, not even for the third baby or the fourth. But if it is explained to them quite frankly that the godparents have to make, in the name of the child, an act of faith in the Catholic religion—which only a Catholic can honestly do—the non-Catholic grandparents usually will see the reasonableness of the situation.

Since the godparents are supposed to substitute for the parents should the necessity arise, it is obvious that a child's own parents cannot be sponsors for their baby; they cannot be substitutes for themselves. Also, in the case of an adult's being baptized, the husband or wife of the person being baptized may not be sponsor.

Aside from these exceptions, any good Catholic, thirteen years old or older, is eligible to be a godparent at Baptism, including brothers and sisters. In Baptism, however, a spiritual relationship is contracted between the person baptized and his godparents, a relationship which is very real and which is an impediment to marriage between the two. If an adult is to be baptized, the fiancé or fiancée should not act as sponsor; otherwise, it would be necessary to obtain a dispensation for the future marriage.

Sometimes it may happen that parents wish to have a cer-

tain person as godparent for their child, but the person cannot be present. It may be that the person chosen is sick in
the hospital, or lives at a great distance, or is overseas in the
armed forces. In such circumstances, the absent person can
be godparent by proxy. All that is necessary is that he know
about the Baptism, give his consent to be godfather or
godmother, and agree to have someone represent him. Even
from overseas such a consent can be air-mailed in a very
few days and need not delay the Baptism. It is best to have
the consent in writing (with a particular person designated
as representative), and show it to the priest when the arrangements for the Baptism are made.

The absent person will be the real godparent. It is his
(or her) name which will go down in the baptismal record.
It is he (or she) who will contract the spiritual relationship
with the child. It is he (or she) who will have a lifelong
responsibility to the godchild. A sponsor should retain a
friendly interest in his godchild as long as both shall live.
Anyone, even one of the parents, may take the place of the
absent person at the baptismal font. No spiritual relationship is contracted by the one who "stands in" for the absent
godparent.

Before Childbirth—and After

While we are on the subject of Baptism, it might be
useful to digress for a moment to call attention to three very
beautiful blessings of the Church which are not as widely
used as they might be. One is the "Blessing of a Woman
before the Birth of a Child." It is a blessing which any
prospective mother can receive if she will just step into the
sacristy any morning after Mass and ask the priest to give
her this special blessing. Or if sickness confines her to the
house or hospital, she can easily arrange by telephone to
have the priest come to give her this blessing.

Modern medical science makes childbearing comparatively safe, but it is well, also, to let God know that we still look to Him with confidence in His loving care. A prospective mother would seem to be very foolish were she to neglect to receive this blessing. It is an *official* blessing of the Church. Consequently, it carries with it the prayer-power which only the liturgical blessings of the Mystical Body of Christ contain.

The blessing requires no more than five minutes. There are some short versicles, such as, "Our help is in the name of the Lord—Who made heaven and earth." Then there are two longer prayers for the mother, followed by Psalm 66, which begins "May God have pity on us and bless us. . . ." This is followed by more short versicles, then the final prayer and blessing. Our space does not permit us to give the words of the entire blessing here, but let us quote a portion of the longest of the prayers:

"O Lord God, Creator of all things . . ., receive the sacrifice of the contrite heart and the ardent desire of Thy servant [mother's name here], who humbly asks Thee for the welfare of the child which Thou didst grant her to conceive . . ., so that the hand of Thy mercy may assist her delivery and her child may come to the light of day without harm, be kept safe for the holy birth of Baptism, serve Thee always in all things, and attain to everlasting life." More than that, no mother can desire. For less than that no mother should ask.

Another blessing, somewhat more familiar, is the blessing of a mother *after* childbirth. This often was popularly referred to as the "churching" of a mother, and I am afraid that for some the word "churching" carried undesirable connotations—as though motherhood had in some way defiled the woman and now she must be purified before she can rightly resume her church-going. That is a very mistaken notion of the blessing after childbirth. It has no more to do with the ancient Jewish rite of legal purification of the mother after delivery than the holy water at the doors of our churches has to do with the "water of purification" which was provided in the Jewish Temple of old. There is perhaps a dim relationship of origin, nothing more. Once Christ had broken the bonds of original sin by His death, there was no longer any meaning to the purification of mothers, by which mankind's sad and sin-bound estate had so long been symbolized.

In the new English Ritual (for which we thank Pope Pius XII), the blessing after childbirth is not just for the mother; it now is for the mother and child. If the mother is well enough to accompany the baptismal party to church, she and the baby can receive this blessing after the child's Baptism. Otherwise she can ask for the blessing later, when she is able to take the baby to church.

Like the blessing before delivery, the blessing after childbirth also has several parts, including the recitation of Mary's joyful hymn, the Magnificat: "My soul magnifies the Lord, and my spirit rejoices in God my Saviour." Here let us just quote briefly from the two central prayers. For the mother: "Almighty, everlasting God, . . . look with kindness on this Thy servant, who comes rejoicing to Thy holy temple to give thanks to Thee, and grant that after this life she and her child may, by the merits and intercession of the Blessed Virgin Mary, attain to the joys of everlasting life."

And for the child: "O Lord Jesus Christ, . . . anticipate the needs of this child . . . with Thy tender blessings, and grant that no evil may corrupt his (her) . . . mind, but that, advancing in age, in wisdom, and in grace, he (she) . . . may live so as to please Thee always. . . ."

The Holy Father has given us one entirely new blessing in the new English Ritual. It is a special blessing after childbirth for a mother whose child has died. The blessing is built around Psalm 120, which begins, "I lift up my eyes toward the mountains; whence shall help come to me?"

For the grief-stricken mother there is comfort and hope

as the Church, in the fullness of her power as Christ's own voice, prays, "Almighty, everlasting God, Lover of holy purity, Who in Thy kindness has called the child of this woman into Thy heavenly kingdom: in Thy kindness also, O Lord, be merciful to Thy servant so that, strengthened by the merits of Thy passion and by the intercession of the Blessed Virgin Mary and all the saints, she may triumph over her sorrow, bravely resume her duties, and rejoice with her child forever in Thy kingdom."

All of us have been present at least once at a Baptism: our own. Unless we are converts, we probably were too young to be aware of what was going on. But most of us probably have been present at Baptisms since our own; as parent or godparent or interested observer. However, even though we may be quite familiar with the baptismal rite, I think it may be profitable to review briefly the ceremonies of Baptism, with a word or two as to their significance.

Before doing so, however, I should like to offer a suggestion to parents who may see a promise of a Baptism in the future. At one point in the baptismal rite (near the end) the officiating priest will lay a linen garment across the infant's shoulders or will touch a linen cloth to the child's head. This is a survival of the custom of clothing the newly baptized person in a baptismal robe to symbolize the robe of innocence with which his soul has been clothed. Even more, it symbolizes the fact that he has clothed himself with Christ, identified himself with Christ. Henceforth he will carry Christ with him wherever he goes. Christ will live in him and will be able to speak and to act through him. This is the significance of St. Paul's words, "For all you who have been baptized into Christ, have put on Christ" (Galatians 3:27).

This custom goes back to the very earliest days of the Christian Church. Converts to the faith were baptized on the day before Easter Sunday. Each was vested with a baptismal robe, which was worn in joy for the ensuing eight days. In the official calendar of the Church, the Sunday after Easter still is called "Dominica in Albis—the Sunday of the White Robes"—because it was on that day that the neophyte Christians laid aside their baptismal robes.

All of which leads up to the suggestion I wish to make. There is no reason why the baby to be baptized (or the adult convert, for that matter) should not have his own baptismal robe. It would add much more significance to this part of the baptismal ceremony. During the months when she is preparing for the arrival of the newcomer, mother might make (or have made) a baptismal robe for the baby. It should be made of linen, and made simply: a sleeveless garment that will drop easily over the baby's head. It can be made somewhat along the lines of a chasuble, the outer vestment which a priest wears when celebrating Mass. Indeed it would be very appropriate to make it so, since by Baptism we become sharers in the priesthood of Christ, and are destined to join with Him in sacrifice to almighty God.

Here is a rough sketch of what a baptismal robe might be like. It could be decorated as the mother might wish; perhaps with a colored border and with liturgical symbols worked in color on the front and back—perhaps a cross or a dove (symbol of the Holy Ghost) or a triangle or three intersecting circles for the Blessed Trinity or a Chi Rho for Christ. Ties could be provided at the sides to keep the robe in place on the infant after the priest has placed it on the child. The godparents should take the robe with them when they go to the church for the Baptism. Before the ceremony begins, they should ask the priest to use the robe when he comes to that part of the ceremony. The robe will be a meaningful memento of the child's Baptism. Perhaps when he has grown to adulthood and has a family of his own, he will want to use the same robe for *his* children.

Immediately after clothing the newly baptized infant with the baptismal robe, the priest presents the child with a candle, which the godparents hold for the child. The candle is a symbol of the light of faith which henceforth will guide the new Christian through life. It also is a symbol of Christ the Light of the World. Here again it would be a fitting thing for the parents to provide the child with a candle of his own, so that it can be taken home after the ceremony and kept for him. In many Catholic homes where the significance of Baptism as a spiritual rebirth is understood and appreciated, the baptismal anniversaries of the children are celebrated even more joyfully than the birthdays. Each year on the baptismal anniversary the godparents are invited (if they can come) for a "party" dinner or supper. There is a special cake, and in the center of the cake the child's baptismal candle stands brightly burning. At the rate of half an hour or so each year, the candle will last for twenty years or more.

Specially decorated candles can be procured at most stores which specialize in church goods and devotional articles. Or the parents can obtain a wax candle from the pastor and decorate it themselves. The candle of course does not *have* to be decorated—but it should be a wax candle, the kind that is used on the altar.

The Birth of a Soul

"Peace be with you." That is the greeting which the priest speaks, in the name of the Church, to the infant who has been brought for Baptism. It is an appropriate greeting. The peace of soul which only the grace of God can give will be the inevitable result of Baptism, if no obstacle is placed to the operation of grace. For centuries little Switzerland has been an island of peace amid the warring nations of Europe, a last point of contact and communication in troubled times. Similarly is a baptized Christian who knows and loves and lives his faith a little island of peace—and strength—in that small segment of the world which is his.

To the troubled souls among whom he lives and works, the vital Catholic often is the last point of contact with the supernatural. In the midst of confusion and unhappiness he is a beacon of hope, a calm reminder that life does have a meaning and a destiny which no pettiness of men can destroy.

"Peace be with you." That is the way the rite of Baptism begins, as the priest greets infant and godparents at the door of the church. "What is your name?" the priest asks next, and the godparents answer (as they do throughout the rite) for the child who cannot speak. They give the child's name. "What do you ask of the Church of God?" the dialogue continues. "Faith," is the simple answer of the child. "What does Faith offer you?" asks the priest, testing the sincerity of this seeker after Baptism. "Everlasting life," is the prompt reply. The priest responds by presenting the whole plan of Christian living in capsule form: "If, then, it is life that you wish to enter, keep the commandments. Love the Lord your God with your whole heart, and with your whole soul, and with your whole mind; and love your neighbor as you love yourself."

The priest now prepares the infant for entrance into the church by detaching him from any claim that Satan may have upon him. Breathing three times lightly on the child's face, the priest commands, "Depart from him (her), unclean spirit, and give place to the Holy Spirit, the Consoler." The priest immediately proceeds to put the mark of Christ's ownership upon the baby by tracing a cross, with his thumb, upon the infant's forehead and breast, with the charge: "Receive the sign of the Cross on your forehead and in your heart. Have faith in the teachings of God, and live in such a way that from now on you may be enabled to be a temple of God."

(Perhaps it would be well to call the godmother's attention to the need for having the child's clothing loosened at the throat, with the top buttons unbuttoned if necessary

Not only at this point, but again later, the priest must trace the sign of the Cross on the baby's breast. The dress must be loose enough to pull down an inch or two below the throat.)

After two further prayers for the child, the priest next drops a pinch of blessed salt on the baby's tongue, and says, calling the infant by name: "Receive the salt of wisdom. May it win for you mercy and forgiveness, and life everlasting." The symbolism of the salt is rather obvious. Just as salt preserves from corruption all that it touches, so will God's grace preserve the baptized person from the corruption of sin. And just as salt gives savor to food, so will God's grace give a taste for divine truths.

There is no need to quote at length all the beautiful prayers with which the Church has surrounded the sacrament of Baptism. Now that we have the Ritual in English, those who assist at a Baptism will find the prayers self-explanatory. Aside from the actual words of Baptism, and the prayers which accompany the anointings, the only other prayers of the baptismal ceremony which remain in Latin are the exorcisms. The exorcisms are two prayers in which the priest, at some length, solemnly commands Satan in the name of the Most Blessed Trinity to depart from this child and to leave him alone forever henceforth.

After the giving of the salt, the first exorcism, and a prayer invoking God's blessing upon the child, it is time for entrance into the church—or into the baptistry, if these ceremonies have taken place outside the baptistry gates. The priest places the end of his stole upon the infant's shoulder and says (calling him by name), "Enter the temple of God, so that you may take part with Christ in everlasting life."

But first, on the threshold the priest and godparents together make for the baby a profession of faith by reciting the Apostles' Creed, the ancient prayer in which the basic truths of our Faith are enshrined. Together also priest and godparents recite the Our Father. Then follows the second exorcism, which concludes with the priest touching the child's ears and nostrils saying the word which Jesus spoke when he healed the deaf mute, "Ephphetá"—adding, "which means 'Be opened' "—and continuing: "so that you may perceive the fragrance of God's sweetness. But you, O devil, depart; for the judgment of God has come."

The time has come now, in the baptismal ceremony, for the pronouncing of the baptismal vows. Addressing the child by name, the priest asks him, "Do you renounce Satan?" and the godparents answer for the child, "I do renounce him." "And all his works?" the priest asks. "I do renounce them." "And all his display?" the priest continues. "I do renounce it." (In families where baptismal anniversaries are celebrated each year, it is an admirable practice for the entire family to renew their baptismal vows together before they sit down for the festive meal, with the father asking the questions and all answering together.)

Immediately after the renunciation of sin, the priest proceeds to anoint the child on the breast and on the back between the shoulders, with the oil of catechumens, also called the oil of salvation. This is one of the three holy oils consecrated by the bishop of the diocese at his Mass on Holy Thursday each year. The other two holy oils are sacred chrism and the oil of the sick (for Extreme Unction). The anointing of the child on breast and back represents the spiritual "armor" with which Baptism will clothe him. Its meaning is found in the words of St. Paul, who says (Ephesians 6:13–16): "Therefore take up the armor of God, that . . . having put on the breastplate of justice . . . you may be able to quench all the fiery darts of the most wicked one." And again (in I Thessalonians 5:8), "Let us put on the breastplate of faith and charity." The meaning of the Latin words which the priest speaks as he makes this anointing is: "I anoint you with the oil of salvation, in Christ Jesus our Lord, so that you may have everlasting life."

The moment of actual Baptism now is here. But first the

priest pauses beside the font to extract from the child a final and formal profession of faith. Again addressing the infant by name, the priest questions, "Do you believe in God, the Father almighty, Creator of heaven and earth?" "I do believe!" answers the infant through his godparents. "Do you believe in Jesus Christ, His only Son, our Lord, who was born into this world and suffered for us?" "I do believe!" "And do you believe in the Holy Ghost, the Holy Catholic Church, the communion of saints, the forgiveness of sins, the resurrection of the body, and life everlasting?" "I do believe!" "Do you wish to be baptized?" "I do."

And the climax of the great event, to which all else has been leading, is here. The godmother holds the baby, face up over the font, with the head tilted down a little so that the water will run from the forehead over the infant's head (and not into his eyes). The godfather places a hand upon the baby. This is very important, as he will not truly be the godfather unless he is touching the baby when the water is poured.

To me, who have baptized so many babies, this has always been a most solemn moment. I think of all the host of heaven gathered around the font, in eager anticipation as a new member is about to be added to the Mystical Body of Christ and the communion of saints. I think of almighty God Himself standing by, waiting, we might say, in impatient love for the moment when He can enter into this soul. I think of the tremendous miracle of grace that is about to occur, and almost can feel the warmth of the Holy Spirit's presence. (And we take it all so casually: "We had the baby baptized last Sunday.")

With hand poised the priest now tips the baptismal shell, and the saving water flows over the child's head as the priest, speaking again in Latin, pronounces the words which Christ Himself gave for this sacrament: "I baptize you in the name of the Father, and of the Son, and of the Holy Spirit," thrice making the sign of the cross with the water as he speaks the words. In imagination we think of the life-saving waters as closing over the child's head to bury forever man's ancient burden of sin, so that the child may rise triumphantly from the waters, a new man in Christ. This particular symbolism of Baptism was more graphic in ancient times, when Baptism was often given by complete immersion. But even in today's Baptism by infusion (pouring) the meaning still is there.

The climax past, the ceremony moves rapidly to a conclusion. The child now is a child of God, a prince or princess in the royal family of heaven. The child also is a sharer in Christ's eternal priesthood. Just as kings and queens of old were anointed, and priests, too, the child now is anointed. With holy chrism the priest traces a cross on the top of the baby's head with the accompanying Latin prayer which consecrates the child to God. Holy chrism is specifically the oil of consecration. A new altar is consecrated with holy chrism. A new chalice is consecrated with holy chrism. And so is this new Christian.

Then the white baptismal robe is placed upon the child. "Receive this white robe and carry it unstained to the judgment seat of our Lord Jesus Christ. . . ." The candle is presented to the child. "Receive this lighted candle, and keep your Baptism above reproach. . . ." And on the same note of peace with which he welcomed the child at the door, the priest bids him farewell: "Go in peace . . . and may the Lord be with you. Amen."

The parents have offered their child to God. God has given the child back to them, a saint.

Who Can Baptize?

Are you prepared, in an emergency, to administer the sacrament of Baptism? Probably you are. There are few Catholics who get through a course of religious instruction —even the First Communion class—without having drilled into them the importance of knowing how to give Baptism in case of necessity. Ordinarily it is the priest who must administer the sacrament of Baptism, and it would be very wrong for a lay person to do so without serious reason. At the same time it is essential that no person who is qualified to receive it should be allowed to die without Baptism. Baptism is an absolute prerequisite to heaven.

That is why our Lord Jesus Christ has thrown this sacrament "wide open" in case of urgent need. In such a case— when an unbaptized person is in danger of death, is eligible to receive the sacrament, and no priest is available—then just *anybody* may baptize. Even a non-Catholic, even an atheist, can validly administer Baptism, so long as he has the intention at least of "doing whatever it is that the Catholic Church does" by this ceremony, and performs the act correctly.

The act itself is as simple as any act could be. It consists in pouring plain tap water on the forehead of the person to be baptized and at the same time pronouncing audibly the words (*while the water is being poured*), "I baptize thee in the name of the Father, and of the Son, and of the Holy Spirit." These are words that every Catholic should know as well as he knows his own name. Someone's eternal salvation may one day depend upon the knowing of these words. In solemn Baptism administered in church, the water used is of course the baptismal water, especially blessed each year on Holy Saturday. In private Baptism, however, plain water is used, in preference even to holy water.

Quite frequently, private Baptism is administered in hospitals to newborn babies whose survival seems to be in doubt. If it is a Catholic hospital, then the parents need have no worry. One of the Sisters or one of the nurses will see to it that a baby is baptized if its life appears to be in danger. However, a prospective mother who must go to a non-Catholic hospital, particularly if her physician is not a Catholic, should make provision for the baptism of her infant in rase of necessity. Under such circumstances it would be well for the mother to have the words of Baptism written out on a card or a piece of paper. Before going to the delivery room she could give the card to the doctor (or nurse) with this request: "Doctor, if it looks as if the baby may not live, will you please pour a little water on the baby's head and say these words while you are pouring the water; and just have the intention of doing what my Church wants done by Baptism?"

If the baby should become suddenly ill at home before he has been baptized, then a member of the family can (and should) baptize the child. An infant's hold on life is pretty frail at best, and sometimes the margin between life and death is rather narrow. In such an event there is no need to wait for the priest. The Baptism will be just as effective, no matter who gives it. And the Baptism should be given unconditionally—that is, without any *ifs* or *ands*. Whether he lives or dies, this is the child's Baptism. It will not be repeated.

However, if the privately baptized baby survives the danger of death, then the pastor should be notified of the Baptism—the date, and by whom performed—so that he can enter it in the baptismal record book. Remember that later on the child will need a certificate of Baptism in order to receive his First Holy Communion and other sacraments. When the child recovers, the parents should also arrange with the pastor to have the child receive the other ceremonies of Baptism. The child will be brought to church at the time scheduled for Baptisms and will receive all the ceremonies of solemn Baptism—the blessed salt, the exorcisms, the anointings, the candle, and the robe—all except the actual pouring of the water, unless there is some reason to fear that this was not done properly.

When a child is baptized privately, he should have godparents (at least one) if it is convenient to secure them; perhaps Catholic neighbors or relatives who are at hand. All that is necessary is that the persons have the intention of being godparents and touch the child while the water is being poured. In this case, the same couple (if they can) should accompany the child to church when the supplemental ceremonies are performed. In practice, however, it seldom is feasible to have godparents at a private Baptism, especially in a hospital. In that case the godparents at the supplying of the ceremonies may be whatever couple the parents may wish to ask. It is a point of minor interest to note that only godparents who assist at the actual Baptism, whether in person or by proxy, contract a spiritual relationship with the child. Those who assist only at the supplying of the ceremonies do not establish such a relationship.

It is unlikely that we ever shall have occasion to give private Baptism to an adult. But it could happen. A prospective convert might suddenly become gravely ill before being received into the Church. Or an unbaptized friend might on his deathbed express a desire to be baptized, and have the necessary faith to receive Baptism: faith in God the Blessed Trinity as the rewarder of the just and the punisher of the wicked and in Jesus Christ as God's own Son and our Redeemer, and the willingness to accept all that the Catholic Church teaches. Such opportunities to administer Baptism may never come to us, but it is of profound importance that we be prepared.

If Baptism is so absolutely necessary in order to get to heaven (and it is), then what about all those people who die without even having a chance to be baptized; who perhaps don't even know about Baptism? Will they lose heaven when it's no fault of theirs at all?

No one who has reached the age of reason loses heaven except through his own fault. It is an article of Christian faith, defined by the Church, that God gives to every soul He creates sufficient grace to be saved. No one ever will be able to say: "I lost heaven because I couldn't help it."

For those who have no opportunity to be baptized, the

path to God is the path of love. A person who loves God above all things else and desires to do all that God wants him to do has Baptism of desire. If circumstances make it impossible for him to receive sacramental Baptism, his Baptism of desire will be sufficient to open for him the gates of heaven. Just as supreme love for God forgives all sin, even mortal sin, in the soul of a baptized person who cannot get to confession, so also supreme love for God will take away all sin, original as well as actual sin, from the soul of one who cannot yet receive Baptism.

When a person who loves God knows about Baptism and wants to be baptized, we call that *explicit* Baptism of desire. When a person ignorant of Baptism loves God and has the desire to do all that God wants, we call that *implicit* Baptism of desire. In other words, the desire for Baptism is contained implicitly in the desire to do God's will. If the person knew about Baptism and knew that God wanted him to receive it, the person would be baptized; what God wants, he wants.

A person taking instruction in preparation for Baptism would have *explicit* Baptism of desire if his faith were accompanied by a love for God for His own sake. A devout Jew or Mohammedan with supreme love for God might well have *implicit* Baptism of desire.

The highest form of substitute for sacramental Baptism of desire is that which we call Baptism of blood. "Greater love than this no one has, that one lay down his life for his friends" (John 15:13). Even without Baptism, anyone who suffers martyrdom for the sake of Christ is certain of his eternal reward. Martyrdom is defined as "the suffering, from a supernatural motive, of death or a mortal wound inflicted out of hatred for Christ, His religion, or a Christian virtue."

The term "martyr" is reserved officially for one who has suffered a bloody or a violent death for Christ. In the days when the Church was formulating her definition of martyrdom, death at the hands of Christ's enemies was usually quick, if not always merciful. It remained for our modern "civilized" age to refine methods of torture by which death could be made to last for years and a man could be killed without leaving a mark upon his body. There are many souls today in Communist prisons and slave-labor camps who are suffering what Bishop Fulton Sheen has called "dry martyrdom." There can be no questioning the reality of their martyrdom. Their agony of mind and body may last for years. Whether they die of dysentery or other prison-contracted disease or are left to freeze to death where they drop of exhaustion—it will be a martyr's palm that they bear with them into eternity. And doubtless many among them—especially in China—are catechumens who never had the opportunity to be baptized before their imprisonment.

CHAPTER XXV

Confirmation

The Sacrament of Confirmation

Being born and growing up are two different events in a person's life. We all recognize that fact. We also recognize that there is a close dependency between the two events. It is obvious that a person cannot grow up unless first he has been born. It is almost as obvious that the purpose of birth has been to some extent frustrated if the process of growing up does not follow. We feel sympathy for the dwarf, whose full physical development has been thwarted by some glandular defect. We feel pity for the idiot, whose mental growth has been arrested by some defect of the brain cells. We are born in order to grow, and in growth our birth is perfected.

These very evident facts of physical life may help us to understand, in our spiritual life, the close relationship between the sacraments of Baptism and Confirmation. While Confirmation is a distinct and complete sacrament in its own right, yet its purpose is to perfect in us that which was

331

begun in Baptism. We might say—in a sense—that we are baptized in order to be confirmed.

We are born spiritually in the sacrament of Baptism. We become sharers in the divine life of the most Blessed Trinity. We begin to live a supernatural life. As we practice the virtues of faith and hope and love and as we unite with Christ in His Church in offering worship to God, we also grow in grace and goodness. But at this stage our spiritual life, like the life of a child, is largely self-centered. We tend to be preoccupied with the needs of our own soul, with the effort to "be good." We cannot be *wholly* self-centered, of course; not if we understand what it means to be a member of Christ's Mystical Body; not if we understand the significance of the Mass as an act of *group* worship and Holy Communion as the bond of union with our fellows. But in general our religious life does revolve around self.

Then we are confirmed. We receive a special grace by which our faith is deepened and strengthened, so that it will be strong enough not only for our own needs but for the needs of others with whom we shall try to share it. With the onset of adolescence a child begins to assume, progressively more and more, the responsibilities of adulthood. He begins to see his place in the total family picture and in the community at large. Similarly, the confirmed Christian begins to see more clearly (or *ought* to) his responsibility to Christ for his neighbor. He becomes deeply concerned (or *ought* to) with the welfare of Christ-in-the-world—which is the Church—and the welfare of Christ-in-his-neighbor. It is in this sense that Confirmation is a spiritual "growing up."

In order that we may have such a concern for Church and neighbor, in deed as well as in feeling, the sacrament of Confirmation gives us a special grace and a special power. Just as the "mark" or character of Baptism made us sharers with Christ in His role of priest, giving us the power to participate with Him in divine worship, so also the character of Confirmation makes us sharers with Christ in His role of prophet or teacher. We now participate with Him in the task of extending His kingdom, of adding new souls to His Mystical Body. Our words and our works are directed not merely to our own sanctification but also to the purpose of making Christ's truths alive and real for those around us.

The Catechism defines Confirmation as "the sacrament through which the Holy Ghost comes to us in a special way and enables us to profess our faith as strong and perfect Christians and soldiers of Jesus Christ." The analogy by which the confirmed Christian is compared to a soldier is one that has been hallowed by long usage. It is a meaningful analogy if it is understood aright. The confirmed Christian has a soldier's unshakable loyalty to the King Whose cause he serves. He is prepared to undergo any suffering in the service of that King. He will resist evil wherever he may find it—to the death if necessary. He will do all that he can to expand his Sovereign's kingdom.

It is to be feared, however, that many Catholics see their role of soldier in a negative light. They see themselves as being on the defensive, ready to fight for the faith if the fight is brought to their own doorstep. Or they see Christ's kingdom—and themselves—as being in a state of siege, surrounded by the enemy, fighting for mere survival.

That definitely is not the true and dynamic concept of the grace and the power of Confirmation. The confirmed Christian—whether we call him a spiritual soldier or a spiritual adult—goes forth joyfully in the fulfillment of his vocation. Strong in his faith and with an ardent love for souls which stems from his love for Christ, he feels a continual *concern* for others. He feels a restless discontent unless he is doing something worth-while for others—something to ease their burdens in this life, and something to make more secure their promise of life eternal. His words and his actions proclaim to those around him: "Christ *lives*, and He lives for you." The grace to do this is the grace which Jesus promised to His Apostles (and to us) when He said: "You shall receive power when the Holy Spirit comes upon you, and you shall be witnesses for Me. . . . even to the very ends of the earth" (Acts 1:8).

We do not know exactly when, during His public life, Jesus instituted the sacrament of Confirmation. This is one of the "many other things that Jesus did" which, as St. John tells us, are not written down in the Gospels (see John 21:25). We know that the tradition of the Church (the teachings of the Church which have been handed down to us from our Lord, or from His Apostles inspired by the Holy Ghost) is of equal authority with Sacred Scripture as a source of divine truth. If a "Bible-only" friend thrusts out his jaw and says, "Show it to me in the Bible; I don't believe it unless it's in the Bible," we do not fall into *that* trap. We answer sweetly by saying: "Show me in the Bible where it says that we must believe only what is written there."

However, it does happen that the Bible tells us about Confirmation. Not under that name, of course. Aside from Baptism, our present names for the sacraments were developed by the early theologians of the Church; "Laying on of hands" was the earliest name for Confirmation. This is the name which the Bible uses in the following passage taken from the Acts of the Apostles: "Now when the Apostles in Jerusalem heard that Samaria had received the word of God, they sent to them Peter and John. On their arrival they prayed for them, that they might receive the Holy Spirit; for as yet He had not come upon any of them, but they had only been baptized in the name of the Lord Jesus. Then they laid their hands on them and they received the Holy Spirit. But when Simon [the magician] saw that the Holy Spirit was given through the laying on of the Apostles' hands, he offered them money, saying, 'Give me also this power, so that anyone on whom I lay my hands may receive the Holy Spirit'" (Acts 8:14–19).

It is from this passage, and the attempt of the magician

Simon to buy the power to give Confirmation, that we get the word "simony"—the name given to the sin of buying and selling sacred things. That, however, is a very minor point. The real significance of this passage lies in what it tells us about the sacrament of Confirmation. It tells us that while Confirmation is a *complement* to Baptism, a completing of what was begun in Baptism, nevertheless Confirmation is a sacrament *distinct from* Baptism. The Samaritans already had been baptized, yet it still was necessary for them to receive the "laying on of hands." The passage also tells us the way in which Confirmation was to be given: by the placing of the hand of the one who confirms, upon the head of the one to be confirmed, with a prayer that he may receive the Holy Spirit.

For the moment, though, we are particularly interested in *this* fact which the passage makes plain: the fact that it was the Apostles—that is, the *bishops*—who did the confirming. Whoever it was who had baptized the Samaritans very evidently did not have the power to "lay hands" upon them and to impart to them the Holy Spirit. Two of the Apostles, Peter and John, had to travel from Jerusalem to Samaria in order to give the sacrament of Confirmation to these new Christians.

As it was in the beginning, so it is now. Ordinarily it is only the bishop who may confirm. No one below a bishop can give the sacrament of Confirmation unless he is given permission to do so by the Pope himself. The Holy Father does sometimes give this permission to priests in missionary lands where bishops may be few and far between. From ancient times the Popes also have given permission to the priests of the Greek Catholic Church to administer the sacrament of Confirmation. In the Greek Catholic Church the priest who baptizes a child also gives Confirmation immediately afterwards. In the Latin Catholic Church, as we know, Confirmation is not customarily given until after a child has made his first Holy Communion.

Pope Pius XII, who did so much to make the sacraments more easily available to the people, did a most fatherly thing in 1947. He gave permission to all pastors, everywhere —when a bishop is not available—to administer the sacrament of Confirmation to any unconfirmed person within their parish who might be in danger of death from sickness, accident, or old age. In our own country it does not often happen that a person reaches adulthood without being confirmed. However, if it ever should happen that a member of the family is in danger of death and has not been confirmed, the pastor should be informed of that fact. He will administer the sacrament of Confirmation along with the Last Sacraments.

This will hold true even if it is a baby who is in danger of death. While Confirmation in the Latin Catholic Church is given normally only to children who have reached the age of reason, that limitation does not apply to children who are in danger of death. So long as a child has been baptized, he has a right also to Confirmation if he is threatened by death. Parents should be quick to notify the pastor if such a crisis should occur in their family. If God should take the child, let him enter heaven with the glorious character of Confirmation, as well as the character of Baptism upon his soul.

Incidentally, it is only the pastor, or a priest taking his place, with the powers of a pastor, who has this power to give Confirmation in virtue of the concession granted in 1947 by Pope Pius XII. The Holy Father did not extend this privilege to assistant pastors.

The Meaning of Confirmation

Most of us probably have witnessed the giving of the sacrament of Confirmation several times—as recipients, as parents, perhaps as sponsors. We know that, as the ceremony begins, the bishop stands facing those who are to be confirmed, with his hands extended towards them, symbolically extended *over* them. With his hands extended, the bishop invokes the Holy Spirit upon the Confirmation candidates, saying (in Latin) the following prayer: "Almighty and eternal God, Who in Thy kindness hast given to these Thy servants a new birth through water and the Holy Spirit, and granted to them remission of all their sins: send forth from heaven upon them Thy sevenfold Spirit, the Holy Paraclete. Amen. The Spirit of wisdom and understanding. Amen. The Spirit of counsel and fortitude. Amen. The Spirit of knowledge and piety. Amen. Mercifully fill them with the Spirit of Thy fear, and seal them with the sign of the cross of Christ, that they may obtain everlasting life. Through our Lord Jesus Christ. . . ."

Then comes the essential part of the ceremony, in which the bishop places his hand upon the head of each individual. For this part some bishops sit at the altar and the candidates come one by one to kneel before the bishop. Other bishops prefer to have the candidates kneel at the altar railing while the bishop himself proceeds from one to the other. In either case, as he places his hand upon the head of the *confirmandus* (the one to be confirmed), the bishop simultaneously traces, with his thumb, the sign of the cross on the person's forehead—having first dipped his thumb in the holy chrism. While doing this he says (in Latin), "I sign you with the sign of the Cross and I confirm you with the Chrism of salvation, in the name of the Father and of the Son and of the Holy Spirit."

Chrism is one of the three kinds of holy oil which a bishop blesses each year at his Mass on Holy Thursday. The other two kinds of holy oil are the oil of catechumens (used in Baptism) and the oil of the sick (used in Extreme Unction). The holy oils, all of them, are composed of pure olive oil. From ancient times, olive oil has been looked upon as a strengthening substance; so much so that athletes were accustomed to bathe in olive oil before taking part in athletic contests. The significance of the holy oils used in the administration of the sacraments is then very evident: the oil represents the strengthening effect of God's grace. Besides the distinct and special blessing which each holy oil receives, chrism has another difference: balm has been mixed with it. Balm is a fragrant substance procured from the balsam tree. In the holy chrism it symbolizes the "sweet odor" of virtue; it tells of the spiritual fragrance, the *attractiveness* that should characterize the life of him who puts his Confirmation graces to work.

The cross which is traced upon the forehead of the person being confirmed is a powerful symbol if it is really understood and acted upon. It is quite easy to know whether I do understand and act accordingly. I have only to ask myself: "Do I actually live as though there were a visible cross branded on my forehead, marking me as 'Christ's man' or 'Christ's woman'? In my daily life, do I really bear witness to Christ? By my attitude towards others, by my treatment of those around me, by my actions in general do I proclaim: 'This is what it means to be a Christian; this is what it means to live by the Gospel'?" If the answer is no, then it means that there is a lot of grace being wasted—the special grace of Confirmation. It is a grace which is available to me in abundance if I will but use it; the strengthening grace which will enable me to overcome my human pettiness, my cowardice in the face of human opinion, my fearfulness of sacrifice.

If there is one thing which all of us remember from our own Confirmation, it is the "slight blow on the cheek"—a gentle tap, really—with which the bishop finished. This is not an essential part of the ceremony; in fact it was only in the twelfth century that it was added to the rite of Confirmation. Very likely this "blow on the cheek" was taken over from the medieval custom of "dubbing" knights. When a man was elevated to knighthood, his sovereign would tap him on the neck or shoulder with the flat side of a sword. This was called the accolade. In Confirmation we become knights of Christ ("soldiers" is the word the Catechism uses). We pledge our loyalty to Christ. We are ready to suffer anything rather than betray Him. But let us emphasize again that it is not a mere *passive* suffering that we undertake to endure for our Sovereign. It is the inevitable suffering, the self-sacrifice involved in the active giving of ourselves to His service.

It is customary, in Confirmation, to add a new name to those we already possess; or rather, to place ourselves under the patronage of an additional patron saint. It is almost as though, in awe of the new dignity to which we are raised —that of apostles, of witnesses to Christ—we realize our need of powerful friends in heaven. And so we add another patron saint to those we already have. It is by this new name that the bishop addresses us as he places his hand upon our head and calls down upon us the Holy Spirit Who can, if we will let Him, transform our lives.

Without Baptism we cannot go to heaven. Without Confirmation we *can* get to heaven, but the going will be much rougher. In fact, without Confirmation it would be easy to lose our way entirely, easy to lose our faith. That is why it is of obligation for every baptized person to be also confirmed if he has the opportunity of receiving the sacrament of Confirmation. We know that Jesus did not institute any of the sacraments "just for the fun of it." Jesus instituted each individual sacrament because He foresaw, in His infinite wisdom, that we would have need of certain special graces under certain particular circumstances.

He foresaw, among other things, the dangers to which our faith would be exposed. Some of the dangers would be from within, as when passion or self-will wars with belief. We may wish to pursue some course of action which our faith forbids. We cannot live with a continual conflict raging inside ourselves. We want interior peace. Something has to give. If we could just convince ourselves that our faith is wrong, then we could follow our desires and still be at peace. It is at a time like this that the grace of Confirmation comes to our aid (if we will let it) and irresistibly pushes back the urgings of self-will so that faith may triumph. The peace we find then is a *real* peace.

Sometimes the dangers to our faith are from without. The dangerous state of the person who is suffering active persecution by imprisonment or torture—as are so many Christians in Communist countries—is obvious. We plainly can see his need for the grace of Confirmation. The dangerous state of those of us who live—as in America—in an atmosphere of religious indifferentism is not so obvious but is just as real. The danger of contagion always is present. We do so want to be a "good fellow" like everyone else. The temptation to soft-pedal our faith, to "not take it so seriously," is almost inescapable. It is the grace of Confirmation which will help us to preserve our sense of values and keep us on an even keel.

There also is danger from without which is peculiarly the danger to which an educated Catholic is exposed, particularly if he attends a secular university. Such a Catholic has to carry on his shoulders the whole burden of the Church's past, the human errors made by Christ's human agents. There were the bad Popes and the luxurious churchmen, the Galileo condemnation and the Spanish Inquisition. Forgetting that it is not Christ's agents who are divine, but rather Christ Himself in His Church, the Catholic begins to feel defensive and a little ashamed. Then there is the thinly veiled contempt of many non-Catholic scholars for religious belief in general, and for Catholic belief in particular, and their airy dismissal of religion as something which primitive man thought up for himself. From being a little ashamed, the intellectual Catholic now begins to feel a little resentful against the faith which seems to make him the laughing-stock of men whom he admires as learned and wise. It is here again that the grace of Confirmation proves equal to the need. The Catholic remembers that today's human wisdom is tomorrow's human folly—while God and His truths endure forever. Strong in his faith, he listens undisturbed to the profundities of the professors.

Yes, we all have need of the grace of Confirmation. So much so that it is a sin for us to neglect receiving this sacrament when we have the opportunity to receive it. The sin would be a mortal sin if our neglect were due to a disdain for the sacrament itself. Parents who would carelessly fail to provide for the Confirmation of their children also would be guilty of a serious sin of neglect.

While it is the custom in the Eastern Church to confirm children at the time of their Baptism, it is the tradition of the Latin Church to confirm children after they have reached the age of reason—at or near the age of seven. Adults who never have been confirmed, whether converts or otherwise, can easily arrange to be confirmed by consulting with their pastor. In either case, whether child or adult, the candidate for Confirmation will have a sponsor. The sponsor must be of the same sex as the person for whom he stands and at least thirteen years of age. The sponsor must be a practicing Catholic who already has been confirmed— and he may not be one of the Confirmation candidate's baptismal godparents. Like the baptismal godparents, the Confirmation sponsor has the duty to do all in his power, especially by example and encouragement, to help his spiritual "ward" achieve a fully Catholic life.

The special *sacramental* grace of Confirmation is, as we have seen, a strengthening of our faith. On the negative side, our faith is strengthened against temptation and persecution; on the positive side, our faith is strengthened to the end that we may become active witnesses to Christ. Confirmation also gives to the soul an increase in that basic source of life, *sanctifying* grace. God cannot increase what is not already there; hence the person to be confirmed must be in the state of sanctifying grace when he receives this sacrament. To receive Confirmation while in the state of mortal sin would be an abuse of the sacrament—the grave sin of sacrilege. The sacrament still would be valid, however. The moment the person received forgiveness of his sins, at that very moment the delayed graces of Confirmation would come to him.

CHAPTER XXVI

The Eucharist

The Greatest Sacrament

As we undertake to discuss the sacrament of the Holy Eucharist, we are somewhat in the position of the traveler who returns to revisit a well-known land. We shall encounter many remembered sights—in this case truths—which we have seen before. Yet in these remembered truths we can expect to perceive facets of interest previously missed. We also can expect to discover other sights—other truths—which had entirely escaped our observation on former visits to this familiar and beloved land, this topic of greatest of all the sacraments.

In saying that the Holy Eucharist is the greatest of all the sacraments, we are stating the obvious. Baptism of course is the most *necessary* sacrament; without Baptism we cannot get to heaven. Yet, despite all the wonderful things that Baptism and the other five sacraments accomplish in the soul, they still are but instruments of God for the giving of grace; while in the Holy Eucharist we have not merely an instrument for the giving of grace—we have the actual Giver of grace Himself, Jesus Christ our Lord truly and personally present.

The sacrament of Christ's Body and Blood has had many names in the course of Christian history. Such names as Bread of Angels, Lord's Supper, and Sacrament of the Altar are familiar to us. But the name which has endured from the very beginning, the name which the Church officially gives to this sacrament, is that of Holy Eucharist. This name is taken from the account of the institution of the Holy Eucharist as it is given in the Bible. All four of the sacred writers—Matthew (26:26–28), Mark (14:22–24), Luke (22: 19–20) and Paul (I Corinthians 11:23–29)—who describe the Last Supper, tell us that Jesus, as He took the bread and wine into His hands, "gave thanks." And so from the Greek word "eucharistia" which means "a giving of thanks" we have the name of our sacrament: the Holy Eucharist.

The catechism points out that the Holy Eucharist is both a *sacrifice* and a *sacrament*. As a sacrifice the Holy Eucharist is the Mass, that divine action in which Jesus, through the agency of the human priest, changes the bread and wine into His own Body and Blood and continues through time the offering which He made to God on Calvary—the offering of Himself for mankind. It is at the consecration of the Mass that the *sacrament* of the Holy Eucharist comes into being (or is "confected" as the theologians say); it is then that Jesus becomes present under the appearance of bread and wine. As long as the appearances of bread and wine remain, Jesus remains present and the sacrament of the Holy Eucharist continues to there exist. The act by which we *receive* the Holy Eucharist is called Holy Communion.

We might say that the Mass is the "making" of the Holy Eucharist and Holy Communion is the receiving of the Holy Eucharist. In between the two, the sacrament of the Holy Eucharist continues to exist (as in the tabernacle) whether we receive It or not.

In undertaking to deepen our knowledge of this sacrament, we could not do better than to begin where Christ began: with that day in the town of Capharnaum when Jesus made the almost unbelievable promise that He would give His own Flesh and Blood to be the food of our souls.

Jesus had laid the foundation for His promise the preceding day. Knowing that He was going to put a tremendous strain on the faith of His hearers, He prepared them for it. Seated on a mountain side, across the Sea of Galilee from Capharnaum, Jesus had been preaching to the great crowd that had followed Him there. As evening drew near He prepared to dismiss the crowd. However, moved both by compassion and in preparation for the morrow's promise, Jesus worked the miracle of the loaves and fishes. He fed the vast crowd (the men alone numbering five thousand) with five loaves and two fish; and when it was over His disciples gathered up twelve baskets of left-over scraps. This miracle would (or should) be in the minds of hearers when they would listen to him the next day.

Having sent the crowd away, Jesus went further up the mountain to pray, as He so often did, in solitude. The crowd however was not so easily got rid of; they wanted to see more miracles and hear more words of wisdom from this Jesus of Nazareth. So they camped there for the night, and watched the disciples put off from shore (without Jesus) and head for Capharnaum in the only boat that was there. That night Jesus, having finished His prayer, came walking across the stormy waters to join His disciples in their boat, and arrived at Capharnaum with them.

The next morning the crowd could not find Jesus. When boats from Tiberius came along, the discouraged searchers gave up their quest and took passage on the boats to Capharnaum. They were amazed to find Jesus there ahead of them; He had not been in the only boat which departed the previous night. It was another wonder, another miracle by which Jesus sought to strengthen their faith (and the faith of His disciples) for the test that was soon to come.

His disciples and such of the crowd as could find entrance, gathered about Him in Capharnaum's synagogue. It was there and then that He made the promise from which we today draw strength and life: the promise of His own Flesh and Blood as our food; the promise of the Holy Eucharist.

If He had the power to multiply five loaves of bread so as to feed five thousand men, why could He not feed all mankind on a heavenly Bread of His own making. If He could walk on water as though it were dry land, why could He not also command the elements of bread and wine to do His bidding—to lend their outward seeming as a cloak for His own Person? Jesus had prepared His hearers well for His promise of the Holy Eucharist. As we shall see, He needed to.

If we have a copy of the Bible or of the New Testament, it would be well for us to read the entire sixth chapter of St. John's gospel. Only by doing so can we get the full flavor, with its background and its build-up, of this scene in the synagogue at Capharnaum. Here we can quote only the most pertinent lines, beginning with verse 52 and ending with verse 67.

"I am the living bread that has come down from heaven," Jesus says. *"If anyone eat of this bread he shall live forever; and the bread that I will give is my flesh for the life of the world." The Jews on that account argued with one another saying, "How can this man give us his flesh to eat?" Jesus therefore said to them, "Amen, amen, I say to you, unless you eat the flesh of the Son of Man, and drink his blood, you shall not have life in you. He who eats my flesh and drinks my blood has life everlasting and I will raise him up on the last day. For my flesh is food indeed and my blood is drink indeed . . . This is the bread that has come down from heaven; not as your fathers ate the manna, and died. He who eats this bread shall live forever." . . . Many of his disciples therefore, when they had heard this, said, "This is a hard saying. Who can listen to it?" But Jesus, knowing in himself that his disciples were murmuring at this, said to them, ". . . The words that I have spoken to you are spirit and life. But there are some among you who do not believe." . . . From this time many of his disciples turned back and no longer went about with him.*

This brief extract from St. John's sixth chapter contains the two points which most interest us at the moment: the two points which tell us, months before the Last Supper, that it will be the true and real Body and Blood of Jesus Christ which will be present in the Holy Eucharist. We know that Martin Luther rejected the doctrine of the true and substantial presence of Jesus in the Holy Eucharist, a doctrine which had been firmly believed by all Christians for fifteen hundred years. Luther did admit some sort of presence of Christ, at least at the actual moment of receiving Holy Communion. But as other Protestant churches sprang up in the fields fertilized by Luther, more and more they refused to accept belief in the Real Presence. In most Protestant churches today, the Lord's Supper or the communion service is held to be merely a memorial rite commemorative of the Lord's death; with the bread still remaining bread and the wine still remaining wine.

In trying to escape from the doctrine of the Real Presence, Protestant theologians have tried to explain away Christ's words as not being meant in a real sense, but only in a spiritual sense, or figuratively. But there can be no "watering down" of Christ's words without doing violence to their very evident meaning. Jesus hardly could have been more emphatic: "My flesh is food indeed, and my blood is drink indeed." There just was no way in which our Lord could have put it more plainly. In the original Greek in which St. John wrote his gospel, the Greek word which in verse 55 is translated as "eat" is really closer, in its original meaning, to the English words "crunch" or "munch."

Trying to explain Christ's words as being only a figure of speech, runs into another snag. Among the Jews, to whom Jesus was speaking, the only time that the phrase "to eat someone's flesh" was used figuratively was when it meant to hate that person, to persecute him vengefully. Similarly "to drink someone's blood" meant to visit severe punishments upon him. Neither of these meanings—the only figurative meanings known to the Jews—would make sense in this discourse of Christ.

Another forceful proof that Jesus really meant what He said—that it would be His real Flesh and Blood in the Holy Eucharist—is the fact that some of Christ's disciples deserted Him because they found the idea of eating Him too repulsive. They did not have enough faith to see that if Jesus gave His Flesh and Blood as their food and drink, He would do it in a way that would not be repugnant to human nature. So they left Him, "and no longer went about with Him." Jesus never would have let these disciples go if their defection was simply the result of a misunderstanding. Again and again at other times He took the trouble to clarify His words when they were misunderstood. For example when He told Nicodemus (John 3:3) that a man must be born again, and Nicodemus asked how a grown man could enter again into his mother's womb, Jesus very patiently set Nicodemus straight on the matter of Baptism. Here however at Capharnaum Jesus did not call His deserting disciples back to explain that they had misunderstood Him. He could not call them back. They had understood Him aright. It was their faith that was wanting, and sadly Jesus had to watch them go.

That is why we say that the doctrine of the Real Presence is inescapably contained in Christ's words of promise. Otherwise words have lost their meaning and Jesus speaks in hopeless riddles.

The Promise Is Kept

Almost a year before He died Jesus, in the synagogue at Capharnaum, promised that He would give His own Flesh and Blood to be the saving Food of mankind. At the Last Supper, the night before His crucifixion, Jesus fulfilled that promise. It was then that He made His last will and testament. To His Church and each member of it He bequeathed, not lands and buildings and money, but a legacy such as only God could make: the gift of His very own living Self.

There are four accounts of the Last Supper given in the Bible, by Matthew (26:26-28), Mark (14:22-24), Luke (22:19-20) and Paul (I Corinthians 11:23-29). St. John, who gives us the account of the promise of the Holy Eucharist, did not bother to repeat the story of the institution of this Sacrament. He was the last of the apostles to write a Gospel, and knew of the other descriptions which already had been written. St. John chose instead to give us the beautiful words of Our Lord's final talk with His disciples at the Last Supper.

Here is the account of the institution of the Holy Eucharist as it is given by St. Paul: ". . . the Lord Jesus, on the night in which He was betrayed, took bread, and giving thanks broke, and said, 'This is my body which shall be given up for you; do this in remembrance of me.' In like manner also the cup, after he had supped, saying, 'This cup is the new covenant in my blood; do this as often as you drink it, in remembrance of me.' "

No words of Jesus could have been plainer than these. "This": that is, "This substance which I hold in My hands, which as I begin speaking is bread, and as I finish speaking is no longer bread, but My own Body." "This cup": that is, "This cup which as I begin speaking contains wine, but which as I finish speaking contains no longer wine, but My own Blood."

"This is my body," and "This cup is . . . my blood." The apostles took Jesus literally. They accepted the fact (and what an act of faith it was!) that the substance which still looked like bread, was now the Body of Jesus; and that the substance which still had all the appearances of wine, now was the Blood of Jesus. This was the doctrine which the apostles preached to the infant Church. This was the universal belief of all Christians for a thousand years. In the eleventh century a heretic named Berengarius questioned the truth of the Real Presence and taught that Jesus was speaking only figuratively, that the consecrated Bread and Wine wasn't *really* His Body and Blood. This heresy of Berengarius was condemned by three Church Councils, and eventually Berengarius retracted his error and returned to the fold. The doctrine of the Real Presence remained the undisputed belief of Christians for another five hundred years.

Then, in the sixteenth century, came Martin Luther and the Protestant Reformation. Luther himself did not entirely deny the Real Presence of Jesus in the Holy Eucharist; Luther admitted that the words of Jesus were too plain to be explained any other way. But Luther wanted to abolish the Mass, and also any adoration of Jesus as being present on the altar. Luther solved his dilemma by teaching that, although the bread is still bread and the wine still is wine, Jesus does become present along with the substance of the bread and wine; but, Luther maintained, Jesus is present only at the moment the bread and wine are received; not before or after.

Other Protestant Reformers went much farther than Luther, and completely denied the Real Presence. They—and Protestant theologians since their time—maintained that when Jesus said, "This is My Body," and "This is My Blood," Jesus was using a figure of speech. What He really meant, they say, was "This *represents* My Body," or "This is a *symbol* of My Blood." In an attempt to escape the obvious meaning of Christ's words, these Protestant divines have resorted to all sorts of unlikely explanations and interpretations; but they leave unanswered the really solid arguments which prove that Jesus said what He meant, and meant what He said.

The first such argument is found in the seriousness of the occasion. On this, the night before His death, Jesus is making His last will and testament. A last will is no place for figurative speech; under the best of circumstances courts sometimes have difficulty in interpreting a testator's intentions aright, even without the confusion of symbolic language. Moreover, since Jesus is God, He knew that as a result of His words this night, untold millions of people would be worshiping Him through the centuries under the appearance of bread. If He would not really be present under those appearances, the worshipers would be adoring a mere piece of bread, and would be guilty of idolatry. Certainly that is not something that God Himself would set the stage for, by talking in obscure figures of speech.

That the apostles did believe that Jesus meant exactly what He said, is evident from the fact that Christians, from the very beginning, believed in the real presence of Jesus in the Holy Eucharist. They could have got this belief no where else except from the apostles. And who, better than the apostles, should know what Christ did mean? They were there. They could—and surely did—ask all the questions they might wish, as to what Jesus meant by these words. We sometimes forget that very little of what passed between Jesus and his disciples is found in the Gospels. It would take a tall stack of books to contain three years of conversation, of questions and answers, of teachings.

When Jesus, on Holy Thursday night said, "This is My Body," over the bread, and, "This is My Blood," over the wine, the apostles took His words at their face value; their later conduct proves that clearly. If Jesus was using a metaphor; if what He really meant was, "This bread is a sort of symbol of My Body, and this wine a symbol of My Blood; hereafter, any time that My followers get together and partake of bread and wine like this, they will be honoring Me and representing My death"; if that is what Jesus meant, then the apostles got Him all wrong. And through their misunderstanding, mankind for centuries has worshiped a piece of bread as God.

It is beyond belief that Jesus would have left His disciples in such error. At other times, many other times, Jesus corrected His apostles when they misunderstood Him—and in matters much less serious than this. To cite but one example, in Matthew's Gospel (16:6-12) Jesus tells the disciples to beware of the leaven of the Pharisees and Sadducees. They think Jesus is talking of real bread, and begin to mumble that they have none. Jesus patiently points out that He is talking about the *teachings* of the Pharisees and Sadducees, not about edible bread. At other times when Jesus uses metaphors, the sacred writer himself will make the meaning plain; as when Jesus says, "Destroy this temple, and in three days I will raise it up"; and John (2:19-21) explains that Jesus was speaking of the temple of His body. So often we find such incidents in the Gospels; and yet we are asked to believe that at the solemn moment of the Last Supper Jesus is using a new and strange figure of speech without explaining what His meaning really is.

It *is* a new and strange figure of speech. Bread is not a natural symbol of a man's body, nor wine of a man's blood. If I were to hold out a slice of bread towards someone and say, "This is my body," my companion would know that I was either joking or crazy. It is blasphemous to suppose that Jesus was either.

As a literary device, a figure of speech is usable only when its meaning is understandable. This may be the case either from the nature of the remark, as when I point to a picture and say, "This is my mother," or say of an active child, "He's a perpetual-motion machine," or of a fast horse, "That nag is greased lightning"; or the metaphor may be understood because its meaning is explained, as when I arrange some matches on the table and say, "Now this is my house, and the bedroom is right here." But neither by the nature of the case nor by explanation given, can the words, "This is my Body" have any meaning as a metaphor.

The idea of Jesus speaking in metaphors at the Last Supper becomes all the more incredible when we remember that He was addressing men who were—most of them—poor, uneducated fishermen. They were not trained in the niceties of rhetoric. Indeed we almost marvel at their slow-wittedness up to the time that the Holy Spirit came upon them. An instance is that of the raising of Lazarus to life. We read (John 11:11–14) that Jesus said, "Lazarus, our friend, sleeps. But I go that I may wake him from his sleep." The disciples answered that it would be good for Lazarus if he was sleeping; the rest would help him to recover. "So then Jesus said to them plainly, 'Lazarus is dead.' " These were hardly the men for metaphors.

Another indication that Jesus was not speaking in metaphors when He said, "This is My Body," and "This is My Blood," is found in the words which St. Paul appends to his account of the Last Supper (I Corinthians, 11:27–30): "Therefore whoever eats this bread or drinks the cup of the Lord unworthily, will be guilty of the body and blood of the Lord. But let a man prove himself, and so let him eat of that bread and drink of the cup; for he who eats and drinks unworthily, without distinguishing the body, eats and drinks judgment to himself." A man hardly could be said to be guilty of the Body and Blood of the Lord, or to bring judgment (that is, grave condemnation) upon himself, if the bread that he ate was merely bread, even blessed bread; and if the wine still was just wine, even prayed-over wine.

We of course do not need any proofs such as those which so briefly have been sketched here, to bolster up our faith in the Real Presence of Jesus Christ in the Holy Eucharist. We believe this truth primarily, not because of rational proofs, but because Christ's Church, which cannot err in matters of faith and morals, has told us that it is so. But it is well to know some of the difficulties they are up against, who try to read meanings of their own into the words of Our Lord.

For ourselves, we prefer to follow this sound principle in

determining the meaning of something that was said: "Ask the man who heard it; ask the man who was there." The Apostles were there. The first Christians who listened to the preaching of the Apostles were, in a sense, there. Even we who have inherited that unbroken tradition were, in a sense, there. Aside from any formal dogma of the Church, we prefer to believe in the teaching of the Aopstles and in the all-but-unanimous belief of the Christian world for one thousand five hundred years, than to believe the strained explanations of the Protestant Reformers. Such men as Luther, Carlstadt, Zwingli and Calvin are asking a lot in asking men to believe that for fifteen centuries all Christians were wrong, and that now suddenly they, the Reformers, have found the right answer.

Bread No Longer

Exactly what did happen when Jesus at the Last Supper (and the priest this morning at Mass) said, "This is My Body," over the bread, and "This is My Blood," over the wine? We believe that the substance of the bread completely and totally ceased to exist, and that the substance of Christ's own Body replaced the annihilated substance of the bread. We believe that the wine entirely ceased to exist as wine, and that the substance of Christ's own Blood replaced the wine. We also believe that Jesus, by His almighty power as God, preserved the *appearances* of bread and wine, in spite of the fact that their substances were gone.

By "the appearances" of bread and wine we mean all those outward forms and accidentals which can be perceived in any way by our bodily senses of sight, touch, taste, hearing and smelling. The Holy Eucharist still looks like bread and wine, feels like bread and wine, tastes like bread and wine, smells like bread and wine, and if broken or splashed would sound like bread and wine. Even under a microscope or under electronic or radiological examination, it still would be only the qualities of bread and wine that we could perceive. Indeed, it is only the outward appearance of *any* thing that can be attained to by human observation. How a thing seems, how it behaves under specified circumstances, what qualities it possesses, what physical laws it seems to obey— these are the questions that science can investigate. But the underlying substance of anything, substance *as* substance, is beyond the reach of human senses and human instruments. Nowadays the science of nuclear physics theorizes that all matter is a form of energy; all matter is composed of electrically-charged particles in motion. The difference between a piece of wood and a piece of iron is simply the difference between the number and speed and direction of the electrically-charged particles which compose these two materials. But when the physicist succeeds, with an electronic camera, in photographing the path of some of these particles, it still is only with appearances that he is dealing. Substance *as* substance, that by which a thing is what it is and is not something else, still would be beyond the scientist's ken.

This whole matter of the relationship of "substance" (the *thingness* of a thing) to "accidents" (the perceivable qualities of a thing) is a philosophical question. To go into it here would carry us too far afield. For us it is enough to know, as we do know, that by the words of consecration the substance of Christ's Body replaces the substance of the bread, and the substance of Christ's Blood replaces the substance of wine, while the appearances of bread and wine still remain.

It is a miracle, of course; a continuing miracle wrought a hundred thousand times a day by God's infinite power. In fact it is a double miracle: there is the miracle of the change itself from bread and wine into Jesus Christ; and the further miracle by which God supports in existence the appearances of the bread and wine, although their underlying substance is gone—like the face of a man remaining in the mirror after the man has walked away.

This change which takes place, by the words of consecration, is such a special kind of change that the Church has to coin a special word to describe it. The word is "Transubstantiation," written always with a capital letter. It means, literally, a crossing from one substance to another; but in this case a unique and unparalleled kind of crossing.

We are familiar with many changes which things undergo in everyday life. Sometimes these are changes only in the *appearances*, as when water is frozen and becomes ice, or a lump of clay is molded and becomes a statue. We also see changes in which *both* substance and appearances are transformed, as when cider becomes vinegar, or carbon under pressure becomes coal or diamonds. And there have been miraculous changes of this kind, as when at Cana Jesus changed water into wine.

However, nowhere in the natural order, and as far as we know nowhere in the supernatural order, is there a change which takes place like the change that occurs in the bread and wine at the words of consecration: a change of substance without a change of appearances. That is why the word, "Transubstantiation" stands alone as a description of this daily miracle.

Although, by virtue of the words of consecration, it is the Body of Jesus which becomes present under the appearances of bread, and the Blood of Jesus under the appearances of wine; yet we know that the Person of Jesus, now that He is risen from the dead, cannot be divided. Where His Body is, His Blood also must be, and with His Body and Blood must also be His Soul and His Divine Nature to which His Body, Blood and Soul are united. Likewise where the Blood of Jesus is, all of Jesus must be. Consequently by the words, "This is My Body," the Body of Jesus becomes present, and by what theologians call *concomitance*—that is by the very nature of His unity of Person—the Blood, Soul and Divinity of Jesus also become present. By the words, "This is My Blood," the Blood of Jesus becomes present, and by concomitance also His Flesh, Soul and Godhead.

That is why it is not necessary to receive Holy Communion under the forms both of bread and of wine. If we receive under either form, of bread or of wine, we receive the *whole* Jesus, complete and entire.

Jesus Christ is present in the Holy Eucharist, whole and entire, under the appearance of bread and wine. He is simultaneously present in every single Sacred Host on every altar throughout the world, and under the appearance of wine in every single Consecrated Chalice wherever Mass is being offered. Moreover Jesus is present, whole and entire, in every part of every Sacred Host, and in every drop contained in the Consecrated Chalice. If a Sacred Host is divided—as the priest does divide the large Host at Mass— then Jesus is wholly present in each of the divided parts. If a crumb were to drop from the Sacred Host, or a drop were spilled from the Chalice, Jesus would be present in that crumb and in that drop.

This is one reason why the sacred linens have to be washed by a priest, deacon or subdeacon, once they have been used at Mass, before they can be laundered by anyone else; there might be some particle of the Sacred Species still clinging to them. The sacred linens include the corporal, upon which the Sacred Host and Chalice rest during Mass; the pall, the square linen cloth which covers the Chalice during Mass; and the purificator, the little linen towel with which the priest wipes his lips after consuming the Precious Blood, and with which he dries his fingers and the Chalice after washing out the Chalice with wine and water.

Jesus of course does not leave His place "at the right hand of God" in heaven to become present in the Holy Eucharist. He still is in heaven as well as on the altar. In fact it is the *glorified* Body of Jesus, His Body as it is in heaven today, which is present under the appearance of bread and wine. In the Holy Eucharist Jesus is present just as He is *at the time* of His presence. At the Last Supper for example it was the "passible" (that is, still mortal) Body of Jesus which was present after He spoke the words of consecration, since Jesus had not yet died. If the apostles had celebrated Mass during the three days Jesus was in the tomb, it would have been His dead Body which was present. His bloodless Body only would have been present under the appearance of bread, and His bodiless Blood only (soaked into Calvary's soil) under the appearance of wine. His Divine Nature would have been present also, since both Body and Blood were inseparably united to His Godhead; but His Soul would not have been present; His Soul was in Limbo.

This presence of Jesus in the Holy Eucharist, under such small dimensions and in so many places at once, would seem to pose two apparent difficulties: How can a human body be present in such a small space? And how can a human body be present many places at once? The difficulties are only apparent, of course. God has done it, so it can be done. We have to remember that God is the Author of nature, the Lord and Master of all creation. The physical laws of the universe were established by God. He can suspend their action if He so wills, and without any strain upon His infinite power.

It is true that in our human experience every physical body must have what we call "extension"; it must occupy a certan definite amount of space. In our experience also a body can be in only one place at any one time. Multilocation (being in many places at the same time) is unknown to us. It is correct for us to say that a body without extension in space, and a body in many places simultaneously, are physical impossibilities; impossible, that is, by the laws of nature. But these phenomena are not *metaphysical* impossibilities; that is, there is no inherent contradiction in the idea of body-without-extension, or in the idea of multilocation. An inherent contradiction would make these absolutely impossible; as for example the idea of a square circle is impossible, being a contradiction in terms.

Perhaps this is getting us too far into the realm of philosophy. The points that we wish to make are, first of all that Jesus is not present in the Sacred Host in miniature, a tiny and shrunk-up Jesus. He is there in the fulness of His glorified Person, but in a spiritualized way, without any extension in space. He has no height nor breadth nor thickness.

The second point is that Jesus does not multiply Himself so that there are many Jesus's; nor does He divide Himself up among the many Hosts. There is but the one Jesus, whole and undivided. His multilocation is not the result of multiplication or division; it is the result of the suspension of the laws of space as far as His Sacred Body is concerned. It is as though He Himself stayed in one place, and all parts of space were brought to Him, were pinpointed in Him. It is easy to see why the Holy Eucharist is called—and is—the Sacrament of Unity. When we receive Holy Communion we are where Jesus is; we and our fellow-communicants all over the world. Space has dissolved for us, and we are there together—one in Christ.

How long does Jesus remain present in the Holy Eucharist? Only as long as the appearances of bread and wine remain. If a sudden fire were to destroy the Sacred Hosts in the tabernacle, Jesus would not be burned. The appearance of bread would be changed to the appearance of ashes, and Jesus would be gone. When, after Holy Communion, our digestive processes have destroyed the appearance of bread within us, Jesus no longer is bodily present; only His grace remains.

Bread and Wine and Priest

At the Last Supper Jesus changed bread and wine into His own Body and Blood. At the same time He commanded His apostles to repeat this same sacred action in time to come. "Do this in remembrance of Me," was the solemn charge which Jesus gave to the Apostles. Obviously Jesus does not command the impossible; consequently with this command went also the necessary power, the power to change bread and wine into His Body and Blood. With the words, "Do this in remembrance of Me," Jesus made His apostles priests.

This power to change bread and wine into the Flesh and Blood of the Savior was passed on by the apostles to the men whom they chose to share their labors and to carry on after they would be gone. These successors of the apostles passed their priestly power on, in turn, to others. Generation after generation, through nineteen hundred years, the power of the priesthood (the power to change bread and wine into the Body and Blood of Jesus) has been transmitted through the sacrament of Holy Orders. From bishop to bishop to bishop, to the priests of today the power has come.

The action by which the bread and wine is changed into Our Lord's Body and Blood, is called the Mass. Our Lord Himself, at the Last Supper offered the first Mass. The word "Mass" is of course an English word, and comes from the Latin word "Missa," which means "dismissal." The word Missa as a name for the sacred Action by which Jesus becomes present in the Holy Eucharist, was the result of a custom in the early Christian Church. No one except baptized Christians was allowed to assist at the complete Eucharistic sacrifice. Prospective converts (called "catechumens") had to leave after the gospel and sermon were finished. Both to them after the sermon, and to the rest of the assembly at the end of the service, the priest gave an official admonition: "Go, it is the dismissal"; which in Latin is "Ite Missa est," even as we have it at the end of Mass today. By a quirk of language the word Missa came to be used as the name for the complete Eucharistic service.

We shall have occasion later on to discuss the Mass as a sacrifice. Here we merely wish to indicate that it is at Mass that the change of bread and wine into the Body and Blood of Christ takes place. It takes place when the priest, making himself the free and willing instrument in the hands of Christ, pronounces over the bread and wine Christ's own words, "This is My Body," and "This is the Chalice of My Blood." Standing at the altar as the visible representative of Jesus and pronouncing Jesus' own words, the human priest "triggers" as it were the infinite power of Jesus, Who at that instant becomes present under the appearances of the bread and wine.

It is in these words—"the words of Consecration" as they are called—that the essence of the Mass resides. Stripped of all other prayers and ceremonies (except the priest's communion which completes the Mass) these words of Consecration *are* the Mass. This assumes of course that the priest has the *intention* to consecrate the bread and wine. If a priest for example were to describe the Last Supper to fellow-guests at a dinner table on which there were bread and wine, patently the bread and wine would not be changed into Our Lord's Body and Blood; the priest would have no such intention.

It is only bread made from wheat flour that can be changed into the Body of Christ. It was wheaten bread that Jesus used at the Last Supper; it must be wheaten bread always that is used for the Holy Eucharist. If the words of Consecration were pronounced over bread made from any other kind of grain, rye or oats or barley for example, Transubstantiation would not take place.

Any kind of wheaten bread will do. In the Latin Catholic Church however it is required that unleavened bread only be used; that is, bread made without yeast. This ancient law of the Latin Church is based on the great likelihood that Jesus Himself used unleavened bread, since He celebrated the Last Supper on the "first day of the azymes," the seven-day period during which the Jews ate only the unleavened bread called "mazzoth."

However, it is leavened bread—bread made with yeast—that is used for the Eucharistic Liturgy in the Greek Catholic Church and in most of the other Oriental Churches; and their Mass is as truly the Mass as is that of our own Latin rite. Leavened or unleavened, it is wheaten bread that must be used.

Because it was grape wine that Jesus used at the Last Supper, it is only grape wine that can be used for Mass. If the words of consecration were pronounced over wine made from any other fruit (such as cherry wine or elderberry wine), or over any other kind of wine at all, the words would have no effect. Our Lord's Body and Blood would not become present. It is only the pure, fermented juice of the grape that can be used for Mass.

The thin, white wafers of unleavened bread that are used in the Mass of the Latin rite, are made of pure wheat flour with nothing added but water. They are prepared and baked by communities of Sisters who specialize in this holy work. Each week the Sisters fill the standing orders which they have from the various parishes which they supply.

The wine that is used at Mass—pure fermented grape juice with nothing added—is purchased only from designated wineries which specialize in altar wine. These wineries must be periodically inspected by the bishop (or his delegate) of the diocese in which the winery is located, and must have the approval of the bishop.

Once the bread and wine have been changed into the Body and Blood of the Lord Jesus, our Savior remains present as long as the appearances of bread and wine remain intact. In other words Jesus is present in the Holy Eucharist, not just during Mass, but as long as the Sacred Hosts consecrated at Mass continue to retain the appearance of bread. This means that we owe to the Holy Eucharist the adoration which is due to God, since the Holy Eucharist contains the Son of God Himself. We adore the Holy Eucharist with the worship of *latria*, the type of worship which may be accorded only to God.

In the early Christian Church the adoration of Jesus in the Holy Eucharist was practiced by Christians only at Mass. Devotion to Jesus in the Blessed Sacrament outside of Mass —so familiar to us today—developed slowly and gradually in the Church. It seems that it took some time for Christians to realize what a treasure was theirs in the Holy Eucharist. It is only about eight hundred years ago, in the twelfth century, that the custom originated of reserving the Holy Eucharist for the adoration of the people outside of Mass. After that, outside-of-Mass devotion to Jesus in the Blessed Sacrament developed very rapidly.

Nowadays in every Catholic church there is a tabernacle upon the altar. The tabernacle (from the Latin word "tabernaculum," meaning "tent") is a cupboard-like safe covered with a veil and marked by a burning light called the tabernacle lamp. Inside the tabernacle Jesus Christ is present. He is present in the large Sacred Host (used at Benediction) enclosed in a gold-and-glass case called a pyx. He is present also in the small Sacred Hosts (enclosed in a covered gold cup called a ciborium) which are available for Holy Communion.

Since the twelfth century when adoration of the Holy Eucharist outside of Mass began to spread, three devotional practices have become universal in the Church: the Feast and Procession of Corpus Christi, Benediction of the Blessed Sacrament (also called Solemn Exposition) and the Forty Hours Devotion.

The Feast of Corpus Christi (Body of Christ) came first. It originated in the diocese of Liege in Belgium in the year 1246, and eighteen years later was extended by Pope Urban IV to the entire Church. Corpus Christi is celebrated always on the Thursday after Trinity Sunday. Part of the celebration consists of the Corpus Christi procession, which may be held either on the feast itself or on the Sunday following the feast. In this procession the Holy Eucharist is carried by the priest in a sacred vessel called the ostensorium or monstrance. Both words—ostensorium and monstrance—literally mean "show case." The ostensorium is a circular glass case surrounded by gold or silver metalwork, and mounted on a standing column. For processions or Benediction of the Blessed Sacrament, the pyx containing the large Sacred Host is inserted in the ostensorium so that It is visible to those participating.

The Eucharistic rite which we call Benediction of the Blessed Sacrament, evolved gradually after the institution of the Feast of Corpus Christi. It became the custom to expose the Blessed Sacrament for the adoration of the faithful, and then there developed the further custom of ending the period of exposition with a blessing which the priest, holding the Blessed Sacrament in his hands, would impart to the people. The rite of Benediction as we know it today, goes back to the fourteenth century. It consists of a period of exposition and adoration during which hymns are sung and prayers may be said, ending always with the singing of the hymn, "Tantum Ergo," with a concluding oration chanted by the priest. Then the priest, vested in surplice, stole and cope, with the broad shawl called the humeral veil around his shoulders, ascends the altar. Holding the ostensorium with the ends of the humeral veil covering his hands, he turns towards the congregation and silently makes the sign of the cross with Jesus enshrined in the ostensorium. It is the blessing of Our Lord Himself in the Holy Eucharist. During solemn Expostion and Benediction, at least twelve candles must burn upon the altar. Before returning the Sacred Host to the tabernacle, priest and people recite the Divine Praises.

The Forty Hours Devotion was first introduced in Milan, Italy, in the sixteenth century. Originally it was actually forty continuous hours of adoration before the Holy Eucharist solemnly exposed, in memory of the forty hours during which the Sacred Body of Jesus lay in the tomb. In our part of the world the Forty Hours Devotion usually is spread over three days, with no adoration during the night hours, and with the total time of adoration often less than forty hours. The Forty Hours Devotion is held in every parish and house of religion once each year. The bishop assigns the dates to each parish and religious community so that every week, someplace in the diocese (unless it be a very small diocese) the Forty Hours Devotion is being held. Thus a continuous year-around adoration is offered to Jesus in the Most Blessed Sacrament. The Forty Hours begins and ends with the singing of the Litany of the Saints and with a procession of the Blessed Sacrament. Twenty candles burn upon the altar during the hours of exposition.

CHAPTER XXVII

The Mass

We Begin the Mass

In the previous eight chapters we have discussed the Holy Eucharist as a sacrament—the sacrament in which Jesus Christ nourishes our soul with His own Flesh and Blood. During that discussion we referred to the Mass very briefly, simply pointing out that the Mass is the sacred action by which Jesus makes Himself present under the appearances of bread and wine. We noted in passing that our English word, "Mass," evolved from the Latin word, "Missa," in the "Ite Missa Est," by which the congregation is dismissed at the end of Mass. The name which the early Christians gave to the Mass was, "Giving of thanks." They chose this name from the Gospel description of the Last Supper, which tells us that Jesus, having taken bread, "gave thanks and broke, and gave it to them, saying, "This is my body, which is being given for you; do this in remembrance of me" (Luke 22:19). From these same words of Jesus, the first Christians also gave to the Mass the name of "Breaking of Bread."

It is time for us now to turn to a more detailed consideration of the Mass. It would be a great mistake for us to think of the Mass simply as a necessary tool for the providing of Holy Communion. The Mass is much, much more than that, as we shall see. It is true that it is at Mass that the bread is changed into the Body of Christ. But we should see the Mass as the greater whole, of which our union with Jesus in Holy Communion is a wonderful part. Even when we receive Holy Communion outside of Mass, we should consider our Holy Communion as an extension to us of the Mass in which was consecrated the Sacred Host which we now receive. During the Church's infancy (when congregations were much smaller) it was the custom for the priest to send Holy Communion immediately after Mass to those members of the Christian community who were unable to be present. To these absent brethren Holy Communion brought sacramental grace; but it also was the bond of union which joined them with Christ in the Mass which had been offered, and with their fellow Christians who had eaten of this same Holy Bread. It is in this light that we should perceive our own Holy Communion when circumstances make it necessary for us to receive outside of Mass.

Well, if the Mass is not merely the preparatory ceremony which makes Holy Communion possible, what else *is* the Mass? First of all the Mass is a memorial of our Lord. "Do this," Jesus says as He makes His apostles priests, "Do this in remembrance of me." It is natural to the human heart to want to keep fresh the memory of those whom we have loved and admired. Whether it be the faded picture on our dresser of our dear dead parents, or the brooding figure in the Lincoln Memorial, the world is full of remembrances. Our Lord Jesus Who loves us so, and Who so much wants our love, has left us a memorial of Himself such as only God could fashion. It is not a picture, not a monument or statue; it is the living Presence of Himself, coming daily among us in the Mass. Here in the Mass is the same Body and Blood which Jesus immolated on the Cross. Here in the Mass Jesus continues through time that offering of Himself on Calvary, applying now to our souls the merits which He gained for us on Golgotha. It is not only His death which we memorialize in the Mass, but Christ's resurrection, too, by which He has forever conquered death; and His ascension into Heaven likewise, to the glory which He is determined (be we willing) to share with us.

In addition to being a remembrance of our Lord, the Mass is a holy banquet. At His table Jesus feeds us upon His own Body and Blood. We already have examined at some length this aspect of the Holy Eucharist. It may however be of some historical interest to us to note how closely the first Christians followed the example of Jesus in annexing the celebration of the Eucharist to an actual supper. It was a special kind of supper, called the "Agape" (pronounced ah-gah-pay, from the Greek) or "feast of love." The Christian community would gather in the home of one of their members, since of course there were no churches as yet. Each member would bring food and wine according to his means, some much and some little or none. The food would be shared by all alike to manifest their love for one another. At the conclusion of the meal the "president"—that is, the bishop—would celebrate the Eucharist after the example of Christ.

However, abuses gradually began to creep into this custom. Some of the wealthier Christians would consume their own food and drink without regard for their poorer brethren, and some even would drink to excess. It is for such abuses that St. Paul scolded the Corinthians in his First Epistle to them (11:20–22): "So then when you meet together, it is no longer possible to eat the Lord's Supper. For at the meal, each one takes first his own supper, and one is hungry, and another drinks overmuch. Have you not houses for your eating and drinking? Or do you despise the church of God and put to shame the needy?"

Because of such abuses the "Breaking of Bread" was very

early disjoined from the ceremonial meal of brotherhood called the Agape. The Agape was eaten in the evening, and the Eucharist was celebrated in the morning. By the middle of the second century the custom of fasting before Holy Communion had become fixed, and within another two hundred years the custom of the Agape had ceased entirely. The lesson of the Agape however—the need for the practice of charity as a continuing preparation for Holy Communion —is one that must never be forgotten.

The Mass is a memorial of our Lord Jesus. It is the perfect memorial, in which His own living Presence keeps always vivid our consciousness of Him. The Mass is a divine banquet, too. It is a banquet in which God spreads the table with His own Flesh and Blood. But the Mass is more than a memorial and more than a banquet. It is a sacrifice.

In the course of centuries the word, "sacrifice," has lost much of the sharpness of its meaning. It even has come to signify something rather painful and therefore distasteful: the giving up of something we would like to have or would like to do.

Originally however the word, "sacrifice," had only one meaning. It was applied to the action by which a gift was offered to God. That still is the strict and most proper meaning of the word. It is from two Latin words, *sacra* meaning holy, and *facere* meaning to do or to make, that our English word "sacrifice," comes. A thing was made holy by being taken from human ownership and human use, and offered to God by a symbolic act of giving.

The desire to offer gifts to God seems to be an instinct rooted deep in the human heart. The first recorded sacrifices were those offered by Adam's sons, Cain and Abel. That God willed to be honored by gifts offered by His creature, man, certainly is a truth which Adam and Eve carried with them from Paradise. However, even without divine revelation, mankind seems to feel an irresistible urge to offer sacrifice. In the whole range of history there is no people or tribe of whom we have knowledge, who have not

offered sacrifice. Sometimes people have been in great ignorance of God and have worshiped false gods and many
gods. Sometimes they have been in great ignorance as to
what might please God, and even have offered human sacrifices. But always and everywhere man has felt the need to
offer gifts to God—or to his gods.

Among the people who have worshiped the true God, we
distinguish three periods of history. The period from Adam
until the time of Moses is called the Patriarchal Age. During
this era the people of God tended to live in tribes, bound together by ties of blood. They were ruled by the patriarch
of the tribe, who was the living ancestor from whom the
members of the tribe had descended. Noah for example was
a patriarch, as was Abraham. The patriarch was also the
priest for his family (or tribe) and presided at the offering
of sacrifices to God.

When God raised up Moses to lead His people from
Egypt to the Promised Land, God made some changes. God
specified exactly the kinds of sacrifices that were to be offered to Him from then on; and God established an official
and hereditary priesthood. Henceforth Aaron (the brother
of Moses) and Aaron's male descendants were to offer the
sacrifices for the whole Jewish nation. This was to continue
until the final period of religious history would begin with
the coming of Christ. This period, from Moses until the
advent of the Messiah, is called the Mosaic Age.

With the coming of Jesus Christ a new age began, the
Christian Age in which you and I are living. All that had
gone before was but a preparation for this final stage in
God's plan for man's salvation. The Patriarchal Age and the
Mosaic Age were full of prophecies and figures which kept
pointing, like signposts along a highway, to Christ and
His "good tidings" and His perfect sacrifice. We have only
to recall Melchisedech, a priest of the Patriarchal Age who
offered bread and wine (Genesis 14:18–20). Later, in the
Mosaic Age the Psalmist prophesies concerning Jesus:

"Thou art a priest forever according to the order of Melchisedech" (Ps. 109:4). Or we can turn to the prophet Malachias who foretells the day when God no longer will find pleasure in sacrifices of sheep and oxen, because ". . . from the rising of the sun even to the going down, my name is great among the Gentiles, and in every place there is sacrifice, and there is offered to my name a clean oblation: for my name is great among the Gentiles, saith the Lord of hosts" (Malachias 1:11).

This turns our attention to the reason why the Mass is called the *perfect* Sacrifice. All other sacrifices previous to the Mass suffered from one great defect: the gifts which were offered had no real value at all as far as God was concerned. They simply gave back to God things which He Himself had created to begin with—bullocks and lambs and bread and wine. Even all the gold in Fort Knox would in itself mean nothing to God. The Lord was pleased with the gifts of men only because He chose to be pleased; He graciously accepted their little presents as an expression of their love.

But in the Sacrifice of the Mass a new and wonderful element enters. Now for the first time (and daily) mankind can offer to God a Gift that is worthy of God: the Gift of God's own Son, a Gift of infinite value even as God is infinite. Here now is a Gift which God does not merely deign to accept; here is a Gift (we dare to say it) which God has got to accept, a Gift which He cannot refuse, a Gift which is precious even to God; it is the Gift of God to God.

Memorial, banquet and sacrifice; the Mass is all three. But most especially the Mass is a sacrifice; *the* Sacrifice which will endure until time ends.

What Makes a Sacrifice?

"Pete Smith sacrificed to center field," says the sports commentator, "advancing Brown to third." The use of "sacrifice" to describe a bit of baseball strategy gives us an idea of how words acquire new meanings with the passing of the years.

In its original meaning we know that a sacrifice is a gift offered to God. However, not every gift offered to God is a sacrifice. That ten dollars we gave to our parish building fund and that suit of clothes we gave to the St. Vincent de Paul Society: both are gifts offered to God (if our motive is right), but neither is a sacrifice in the strict sense of the word.

In a true sacrifice the gift is removed from human use and in some way *destroyed*, as a symbol of the fact that it is being given to God. In pre-Christian sacrifice the gift (if an animal) was slain upon the altar. Often the gift would be consumed in fire upon the altar. Wine would be offered by pouring it into the ground at the foot of the altar. This destruction of the gift ("God, we give it back to You!") is essential to the idea of sacrifice.

There is a special name for the gift that is offered to God in sacrifice. It is called the *victim* of the sacrifice. The word, "victim," is another word that has acquired new meanings through the centuries. We now speak of the victim of an accident or the victim of a swindler. But originally the Latin word *victima* meant specifically the gift which was offered in sacrifice.

Another significant point concerning sacrifice, is that it is not an act of individual piety. The offering of a sacrifice is an act of *social* worship, of group worship. This means that the one who offers the sacrifice does not offer it as a private individual in his own name only. He offers the gift in the name of the group whom he represents, in the name of the group for whom he is the spokesman. In pre-Christian times the patriarch offered sacrifice for his family or tribe; the king offered sacrifice for his subjects; the sons of Aaron offered sacrifice for the Jews.

This brings us to the final requisite for a genuine sacrifice:

there must be a priest. The one who offers the sacrifice must have the right to represent the group in whose name the gift is offered. Whether he be patriarch-priest, king-priest or Aaron-priest, he must have the right to speak to God in the name of God's people. Directly or indirectly, he must have his mandate from God. Strangely enough the word, "priest," is one word that has not acquired any other meaning. Even today, when used literally, *priest* has only one specific meaning; it is applied only to a man who offers sacrifice. That is why non-Catholic clergymen are not called priests. They do not offer sacrifice; they do not believe in sacrifice.

Step by step we have built up the definition of a sacrifice. We may now describe it as, "The offering of a group-gift (called a victim) to God, and the destruction of the victim to indicate that it is being given to God, by someone (called a priest) who has the right to represent the group."

It should be clear why we call the Mass the Holy Sacrifice. All the essentials of a true sacrifice are here. There is first of all the Gift, the infinitely precious Gift, the infinitely perfect Victim: God's own Son. There is the group which offers the Gift: all baptized Christians in union with Christ's Vicar on earth, the Pope; that is, the Mystical Body of Christ. There is also the priest: the man who in the sacrament of Holy Orders has received from God not only the mandate but also the *power* that is required for the offering of this sublime Gift—the power to change bread and wine into the Body and Blood of Jesus Christ.

This human priest however is but a secondary figure. It is Jesus Himself who *really* represents God's people, a people purchased with His own Blood. It is Jesus Himself who is the real priest in every Mass; Jesus the Priest offering Himself, Jesus the Victim, to God for all of us. The human priest simply is the agent of Jesus. By the sacrament of Holy Orders Jesus has designated and empowered this man to be His free and cooperating instrument; to speak the words by which Jesus, at this particular point in time and space, will renew for us the offering of Himself upon the Cross.

That is where the destruction of the Victim takes place: on the Cross. Each individual Mass is not a new sacrifice in which Jesus dies anew. Each Mass is but a continuation, a prolongation through time, of the once-for-all death of Christ upon the Cross. To use a modern term we might say that the Mass re-activates for us the sacrifice of Calvary. The Mass makes present and effective for us, right here and now, the Victim on the altar of the Cross. The death of Jesus is more than a mere fact of history. It is an *eternal* sacrifice. There are no yesterdays with God. In the infinite Mind of God, to Whom all things past are present, Jesus hangs eternally upon the Cross.

It is not an easy truth to grasp, but it is the truth: that at Mass time and distance are annihilated in a mystical sense; and you and I stand beneath the Cross as the Son of God offers Himself in sacrifice for us.

In the Mass Jesus Christ the Priest offers Himself, the perfect Victim, the infinitely precious Gift, to God for us. Why? What is the significance of the Mass, what is its purpose?

The Mass has a fourfold purpose, and these four purposes or aims are rooted in the relationship that exists between God and ourselves. God is the Lord and Master of all creation. Everything that exists, He has made. We are God's creatures, God's property; body and soul we belong to Him. From the very nature of this relationship of creature to Creator, certain inescapable duties arise.

First of all we have the obligation to acknowledge this relationship: to acknowledge God's infinite power and wisdom and goodness, to acknowledge that He is everything and that we are nothing as compared to Him. The very purpose of our existence, the reason why God made us, is to give glory to God. Below the level of man, created nature gives glory to God by the mere fact of its existence. Minerals and trees and animals bear witness to God's greatness just by being what they are. Something more however is expected of man. With his immortal soul, with his free will and power of thought and speech, man must be more than a mute witness to God's glory. With the freedom that is uniquely his, man must freely give glory to God, must freely voice God's praises.

In short, man must *adore* God. To adore God is man's first duty. Adoration is the most basic element of prayer and is the primary purpose of every sacrifice. Adoration is consequently the primary purpose of the Mass. In the Mass for the first time mankind is able *adequately* to adore God in the Person of God's own Son Who represents us.

After adoration, our second duty to God is one of gratitude. Since God is the source of all good, it follows that everything we are or have or hope for, comes from God. We would not even continue to exist were God to let us out of His mind for a single instant. Physical life and spiritual life, daily graces that come to us continuously, love and friendship, TV waves and water from the kitchen faucet: all these are from God and for all of them we owe Him thanks. Thanksgiving is the second basic element in all prayer and in every true sacrifice. It is the second purpose of the Mass. In the Mass Jesus Christ offers to God for man a thanksgiving that surpasses the gifts which have been given, an infinite thanks that even God's infinite bounty cannot outrun.

Besides adoration and thanksgiving, our relationship to God imposes another duty upon us: we must ask God for the graces which we and others need in order to reach Heaven. Having given us free wills, God makes our salvation dependent upon our free cooperation; He will not force upon us graces which we do not want. We show our eagerness to cooperate by asking God for the graces we need.

God also has made our salvation dependent to some degree upon each other. Jesus Christ has deigned to allow us to share in His work of redemption; our prayers will profit others, even as their prayers will profit us. Since it is God's law that we love our neighbor as ourselves, it follows that we must pray for our neighbor—for the graces he needs—even as we pray for ourselves. We pray of course for those who are bound to us by ties of blood or of duty or of affection; but our prayers must also go beyond them to embrace all mankind. We may pray for temporal favors if we will—God is pleased to have us ask; but we *must* pray for our spiritual needs and the spiritual needs of our neighbor. Petition is the third basic element of prayer and of sacrifice; it is the third purpose for which Mass is offered, Jesus Himself making intercession to God with us and for us.

Besides adoration, thanksgiving and petition, we also owe God reparation for our sins. By the nature of our relationship to God—that of creature to Creator—absolute obedience to God's will is our duty. To rebel by sin against the God Who made us is an act of base injustice as well an act of monstrous ingratitude. If we have so rebelled, it is our duty to restore the balance to justice by making reparation for our sin. Moreover, because of the oneness of the human race and our interdependence upon each other, it also is necessary for us to make reparation for the sins of others. We must remember again that God wills us to participate in the redemptive work of His Son.

None of us of course could make adequate satisfaction for sin. But Jesus Christ could, and on the cross He did. Drawing upon that inexhaustible fund of satisfactory merit, Jesus continues to offer it daily to God in the Mass. The infinite value of Christ's satisfaction for sin does not of course excuse us from making reparation ourselves. It is precisely because of the infinite satisfaction for sin made by Jesus on the cross that our own acts of reparation, offered in union with His, have value in the eyes of God. This is the fourth purpose then for which Mass is offered: to make satisfaction to God for the sins of men.

To adore God, to thank God, to petition God for grace,

and to atone to God for sin: as we assist at Mass, this fourfold purpose should be primary in our own intentions as
we offer the Holy Sacrifice. In our appreciation of the Mass,
God's glory must have precedence over the graces which
the Mass may bring to us.

Every Mass Is Our Mass

The primary purpose of the Mass is to give honor and
glory to God. However the effects of the Mass do not stop
there; even as He offers infinite homage to God, Jesus Christ
in the Mass also bestows great graces upon us. The graces
which God, through the merits of His Son, gives to us
through the Mass are called the "fruits" of the Mass.

Theologians distinguish three kinds of fruitfulness in the
Mass. First of all there is the *general* fruit. In accordance
with the intention of our Divine Lord and His Church, the
priest at every Mass offers the Holy Sacrifice for those who
are present, for the Church, for the Pope, for the bishop of
the diocese, for all faithful Christians living and dead, and
for the salvation of all mankind. By the will of Christ and
His Church these intentions are present in every Mass; the
priest who offers the Mass could not exclude these intentions even if he wanted to. The graces which result from
these intentions might be called the "communal graces" of
the Mass.

The degree to which these communal graces are received
by any particular soul, will depend greatly on the closeness
of the person's participation in the Mass, and on the person's
own interior dispositions. The servers, the choir, the devout
and attentive congregation—these certainly will receive most
fully of the general fruit of the Mass. As the communal
graces spread from each altar like irradiating waves throughout the world, they will find lodgment in the hearts best
disposed to receive them. These graces will accrue especially
to those persons who have united themselves in spirit with

all the Masses being offered everywhere; an intention which all of us ought to make daily in our morning prayers. Somewhere, at every moment of the twenty-four hours, Mass is being offered; we should want to be a part of every Mass.

Obviously the general fruit of the Mass does not depend for its application entirely upon the dispositions of those for whom it is offered. Otherwise the Mass would have no effect on the sinners and unbelievers who are prayed for in every Mass. The application of the graces of the Mass depends upon God's will as well as upon personal worthiness. That the Mass does effect the conversion even of hardened and stubborn souls is a truth known to us all.

Besides the general fruit of the Mass, there also is a *special* fruit which is applied to the person or persons (living or dead) for whom the Mass is offered by the officiating priest. When we give a stipend for a Mass, it is this special fruit which is directed to the person for whom we are having the Mass offered—whether for ourselves or for someone else. We no doubt are aware that the ancient custom of giving a stipend when we request a Mass, has its origin in St. Paul's dictum (I Corinthians 9:13) that they who serve the altar also should have their share with the altar. We never should ask, "How much does a Mass cost?" The Mass is infinite in value and no price can be put upon it. The stipend is not a price that we pay, it is an offering that we give. And once a priest has accepted a stipend, whether for a Low Mass or a High Mass, he is bound in conscience under pain of mortal sin to see to it that a Mass is offered according to the donor's intention.

The custom of giving a stipend for a Mass is in reality a great advantage to the faithful. A priest might promise to say a Mass for someone, and then later forget the promise or change his mind. But once he has accepted a stipend he dare not forget, he may not change his mind. A lay person might be surprised to know how conscientiously priests do keep account of their Mass stipends and Mass intentions. A priest may be careless with his own personal accounts, but never with the Mass stipend account; it weighs too heavily on his conscience. Every priest has a dread of going into eternity with Mass obligations unfulfilled. That is why it is standard practice for priests to leave a sum of money in their wills to provide for any undischarged Mass intentions in case death should be sudden.

This special fruit of the Mass is—as the theologians say— both impetratory and propitiatory in nature. "Impetratory" (from the word "impetrate," to ask) means simply the power to obtain from God the graces and benefits which we ask. "Propitiatory" means the power to propitiate, to atone for sin. Since the souls in purgatory have only one need— to be released from the temporal punishment due to their sins—it follows that the special fruit of the Mass is entirely propitiatory when the Mass is offered for departed souls. We have no way of knowing how much of the propitiatory fruit of any one Mass is applied to any particular soul, so we are following a right instinct in having more than one Mass offered for the soul whom we wish to help. We also have no way of knowing when purgatory ends for any particular soul; consequently it is a good idea to have a secondary intention in mind when having a Mass offered for a deceased person: "Lord, if this soul already is in heaven, then please apply the fruit of this Mass to such-and-such an intention."

Besides the general fruit and the special fruit of the Mass, there is a third fruit which the Mass produces: the graces which are the personal share of the priest who celebrates the Mass and which will contribute to his own sanctification and to the reparation of his own sins. This is called (naturally) the personal fruit of the Mass.

Do the fruits of a Mass vary according to the kind of a Mass that is offered? That is, is a High Mass more fruitful than a Low Mass? Or, to phrase the question in the practical form in which Catholics some times ask it, "Is one High Mass better than five Low Masses?"

Before answering the question, we might recall the various kinds of Masses with which we are familiar. There is first of all the Solemn High Mass, in which the celebrant is assisted at the altar by a deacon and a subdeacon, with solemn and rather elaborate ceremonial. Then there is the ordinary High Mass (sometimes called Sung Mass), less elaborate than the Solemn Mass but with certain parts of the Mass sung by the celebrant and by the congregation or choir. Thirdly there is the simple Low Mass, in which all parts of the Mass are read or recited by the priest with responses from the server. If, instead of the server alone, the entire congregation joins in praying the public parts of the Mass aloud and answering the priest, the Low Mass is called a Dialogue Mass or a Recited Mass.

If any of these Masses are celebrated by a bishop, then the Mass will be a Pontifical Mass—Solemn Pontifical Mass or Pontifical Low Mass as the case may be.

Any of the three kinds of Masses may also be a Requiem Mass, a Mass which is celebrated with black vestments and with special prayers for the dead. It might be well to note that a Mass offered for a deceased person does not have to be a Requiem Mass. Normally the Mass at a funeral will be a Requiem Mass, and if the Church calendar permits, the Month's Mind Mass (thirty days after death) and Anniversary Masses also will be Requiem Masses. However there are many feast days in the Church calendar when Requiem Masses are not permitted, but this is no cause for concern to those who are having Masses offered for departed souls. The special fruit of the Mass will be applied to the deceased person, whether it is a Requiem or a feast day Mass that is offered.

This raises another point that we might comment upon in passing: the custom of offering Masses in honor of our Blessed Mother and the saints. This is a practice that goes back to the early Christian Church, when Masses were offered in honor of the martyrs on the anniversaries of their death. We all are aware that a Mass cannot be offered *to* a saint; Mass can be offered only to God. But it pleases God to have us honor His friends, the saints, by making a special commemoration of them in the Holy Sacrifice on their feast days. This is the same principle underlying all our devotion to the saints: to give glory to God by honoring His masterpieces of grace, His saints. When we offer a Mass in honor of a saint, we are asking the saint to join with us in giving glory to God, and we ask God to grant us, through the intercession of St. So-and-so, the graces which we ask. Consequently we can offer a Mass in honor of our Blessed Mother or a saint and at the same time apply its special fruit to a soul or souls in purgatory.

This brings us finally to the question with which we began: whether a High Mass may be regarded as more fruitful than a Low Mass. We know that it is absurd to ask whether one High Mass is as good as five Low Masses; the Mass is a spiritual entity, not to be weighed or measured or compared like potatoes or flour or gold or silver. As concerns the honor and glory which Jesus Christ in the Mass renders to God, the value of the Mass is infinite. As concerns the extent to which the fruits of the Mass are applied to any individual soul, that depends upon the will of God and is something which we cannot know. We can only do our best to see that the Mass is offered with all the solemnity and dignity which we can contribute, so as to make our claim upon God's bounty as strong (humanly speaking) as we can. When we make the additional sacrifice involved in the offering of a high Mass, both the personal sacrifice and our contribution to the external solemnity of the Mass do fortify our suffrage, our petition.

The Church is not a huckster, vending Low Masses at one counter and High Masses at another. Every Mass is a grand and awesome bridging of earth and heaven, from the Low

Mass of the lonely missionary in a thatched hut to the Solemn Pontifical Mass of the bishop in his cathedral. Whether we request one High Mass or five Low Masses, neither the Church nor any individual priest will try to persuade us one way or the other; the decision is strictly our own.

All that we can say with any degree of certainty is that (all things else being equal) a High Mass does add to the extrinsic honor which the Mass offers to God, and thereby does reinforce our prayer. We should emphasize the word "extrinsic," because nothing of course can alter the essential honor which Christ gives to God in the Mass. If we are going to request a Mass, and we can make it either a High Mass or a Low Mass—then we shall do better to request a High Mass. That is as far as human wisdom can carry us in judging the relative "value" of one Mass against another.

The Mass Has a History

As we read in the Gospels the description of the Last Supper, and compare the simplicity of that scene with the Mass as it is offered in our churches today, we are conscious of the great development that has taken place in the ceremonial of the Holy Sacrifice during nineteen hundred years. It is a development that is easy to understand. The Eucharistic Sacrifice which Jesus instituted on Holy Thursday night was like a precious gem which He presented to His Church. It was a perfect and a flawless jewel, but it needed an appropriate setting, as does every jewel, to make its beauty and its grandeur evident to all. It is not surprising then that the Church, through several hundreds of years, should fashion and embellish that setting which constitutes the ceremonial of the Mass as we know it today.

Here is the description of the Last Supper as recounted by St. Matthew (26:26-28): "And while they were at supper, Jesus took bread, and blessed and broke, and gave it to his disciples, and said, 'Take and eat; this is my body.' And taking a cup, he gave thanks and gave it to them, saying, 'All of you drink of this; for this is my blood of the new covenant, which is being shed for many unto the forgiveness of sins.' "

Here we have the Holy Sacrifice in its essence, in its basic simplicity: the Consecration and the Communion. Besides these essentials of sacrifice there are other incidental circumstances which are of interest to us. There is the fact that Jesus "gave thanks." The words of His prayer of thanksgiving have not been recorded by the Evangelists, but it is this prayer of thanksgiving which is reflected in the Canon of today's Mass, especially in the Preface which introduces the Canon. We also know from the gospel of St. John (13:4–10) that Jesus preceded the Last Supper with the washing of His apostles' feet, a symbolic rite of purification which finds an echo in the *Confiteor* which precedes the Mass. It is St. John also (14–17) who records for us the beautiful address of Jesus to His apostles at the Last Supper—a forerunner surely of the sermon which is a part of our Sunday Mass.

In any event the first Christian communities, when they gathered for the "Breaking of Bread," followed quite closely the simple ceremonial of the Last Supper. However, the first Christians were Jews. They did not at first realize how complete was to be their break with the now abolished (by God) religion of the Old Testament. They continued to attend and to take part in the services of the synagogue, and would meet privately in groups for the "Breaking of Bread." Eventually the Christians were expelled from the synagogues by their fellow Jews. They then began to preface the "Breaking of Bread" with a prayer service modeled on the synagogue service. The synagogue service consisted basically of two readings, one from the books of Moses and one from the books of the prophets, followed by a sermon and with prayers interspersed between them. In adopting this service from the synagogue the Christians "baptized" it, and began to use readings from the New Testament as well as from the Old Testament. This is how the first part of our present Mass (epistle, gospel, sermon and other prayers) originated. This is really a preparatory service for the Mass proper. It is called the Fore-Mass or the Mass of the Catechumens. It gets the name "Mass of the Catechumens" from the fact that in early Christian times this preparatory service was the only part of the Mass that prospective converts were allowed to assist at; not until they were baptized could they remain for the entire Mass.

The elaboration of the Mass ceremonies developed very rapidly. The pattern of the Mass as it is offered today, was pretty well established by the year 150 A.D. A Christian writer of that time, St. Justin Martyr, describes for us the Mass as it was offered at Rome in his day: "On that day, which is named after the sun, all those who live in the city and in the country come together, and then the memoirs of the Apostles (meaning the Gospels) or the writings of the prophets are read, as long as there is time. When the reader has finished, the president (meaning the priest) makes an address (this was the sermon) in which he earnestly admonishes us to practice the beautiful lessons which we have just heard. Then we all rise and pray." This was the Fore-Mass, the Mass of the Catechumens. St. Justin then describes for us the Mass proper.

"Then bread and a chalice with water and wine are brought to the president of the brethren. He receives these and offers praise to the Father of all in the name of the Son and of the Holy Spirit, and continues at some length with a prayer of thanksgiving (this is what we today call the Canon of the Mass which includes the Consecration) because we have been made worthy by Him to partake of these gifts. When he has finished the prayers and the thanksgiving, all the people present answer: Amen." (This is the Great Amen of our own Mass, which comes just before the *Pater Noster*.) "After the thanksgiving of the president and the answer of the people, the deacons, as they are called among us, distribute the bread and the wine over which the thanksgiving has been pronounced . . . we do not receive it as common food and common drink, since we are taught that even as, by a word of God, Jesus Christ our Savior became flesh, so, too, this food over which has been spoken His word of prayer and thanksgiving, is the true flesh and blood of that Jesus who became man, and enters our flesh and blood when we receive it" (chapters 65–67 of St. Justin's First Apology). In this description we see the Mass approaching its final form.

By the year 150 A.D. the fundamental structure of the Mass was established. However, the prayer-content of the Mass continued to be expanded through another four and a half centuries. By the time of Pope St. Gregory the Great, who died in the year 604 A.D., the development of the Mass was pretty well completed.

It was during this period, between St. Justin and St. Gregory, that the element of prayer was added to the element of instruction in the Mass of the Catechumens, the preparatory part of the Mass. In St. Justin's time there were the two readings, one from the Old Testament and one from the Gospels, and the sermon. By St. Gregory's day the *Introit*, the *Kyrie*, the *Gloria* and the *Collect* had been prefixed to the readings and the sermon. Each of these additions has an interesting history of its own upon which we will comment briefly.

The *Introit* is the real beginning of the Mass. This is the prayer which the priest reads from the Missal when he first goes up to the altar. The prayers which the priest now recites at the foot of the altar before beginning the Mass, were unknown at the time of St. Gregory. They developed gradually during the Middle Ages, and originally were recited by the priest privately on his way from the sacristy to the altar, as a part of his preparation for Mass. It was only four hundred years ago that Pope St. Pius V made it obligatory for a priest to recite these prayers before beginning the Mass. That is why we say that the *Introit* is the real start of the Mass.

Originally the *Introit* was a processional hymn. It was one of the psalms, chosen to express the spirit of the day's Mass—joyful, penitent or triumphant, depending upon the day. It was chanted by people and choir as the celebrant of the Mass and his attendants made their way from the sacristy (then located near the door of the church) to the altar. We can see how the *Introit* (from the Latin word "Introitus," meaning "Entrance") got its name. Originally it was an entire psalm, but in the eighth century these solemn entrance processions were gradually discontinued and the *Introit* became shorter and shorter until, in the Middle Ages, it became the mere "stub" of an *Introit* which we find in our missals today. The *Introit* now consists only of an introductory verse (called the antiphon) and one verse of the psalm, plus the Glory be to the Father.

The Introit Procession is one of four processions which were a part of the Mass in ancient times and which have all but disappeared from our Mass at present. The other three processions were the Gospel Procession through the church to the "gradus" or step where the deacon would chant the Gospel; the Offertory Procession when the members of the congregation would bring their offerings of bread and wine and other gifts to the altar; and the Communion Procession when the congregation would come in orderly ranks to partake of the Sacrifice. During each of these processions an appropriate psalm would be sung by the choir and the people. All that now remains in the Mass of these psalms is one or two little verses apiece: the Gradual verse (between the Epistle and Gospel), the Offertory verse just before the priest uncovers the chalice, and the Communion verse after the priest has cleansed and recovered the chalice.

After the *Introit* comes the *Kyrie Eleison* of the Mass. This cry for God's mercy is in the Greek language and goes back to the days (before the fourth century) when

Greek was the liturgical language of Rome. The *Kyrie* is a relic of an ancient Roman custom. The people would gather at one church (the church of assembly) where they would meet the Pope or other bishop and his assistants. All would then go in procession to another church (called the Station church) for the celebration of Mass. During this procession all would join in singing a litany of acclamations to God. When these processions were discontinued (about the sixth century) a shortened form of the acclamations was retained as a part of the Mass: the *Kyrie eleison* and *Christe eleison*. Another survival of these station processions appears in our missals. We notice that each Lenten Mass in the missal is designated as being the station Mass of a certain church. For example, the Third Sunday in Lent is headed, "Station at St. Lawrence Outside the Walls." That is the church where the Pope or other bishop would celebrate Mass on that day.

Just when the *Gloria in excelsis Deo* became a part of the Mass we do not know, except that originally it was chanted only in the Mass on Christmas night. By the sixth century it also was chanted in Mass on Sundays and certain feast days, but only by the Pope. Ordinary priests were allowed to chant the *Gloria* only in their Easter Mass. It was not until the twelfth century that these restrictions were lifted and the *Gloria* became a part of every Mass of joyful character.

The prayer which the priest recites at Mass immediately after the *Gloria* (or after the *Kyrie* if there is no *Gloria*) is called the *Collect*. Nowadays in the missal this prayer is called simply the *Oratio* or prayer. It gets the name *Collect* from the fact that in the era of Station Masses, this prayer was recited by the Pope or bishop in the church of assembly (ecclesia collecta) before the procession set out for the station church. When these processions were discontinued, the *Collect* became an integral part of the Mass.

Rich in the history of our Christian ancestors is the Mass which we offer today.

The Mass of the Faithful

The Mass of the Catechumens is really a prologue to the Mass proper. The Mass of the Catechumens, developed by the early Church out of the Jewish synagogue service, is a service of prayer and instruction to prepare us for the great Action of the Mass. In the prayers at the foot of the altar, and in the *Kyrie*, the *Gloria*, the *Collect* or initial prayer of the Mass, we address ourselves to God. In the Epistle, the Gospel and the sermon God speaks His words of instruction and admonition to us. Now we are ready really to begin the Sacrifice. In the ancient Church, it was at this point that the catechumens and public penitents left the assembly; only baptized Christians in good standing remained for the Eucharist, the Giving of Thanks, the Mass. That is why this part of the Mass, from the Offertory to the end, is called the Mass of the Faithful.

In the Mass on Sundays and certain feast days, there is a transition from the Mass of the Catechumens to the Mass of the Faithful in the form of the Nicene Creed. Although the Creed was sometimes recited during Mass in earlier centuries, it was not until the year 1014 that Pope Benedict VIII made the Creed an official part of the liturgy. After listening to God's Word in Epistle, Gospel and Sermon, we can see how appropriate it is to make a declaration of our faith by reciting the Creed, before we proceed to the holy Action of the Mass. We might look upon the Nicene Creed as the door through which we pass from the Mass of the Catechumens to the Mass of the Faithful.

There are three parts to the Mass of the Faithful. There is first of all the *Offertory*, which begins with the Offertory verse just before the unveiling of the chalice and ends at the Preface of the Mass; then there is the *Canon*, the very heart and center of the Mass, which begins with the Preface and ends just before the *Pater Noster;* finally there is the *Communion* of the Mass, which begins with the *Pater Noster* and ends with the Last Gospel. The significance of these three parts of the Mass is this:

In the Offertory we present our gift, our love, our *self* (represented by the bread and wine); we unite ourselves with Christ Who is about to present Himself, the Perfect Gift, to the Most Blessed Trinity. In the Canon of the Mass Jesus consecrates our gift and carries us with Himself, the infinitely Perfect Gift, to God. In the Communion of the Mass God, having accepted our gift and transformed it into the infinitely precious Person of His Son, returns the Gift to us. In the Offertory we united ourselves with Jesus in spirit; in the Communion we are united with Jesus in reality, to grow and to live unto life everlasting.

We might picture the Mass as a triangle. Up one side of the triangle we go with Christ to God. At the apex of the triangle is the Consecration of the Mass, God's acceptance and transformation. Down the other side of the triangle comes God, in Christ to us.

It would need a large book to describe in detail the historical development of the Mass of the Faithful. We can touch here on only a few outstanding points of interest.

In the early Christian Church the Offertory was an action of the people rather than a set of prayers recited by the priest. After the Mass of the Catechumens, the faithful would come in a procession to the sanctuary, bearing their gifts. They would bring bread and wine, some of which would be used for the Body of Christ in the Eucharist. But they would bring other gifts too, such as fruit and honey and olive oil and cheese and milk. These latter gifts were for the Mystical Body of Christ—for the support of the clergy and for the relief of the poor. Whatever the gift might be, its symbolism was the same: the gift represented the giver, the giver was putting *himself* into the Mass.

At a table near the altar the gifts were accepted by a deacon who placed them on the table, emptying the wine flasks into a larger container and gathering the bread into a large linen cloth. During this Offertory procession the congregation would alternate with the choir in singing an appropriate psalm. The Offertory verse which the priest nowadays recites just before he unveils the chalice, is all that remains of the longer psalm which once was sung by all the people.

When all the gifts had been presented, the deacon would take to the celebrant at the altar as much of the bread and wine as would be needed for the Holy Sacrifice, including that which would come back to the people as God's Gift to them in Holy Communion. After the gifts had been accepted and placed on the altar, those who had handled them would wash their hands; this is the origin of the washing of the priest's fingers which occurs in today's Mass. Then the celebrant would offer a prayer over the bread and wine which had been selected for the Sacrifice. This was the only Offertory prayer offered by the priest. It appears in our present Mass as the "Secret" prayer just before the Preface. It gets its name from the fact that the gifts chosen for the Sacrifice were called in Latin the "secreta," "the things selected and set aside."

Because of its meaningfulness the Offetrory Procession was a beautiful ceremony, but in the Middle Ages it was gradually abandoned, perhaps because of the difficulty of managing it in a large congregation. To fill in the gap, extra prayers were introduced to be recited by the priest. The present Offertory prayers which the priest recites were made a part of the Mass in the fourteenth century. The ushers with their collection baskets now substitute for the Offertory Procession.

The gifts have been made ready on the altar, and a preliminary offering of the gifts has been made. The Offertory of the Mass has ended with the pronouncing of the Secret prayer over the bread and wine. We have come now to the most solemn part of the Holy Sacrifice, the *Canon* of the Mass. The Canon is introduced by the hymn of praise called the Preface; a hymn of praise to the King Who is about to come and to ascend His throne, the Cross. The Canon ends with the "Little Elevation" just before the *Pater Noster*.

The word Canon means "rule." In the Greek language from which it comes, Canon could mean either a carpenter's rule or a rule of conduct. This central part of the Mass is called the Canon because it is now a fixed and relatively unchangeable part of the Mass. In the early days of the Church this part of the Mass was called the *Eucharistia* or prayer of thanks, and was not a fixed prayer. It was largely an extemporaneous prayer on the part of the priest in which the priest would give detailed thanks to God for His many benefits and graces, climaxed by the description of Christ's wondrous Gift of His Body and Blood at the Last Supper. Gradually some of these prayers (probably those of bishops who were especially revered) came to be generally adopted and widely used. Little by little the Canon as we know it began to take form and to "jell." Since the year 600 there has been no notable change or addition in the Canon of the Mass.

It is interesting to know that the early Christians regarded the entire Canon as the prayer of Consecration. We today are keenly aware that the bread and wine become the Body and Blood of Jesus at the moment when the priest pronounces the words, "This is My Body," and "This is the Chalice of My Blood." In earlier times however the Christians did not advert to this precise moment in the Canon as *the* moment. To them this entire part of the Mass was an *action*, the sacrificing Action, and they did not consciously distinguish between the various parts of it as do we. That is why the Church ended the Action with the elevation of the Sacred Host and Chalice, just before the *Pater Noster*, for the adoration of the people. For a thousand years this was the only elevation in the Mass. It was not until the eleventh century that there was introduced into the Mass the elevation of the Body and Blood immediately after the words of Consecration. The original elevation still remains in the Mass, but very few notice it; often the priest does not raise the Sacred Host and Chalice high enough for anyone but himself to see.

With the *Pater Noster*, the Communion, the third part of the Mass of the Faithful begins. Like other parts of the Mass, this also developed gradually through the centuries. It should be noted first of all that in former times, in fact up until the Middle Ages, it was taken for granted that everyone who assisted at Mass would also receive Holy Communion. For the first thousand years of Christian history the people had a true understanding that the Mass is *"our* Mass." All participated in the Mass to the fullest possible extent, which meant of course partaking of the Victim of the Sacrifice, receiving back from God the transformed Gift which had been offered; in other words, receiving Holy Communion. During the Middle Ages this sense of active participation seems to have diminished, and as a consequence the people became lax and neglectful in the matter of receiving Holy Communion. Pope St. Pius X and Pope Pius XII both have labored mightily to bring back the concept of Holy Communion as an integral part of the Sacrifice, urging all of us to make every Mass a Communion Mass insofar as we possibly can.

Historically the Communion rite of the Mass was originally very simple. In fact the Communion was not even looked upon as a separate part of the Mass by the early Church; it simply was the completion of the Sacrifice. When the first Christians sat or reclined at table for the Eucharistic Sacrifice, the Holy Bread and Chalice were passed from one to the other. As congregations grew in size, it became necessary for the people to come forward to receive Communion from the celebrant or his assisting deacons. As the people came in procession to the Communion table near the altar, they would sing an antiphon and psalm in keeping with the spirit of the season or the feast. A relic of this Communion psalm survives in our present Mass in the form of the Communion verse which is recited by the priest (and sung by the choir) after priest and people have received Communion. The *Pater Noster* (Our Lord's own prayer) first appears in the Mass about the year 350. The *Agnus Dei* was added to the Mass about the year 700, to cover the time required for the celebrant to break the large Sacred Hosts into smaller pieces for the people. The Postcommunion prayer which the priest recites (or sings) just before closing the missal, is an ancient prayer of the Mass. However, most of the other prayers which appear in our Mass between the *Pater Noster* and the Last Gospel were of much later origin; some of them did not become a fixed part of the Mass until the time of Pope St. Pius V in the sixteenth century.

Up until the fourteenth century, Holy Communion was given to the people under the appearance of wine as well as under the appearance of bread in the Latin Catholic Church, and this still is the practice in the Greek Catholic Church. However, we know that Jesus is present, whole and entire, under each of the two Species; to receive Holy Communion, it is sufficient to receive under one appearance or the other. It no doubt was the practical difficulties posed by large congregations that led to the discontinuance of Holy Communion under the appearance of wine in the Latin Catholic Church.

Why Have Vestments?

"The eyes are the windows of the soul." This ancient aphorism reminds us that we are humans, not angels. All our knowledge comes to us through our physical senses. If it were possible for a person to be born and to survive minus all sense perception—with no sense of sight, of hearing, of taste, of smell, of touch—that person's mind would be an absolute blank, regardless of how well-formed a brain he might have. The spiritual soul would be present, but all avenues to knowledge would be closed. Not only our knowledge, but our emotions and our internal attitudes also depend upon our bodily senses. We want sweet music for our sentimental moods, and peppy marches for our parades. We want soft lights for restfulness, and bright lights for excitement.

It is no wonder then that external accessories can be of such importance in our religious life and worship. If caps and gowns can add to the seriousness of a graduation, colorful robes to the solemnity of a fraternal society's initiation, and white tie and tails to the glamor of a formal ball—it is to be expected that special garments will foster our sense of awe in our worship of God. No one knows this better than the God Who made us. That is why God in the Old Testament specifically prescribed certain vestments to be worn by the Mosaic priesthood. That is why God's Church in the New Testament has evolved, under God, special garments to be worn by priests in the discharge of their sacred duties, particularly when they celebrate Mass.

During the first three or four hundred years of Christian history, when the faithful gathered for the celebration of the Eucharist the priest wore the ordinary clothing of the layman. In those days a man's ordinary garment was a long flowing robe, a form of the Roman "toga." When the Roman empire was conquered by the barbarian tribes from northern Europe towards the end of the fourth century, the style of men's dress began to change, but priests continued to wear the long flowing robe when celebrating Mass. Thus the oldest of the Mass vestments is the *alb* (from the Latin word *albus* which means white), the long white robe which the priest puts on over his cassock, his "everyday" clothes. The alb signifies purity of heart, and in symbol the priest puts the world behind him as he dares to offer the holy Lamb of God. In ancient times the Roman toga was bound about the waist with a cord or girdle, and this girdle also survives as a Mass vestment which is called the *cincture*. The cincture is a cord of braided linen or wool and is a symbol of chastity, of restraint of physical desire.

Along about the eighth century it became the custom for the priest to come to the altar with his head covered by a hood. Eventually this hood became stylized as the vestment which now is called the *amice* (from the Latin word *amic-tus* meaning simply a covering). The amice is a white linen cloth of oblong shape, about 16 x 20 inches in size, with long tapes sewn to two of its corners. In a few religious Orders the amice still is worn as a head-covering at the beginning of Mass. For other priests however the rule is to touch the amice to the top of the head as the priest begins to vest for Mass, and then to bring it down around the shoulders and tie it about the chest with the tapes provided for the purpose. The Church has made the amice a symbol of the "helmet of salvation" of which St. Paul speaks: armor for the head against the attacks of Satan.

While the alb is the oldest of the vestments, the amice is the first vestment which the priest puts on. With the amice about his shoulders the priest then dons the alb, and then fastens the cincture about his waist. Clothed in white, the priest now is ready to assume the vestments which vary in color from day to day, from feast to feast. There are three of these colored Mass vestments: the *maniple*, the *stole*, and the *chasuble*.

The maniple is a band of cloth which the priest wears hanging from his left arm. The maniple has a very homely origin. It began as a handkerchief which the priest wore across his arm so as to have it readily accessible when he needed it. That in fact is how the maniple got its name— from the Latin word *manipulus* which means (among other things) a handkerchief. In time the maniple became stylized into a prescribed vestment. The Church points to it as a symbol of the tears of human sorrow and suffering which one day will be dried by God's own handkerchief of heavenly joy.

The priest next puts on the stole, a long band of colored cloth which goes over the shoulders and hangs down in front, crossed upon the priest's breast. The stole came into use about the fourth century, and seems to have derived from the official robe worn by Roman court judges; it was adopted by the Church as a symbol of priestly authority. From a robe it evolved into the narrow band of cloth which is its form today. In her liturgy the Church equates the stole with the "robe of immortality" which clothes the Christian soul.

The last vestment which the priest puts on is the chasuble. This is the large colored vestment, usually ornamented, which hangs from the shoulders front and back. Because of its enveloping nature it gets its name from the Latin word *casula* which means "little house." In Christian symbolism it denotes the yoke of Christ, the yoke of Christian and priestly responsibility. Chasubles are made in two styles. The voluminous chasuble which hangs down at the sides over the arms is called a Gothic chasuble; a chasuble which is cut away at the sides so as to leave the arms free, is called a Roman chasuble. In its origin, the chasuble is simply a gradual adaptation of the outer cloak worn by men in the early centuries of Christian history.

It may be of interest to look with an examining eye upon the celebrant and the altar as the priest comes from the sacristy, vested and ready to begin Mass.

We notice at once that the priest's outer vestments are colored, and that the color of the vestments may vary from one day to another. There are five colors which lend variety to the Church's liturgy: white, red, green, violet (or purple) and black. White is a symbol of purity and holiness, and is also expressive of joy. It is the color used on feasts of Our

Lord, feasts of the Blessed Virgin Mary, feasts of saints who were not martyrs, and during the Easter season. Red is symbolic of fire and of blood. Because it is expressive of the burning fire of love red is the color used on feasts of the Holy Spirit, who on Pentecost descended upon the apostles in the form of tongues of fire. Red also is the color assigned to feasts of martyrs—those saints whose love for Christ was proven in the shedding of their blood for Him.

Green is the color which clothes the earth when nature rises from the death of winter. Green therefore is the color of hope, expressive of our hope for eternal life. Green is the color used on the Sundays-after-Pentecost, and on weekdays also during the post-Pentecost season when the Mass is not that of a saint or of another feast. The somber shade of violet has become associated with penance, and so it is used on Sundays and weekdays (which are not feast days) of Advent and of Lent, and on other penitential days such as the Ember Days. Black of course is a symbol of mourning; it is the color worn by the priest at funeral Masses and at other Requiem Masses.

Besides these five liturgical colors there are two substitute colors. For festive occasions cloth-of-gold vestments may be worn in place of white, red or green. On two Sundays of the year, Gaudete Sunday (the third Sunday of Advent) and Laetare Sunday (the fourth Sunday of Lent) rose colored vestments may be worn instead of violet. On these two Sundays the Church takes a peek ahead to the joy that is coming, and lightens a little the dark color of penance.

As the priest approaches the altar, we observe that he carries in his hands the chalice, covered with a veil which is the same color as that of the vestments. On top of the veiled chalice there rests a square-shaped pocket or pouch which is called a burse. Inside this burse is the folded corporal, the square linen cloth which the priest will unfold upon the altar beneath the chalice. This square of linen is called a corporal because upon it will rest the Body (Latin: *corpus*) and the Blood of Jesus. Like the chalice veil, the burse also is of the color of the day's vestments.

The veil over the chalice reminds us that this is a sacred vessel, to be shielded reverently from view except when in actual use. All the vessels of the altar are treated with equal reverence. The ciborium (which in Latin means "bread-container"), the golden cup which contains the small Sacred Hosts which are distributed in Holy Communion; and the monstrance in which Jesus is enshrined at solemn exposition and Benediction of the Blessed Sacrament: these vessels also are veiled (in white) when not in use.

The chalice or cup which the priest now places upon the altar is made of gold or of gold-plated silver. If other metals are used, as a very minimum the inside of the cup must be plated with gold, since we deem that nothing less than precious gold is worthy to have contact with the Precious Blood of God. The same rule applies to the small shallow plate called the *paten*, which at present is nested upon the chalice, and upon which rests the large altar bread which is to be changed into the Body of Christ. If the paten is not of solid gold, its upper surface at least must be gold-plated, since hereon will lie the Sacred Host.

Resting on the top of the paten beneath the chalice veil is a stiffened square of linen cloth, called a *pall*. The pall will be used as a cover for the chalice during the Mass. Underneath the paten and lying across the chalice is another accessory, the purificator. This is a small towel of fine linen with which the priest will wipe out the chalice, before the Offertory and after the chalice has been purified with wine and water at the end of Mass. Corporal, pall, and purificator: these are the sacred linens of the Mass.

We can plainly see the pure beeswax candles (Christ the Light of the world) which burn upon the altar, two for a Low Mass and six for a High Mass. We can see also the crucifix above the altar to which the priest often will raise his eyes as he offers the Sacrifice of Calvary. We can see too the linen altar cloth which covers the altar, and know that there are (and must be) two shorter linen cloths beneath it. We cannot however see the altar stone upon which, in the Latin Rite, Mass always must be celebrated. If the altar is a fixed altar, of stone or marble and with its foundations sunk into the ground, then the whole altar top will be the altar stone. If the altar is of wood or composition, then the altar stone will be imbedded in the middle of the altar's table. In either case the altar stone will be a slab of stone or marble consecrated by a bishop. On its surface will be engraved five crosses, and in a hollowed-out cavity near its front edge will be imbedded and sealed a small silver or gold box which contains martyrs' relics from the Roman catacombs. Upon this stone must rest the Chalice and the Sacred Host at Mass.

The Roman Missal

All the prayers and readings that are recited and sung in Mass of the Latin rite, are contained in a book called the Roman Missal. This book also contains the detailed directions for the ceremonies which the Church prescribes for the offering of the Mass. In the Latin Missal the prayers and readings are printed in black, while the directions are printed in red. The directions or instructions are called the *rubrica* of the Mass, from the Latin word *ruber* which means "red."

Our Mass book is called the Roman Missal to distinguish it from the Mass books used by the Catholic Church of the Oriental or Eastern rites. We must remember that Latin is not the only language in which the Mass is offered, nor are the ceremonies of the Latin rite the only ceremonies that are used in the celebration of Mass. It is only by what we might call an accident of history that Latin is now the dominant language of the Catholic Church. Even at Rome itself, Greek was the official language of worship for the first three hundred years of Christian history. It was in the fourth century that the Church adopted Latin, which had replaced Greek as the language of the people, so that the people might participate more fully in the Holy Sacrifice.

While at Rome the ceremonies of the Mass were developing along the lines now so familiar to us, the Christian communities at Jerusalem, at Antioch in Syria, at Alexandria in Egypt, and at Constantinople in Greece were evolving other sets of prayers and ceremonies for the Mass. We might say that they were fashioning other styles of settings for the precious gift which Jesus presented to us at the Last Supper. Out of the liturgies of these eastern communities, there developed the Mass prayers and ceremonies which we now call the Eastern or Oriental rites.

Various bishops adapted one or the other of these Eastern liturgies to the language of their own people, which made for still greater diversity. As a result we have the Byzantine (or Greek) rite, the Syriac rite, the Chaldean rite, the Armenian rite, to mention a few. What makes the situation still more confusing for Latin Catholics is the fact that some of the bishops in these eastern lands eventually renounced their allegiance to the Bishop of Rome, the Pope. Many of the people in their ignorance followed the bishops in their disloyalty. This was the beginning of the schismatic churches; that is, churches cut off from unity with the true Church of Christ which has the Bishop of Rome as its head. We cannot here go into the historical reasons for these breaks with Rome. We can only observe that the Oriental churches which broke away from Rome are now usually called the Orthodox churches, while the Oriental churches which remained loyal to Rome now are called the Uniate (that is, united) churches. As a consequence we have such divisions as the Greek Catholic rite and the Greek Orthodox church; the Armenian Catholic rite and the Armenian Orthodox church.

It should be emphasized that *Catholics* of the Oriental or

Eastern rites are just as truly Catholics as are we. They acknowledge the Pope as their supreme spiritual head, and have the true Mass and all the sacraments, even though the language and the ceremonies of their liturgy may seem strange to us. We are quite free to attend one of their churches, just as they are quite free to attend Mass in a Latin church.

In fact, it might be a good idea for us to assist at Mass once a year (or at least once in a lifetime) in a church of the Eastern rite. It will serve to renew our understanding of the meaning of the word Catholic, universal; embracing all men and adapted to every culture. It would be well also for Latin Catholic parents to take their children to a church of the Eastern rite. The children's vision of their Church will be enlarged. They will realize that Christ's Church is not inescapably tied to one language or to one set of cere-monies. They will realize that it is what happens at Mass that matters: the offering of one's self in union with Christ the perfect Gift—and not the language or the motions with which it is done. For the Latin Catholic too there may be a freshened reverence for the Body and Blood of Jesus as he receives Holy Communion under both forms, as the priest with a golden spoon drops upon the communicant's tongue the Sacred Host (a Cube rather than a Wafer) which has been dipped into the Precious Blood of the chalice. There are churches of the Eastern rite in all the large cities of our country, and in some of the smaller cities too. However, anyone planning to fulfill his Sunday obligation in an East-ern rite church should first make sure that it is a *Catholic* church, a Uniate church. An Orthodox church is a non-Catholic church and is forbidden to Catholics.

We have said that it is only an accident of history which has made Latin the dominant language of the Catholic Church. That of course is not strictly true, if we believe as we must in the providence of God. Under God, however, it is a historical fact that the vigorous new pagan nations of the West were evangelized by Latin rite missionaries from Rome, rather than by Eastern rite missionaries from Constantinople. It is due to Patrick, Boniface, Augustine and Cyril and Methodius that the Roman Missal is the Mass book of the great majority of Catholics today.

When a person first begins to use a daily missal, he may find the Roman Missal (even in its English translation) a confusing book. The structure of the Mass itself is fairly simple. There is first of all the Mass of the Catechumens which is the prayer-and-instruction preparation for the Sacrifice. Then there is the Mass of the Faithful which includes the Offertory, the Canon or Consecration, and the Communion of the Mass. If the structure of the missal followed this structure of the Mass itself, it would be no trick at all to use a daily missal.

However the structure of the missal is complicated by the fact that, while most parts of the Mass are the same every day, there are some parts which change each day according to the season of the year or the feast which is being celebrated. It is in fitting the changeable and the unchangeable parts of the Mass together that the beginner (and sometimes the veteran) encounters difficulty.

In using the Roman Missal it is necessary to remember that there are three broad divisions of the missal: the *Ordinary* of the Mass, which contains the unchanging prayers of the Mass, from the beginning up to the Preface; the *Canon* of the Mass, which in the Missal contains not only the prayers of the Canon proper (from the Preface up to the *Pater Noster*) but also the prayers of the Communion part of the Mass (from the *Pater Noster* to the end); and the *Proper* of the Mass.

The Ordinary and the Canon offer no difficulty. In these two sections of the missal we go smoothly and easily from prayer to prayer—until suddenly we come to a point where we have to insert a reading or a prayer from the Proper of the Mass. It is here that the beginner is likely to be tempted to discouragement in his use of the daily missal. It still would be comparatively simple if there were just one set of Propers in the missal, following neatly one after the other according to dates. However in the Catholic Church we have two calendars: the Calendar of the Saints and the Calendar of the Season. The technical names for these are the Sanctoral Cycle (from the Latin word "sanctus" meaning saint) and the Temporal Cycle (from the Latin word "tempus" meaning time).

In the sanctoral cycle the feasts of the Saints, of our Blessed Mother and of Our Lord follow nicely in succession according to dates. But in the temporal cycle the structuring of the missal faces two obstacles. First of all any designated Sunday will fall on a different date each year, since the number seven does not divide evenly into 365. For example the First Sunday of Advent (the fourth Sunday preceding Christmas) will be on a different date from year to year.

The second obstacle to an easy Church calendar lies in the fact that Easter is what we call a "movable" feast, and varies from year to year. This is because Jesus rose from the dead the day after the Jewish feast of the Passover, and the date of Easter is fixed by the same ancient rule which fixed the date of the Passover. Consequently Easter is the first Sunday after the first full moon after the spring equinox—the spring equinox being March twenty-first. The date of Easter Sunday thus may vary by as much as a month from year to year, depending upon the phase of the moon after the twenty-first of March.

This makes all the feast days which depend upon Easter (such as Pentecost, Trinity Sunday, Corpus Christi) vary also from year to year. The same is true of the Sundays which precede Easter (beginning with Septuagesima Sunday) and of the Sundays which follow after Pentecost (first Sunday after Pentecost, second Sunday after Pentecost, and so on). This is why, in using our daily missal, we cannot always pick the right Proper for the Mass of the day just by turning to a certain date in the missal. If the Proper of the Mass at which we are assisting is taken from the Proper of the Season, we have to know what week it is in the temporal cycle: whether for example it is the third week after Epiphany, the third week in Lent, or the third week after Pentecost.

Even when the Mass at which we assist is a feast day Mass with a fixed date, we may encounter complications. We discover that not every feast day has a Proper all its own. Sometimes the same Proper does for many saints or for several feasts. These Propers which are shared in common by many saints or feasts are found in a separate section of the missal which is called the Common of the Saints. Thus the Proper of the Mass in honor of St. Anselm on April 21 is found in the Common of the Saints and is the Mass for a Bishop-Confessor and Doctor of the Church. The Proper of the Mass in honor of Our Lady of the Snows on August 5 is found in the Common of the Saints under the title, Common of Feasts of the Blessed Virgin Mary. It may seem like a contradiction in terms to speak of a Proper which is common, but not as the missal uses the words.

Ordinary, Canon, and Propers—with some Propers proper and some Propers common—this is the overall structure of the Roman Missal.

Participating in the Mass

Basically there is only one right way to assist at Mass. The one right way is to unite ourselves with Jesus Christ, solidly and sincerely, as He offers Himself for us and in our name to the Most Blessed Trinity. This means to put our *self* into the Mass, to make ourselves a part of the Gift that is being offered. It means to make ourselves co-victims with Christ the infinitely perfect Victim as He offers Himself to God. As the Mass begins and as the Mass proceeds our disposition ought to be this: "Most holy God, I am all Yours.

Help me to realize the fact that I am all Yours. Use me as Your instrument in any way You want, no matter what the cost to me may be. Give me the light to know Your will, and the strength to do Your will. But if You find me blind or stubborn or weak, then *make* me do Your will in spite of myself. To love You and to do Your will; this is what matters the most to me."

To say such a prayer and to mean it all the way, with all its implications, is not easy. But it is the disposition of heart which really does unite us with Jesus Christ and which makes the Mass our own.

Basically there is only one right way to assist at Mass, but there is more than one form of assistance. Having established our oneness with Jesus, we may for example choose to pray our rosary during Mass. As we meditate upon the mysteries of the rosary, we unite ourselves with Christ in the incidents of His life and death and triumph. We shall pause of course to renew the offering of ourselves at the Offertory of the Mass, to adore Christ our King as He becomes present in the Holy Eucharist at the Consecration of the Mass, and to renew our expressions of faith and love and gratitude as Jesus comes to us in the Communion of the Mass. Indeed we shall do this regardless of what method of prayer we may use at Mass.

Rather than our rosary, we may choose at Mass to use a prayer book, and to make our own the Mass prayers which we find therein. At other times we may prefer to use prayers that are not explicitly Mass prayers but which are Christ-centered, such as the litany of the Sacred Heart and acts of consecration and reparation and self-oblation. There are no prayers that are "bad" prayers to say at Mass. There are however some prayers which are better keyed to keeping us mindful of the full significance of the Mass. For this purpose the prayers of the Mass itself are ideally suited. These are the prayers of the Roman missal, the prayers which the priest is reciting at the altar.

The fact that an increasingly large number of Catholics do choose to make the Roman missal their own Mass prayer book, is a good sign that the Mass is becoming better understood and appreciated as *our* Sacrifice, the Sacrifice of Christ and His Mystical Body. As we pray from our English missal the same prayers which the priest is reciting in Latin at the altar, we become more conscious of our unity, of our unity with Christ and with one another. We become more conscious of the fact that the Mass is an act of corporate worship, of group worship. The idea that we all are in this together—the priest at the altar and the people around us—comes more alive for us. We are in this together, one Body in Christ. We support each other with our prayers, we share with each other our graces. We see the Mass as we should see it: a community act, the Christian family at prayer. As we leave church we can smile and speak to the stranger next to us because we know that he is not really a stranger; he is a brother in Christ with whom we have prayed and sacrificed.

This meaning of the Mass is made still more vivid when we assist at a dialogue Mass. In the dialogue Mass the entire congregation makes the responses of the Mass instead of delegating this privilege to one or two servers at the altar. In a sung Mass also the sense of community is made keen when the Mass is sung by the whole congregation rather than by a select choir. Dialogue Masses and High Masses sung by the congregation are on the increase, thanks be to God. If and when our own parish makes a start in this direction, our whole-hearted support and participation should be forthcoming.

Some of us who already are in the habit of assisting at Mass with an English missal may sometimes experience a sense of frustration which is fairly common. This sense of frustration results from the inability to "keep up with the priest." Just as some people speak more rapidly and move more nervously than others, so do some priests celebrate

Mass more quickly than other priests. Even when the priest is deliberate in speech and motion, there remains the fact that the Latin language is more compact (and therefore more brief) than the English tongue. There is the further fact that the priest has many of the Mass prayers in plain sight before him on the altar cards and does not have to spend time in paging through the missal as does the man in the pew.

However, we should not let ourselves become anxious just because we cannot keep abreast of the priest when using our daily missal. We should not feel that we *must* read every word of every prayer. There was a time when Mass was offered with far fewer prayers than we have in our missals today. It will be much more profitable for us to read just a few of the prayers for each major part of the Mass, and to read them thoughtfully and reverently, than to exhaust ourselves in a losing race.

Fifteen hundred years ago in the Roman empire, Latin was the everyday language of the people. When the people assisted at Mass they knew what was happening. More than that, they helped to make it happen. They prayed with the priest and they sang with the priest, and they did so with complete understanding because the Mass was in their own tongue. In the Offertory and Communion processions they moved back and forth to the altar, bringing their gifts and receiving their Gift. Taking such an active part in the Mass, it was easy for them to realize that they were members of a community, the Christian community, engaged with Christ as their Head in His work of reconciling man with God.

Then out of the wildernesses of northern Europe came the barbarian tribes. These pagan peoples invaded the Roman empire, bringing their own languages out of which developed the modern languages of present-day Europe. Little by little Latin ceased to be the language of the people. It became a "dead" language, spoken by no one except scholars. Gradually the people receded into the background at the offering of the Mass. The Mass became the work of the priest alone, of the priest assisted by a few servers and by a professional choir. The Mass was no longer so visibly the *action* of the whole Mystical Body of Christ. To the people it became more like a spectacle; something at which they were present and at which they looked, but in which they had no part.

The Mass lost none of its essential value. In it Jesus Christ still offered Himself through the ministry of the priest as the perfect Gift, the perfect Sacrifice to God. The Mass still was (and is) the great Action, the great Work of Christ in His Church, adoring God and redeeming man. But when the people ceased to take an active part in the Mass, the Mass did lose much of its secondary value: its value as an instructor in Christian living and as a builder of the Christian mentality. When they participated actively in the Mass, the Christian people had a constant living reminder of their oneness with Christ and with each other.

As they spoke and chanted the prayers of the Mass, the people relived with Christ His Passion, His death and resurrection. Theirs was a joyous religion because they were reminded so vividly that Christ had conquered sin and death, and by His resurrection had pledged them eternal life. Theirs too was a Christ-centered religion; they went from church conscious of their obligation to share in Christ's work of redemption, conscious of their responsibility to their neighbor.

When the people ceased to have an understanding part in the liturgy ("liturgy" is a Greek word meaning "work") their spiritual life underwent a gradual change. For one thing their spiritual life became less Christ-centered and more self-centered. They became more preoccupied with the business of saving their own soul, and less mindful of their neighbor and his needs. In their own thinking they became individuals rather than interdependent members of the one Mystical Body. Religion lost much of its joyfulness too, as Christians lost some of their happy confidence in the effectiveness of Christ's redemption as applied to themselves. They began to worry more about their own sinfulness, and to see "goodness" as a matter of keeping from sin. It is of course necessary to keep from sin, but that is only the beginning. We must not only keep from betraying Christ through sin; we also must work with Christ through the exercise of charity, of love.

The loss of intimate participation in the liturgy on the part of the people had another effect. As the significance of the Mass became obscured, private devotions of all kinds began to flourish. The human desire to participate in worship found outlet in novena services and other forms of non-liturgical piety. None of this was bad—all prayer is good and pleasing to God—but all too often these private devotions became more important than the Mass itself; first things ceased to be first.

We can be grateful that recent Holy Fathers, St. Pius X and Pius XII in particular, labored so devotedly to restore the liturgy to its rightful place as the center of Christian life and worship. The twentieth century probably will be recorded in church history as the age of the liturgical revival. It is almost incredible how much was accomplished within the reign of Pope Pius XII. He first laid the groundwork with those wonderful encyclical letters on the Mystical Body and on the Liturgy. Then came the relaxation of the Eucharistic fast, permission for evening Mass, approval of the vernacular ritual, which permits the use of our own language in many of the sacramental ceremonies and blessings of the church, the restoration of the Holy Week services so that the people might take an active and meaningful part in them.

There is still more to come. Liturgical scholars commissioned by the Pope are even now busy at Rome, reshaping the liturgy so that the Mass may once again exert the fullness of its attraction as the focal point of Christian piety and Christian action. In the meantime it is for us to enlarge our understanding of the Mass and to deepen our love for the Mass. It is for us to make more complete the giving of *self* in union with Christ in the Mass—and to live the Mass by carrying our self-giving into our everyday activities.

CHAPTER XXVIII

Holy Communion

So Close to Christ

It is in that august Action which we call the Mass, that bread and wine are changed into the Body and Blood of Jesus. Yet it would be a great mistake to think that the Mass is merely the means or the tool by which the Holy Eucharist comes into being. The Mass has a purpose of its own. It is a sacrifice which renews for us, through all time, the sacrifice of the cross. However, the Mass is such a big topic that we should like to defer discussion of it until later. Before we take up a consideration of the Holy Eucharist as a sacrifice, we should like to pursue our investigation of the Holy Eucharist as a sacrament.

A question that quite naturally proposes itself to us at this point is: What is the purpose of the sacrament of the Holy Eucharist? What effects does It produce in the soul? We know that every sacrament does produce its own special effect or effects. If the purpose of all sacraments were simply to give a single kind of grace, one sacrament would be enough; there would have been no need for our Lord Jesus to have instituted seven.

The sacrament of the Holy Eucharist was instituted as a food, a spiritual food. That is why the outward sign of this sacrament—the appearances of bread and wine—is a sign of nourishment; just as in Baptism the outward sign is water, a sign of cleansing. The action by which we as individuals receive the Holy Eucharist is an act of eating; we swallow the appearances of bread and wine under which Jesus is present. This is the action which we call Holy Communion. Since the Holy Eucharist is a spiritual food, we would expect It to do for the soul what physical food does for the body. In supposing that, we are right.

The first and principal effect of physical food is that it becomes united to him who eats it. It is changed into the person's own substance and becomes a part of him. In Holy Communion something analagous happens to us spiritually, but with a great difference. A union is effected between the person and the Food, but in this case it is the individual who is united to the Food, not the Food to the individual. The lesser is united to the Greater. We become one with Christ.

This sacramental union of ourselves with Jesus does not consist in the mere physical union between our body and the Sacred Host which we have swallowed. The union consists rather in the mystical and spiritual union of the soul with Jesus by the divine virtue of love, which is produced in the soul by our physical contact with the sacred Body of Jesus. This effect—a mystical incorporation of the soul with Jesus through an access of charity, is produced "ex opere operato" as the theologians say. That is, it is produced by the Sacrament itself, not by any effort on our part. If we place no obstacle in the way, we invariably become more closely united with Jesus by the bond of charity, when we receive Holy Communion.

This marvelous blending of the soul with Jesus is a very special kind of union. Obviously we do not become "part of

God." We are not united to Jesus by a hypostatic union, such as the union which exists between the sacred Humanity of Christ and His Divine Nature. The union with Jesus which Holy Communion effects in us is however in a class by itself. It is much more than the "ordinary" union with God which the Holy Spirit establishes in us by sanctifying grace; yet it is less than the ultimate and most intimate union with God which will be ours in the beatific vision in heaven. It is neither hypostatic nor beatific; it is simply *Communion*.

Being united with Christ in this close and personal, this very special union, we are necessarily united also with all others who are "in" Christ, all others who are members of His Mystical Body. Union with Christ in Holy Communion is the bond of charity which makes us one with our neighbor. We cannot experience the growth in love for God which our union with Jesus imparts, without also experiencing a growth in love for our fellow man. The fruitfulness of our Holy Communions is suspect if we find in ourselves no lessening of racial and national prejudices, of neighborhood resentments; if we find in ourselves no increase in neighborliness, in compassion, in patience and forbearance towards others.

The very sign of the sacrament symbolizes our total oneness in Christ. Many grains of wheat have been compounded together to make the one bread which has become the Body of Christ. Many grapes have been crushed together in the press to make the contents of the one chalice which has become the Blood of Christ. We are many in One—and that One is Christ. "And the bread that we break," says St. Paul, "is it not the partaking of the body of the Lord? Because the bread is one, we though many, are one body, all of us who partake of the one bread" (I Corinthians 10:17).

One observation perhaps we should make. The love for God and neighbor of which we are speaking is not a sentimental love, not necessarily even an emotional love. We may grow in love for God and neighbor, and grow greatly, without "feeling" the love in an emotional way, as we do feel our human attachments. Even at best, mere feeling is an unreliable guide. Let us not worry because our emotions seem untouched. It is by what we become and what we do that we must gauge the effectiveness of our worthy and frequent Holy Communions.

When our organism takes in food, and transforms the food into our own substance, what is the result? In the earlier years of our life the most noticeable result is growth; as we eat, we gain in stature and in strength. Another effect of food is that it preserves life; it constantly replenishes the burned-up and wornout cells of the body, and provides the body with the elements which will ward off infection. Food has a medicinal value, too; many illnesses need no other medication than a proper balancing of the sick person's diet.

Since the Holy Eucharist is a food, we can expect it to accomplish for the soul that which physical food effects in the body. We already have observed that in Holy Communion there is a reversal of the process by which physical food is united to the eater; in Holy Communion it is the eater who is united to his Food. From this unique and intimate union with Jesus in the Holy Eucharist, other consequences flow.

First of all there is the spiritual growth which follows upon the repeated increases in sanctifying grace which our Holy Communions impart. It is characteristic of every sacrament either to give or to increase sanctifying grace. Each of the other sacraments however has a specific purpose of its own in addition to the bestowal of sanctifying grace. Baptism cleanses from original sin, Penance forgives mortal sin, Confirmation strengthens faith, Matrimony sanctifies marriage, and so on. But in the Holy Eucharist we have the one sacrament whose *principal purpose* is to increase sanctifying grace, repeatedly and often, through personal union with the Giver of grace Himself. That is why the Holy

Eucharist is pre-eminently the sacrament of spiritual growth, of increase in spiritual stature and strength.

That also is why the soul already must be in the state of sanctifying grace when we receive Holy Communion. Physical food cannot benefit a dead body, and the Holy Eucharist cannot benefit a dead soul. Indeed, a person who knowingly would receive Holy Communion while in the state of mortal sin, would add a new dimension of guilt to his already sinful state: he would commit the grave sin of sacrilege. In the very act of outwardly offering himself to Jesus for the union-in-love which is the essence of Holy Communion, he would be opposing Jesus by that rejection of God which is inherent in all mortal sin.

Material food will not restore a dead body to life, but it will restore a weak body to health. Similarly the reception of the Holy Eucharist will not forgive mortal sin, but it will forgive venial sin—presuming of course that the communicant has sorrow for his venial sins. Here again it is love that does the work. What we might call the "charge" of love which Jesus unleashes upon the soul in this moment of personal union, is a purifying force; it purges the soul from all lesser infidelities. Whatever accumulation of venial sin may encumber the soul, it is dissolved and annihilated (if repented) as Christ's love makes contact with the soul.

Food will not restore life, but it will preserve life. It follows then that another effect of Holy Communion is to preserve the soul from spiritual death, to preserve the soul from mortal sin. One step in that direction already has been taken when venial sin has been forgiven, since venial sin is the easy gradient which leads to the sharp and sudden drop of mortal sin.

However, Holy Communion has an additional effect which helps to preserve us from mortal sin. This effect is what theologians term, "the allaying of concupiscence." Concupiscence is that tendency to sin which is human nature's common heritage as a result of Adam's fall. It is the downward drag of disordered passions, the rebellious thrusts of impulses which we inadequately control, the prideful effort of the human will to go its own way regardless of God.

It is this concupiscence, this inclination to sin, whose strength is lessened when we receive the sacrament of the Holy Eucharist. As the rocketship travels into outer space, the pull of the earth's gravity weakens as the ship travels on towards the sun. There comes a point, in fact, where the force of gravity ceases entirely and bodies float freely in space. Somewhat similarly, as we draw closer and closer to Jesus through frequent Holy Communion, we find that the counterdrag of concupiscence lessens and the power of temptation is weakened. It isn't simply that we ourselves are stronger (we are, of course); but to a larger extent sin begins to lose its attractiveness; we begin to recognize the self-attachments of yesterday for the baubles that they really are. It isn't likely that in this life we ever shall reach the point of no-gravity; but we can come very close.

Holy Communion unites us with Christ and intensifies our love for God and for neighbor. It increases sanctifying grace. It remits venial sin, lessens concupiscence, and thus preserves us from mortal sin. Finally, as good food should, it readies us for work. A frequent communicant who receives worthily and fruitfully cannot possibly remain wrapped up in himself. As love for Christ more and more fills his horizon, he feels the urge to *do* things for Christ and with Christ. Powered by the graces of Holy Communion, he becomes an apostolic Christian.

Who May Receive?

Every baptized Catholic who has attained to the use of reason and who has the necessary knowledge, may and should receive the sacrament of the Holy Eucharist.

A child is considered to have attained to the use of reason when he becomes capable of understanding (at least to some extent) the difference between moral right and moral wrong. A child of four may know that an action is "naughty" because it is displeasing to his parents, and that an action is good because it wins him praise. But he cannot grasp the fact that certain actions are good or bad because they are what God does or does not want him to do; he cannot grasp the abstract ideas of virtue and sin. As a rule-of-thumb, the age at which a child comes to the use of reason has been established at seven years. However, very few children are "average." Mentally as well as physically, some children develop more rapidly or less rapidly than others. Each child has his own individual rate of growth. It is the responsibility of parents and pastor to determine when a child has reached an age at which he can and should receive Holy Communion.

Mentally ill persons who are completely out of touch with reality may not receive Holy Communion. If they have lucid intervals, periods of rational awareness, they may and should receive Holy Communion at such times, Or, if their mental illness is only partial and they still are capable of distinguishing between the Holy Eucharist and ordinary bread, then also they may receive Holy Communion.

The amount of knowledge required for the reception of Holy Communion will depend upon the individual's mental capacity. Obviously a child of seven will not understand the nature of the Holy Eucharist as fully as will an adult, and an illiterate person may not grasp the truths of faith as clearly as will a college graduate. At a minimum, a person must have a knowledge of (and a belief in) those divine truths which are necessary for salvation: a knowledge of God the Blessed Trinity Who rewards virtue and punishes sin, and a knowledge of Jesus Christ as God-Man and Redeemer. In practice of course children are given more knowledge than this when they are being prepared for their first Holy Communion. However, parents should know that a child who is in danger of death may and should receive

Holy Communion, even though he has not made his first Holy Communion; provided he is old enough to distinguish between the Holy Eucharist and ordinary bread. If a pre-Communion child becomes dangerously ill, parents should by all means consult the pastor on this point.

Assuming that a person has the use of reason and possesses the necessary knowledge, what else is required for a worthy Holy Communion? One primary requisite is freedom from mortal sin. The Holy Eucharist is the sacrament of spiritual growth, not the sacrament of spiritual birth or of spiritual medicine. It presupposes that he who receives It is already living the life of grace. The Holy Eucharist is the sacrament of loving union between Jesus Christ and the soul; it would be monstrous to attempt such a union when the soul is at enmity with God by grave and unrepented sin. Knowingly to receive Holy Communion while in the state of mortal sin would in itself be a new mortal sin. It is the sin of sacrilege, an abuse of God's most gracious Gift to us: the gift of Himself.

If we have committed a mortal sin, it is not enough to make an act of perfect contrition before receiving Holy Communion. It is true that an act of perfect contrition (sorrow for sin out of love for God) would restore the soul to the state of grace. However, to protect us against the danger of self-deception in the matter, and to protect the Holy Eucharist against the danger of profanation, the law of the Church explicitly requires that if we know ourselves to have committed a mortal sin, we must receive the sacrament of Penance before receiving Holy Communion. This law binds us even though we may be quite sure that we have perfect contrition for the sin.

This does not mean that we must precede every Holy Communion with the sacrament of Penance. It is a good and highly desirable practice to go to confession regularly and frequently; but as long as we are not conscious of having an unforgiven mortal sin on our soul, we may continue to receive Holy Communion as often and as long as we wish, without going to confession.

It should be mentioned, too, that it is only when we are quite sure that we have been guilty of a mortal sin, that confession is necessary before receiving Holy Communion. It could happen that a person would commit a sin, and then be honestly doubtful afterwards as to whether it was a mortal or a venial sin. A person might give way to a fit of temper, for example, and afterwards be doubtful whether his unjustified anger was fully conscious or fully deliberate, or sufficiently serious to be a grave sin. The same doubt might occur as a result of strong temptations against purity or against some other virtue. If the doubt is an honest doubt and not a transparent self-deception, then the person may make an act of perfect contrition and receive Holy Communion without first having to go to confession. Of course we never can be *absolutely* sure that our contrition is perfect; but in this instance a reasonable certainty is sufficient.

Strictly speaking, no human being (excepting our Blessed Mother) could be genuinely worthy to receive Holy Communion. To be truly worthy of such an intimate union with the Incarnate God would require an angelic holiness beyond the reach of ordinary mortals. When we here speak of a worthy Holy Communion we are using the word "worthy" in a relative sense; we are speaking of that minimum degree of readiness which Jesus Christ and His Church have established as being necessary for a fruitful Holy Communion. It is that degree of readiness without which the sacrament of the Holy Eucharist would not impart grace to our souls.

We should not require of ourselves more than Jesus Himself asks of us. If a person can fulfill the minimum requirements for a worthy Holy Communion, it would be a great mistake to abstain from Holy Communion, or from frequent Holy Communion, through an exaggerated feeling of unworthiness. We must remember that Jesus does not ask us to become saints in order to receive Holy Communion frequently. Rather He asks us to receive Holy Communion frequently in order to become saints.

Some three hundred years ago there arose in the Church a heresy known as Jansenism. This heresy took its name from a French bishop, Jansen, who wrote a book on the topic of Grace, a book which was over-rigorous in its teachings. The Jansenist heresy maintained that only the most holy people should receive Holy Communion frequently, and that no one should dare to approach the Holy Table without extensive preparation and long practice of virtue. In spite of its condemnation by several Popes, this heresy spread widely through the Church and persisted, to some degree, up to our own century. It was not until Pope St. Pius X issued his famous decree on frequent Holy Communion, that Jansenism really received its death blow.

Pope St. Pius made it plain that, in addition to being free from mortal sin, the only other spiritual requirement for a worthy Holy Communion is that we receive Holy Communion with a right intention. The most perfect intention would be an eager desire to be united with Jesus because of our great love for Him. It may be that we have not as yet reached this perfection of disposition, this state of hungering love. However, there are lesser intentions that still are *right* intentions. To receive Holy Communion out of a desire to conquer temptation and keep from sin, is a right intention. To receive Holy Communion because we want to grow in grace; to receive Holy Communion because Jesus has promised heaven to those who do receive Him in this Sacrament; indeed, to receive Holy Communion in a spirit of obedience, simply because we know that Jesus wants us to—all of these are right intentions. All of these reasons, or any one of them, qualify us to receive Holy Communion.

We can recognize that it would be extremely stupid to abstain from Holy Communion on the plea that we are not in a pious mood, on the plea that we seem to have no taste for things spiritual. Our emotions are a very poor measure of our worthiness for Holy Communion. We receive Holy Communion—at a minimum—because it is what Jesus wants; the present state of our feelings should have no bearing on the matter. We can achieve a high degree of spiritual growth without having palpitations of the heart, without experiencing any moments of sweet ecstasy. It is what we are willing to do for Jesus Christ, not how we feel towards Jesus Christ, that is the acid test of our love for Him.

It is of course possible to receive Holy Communion from an unworthy motive. To receive Holy Communion simply and solely because everyone else was doing so (on Christmas or Easter for example) and it seemed the thing to do; that is, to receive Holy Communion as a mere matter of form without any real desire for grace or advertence to what we were doing—this would not be a right intention. To receive Holy Communion reluctantly just to still someone's nagging tongue, would not be a right intention. To receive Holy Communion in order to gain someone's good will (teacher, employer, or perhaps the voters) and for no other reason, would be a downright unworthy intention. To receive Holy Communion only as an outward display of piety, is the sin of hypocrisy.

However, it should be observed that the lack of a right intention in receiving Holy Communion does not result in the sin of sacrilege, presuming that the person is in the state of sanctifying grace. The total lack of a right intention means that the communicant will receive no grace from the sacrament of the Holy Eucharist; or, if the intention is downright unworthy (such as an outward display of piety) there is a venial sin of irreverence in addition to the loss of grace.

With any kind of a right intention, and with a soul that is free from mortal sin, we infallibly will receive grace from our Holy Communion. The amount of grace we receive will depend upon the perfection of our dispositions. The more ardent our love for Jesus Christ, the fewer our unrepented venial sins, the more unreserved the offering of self which we make to Jesus Christ—then the greater shall be our grace.

The Eucharistic Fast

We Catholics have reason to bless, again and again, the name of His Holiness Pope Pius XII. For several hundred years it was the law of the Church that anyone wishing to receive Holy Communion must abstain from all food and drink, even from water, beginning at midnight on the day of Holy Communion. There were exceptions for the sick and the dying, but that was the general law for the rest of us.

The reasons for this law, as also for the present law governing the Eucharistic fast, are both spiritual and practical. The spiritual reason is the Church's desire that we show special reverence towards Jesus in the Holy Eucharist, and that we show that reverence by an act of self-denial—by abstaining from other food and beverage for a specified time before partaking of the Body of Christ. The practical reason is the Church's desire to guard against possible irreverence to the Holy Eucharist, an irreverence which could result from stomach sickness if food and drink, particularly alcoholic drink, were consumed too close to the time of our Holy Communion.

It was in 1953 that Pope Pius XII took the first step in relaxing the centuries-old "From midnight on" law for the Eucharistic fast. Then in 1957 the same Holy Father promulgated the final and definitive laws prescribing the fast which we now must keep before receiving Holy Communion.

The basic law is this: Regardless of when we receive Holy Communion (midnight Mass, morning Mass or evening Mass) we must abstain from all solid foods and from alcoholic beverages for a full three hours before receiving Holy Communion; and we must abstain from all beverages (excepting water, which may be drunk at any time) for one full hour before receiving Holy Communion. It should be noted that this law specifies for the laity three hours and one hour before Holy Communion; not three hours and one hour before Mass. Thus if a person plans to receive Holy Communion at a 12 o'clock Mass and knows that Holy Communion will not be distributed until 12:30, he then could eat solid food up until 9:30 and take liquids up until 11:30. By "liquids" is meant not only beverages such as tea and coffee, but also liquid foods such as clear soup, egg-nogs and malted milks.

For the priest who celebrates Mass however, the law has a special restriction. The priest must measure his three hours and his one hour from the time he will begin Mass; not from the time he will be receiving Holy Communion during the Mass.

The time involved must be measured very strictly and to the last second. It would be very wrong to reason, "I'm only two or three minutes short, so I'll receive Holy Communion anyway." We may not "chisel" in this matter of Eucharistic fast. If, as the priest finishes giving Holy Communion at Mass, we still are a minute or two short of the full three hours since our last solid food, or the full one hour since our last beverage (water excluded) then we just may not receive Holy Communion. Of course the principle of honest doubt still holds here. If we forgot to look at the time as we took our last mouthful of food, and we now are sincerely in doubt as to whether it was or was not a full three hours ago, we may give ourselves the benefit of the doubt and still receive Holy Communion.

Concerning the abstinence from all alcoholic beverages for three hours before Holy Communion, it might be in place to sound a note of caution because of the American penchant for hard liquor. A person might fulfill the law by abstaining from alcoholic drinks for three hours before Holy Communion, and still be under the influence of liquor at Communion time if he had drunk heavily up until the three hour limit. It would of course be gravely scandalous for such a one to receive Holy Communion, even though he had fulfilled the letter of the law with regard to keeping the fast.

In revising the Eucharistic fast law, Pope Pius XII made special provision for the sick. Anyone who is sick may take any needed medicine (even in solid form, such as pills) and any kind of non-alcoholic beverage right up to the time of Holy Communion. The sickness in question here need not be of such a nature as to confine us to bed. A severe headache would justify the taking of aspirin before going to Mass even though an hour will not elapse before the time of Holy Communion; a stubborn cough would permit the taking of cough medicine; a chronic heart condition would allow the use of heart pills. Even old age may be considered an infirmity within the meaning of the law. An aged person might need the fortification of a hot or nourishing drink (non-alcoholic of course) before leaving for Mass. If so, the drink is allowable even though an hour will not elapse before Holy Communion.

While the beverages which are taken for their nutritive or stimulative value must be non-alcoholic, this is not true of the medicine that is taken. Whatever remedy the sick person may use, its ingredients do not matter and it even may include alcohol, so long as the remedy is truly and properly a medicine.

In order to avail ourselves of these special concessions for the sick, we do not have to have the permission of a priest. The Holy Father has left us to be our own judges in the matter. If we are sick then we may use the privileges accorded the sick, without further ado. And, since no particular degree of sickness is established in the law, we may make use of the privileges even though our sickness is a slight one.

In his decree (officially called a "Motu Proprio") establishing the new Communion-fast regulations, the Holy Father did say, "We strongly exhort priests and faithful who are able to do so, to observe the old and venerable form of the Eucharistic fast before Mass and Holy Communion. All those who will make use of these concessions should endeavor to lead an exemplary life and engage in works of penance and charity." These words of the Holy Father are an exhortation, not a command. They leave us full liberty to observe the law of Eucharistic fast as it now stands, or to observe in a spirit of devotion and mortification, the former and stricter fast from midnight. Continuing to fast from midnight will be a source of greater merit, but it is not of obligation. Obviously it is much better to receive Holy Communion after a fast of only three hours, than not to receive Holy Communion at all.

The law pertaining to the reception of Holy Communion when in danger of death, remains unchanged. For a person in danger of death, there is no fast required before receiving Holy Communion. This "danger of death" differs somewhat from the "danger of death" required for the reception of the sacrament of Extreme Unction. To receive Extreme Unction a person must be in danger of death from causes within himself: sickness, injury or old age. However the danger of death which justifies Holy Viaticum (Communion when in danger of death) may also be from outside ourselves. For example, soldiers about to go into battle may receive Holy Viaticum, as also a person who is about to be executed.

In addition to relaxing the strictness of the Eucharistic fast, Pope Pius XII also accorded us the great privilege of having Mass in the afternoon or evening, whenever such Masses contribute to the spiritual good of a considerable number of people. It is left to each bishop to decide whether and on what days afternoon or evening Masses may be offered in his own diocese. It should be observed that we still may receive Holy Communion only once a day—except of course when in danger of death. If we have received Holy Communion at a morning Mass, obviously we may not receive again at an evening Mass.

To two Popes by the name of Pius do we owe a great debt

of gratitude. St. Pius X restored to little children the right to receive Holy Communion, and called all of us back to the practice of frequent Holy Communion—back from the lax custom of receiving Holy Communion once a year or once a month. Pius XII pressed on for even greater conquests for our Eucharistic King. The late Holy Father tried to remove every obstacle that might impede any of us —the sick and the weak, night workers and late sleepers— from uniting ourselves often with Jesus in the Holy Eucharist. It now takes a cold and selfish heart indeed to find an excuse for not receiving Holy Communion.

As time goes on and more and more people awaken to the possibilities in the privileges which the late Holy Father granted, we may hope that the day will come again when, as in the early Christian Church, all present at Mass will receive Holy Communion. Then will the Holy Sacrifice have its full significance as the whole congregation, having offered their Gift of Jesus to God, receive back God's Gift of Jesus to themselves.

Practical Pointers for Communicants

The essential requirements for worthy Holy Communion are familiar to us: that we be free from mortal sin, that we have a right intention in receiving Holy Communion, and that we keep the Eucharistic fast as it applies to us. If we fulfill these requisites, then we shall infallibly receive an increase in sanctifying grace, together with many actual graces, each time that we receive the sacrament of the Holy Eucharist.

It should hardly need mentioning that our external appearance should be in accord with our internal fitness. Mere courtesy would dictate that we be clean of body and of clothing when we approach the Communion railing. We need not be nattily dressed; our Lord certainly would welcome the worker in his working clothes who stops in for

Mass and Holy Communion on his way to or from work; or the poor man who must come with mends and patches. But cleanliness and neatness are within the reach of all.

So also is decency of attire. Rigid protocol governs the dress of those who are received at England's court; and no one would dream of attending a personal interview with the President of the United States clad in shorts and a halter. The King of Kings has even more right to expect that our dress shall express outwardly the reverence and respect we have for Him. It is basic piety, not prudery, that bars scanty sports attire and extreme types of dress from the Communion railing.

Not so pertinent perhaps, but still a point of practical value is the exercise of moderation in the use of lipstick when preparing for Holy Communion. It is disconcerting to the priest who, faced with a pair of heavily coated lips, has to manipulate the Sacred Host gingerly past the crimson grease; it is even more disconcerting to him to find his fingers smeared with scarlet as he moves on to the next communicant.

While we are ticking off such practical items, it may be useful also to mention the special love which priests have for those communicants who, at the railing, put back their heads, open their mouths wide, and extend their tongues out beyond the lower lip. Fortunately most communicants do just this. However, it is surprising how often at a crowded Communion railing the priest is obliged to falter and fumble before an unraised head, or barely parted teeth, or a tongue that does not protrude. If we are in doubt as to our own cooperation here, a mirror will afford us an easy check upon ourselves.

Some persons worry themselves unnecessarily in fear that the Sacred Host may touch their teeth. Actually it does not matter at all if the Sacred Host happens to touch the teeth. We should not chew the Sacred Host, however, because of the danger that particles of the Sacred Host might lodge between the teeth.

We should not chew the Sacred Host, but we must be sure to swallow It. The Holy Eucharist is a spiritual food. The act of receiving the Sacrament of the Holy Eucharist consists in the act of swallowing. If we allowed the Sacred Host to dissolve completely in our mouth so that It no longer had the appearance of bread, then we would not receive Holy Communion, we would not receive the graces of the sacrament of the Holy Eucharist. We should allow the Sacred Host to remain in the mouth only until It is moist enough to swallow.

It would be very wrong for anyone to receive Holy Communion while suffering from a digestive disturbance that may easily result in vomiting. If a person should happen to be struck by an unexpected attack of nausea after receiving Holy Communion and should vomit the Sacred Host—then the Sacred Host should be gathered up in a clean linen cloth and given to the priest for disposal. If the priest is not available, or it is doubtful whether the appearances of bread still remain—then the stomach-contents should be enclosed in a linen cloth and burned.

Turning now to a pleasanter and a still more practical point, we may raise the triple question: "How often may I receive Holy Communion; how often must I receive Holy Communion; how often should I receive Holy Communion?"

We *may* receive Holy Communion once every day, but only once in a day. The only persons allowed to receive Holy Communion more than once in a day, are priests who celebrate Mass more than once, and those who receive Holy Viaticum in danger of death even though they may have communicated earlier in the day.

We *must* receive Holy Communion once a year during the Easter time (from the first Sunday in Lent to Trinity Sunday inclusive) and when in danger of death. Deliberately to neglect to receive Holy Communion in either of these in-stances would be a grave sin.

We *should* receive Holy Communion as often as we pos-sibly can. The Holy Eucharist is our spiritual Food. We should have at least as much zeal for nourishing our soul as we have for nourishing our body—and certainly no one omits his meals for very long. The Holy Eucharist also is our guarantee of eternal happiness, if we receive It regularly, and with reasonable frequency. "He who eats this bread," Jesus promises, "shall live forever" (John 6:59). With the privileges which the late Holy Father granted to those who find it difficult to fast, we should aim to receive Holy Com-munions (as did the ancient Christians) *at every Mass at which we assist.*

Let us assume that we are prepared inwardly and out-wardly for a worthy Holy Communion. We then may wish to ask ourselves, "How much grace can I expect to get when I receive Holy Communion?"

We have heard it said that there is an infinite amount of grace available in a single Holy Communion. We have heard it said that the grace of a single Holy Communion, well received, is enough to make a person a saint. We have heard these and similar statements; and we may feel a bit guilty because, in spite of our rather frequent Holy Com-munions, we seem still to be plodding along on a pretty mediocre level of sanctity.

It is true that there is an infinite amount of grace available in a single Holy Communion. In the Holy Eucharist Jesus Christ is present, and He is God, and God is infinite, with infinite graces at His disposal. BUT the amount of grace which any particular individual receives in any single Holy Communion will depend upon that individual's *capacity* for grace.

There is a lot of water in the Pacific Ocean; but a pint bottle will hold only a pint of that water, no matter how deep in the ocean we may dip the bottle. Similarly is our soul limited in its capacity for grace. Being a finite creature, no human soul ever can have an infinite capacity for grace; no human soul ever can absorb all the grace available in Holy Communion.

This does not mean that we at present are getting from Holy Communion all the grace that we can get. It does not mean that we cannot increase our capacity for grace. If it is not an empty bottle, but rather a bottle three-quarters filled with sand which we lower into the ocean; then we shall come up, not with a pint of water but with only a fourth of the bottle's real capacity. Only God can know what is the top capacity for grace of any individual soul. But we all can be sure that none of us has reached his top capacity.

We increase our capacity for grace as we empty the sand out of the bottle, as we remove the obstacles to grace which clutter up our soul. The first and most bulky of these obstacles is attachment to venial sins (a worthy Holy Communion presupposes freedom from mortal sin). So long as there is a single deliberate venial sin which we are unwilling to abandon (a continuing grudge perhaps against the boss, alcoholic intemperance short of drunkenness, or tea-cup gossip with a tinge of malice?) just so long are we contracting our soul's capacity for grace.

After the venial sins are gone, there still are the imperfections to deal with, the failings which show that our love for God still is short of being whole-hearted. There is stinginess and half-heartedness in prayer, for example, or selfish reluctance to inconvenience ourselves for the good of our neighbor; there is lack of effort to resist our irritability and impatience, or childish conceit in our appearance or our talents. Whatever our own imperfections may be, they probably add up to a good many grains of sand in the bottle.

What can we do about these sins and imperfections? We can try a little harder, and we can receive Holy Communion more frequently. One wonderful thing about the grace of

Holy Communion is that it purifies and strengthens against the very things that block it. With any effort at all on our part, each Holy Communion paves the way for more grace in the next Holy Communion. One Holy Communion builds upon another.

This fact illuminates also the statement that, "One Holy Communion can make a saint." It is true that Our Lord could, by a very miracle of grace, transform a sinner into a saint in one Holy Communion. Normally however God permits that growth in sanctity be an organic growth, gradual and steady like the growth of a child, hardly perceptible from day to day. Again, one grace builds upon another. It is better for our humility that we do not see too clearly the progress that we make.

Surely one conclusion that emerges here, is the need to make every Holy Communion count just as powerfully as we can. This entails a good *immediate* preparation for each Holy Communion, arousing ourselves to sentiments of repentance, of faith, of love, of gratitude; trying hard to push ourselves into a genuine act of self-giving, to make our own will one with God's. All this we do, of course, if we join prayerfully and with sincerity in the offering of the Mass.

Then there are those precious minutes after Holy Communion, when our Lord Jesus has us, we might say, in His embrace. "Thanksgiving after Communion" means renewed avowals of love as well as of gratitude. It means a brave asking of the question, "Lord, what wilt Thou have me to do?" and an even braver listening for the answer that will come. If the Last Gospel finds us with one foot in the aisle, poised for a quick flight home to our coffee—then we are short-changing ourselves pitifully of graces that our Lord Jesus has not yet finished giving to us. Barring exceptional circumstances, fifteen minutes of thanksgiving after Holy Communion should be our habit, even if it means remaining for a few moments after the Mass is ended.

There is one final (and comforting) point to remember.

We may be receiving Holy Communion with great frequency. We may be making an adequate preparation and a generous thanksgiving for our Holy Communions. We may be trying honestly, from Communion to Communion, to keep some of our resolutions. In spite of all this (or perhaps because of it) we shall be dissatisfied with ourselves—as we should be. But let us not merely exclaim, "How much better I should be, with so many Holy Communions!" Let us also ask, "How much worse I might be, if it were not for my Holy Communions?"

CHAPTER XXIX

Penance

The Sacrament of Penance

It is a strange paradox. Converts quite frequently say that one of the hardest things about becoming a Catholic is the thought of having to "go to confession." And yet, for those of us who have grown up in the Church, the sacrament of Penance is probably the one that we would least want to abandon—except for Baptism. The peace of mind and soul which the sacrament of Penance imparts to us is one for which there is no substitute. It is a peace that flows from a certainty, rather than from an unsure hope, that our sins have been forgiven and that we are right with God. Of course, even the convert quickly comes to love the sacrament of Penance once he has got over his nameless fears, fears which have grown out of an ignorance of what the sacrament of Penance really is.

The word "penance" has two meanings. First of all, there is the *virtue* of penance. This is a supernatural virtue by which we are moved to detest our sins from a motive made known by faith, and with an accompanying purpose of

433

offending God no more and of making satisfaction for our sins. In this sense the word "penance" is synonymous with "penitence" or "repentance." Before the time of Christ the *virtue* of penance was the only means by which men's sins could be forgiven. Even today, for those outside the Church in good faith, not possessing the sacrament of Penance, it is the only means for forgiveness of sins.

Besides being a virtue, Penance also is a sacrament. It is defined as "the sacrament by which sins committed after Baptism are forgiven through the absolution of the priest." Or, to give a longer and more descriptive definition, we may say that Penance is a sacrament in which the priest, as the agent of God, forgives sins committed after Baptism, when the sinner is heartily sorry for them, sincerely confesses them, and is willing to make satisfaction for them.

By His death on the Cross, Jesus Christ redeemed man from sin and from the consequences of his sin, especially from the eternal death that is sin's due. So it is not surprising that on the very day He rose from the dead Jesus instituted the sacrament by which men's sins could be forgiven. It was on Easter Sunday evening that Jesus appeared to His Apostles, gathered together in the Upper Room, where they had eaten the Last Supper. As they gaped and shrank back in a mixture of fear and dawning hope, Jesus spoke to them reassuringly. Let St. John (20:19-23) tell it: "Jesus came and stood in the midst and said to them, 'Peace be to you!' And when He had said this He showed them His hands and His side. The disciples therefore rejoiced at the sight of the Lord. He therefore said to them again, 'Peace be to you! As the Father has sent Me, I also send you.' When He had said this, He breathed upon them, and said to them, 'Receive the Holy Spirit; whose sins you shall forgive, they are forgiven them; and whose sins you shall retain, they are retained.' "

By way of paraphrasing our Lord's words in more modern idiom, what He said was this: "As God, I have the power to forgive sin. I now entrust the use of that power to you. You will be My representatives. Whatever sins you forgive, I shall forgive. Whatever sins you do not forgive, I shall not forgive." Jesus knew well that many of us would forget our brave baptismal promises and commit grave sins after our Baptism. He knew that many of us would lose the grace, the sharing-in-God's-own-life which came to us in Baptism. Since God's mercy is infinite and unwearying, it seems inevitable that He would provide a second chance (and a third and a fourth and a hundredth if necessary) for those who might relapse into sin.

This power to forgive sin which Jesus conferred upon His Apostles was not, of course, to die with them; no more so than the power to change bread and wine into His Body and Blood, which He conferred upon His Apostles at the Last Supper. Jesus did not come upon earth just to save a few chosen souls. He did not come just to save the people who lived on earth during the lifetime of His Apostles. Jesus came to save *everybody* who was willing to be saved, down to the end of time. He had you and me in mind, as well as Timothy and Titus, when He died on the Cross.

It is evident then that the power to forgive sins is a part of the power of the priesthood, to be passed on in the sacrament of Holy Orders from generation to generation. It is the power which every priest exercises when he raises his hand over the contrite sinner and says, "I absolve thee from thy sins in the name of the Father, and of the Son, and of the Holy Spirit. Amen." We have heard those words often enough. If they do not sound familiar, it is because we usually hear them in Latin. They are called "the words of absolution."

Every priest has the *power* to forgive sins. But in practice he needs something else besides. He needs what is called "jurisdiction." The sacrament of Penance is akin to a legal proceeding; the priest listens to the evidence, the priest pronounces judicial sentence. We know that in civil law a judge from one state cannot try cases in another state unless the governor of the second state appoints him for that purpose. Without such an appointment the out-of-state judge would have no jurisdiction. Similarly, a priest cannot exercise his power as spiritual judge in the sacrament of Penance unless and until the bishop of the diocese gives him permission to do so. Without that permission the priest has no jurisdiction; he cannot validly absolve from sins. His power to absolve, moreover, is limited to the diocese for which he has jurisdiction. A priest from the New York archdiocese, for example, could not validly hear confessions in the Brooklyn diocese unless the Bishop of Brooklyn gave him permission to do so, or unless he was a New York pastor to whom one of his parishioners came in Brooklyn.

It may be that at one time or another we have found the sacrament of Penance a burden. Perhaps we even can remember an occasion when we said, "I wish I didn't have to go to confession." But certainly in our saner moments we find Penance a sacrament that we love, a sacrament we would not want to be without.

Just think of all that the sacrament of Penance does for us! First of all, if a person has cut himself off from God by a grave and deliberate act of disobedience against God (that is, by mortal sin), the sacrament of Penance reunites the soul to God; sanctifying grace is restored to the soul. At the same time, the sin itself (or sins) is forgiven. Just as darkness disappears from a room when the light is turned on, so too must sin disappear from the soul with the coming of sanctifying grace.

If, as is more often the case, a person receives the sacrament of Penance without any mortal sin on his soul, the sacrament still is not received in vain. In this instance, there is imparted to the soul an *increase* in sanctifying grace. This means that there is a deepening and strengthening of that divine-life-shared by which the soul is united to God. And always, whether there have been mortal sins or not, any venial sins which the penitent may have committed and for which he is truly sorry are forgiven. These are the lesser and more common sins which do not cut us off from God but still hinder, like clouds across the sun, the full flow of His grace to the soul.

The restoring or the increasing of sanctifying grace and the forgiving of mortal and venial sins—is there anything else that the sacrament of Penance can do for us? Yes indeed. If it is a question of mortal sin, Penance wipes out the eternal punishment which is the inevitable consequence of mortal sin. We know that a person who rejects God by mortal sin and goes into eternity unrepentant has cut himself off from God forever. He is in hell. But when God, in the sacrament of Penance, reunites the soul to Himself and absolves from the guilt of mortal sin, He also eliminates the threat of everlasting disaster which has been facing the soul.

Besides remitting the *eternal* punishment due to mortal sin the sacrament of Penance remits at least part of the *temporal* punishment due to sin. The temporal punishment due to sin is simply the debt of satisfaction which I owe to God for my sins even after the sins themselves have been forgiven. It it a matter of "repairing the damage," we might say. A homely example to illustrate this would be that of an angry boy who kicks at the table leg and knocks a piece of pottery off onto the floor. "I'm sorry, Mother," he says repentantly. "I shouldn't have done that." "Well," mother says, "if you're sorry, I won't punish you. But get down and pick up the pieces, and I'll expect you to buy a new dish out of your allowance." Mother forgives the disobedience and absolves from the punishment—but she still expects her son to make satisfaction for his rebellious outburst. It is this satisfaction which we owe to God for having offended Him that we term "the temporal punishment due to sin." Either we pay the debt in this life by the prayers, penances, and other good works which we perform in the state of grace or we shall have to pay the debt in purgatory. And it is this debt which the sacrament of Penance at least partially reduces, in proportion to the degree of our sorrow. The more fervent our condition is, the more is our debt of temporal satisfaction reduced.

Still another effect of the sacrament of Penance is that it restores to us the merits of our past good works if these have been lost by mortal sin. As we know, every good work that we perform in the state of grace and with the intention of doing it out of love for God is a *meritorious* work. It entitles us to an increase of grace in this life and an increase of glory in heaven. Even the simplest actions—kind words spoken, thoughtful deeds performed—have this effect, not to mention prayers said, Masses offered, sacraments received. However, mortal sin wipes out this accumulated merit, much as a man might lose his life savings by one reckless gamble. God could with perfect justice allow our past merits to remain forever lost even when He forgives our sins. But in His infinite goodness He does not do so. He does not make us start all over again from scratch. The sacrament of Penance not only forgives our mortal sins; it also restores to us the merits which we had so willfully cast away.

Finally, besides all its other benefits, the sacrament of Penance gives us the right to whatever actual graces we may need, and as we need them, in order that we may make atonement for our past sins and may conquer our future temptations. This is the special "sacramental grace" of Penance; it fortifies us against a relapse into sin. It is a spiritual medicine which strengthens as well as heals. That is why a person intent upon leading a good life will make it a practice to receive the sacrament of Penance often. Frequent confession is one of the best guarantees against falling into grave sin. It would be the height of stupidity to say, "I don't need to go to confession because I haven't committed any mortal sins."

All these results of the sacrament of Penance—restoration or increase of sanctifying grace, forgiveness of sins, remission of punishment, restoration of merit, grace to conquer temptation—all these are possible only because of the infinite merits of Jesus Christ, which the sacrament of Penance applies to our souls. Jesus on the cross already has "done our work for us"; in the sacrament of Penance we simply give God a chance to share with us the infinite merits of His Son.

Preparing for Confession

Most of us probably receive the sacrament of Penance with a fair degree of frequency. If we are afflicted with severe temptations or find ourselves otherwise troubled in spirit, we no doubt find the sacrament a great source of strength and peace. We thank God for having afforded us this opportunity to obtain spiritual guidance and counsel so easily, even aside from the graces which Penance gives. If we are wise, we go to the same confessor regularly, so that he may grow in an understanding of our needs.

However, it is likely that many of us, without any great temptations or discernible problems, receive the sacrament of Penance in a routine sort of way. We go to confession frequently because we take it on faith that it is good for us. We tell our sins and say our penance afterwards, and that is that. We have no feeling of renewal as we leave the confessional; we see no change in ourselves from confession to confession. What could be the reason for what we might almost call our apathy? What is needed, on our part, for a fruitful confession?

The catechism lists five requirements for a worthy reception of the sacrament of Penance. First, we must examine our conscience. Second, we must be sorry for our sins. Third, we must have a firm purpose of not sinning again. Fourth, we must confess our sins to the priest. Fifth, we must be willing to perform the penance which the priest assigns to us. Failure in these points may result, at worst, in a totally unworthy confession, a sacrilegious confession; or, at best, in a less fruitful confession with but little grace accruing to us.

Consider first the examination of conscience. This is described as a sincere effort to call to mind all the sins we may have committed since our last worthy confession. This is a task that we perform before we enter the confessional. If a person—perhaps a recent convert or someone who has been away from confession for a long time—has difficulty in examining his conscience, the priest gladly will lend assistance if asked. But normally we try to have our sins "lined up" in advance, ready to tick them off when the priest is ready to hear us.

The question is, is our examination of conscience as thorough and as earnest as it might be? It is easy, particularly if we receive the sacrament of Penance often, to grow quite casual about this examination of conscience. "It's about the same as last time," we say to ourselves. "Missed my morning prayers, used God's name irreverently a couple of times, got angry maybe once, told two or three lies." With that quick roundup, we hold ourselves ready for confession. We seem to forget that it is a *sacrament* which we are about to receive, a sacrament for whose efficacy Christ died in agony. Our examination of conscience ought to be an unhurried and careful preparation; otherwise, it will be no wonder if our quota of grace is small.

First of all, our examination should be prefaced by a heartfelt prayer, asking God for His assistance, that we may see and recognize our sins clearly, asking for the grace to confess them properly and to be truly sorry for them. Only then do we turn to the actual taking of inventory. Without haste or nervousness (letting others precede us to the confessional if we are not ready when our turn comes), we go through the commandments of God and of the Church, as well as the particular duties of our state of life, applying them one by one to ourselves. We need not worry about remembering the mortal sins; unless our moral prin-

ciples are very lax, a mortal sin will stick out like the pro-
verbial sore thumb. But it is a *very fruitful* confession that
we want to make; so we watch for the venial sins too—the
things that are getting in the way of a fuller love for God.

We may be inclined to dismiss some of the commandments too quickly. We may say, "The first commandment?
I haven't worshiped any false gods." No, but how about
irreverence in church, carelessness in prayers, a bit of superstition, perhaps? "The fifth commandment? I haven't killed
anybody." No, but how about blowing my top at home and
making everybody miserable? How about that resentment
I harbor against so-and-so; that secret hope I cherish that
he may get what's coming to him? "The sixth commandment? I haven't committed adultery or fornication." No,
but how about that roving eye on the bathing beach, that
smutty story at the office, that "daring" gown at the dance?
"The eighth commandment? Oh, one or two little lies
maybe." Yes? And how about that damaging bit of gossip
I passed along? How about those prejudiced remarks I
made against a man (or a woman) of another race? When
we begin to *really* examine ourselves on the virtue of charity,
we may find ourselves spending more time than we first
thought necessary.

How about the completeness of our honesty in matters
of money and property, our willingness, too, to share materially with others less fortunate? How about the fullness
of our acceptance of all that the Church teaches and our
respectfulness in speech towards priests and religious? How
about our temperance in food and especially drink (do we
have to be drunk before we admit to intemperance)? How
about the example in Christian living that we set to those
around us?

There is no need to continue the list here. A weakness
that we all are prone to indulge is to compare ourselves with
the man across the street or with the woman next door—
and to decide that we aren't so bad after all. We forget that

the only one with whom we have any right to compare ourselves is Jesus Christ. *He* is our pattern, and no one else.

It is important to examine our conscience well before receiving the sacrament of Penance; but it is even more important to make sure that we are genuinely sorry for our sins. We might conceivably forget to confess a sin—even a mortal sin—and still make a good confession, still receive forgiveness of our sins. On the other hand, we might confess our sins with the utmost exactness yet leave the confessional with all our sins still on our soul if we did not have true contrition for them.

What then *is* this contrition that is so essential in order to receive the sacrament of Penance worthily? The word "contrition" comes from a Latin word which means "to grind, to pulverize." The idea is that contrition reduces the self to dust, causes the self to stand before God in utter humility. The great Council of Trent, which gave exact wording to so much of Catholic doctrine, defined contrition as "a sorrow of heart and hatred for sin committed, with the resolve to sin no more."

We can understand readily enough the need for sorrow as a condition for forgiveness. If we were to offend someone, we know that it would be folly to expect that person to forgive us if we were not sorry for our offense and the injured person knew that we were not sorry. It does not surprise us, then, that God, whom we have dishonored by our deliberate disobedience to His commands, should require that we be sorry for our offense before He will absolve us from guilt. God will forgive *no* sin, mortal or venial, unless we are truly contrite. But there is another and more comforting side to the picture. In human affairs we sometimes find bitter and vengeful people who will not forgive an insult, no matter how sorry and apologetic the offender may be. God, however, will forgive *any* offense, no matter how heinous, if the sinner has genuine contrition.

In speaking of contrition, we have to distinguish two

kinds: *perfect* contrition and *imperfect* contrition. The difference between them lies in the motives behind them—the "reasons why" we are sorry. Perfect contrition is a sorrow for our sins which springs from a perfect love for God. Loving God above all things else for His own sake, simply because He is so supremely good and deserving of our utmost loyalty, we grieve for having offended Him. That is perfect contrition.

It should be noted that "loving God above all things else for His own sake" does not mean that we necessarily have to *feel* that love in a human way, emotionally. We might easily have a more ardent love, emotionally, for certain human beings than we have for God; but that does not mean that we would choose those human beings in *preference* to God. St. Blanche, mother of St. Louis (King Louis IX of France), provides a good example here. There is no question about the ardent mother-love which Blanche had for her son. And yet she once said to Louis, "I would rather have you dead at my feet than to have you commit a single mortal sin." If we can honestly say that in a pinch, if He required it of us, we would give up anyone and anything for God— then we have perfect love for God. And if it is that kind of love that inspires our sorrow for sin, we have perfect contrition.

Perfect contrition, incidentally, forgives mortal sin instantly so long as we have the intention of confessing the sin when we next go to confession. That is why we ought to make an act of perfect love a part of our daily prayers, reminding ourselves that God *is* the most important Being in our lives not because of what He has done for us but just simply because of what He is. By "keeping in practice" this way, we have a better chance of being able to make an act of perfect contrition, with God's grace, if the time ever comes when we need to.

Imperfect contrition is a more selfish kind of sorrow. It is not a *bad* kind of sorrow, let us remember. Although it is inadequate for cleansing us from mortal sin outside of confession, yet it is a sufficiently genuine sorrow for obtaining God's forgiveness in the sacrament of Penance.

The motives which inspire imperfect contrition are a hatred of sin itself as being essentially evil or a fear of incurring God's justice—the loss of heaven and eternal exile to hell. Sorrow which flows from either or both of these motives constitutes imperfect contrition. For imperfect contrition it does *not* suffice merely to fear hell as the greater of two evils, so that I explicitly decide that, if there were no hell, I would gladly sin. That is the kind of fear that a dog has when he sees the whip in his master's hand. It is an entirely self-centered, slavish fear, with no thought of God nor of one's own greatest good. Our fear of God should be the child's fear of a just but loving father, not the slave's fear of a harsh taskmaster.

Both kinds of contrition, perfect and imperfect, must of course include the firm determination not to sin again. Manifestly, a person is not really sorry for an action when he is quite prepared to commit the same action again if he happens to feel like it or if the same circumstances should arise. This purpose to sin no more must include *all* mortal sins, not just the ones which have been confessed; and it must include any venial sins for which we hope to receive forgiveness.

With reference to perfect contrition, it should perhaps be recalled that, although perfect contrition does cleanse us from mortal sin *immediately*, yet by positive precept we are forbidden to receive Holy Communion until we have confessed that mortal sin (or sins) in the sacrament of Penance.

CHAPTER XXX

Contrition

When Is Sorrow Real?

Sometimes we bump into someone on the street or on the bus and we say, "I'm sorry." We say it for the sake of politeness although really we may not be sorry at all. Privately we are tempted to say, "Why don't you watch where you're going?" Or someone takes offense at something we have said quite innocently, and we say, "I'm so sorry." Actually we may be saying to ourselves, "I wish he wouldn't be so sensitive."

We could multiply examples of occasions when people say, "I'm sorry," without really meaning what they say. The point we want to make, however, is that when we receive the sacrament of Penance our sorrow must be the one hundred per cent genuine article, or we might better not go to confession at all. To receive the sacrament of Penance without genuine contrition would be to make a bad confession. The sacrament would be invalid and fruitless. Unless we have true sorrow, God will not forgive our sins. How can we tell, then, whether or not we have true contrition? What are the essentials of a genuine act of sorrow?

Theologians list four qualities that are essential for true contrition. The first and obvious requirement is that our sorrow be *interior*. When we say to God, "I am sorry for having offended You," it is no mere act of politeness that we are performing. It is not a dutiful bit of courtesy. Our heart must be in our words. Quite simply, we must mean what we say. It does not follow that we must necessarily *feel* our sorrow. Like love, sorrow is an act of the will, not an upsurge of emotion. Just as we may love God quite genuinely without *feeling* our love, so too we may have a very solid sorrow for our sins without having it cause any emotional reaction. If we are quite honestly determined to abstain, with the help of God's grace, from anything that might seriously offend Him, then we have sorrow which is interior.

Besides being interior, our sorrow also must be *supernatural*. This concerns the "reason why" we are sorry. If a man is sorry for getting drunk because it left him with a terrible hangover, that is natural sorrow. If a woman is sorry for her malicious gossip because it lost her her best friend, that is natural sorrow. If a child is sorry for his disobedience because he got a spanking for it, that is natural sorrow. The sorrow in these cases has nothing to do with God or the soul or supernatural motives. Such sorrow is not *bad* sorrow; it just isn't sufficient as far as God is concerned.

Our sorrow is supernatural when it springs from supernatural motives; that is, when the "reason why" stems from our belief in some truth which God has told us. For example, God has told us that we must love Him above all else and that sin is a denial to Him of our love. God has told us mortal sin will cause us to lose heaven and to incur hell and that venial sin must be satisfied for in purgatory. God has told us that it was sin which caused Jesus to die on the cross and that sin is an offense against God's infinite goodness. God has told us that sin is hateful by its very nature.

When our sorrow is based on these truths revealed to us by God, then our sorrow is supernatural. It has risen above the level of merely natural considerations.

In the third place, our sorrow must be *supreme*. That is, we must really see the moral evil of sin as being the greatest evil that exists—greater than any physical or merely natural evil that could occur. It means that, as we tell God we are sorry for our sins, we are determined that we shall, with the help of His grace, suffer *anything* rather than offend Him again. That phrase, "with the help of His grace," is an important one. Supreme sorrow does not rule out a wholesome fear that we might sin again if victory depended upon our own human strength. On the contrary, we *should* have a distrust of ourselves and our self-sufficiency; we *should* acknowledge how much we must depend upon God's grace. At the same time we know that God's grace will never fail us if we do our part. It would be a great mistake to test the supremeness of our sorrow by imagining extraordinary temptations. For example, it would be meaningless for a man to ask himself, "I wonder whether I would be chaste if I were locked in a room with a nude and seductive woman." Without our own fault God will not let us be faced by temptations that are beyond our power of resistance; and if He does allow extraordinary temptations, we can always be sure that He will give the extraordinary graces that will be needed.

Our sorrow must be interior, supernatural, and supreme. Finally, it must be *universal*. That means that we must be sorry for *all* our mortal sins without exception. A single mortal sin cuts us off from God and keeps sanctifying grace out of the soul. Either we are sorry for all or we cannot be restored to God's grace. Either all are forgiven or none is forgiven. If we were to strike a friend in the face four times, we know how ridiculous it would be to say, "I'm sorry for three of those blows, but I'm not sorry for the fourth one."

It should be noted that these four qualities apply to imperfect contrition as well as to perfect contrition. Particularly with regard to the second quality, the supernaturalness of our sorrow, people sometimes make an error. They confuse *natural* sorrow with *imperfect* sorrow. However, the two are not at all identical. Even imperfect sorrow must be supernatural in its motives; it must be based upon a motive made known by faith, such as belief in heaven and hell or the essential hatefulness of sin. A merely natural sorrow is not true contrition at all, not even imperfect contrition.

Let us suppose that I have offended a friend of mine by spreading gossip about him. Wishing to regain his friendship I apologize by saying, "I'm sorry for what I did, Joe; but I reserve the right to do it again if I should happen to be in the mood." We do not need a professor of psychology to point out to us that Joe still will feel hurt, and rightly so. My pretended apology is no apology at all. If I am genuinely sorry for hurting Joe, then I shall resolve very firmly not to hurt him again.

This is equally true of our offenses against God. There is no such thing as a true act of contrition without an accompanying purpose of amendment. A purpose of amendment is simply a firm and honest resolve to avoid sin in the future, and to avoid as far as possible the near occasions of sin. Without such a resolve there can be no forgiveness for sin— not even for venial sin.

A near occasion of sin is any circumstance which might easily lead us into sin. Some occasions of sin are "near occasions" by their very nature; very obscene books and pictures, for example. Other near occasions may be such for certain individuals only. Thus a bar may be an occasion of sin for a man who finds it hard to be temperate in drink; a parked car in the moonlight may be an occasion of sin for a young couple on a date. Past experience usually will tell us what, for us, are the near occasions of sin. All such threats to our spiritual well-being, whether they be persons, places, things, or particular activities, must be resolutely renounced as we make our act of contrition.

It should be noted that our purpose of amendment—our resolve to avoid sin and the near occasions of sin—must extend not only to the mortal sins which we ourselves may have committed but to *all* possible mortal sins without exception. Without such an all-embracing resolution, no mortal sin can be forgiven. The situation is somewhat different with respect to venial sin. Venial sin does not cut us off from God, does not extinguish His grace in the soul. Consequently, it is possible for us to obtain forgiveness for one venial sin, even while another venial sin remains still unforgiven. This means that our purpose of amendment *must* extend to those venial sins for which we hope to secure forgiveness but need not extend to all. Clinging to certain venial sins while renouncing others would obviously mark a rather low level in our love for God. However, we are not speaking here of what is *best* but of the minimum that is necessary.

Without sorrow there can be no forgiveness, and without a purpose of amendment there can be no true sorrow. That is a principle that seems quite plain. Yet it is possible that some persons who would recoil in horror from making a bad confession through the concealment of a mortal sin may not have the same horror of a confession made invalid by lack of a firm purpose of amendment. If a person has been guilty of mortal sins, it is not enough merely to tell those sins to the priest or to recite a routine act of contrition for them. Unless the penitent is sincerely and resolutely determined not to commit any mortal sin again, his confession is an act of hypocrisy. It is just as truly a bad confession as it would be if he purposely failed to tell one or more of his mortal sins.

However, in emphasizing the need for a genuine purpose of amendment, we must avoid the error of confusing the present moment with future possibilities. A person might conceivably feel this way: "I really am sorry for my mortal sins, and I really and truly don't want to commit any mortal sin again. But I know my own weakness, and I know how my good resolutions have cracked under pressure in the past. I resolved before that I wouldn't do it again, but I did. So how can I be sure that I have a firm purpose of amendment now?"

We can be sure that we have a firm purpose of amendment *now* by keeping our mind on the now and not borrowing trouble by peering into an imaginary future. Even though we have failed in the past, a dozen times or a hundred times, it does not mean that we are doomed to failure forever. This present time may be the time that we get over the hump. This may be precisely the time that, with God's patient grace, we finally succeed.

Although it is an axiom hallowed by long use, it is *not* true that the road to hell is paved with good intentions. It is the road to heaven which is paved with good intentions. The road to hell is paved with discouragement and despair. How can we succeed at anything unless we try, and try again, and keep on trying undaunted? The mountain climber may advance three steps and slip back two steps; three steps forward again and back two once more. But if he is dogged enough and stubborn enough, he'll reach the summit at last.

A person who may have had the misfortune to fall into a habit of sin—whether it be a habit of impurity or anger or uncharitableness or some other sin—needs especially to be reassured on this matter of true purpose of amendment. *It is the present moment and the present intention that counts in confession.* There may be further stumbles and further falls before final victory is achieved. But the only sinner who is defeated is the sinner who has quit trying.

Thank God for Confession!

From those who have no understanding of the Catholic faith we sometimes hear some such statement as this: "I never could believe in confession. If I do wrong, I'll tell God I'm sorry in the secrecy of my own heart, and God will forgive me. I don't have to tell my sins to any mere man in order to obtain forgiveness." It sounds like a reasonable remark, doesn't it? And yet it is as full of fallacies as a net is full of holes.

First of all, the question is not whether we *like* confesion or whether we would prefer to have our sins forgiven in some other way. The question is, *how does God want it done?* If Jesus Christ, true God, in instituting the sacrament of Penance as the necessary means for the forgiveness of sins committed after Baptism, made the confessing of our sins to the priest an essential part of the sacrament, then that is the way it must be done. We are not at liberty to pick and choose when God already has spoken. We are not free to say, "I'd rather do it this way or that way."

Jesus did make the telling of our sins an essential part of the sacrament of Penance. In bestowing the power to forgive sins upon His priests on Easter Sunday night, our Lord said, "Whose sins you shall forgive, they are forgiven them; and whose sins you shall retain, they are retained" (John 20:23). Jesus, with the infinite wisdom of God, did not use words carelessly; and His words do not make sense unless they presuppose the confession of sin. How could the apostles and the priests who would succeed them know what sins to forgive and what sins not to forgive if they did not know what the sins were? And how could they know what the sins were unless the sinner himself would tell?

The history of the Christian Church backs up the obvious meaning of these words of Christ. Ancient writings tell us that from the very beginning of the Church forgiveness was granted to penitents only after they had confessed their sins. The principal difference between the first centuries and our own time is that when the Church was in its infancy, forgiveness for grave sins was not lightly granted. If his sin was a publicly known one—such as idolatry, adultery, or murder —a sinner might have to perform a life-long penance and be granted the sacrament of Penance only on his deathbed.

What critics of confession (and of other doctrines of the Church) forget is that not all the words of Jesus are written down in the Gospels. Indeed, when we reflect that Jesus spent almost three years in preaching and teaching, we realize how little of His total discourses can be contained in the few pages left us by the four evangelists. On Easter Sunday night, for example, we may be sure that the apostles took advantage of their opportunity to question Jesus at length as to the exact meaning of His words, "Whose sins you shall forgive . . . ," and as to what would be required for forgiveness.

History shows that the telling of one's sins in order to obtain forgiveness is as old as the Christian Church. Consequently the bigot who says, "Confession is something which the priests invented in order to keep their hold on the people," is displaying his ignorance of history as well as his prejudice. A very obvious answer to such a critic is to ask, "Well, if the priests invented confession, then why didn't they exempt themselves from the necessity of going to confession?" Actually the Pope must go to confession, bishops must go to confession, priests must go to confession, the same as everyone else.

All these objections to confession which we hear from outsiders are based on the supposition that the sacrament of Penance is a horrible ordeal to be dreaded and avoided if possible. We Catholics know that that supposition "just ain't so." We should know, better than any outsider; and we *do* know that the sacrament of Penance is one of God's greatest gifts to us—a gift which we would not be without and for which we shall be everlastingly grateful.

First of all, by requiring explicit confession of our sins, God protects us against the universal human weakness of self-justification. It is all very well to say, "In the secrecy of my heart, I will tell God that I am sorry, and God will forgive me." If that were all that were required of us, it would be so easy for us to fool ourselves into thinking we were sorry, while we went blithely forth to sin again and again. But when we have to drag our evil out into the light; when we have to get on our knees and put our wrongdoing into words—then we have to face the facts. It no longer is easy to deceive ourselves. God, who made us and who knows our deviousness, has blessedly preserved us from the danger of our own self-deceit.

Another noteworthy blessing of confession as a part of the sacrament of Penance is that it provides us with skilled advice in our spiritual problems. Just as we obtain from the physician expert help in the cure and the prevention of our physical maladies, so too we find in confession one who is learned in the ills of the soul, one who can prescribe the remedies and safeguards that will contribute to spiritual health and growth in holiness.

Not to be despised, either, is the psychological help which we obtain from confession: the sense of release from a burden which follows upon the avowal of our sins, the interior peace and comfort which accompany the *certainty* of sins forgiven, the relief from guilt-feelings which might disturb and discourage us. It is not surprising that a prominent psychiatrist (himself a non-Catholic) has said, "If all churches had confession, there would be fewer patients in our mental hospitals." Nor is it surprising that we who know its graces say, "Thank you, God, for confession."

After Baptism there is only one thing which can separate us from God. That is mortal sin: a knowing, deliberate refusal to do God's will in a serious matter. The primary purpose of the sacrament of Penance is to restore to the soul of a sinner the God-life (sanctifying grace) which he has lost. Consequently, the sins which we *must* tell in confession are the mortal sins committed after Baptism which we have not previously confessed.

Since venial sin does not extinguish in us the life of grace, we are not obliged to mention our venial sins in confession. It is profitable to mention them, even though we are under no obligation. Nothing can give us greater certainty that our venial sins have been forgiven than submitting them to the absolution of the priest. Moreover, from the sacrament of Penance we shall receive special graces enabling us to avoid those particular venial sins in the future. The fact remains, however, that venial sins can be forgiven outside confession by an act of genuine sorrow (at least, if it is perfect contrition) and a purpose of amendment.

Neither are we obliged to tell *doubtful* mortal sins in confession. Again, it is by far the wisest thing to avow such sins, for the sake of our own peace of mind and for the sake of the grace which we will receive against a relapse. Nevertheless, the telling of doubtful mortal sins is not essential to a good confession. If we do confess such sins, we should mention our doubt to the priest, and confess them "as God sees me guilty." An example of a doubtful mortal sin would be an outburst of vengeful anger, with uncertainty afterwards as to whether our anger was fully deliberate. Another example would be sinful thoughts, with a question afterwards as to whether we had given consent to them or resisted them quickly enough.

It needs no pointing out, surely, that we must be careful not to deceive ourselves in such matters. We must not try to convince ourselves that a sin was doubtfully mortal when every reasonable judgment indicates otherwise.

In confessing our mortal sins, we are obliged to tell the number of times we have committed each sin. For the practical Catholic who receives the sacrament of Penance frequently, this poses no problem. A person who has not been to confession for a long time, however, might encounter some difficulty in enumerating his sins. He needs only to remember that God does not ask the impossible of anyone. When it is not possible to recall the exact number of times a certain sin may have been committed, it is enough to make an honest estimate. A practical procedure in such a case is to estimate the number of sins that have been committed, on the average, every week or every month.

In telling our mortal sins in confession, it is required that we indicate the *kind* of sins which we may have committed. It is not enough to say, "I broke the second commandment." We must mention (supposing the sin was mortal) whether we sinned by profanity, cursing, false swearing, or blasphemy. We may not simply state, "I sinned against justice." We must distinguish whether we stole, or defrauded, damaged property or damaged a reputation. Most prayer books provide a list of possible sins which will help the penitent to classify his own offenses.

It is not at all desirable to clutter up our confession with the unessential details of our sins. Just why we had hatred for our brother-in-law and what came of it, or just how we worked the sharp business deal that we now acknowledge to have been fraud, are matters not ordinarily pertinent to confession. However, any circumstance which changes the nature of a sin must be mentioned. That means any circumstance which really would add a new kind of wickedness. To say that I stole a gold-plated cup is not sufficient if the gold-plated cup happens to be a chalice from the church; in this case the sin of sacrilege has been added to the sin of theft. It is not enough to say that I took a false oath if my false oath caused someone a grave loss of property or character; in this case injustice has been added to perjury.

Not only the actual telling of our sins but also the *manner* of their telling is important for the making of a good confession. Since the whole spirit of the sacrament of Penance is one of repentance for acknowledged error, it is plain that we should bring to our confession a profound humility of heart. Any such attitude as, "Well, after all, I'm not so bad," or "I guess I'm no worse than anybody else," or "Everybody commits these sins; they can't be so terrible," would of course be fatal to the making of a good confession.

Sincerity is another quality demanded by the sacrament of Penance. This means nothing more (nor less) than the telling of our sins quite honestly and frankly, without any attempt to evade or conceal. Our confession would be lacking in sincerity if we attempted to phrase our confession in vague or ambiguous terms in the hope that the priest might not understand what we were talking about; if we looked about for a hard-of-hearing priest who might be expected to miss our hurriedly mumbled words; if we interlarded our confession with alibis and excuses in an attempt to save our self-esteem.

Defects such as these are mentioned not because they are a common practice but because they aid in an understanding of the essence of a good confession. The vast majority of Catholics, receiving the sacrament of Penance frequently and with grateful appreciation, give constant exemplification of what it means to make a good confession. Their humility and sincerity are a never-ending source of edification to the priests who shrive them.

CHAPTER XXXI

Confession

Telling Our Sins

Our Lord Jesus Christ intended the sacrament of Penance to be also an *act* of penance, an act of humility; but He did not intend it to be an intolerable burden for the members of His flock. It is true that all post-Baptismal mortal sins must be confessed explicitly. This principle remains valid even when, because of urgent necessity, explicit confession must be temporarily postponed. An extremely sick person who is too weak to detail his sins could receive the sacrament of Penance by merely signifying that he has sinned and that he is sorry for his sins. Large numbers of soldiers might be absolved from their sins before going into action, after signifying their guilt in general terms, together with their sorrow. But in these and similar emergencies the sinner still is obligated to tell his mortal sins in detail the next time he goes to confession.

The same principle applies when a person, in making his confession, forgets to mention one or more of his mortal sins. If he should later on remember the omitted sin, he must mention it in his next confession. However, it is not necessary for him to hurry back to confession immediately, and he may receive Holy Communion in the meantime. Because of his all-inclusive sorrow, the penitent's forgotten sin already has been indirectly forgiven; there remains only the obligation to mention it, if remembered, in his next confession, whenever that may be, so that it may be directly forgiven.

It would be very foolish for anyone to be unduly anxious in preparing for confession, or nervous for fear that he may accidentally forget a sin. It would be even more foolish for anyone to let himself be beset by vague anxieties about past confessions. God is a just judge, but He is not a tyrannical judge. All that He asks is that we do our reasonable best to make a good confession. He will not hold us accountable for such human frailties as a bad memory.

There is only one thing that will vitiate our confession and make it a "bad" or sacrilegious confession. That is to omit telling, knowingly and deliberately, a sin which we are certain is mortal and ought to be confessed. To do that is to refuse to fulfill one of the conditions upon which God has made His forgiveness contingent. If we do not "come clean" with God, we cannot go clean from His tribunal of forgiveness.

The tragedy of a bad confession is that it sets off a whole chain-reaction of sin. Unless and until the invalid confession is rectified, each subsequent confession and each Holy Communion is a new sacrilege, as sin piles upon sin. As time goes by, the conscience may become dormant, but it never really can be at peace.

Fortunately a bad confession can be remedied very easily, once the hapless penitent decides to make amends. He has only to say to his confessor, "Father, I once made a bad confession and now I'd like to straighten things out." The confessor will take over from there and by sympathetic questioning will help the sinner to cast off his burden of guilt.

That phrase "sympathetic questioning" is used advisedly. Our reluctance to confess an ignoble deed would be much less if we would remind ourselves that it *is* a sympathetic listener to whom we speak. The priest is not sitting self-righteously on the other side of the screen, ready to cluck his tongue at our misdeeds. He is human, too. He has to go to confession, too. Instead of despising us for what we have to tell, he admires the humility with which we have overcome our embarrassment. The bigger our sin, the happier is the priest in the knowledge of our repentance. If the priest should happen to know who the penitent is, his regard for the person will not decrease; on the contrary, his regard will be the greater because of the trust and confidence which the penitent has shown in his confessor.

Besides these considerations there is the knowledge (comforting to all of us) that the sins which we tell in confession are covered by the strictest bond of secrecy which exists upon earth. This bond of secrecy—"the seal of confession" —forbids the priest to reveal *for any reason whatsoever* what has been told to him in confession. The penitent himself is the only one who can release the priest from that bond. Not even to the penitent himself, outside of confession, can the priest speak of things which the penitent has told in confession; that is, not unless the penitent so wishes and permits. Much less, then, would a priest refer to, or even hint at, confessional matters to a penitent's employer, or parents, or other parties.

Rather than violate the seal of confession a priest must be prepared to suffer death or, what is worse, false accusations and disgrace. Many priests have done so in the course of the Church's history. A priest cannot reveal what has been told him in sacramental confession even to save the whole world from destruction. If a priest were ever guilty of having deliberately broken the seal of confession, he would be penalized with the strictest type of excommunication that the Church can inflict.

Incidentally, this is an obligation which binds the laity,

too. If a person should happen to overhear something told in confession, he must never under any circumstances reveal what he has heard. To do so would be a grave sin. Not even to the person whom he has overheard should he mention the fact. The penitent himself is not bound by the seal of confession; nevertheless he should not, without necessity, discuss with others what he has told in confession.

It may be assumed that bad confessions are a fairly rare occurrence, whether the sacrilegious confession be due to concealment of mortal sin or to lack of adequate sorrow. A person is not likely to waste time performing an action which he knows to be worse than useless.

It also may be assumed that most persons who receive the sacrament of Penance regularly and frequently have no mortal sins to tell. The special sacramental grace of Penance strengthens us against temptation and builds up a resistance to sin, much as vitamins build up a resistance to bodily infection. It would be a great mistake for us to neglect frequent confession on the plea that we have no mortal sins to tell. It is precisely by frequent confession that we receive the graces which will most surely enable us to avoid mortal sin. Moreover, there is the increase in sanctifying grace which the sacrament of Penance imparts to the soul already free from mortal sin—a deepening of spiritual life which must not be despised.

However, *some* actual sin must be confessed or the sacrament cannot be received, since Penance was instituted for the forgiveness of post-Baptismal sins. A person who had committed absolutely no sin at all after Baptism would be incapable of receiving the sacrament of Penance. There would be nothing for the sacrament "to work on." However, it is commonly held that the Blessed Virgin Mary was the only purely human adult who never committed even the slightest venial sin. (Of course, Jesus Christ, even as man, was sinless.)

If we have no mortal sin to confess, then the telling of

one or more of our venial sins (for which we truly are sorry) will enable us to receive the sacrament of Penance with its graces. If we cannot remember even one deliberate venial sin since our last confession, then we can re-confess some sin of our past life. It may be a sin that was confessed and forgiven long ago; but here and now we recall the sin and renew our heartfelt sorrow for it. Our past sin plus our present sorrow qualifies us for absolution and the graces of the sacrament.

In such an event, our confession would run something like this: "Bless me, Father, for I have sinned. It is a week since my last confession. I do not remember having committed any sins since then, but I am sorry for any sins which I may have forgotten and for all the sins of my past life, especially for sins of anger" (for example).

That, in fact, is the proper formula to follow in any confession: to begin by asking the priest's blessing, then to mention the time of our last confession, and to end with an inclusion of the sins of our past life—particularly one or the other past sin for which we are especially sorry. Thus, if it should happen that the current sins which we mention aren't really sins at all but only imperfections, the inclusion of a past sin will make it still possible for the priest to give absolution and for us to receive the graces of the sacrament. If a penitent were to confess, "Father, I forgot my morning prayers twice, missed Mass once on Sunday through sickness, and talked in church three times," and said no more, the priest could not give absolution, at least not without some questioning. There is no evidence of real sin in such a confession. It is not a sin to forget one's morning prayers; indeed, we cannot commit any sin through forgetfulness if the forgetfulness is genuine. One requirement for a sin is that we do the wrong act knowingly and willingly. Neither is it a sin to miss Mass on Sunday because of illness, or for any other serious reason. Neither is it necessarily a sin to talk in church if no deliberate lack of reverence is involved.

In practice, there is no need even to mention such non-sins in confession, no need to "pad" our list to make it seem longer than it is. If we have the habit of ending our confession always with the mention of a sin of our past life, there is material enough for our sorrow to work on. The confessor will not feel that we are wasting his time just because we can't remember any sin since our last confession. However, in such a case we should be sure that we haven't skimped on our examination of conscience. We should never enter the confessional without first spending a reasonable time in examining our conscience and in arousing ourselves to genuine sorrow for our sins.

It might be helpful to list briefly here a few other reminders pertaining to confession:

1. When making your confession, speak to the priest clearly and distinctly, *but in a whisper*. The seal of confession cannot help you much if you speak so loudly as to share your sins with all who are in church. Hard-of-hearing persons should look for a confessional equipped with a hearing aid (nowadays most churches have them) or ask to have their confession heard in the sacristy. Persons with a serious impediment of speech may write out their sins beforehand and hand the paper to the priest through the confessional door. The priest will destroy the paper after reading it.

2. Do not tell anyone else's sins (your husband's or wife's, for example) and especially do not mention names in confession.

3. Except when necessary to repair a bad confession, do not undertake to make a general confession (covering all or a major part of your life) without first consulting your confessor. A general confession rarely is advisable except perhaps at some major milestone such as marriage or religious profession or ordination.

4. Listen attentively while the priest tells you your penance, and also to any advice he may have to offer. If you

cannot hear him well, tell him so. And if you have any questions to ask or counsel to seek, don't hesitate to speak up.

5. Put your heart into your act of contrition but do not say it silently; the priest should hear you say that you are sorry.

6. Finally, spend a little time after confession in thanking God for the graces that have just come to you—and in performing the penance which the priest has assigned.

Sin and Punishment

Sin and punishment go together. We might say of sin that punishment is the "built-in" stabilizer by which the demands of divine justice are met. God is infinitely merciful; He is quick to forgive the repentant sinner. But at the same time God is infinitely just; He cannot be indifferent to moral evil. He cannot "not care" what man does with his freedom. If there were no penalty attached to sin, then good and evil would stand side by side as seeming equals; justice would be an empty word.

God is a *just* God, but He is not a *vengeful* God. In human affairs the administration of punishment often is motivated more by vindictiveness than by charity. Punishment frequently is imposed more to salve the wounded ego of the injured party than to save the soul of the offender. With God the opposite is true. While His justice demands that sin be "evened up" by adequate reparation, God does not seek to "get even" with the sinner. Always His end in view is the salvation of the wrong-doer: before the fact, in making the price of sin too high; after the fact, in making the consequences painful.

In practice it hardly seems accurate even to say that God punishes the individual sinner. Rather, the sinner punishes himself. The sinner freely chooses the penalty along with his sin. The perpetrator of a mortal sin freely chooses to live eternally separated from God (hell) for the sake of doing his own will at the present moment. The doer of a venially sinful act accepts purgatory in advance for the sake of his present petty satisfaction. The choice is something like that of the deliberate drinker who accepts tomorrow's hangover for the sake of tonight's overindulgence.

There are two kinds of punishment attached to mortal sin. There is, first of all, the *eternal* punishment which is its necessary accompaniment—the eternal loss of God. This eternal punishment is forgiven when the *guilt* of the sin is forgiven, whether in the sacrament of Baptism or that of Penance.

Besides this eternal punishment there also is a *temporal* (meaning "for a time") punishment which may remain even after the mortal sin itself is forgiven. Temporal punishment likewise is incurred by venial sin. Temporal punishment is the reparation which we must make to God (through the merits of Christ) for having violated His justice even after the sin itself is forgiven; it is the satisfaction we make to God for whatever inadequacy there may be in the intensity of our sorrow for our sins. We pay this debt of temporal punishment through the sufferings of purgatory unless we discharge the debt during life (as we so easily can) by appropriate works of penance.

In their effect upon the temporal punishment due to sin, there is an important difference between the sacraments of Baptism and Penance. Baptism is a spiritual rebirth, a "new start in life." When received by an adult, it not only forgives mortal sin along with original sin and the eternal punishment due to sin; it also wipes out the temporal punishment due to sin. A person who would die immediately after Baptism would enter heaven immediately. This would be true even though his sorrow for sin at the time of his Baptism were an imperfect sorrow.

A person who happens to die just after going to confession, however, would not necessarily be ready for heaven immediately. While the eternal punishment due to sin is completely remitted in the sacrament of Penance, the amount of temporal punishment taken away will depend on the perfection of the penitent's sorrow. The more fervent is his sorrow the less will be the debt of temporal punishment still remaining; the less satisfaction he will have to make, here or in purgatory.

A story (not real-life, of course) will illustrate this point. It is told that a certain man went to confession after many years of irreligious living. The priest prescribed, as a penance, that the man should pray the rosary every day for a month. "But Father!" the man objected, "I've been so ungrateful to the good God all these years; surely I ought to do much more than that!" "If you are that sorry," answered the priest, "perhaps the rosary daily for a week would be enough." Then the penitent broke down and began to weep. "I am so ashamed," he sobbed. "God has loved me so and borne with me so long in my sinfulness; there's nothing I wouldn't do for Him now." "If you are *that* sorry," replied the priest, "then it will be enough to say for your penance five Our Fathers and five Hail Marys, once."

The story emphasizes the importance of our own interior dispositions as we receive the sacrament of Penance. The deeper our sorrow and the more it is actuated by selfless love of God, the fewer will be the "remains of sin" surviving; the less will be the debt of temporal punishment calling for penitential satisfaction from ourselves.

The more intense our sorrow when we go to confession, the less do we owe God afterwards in the way of temporal punishment. Neither we nor the confessor, however, can judge accurately as to just how intense our sorrow is. It is only God who can look into the human heart and know, at any particular moment, just what our debt to Him is. Consequently, the priest always will impose upon us a penance to be performed after confession: certain prayers to be said or good deeds performed. For our confession to be a good confession, we must accept the penance which the priest prescribes and must have the intention of carrying it out at the time the priest assigns it to us.

The size of the penance will depend upon the gravity of the sins confessed; the greater the number and the seriousness of the sins, the more arduous we may expect the penance to be. Yet the confessor does not wish to prescribe a penance beyond the ability of the penitent to perform. If ever we should be given a penance in confession which we feel is impossible for us to fulfill, we should mention the difficulty, whatever it is, to the confessor. He will adjust the penance accordingly.

Once the penance has been established and given us, we are bound in conscience to discharge it, and to discharge it in the way it was given. For example, if we are told to recite the Acts of Faith, Hope, and Charity each day for a week, it would not be right for us to "get it over with" by saying each one seven times in one day.

To *deliberately* neglect to perform our penance would be a mortal sin if it were a grave penance imposed for grave sins. Deliberate neglect of a lesser penance would be a venial sin. Obviously, it is not a sin to forget one's penance, since one cannot sin through forgetfulness. If we should forget to say or do our penance, it simply would mean that the temporal punishment which the penance was intended to absolve still remains as a debit against us. Because of this very danger of forgetting, we should make it a practice to perform our penance immediately after confession, unless the confessor has assigned some special time for the discharge of the penance.

It should be remembered that the penance prescribed for us in confession has a special efficacy in paying our debt of temporal punishment because it is a part of the sacrament of Penance. We should, of course, perform other penitential works on our own. All our meritorious works can be offered as satisfaction for our sins, and should be so offered.

This does not mean only the prayers we say, the Masses we offer, the acts of religion or charity that we perform. It means every single action of our Christ-centered day; that is, every action (barring bad actions, of course) that is done in the state of grace and from a sense of duty to God. These are the actions that gain merit for us in heaven and at the same time can be offered in satisfaction for sin.

However, prayer for prayer and deed for deed, nothing else will satisfy for the temporal punishment due our sins so certainly and so richly as the sacramental penances given in confession. These official penances have a sacramental efficacy, an atoning power that no privately assumed penance can match.

It should perhaps be pointed out that *none* of our penitential works would have any value in the eyes of God if it were not that Jesus Christ already has made atonement for our sins. The atonement made by Jesus on the Cross is infinite—more than enough to pay the entire spiritual debt of mankind. But God by positive design wills that we should share with Christ in His work of satisfying for sin. God makes the application of Christ's merits to our own debt of temporal punishment dependent upon our willingness to do penance ourselves. The real value of our personal penances is insignificant in God's sight; but their value swells to a tremendous worth because of their union with the merits of Jesus.

That is why, also, our prayers and works and sufferings can be offered in satisfaction for the sins of others as well as for our own. God wills that we should share in the work of redemption. It is part of our privilege as members of Christ's Mystical Body to be able, with Christ, to satisfy for the temporal punishment due to the sins of others. Mindful of the possibilities, we shall be watchful for the opportunities. In every illness (even today's little headache), in every disappointment and every sorrow, we shall see the raw material from which satisfaction may be fashioned and souls saved. And we shall never suffer from the temptation (rare, surely!) to feel that the priest gave us "too big a penance." If we don't need it ourselves, somewhere there is a soul who does.

CHAPTER XXXII

Temporal Punishment and Indulgences

Indulgences

In discharging the debt of temporal punishment still remaining after our sins have been forgiven, indulgences offer a very easy and fruitful form of payment. We can gain indulgences every day. We know that they "shorten our purgatory." Perhaps we even can quote the catechism definition of an indulgence: "The remission granted by the Church of the temporal punishment due to sin already forgiven."

But did we ever try to explain the doctrine of indulgences to a non-Catholic friend? If we did, we know that it isn't an easy task. First of all, there is a lot of dead wood to be cleared away. The word "indulgence" itself has come in modern times to have a slightly unfavorable connotation. An indulgent grandmother is one who lets the youngsters do anything they wish. Self-indulgence means surrender to one's impulses, the ignoring of nobler motives. In short, the word "indulgence" as used today seems to imply a moral softness, a lowering of ideals.

Thus we usually have to begin our explanation of indulgences by explaining what an indulgence *is not*. We point out that an indulgence is *not* a permission to commit sin; it is not even a forgiveness of past sins. In fact, an indulgence has nothing whatever to do with sins as such. An indulgence is concerned only with the debt of temporal punishment which we owe to God *after* our sins have been forgiven in the sacrament of Penance (or by an act of perfect contrition). We emphasize to our inquirer that a person cannot even gain an indulgence unless he already is in the state of sanctifying grace.

After clearing away the misunderstandings, we next undertake to give a positive explanation of the nature of an indulgence. A first step will be to show that the Church has the *right* to remit the temporal punsihment which we owe God for our forgiven sins. We do so by recalling Christ's words to St. Peter, and St. Peter's successors, the Popes: "Whatever thou shalt bind on earth shall be bound in heaven, and whatever thou shalt loose on earth shall be loosed in heaven" (Matt. 16:19); and the very same words, spoken on a later occasion to all the apostles—and to their successors, the bishops of the Catholic Church (Matt. 18:18). Jesus spoke these words without any qualifications or exceptions. In other words, He gives to His Church complete and unrestricted power to remove from men's souls any impediment at all which might hold them back from heaven. This includes not only the impediment of sin, which is removed in the sacrament of Penance, but also the impediment of temporal punishment, which is removed by means of indulgences.

The Church has exercised this power of remitting temporal punishment from the very earliest days of Christian history. In those early times, when Christians had a much greater horror of sin than we have nowadays, repentant sinners had to perform great penances before they would be readmitted to fellowship with the Christian community.

A sinner might have to do public penance for forty days, or three years, or seven years, or even for the rest of his life—depending on the seriousness of his sins and the amount of scandal given. Examples of such penances were the wearing of rough sackcloth with ashes sprinkled on the head, fasting, scourging one's body, retiring to a monastery, kneeling at the church door to beg prayers from those entering, or wandering as a beggar through the countryside.

This was the age of martyrdom, when thousands upon thousands of Christians were arrested and put to death for their faith. It became the custom for penitents to seek the intercession of the martyrs—that is, Christians who were in prison awaiting execution. An imprisoned martyr would give to a penitent a written request for mercy, to be presented to the bishop. These pleading letters from the martyrs were called "letters of peace." When a penitent presented such a letter to the bishop, the sinner would be absolved from the arduous public penance which had been imposed upon him by his confessor. Not only was the sinner absolved from the external penance; he also was absolved internally from his debt to God—from the temporal punishment for which the penance was intended to make satisfaction. This was effected through the transfer to the repentant sinner of the satisfactory value of the martyr's sufferings.

That is how the Church's practice of granting indulgences began. That also is the origin of the system of "measuring" indulgences which the Church uses to the present day. An indulgence of three hundred days, for example, does *not* mean three hundred days less in purgatory. It means that this prayer for which a three hundred days' indulgence is granted will remit as much of the temporal punishment due to sin as would be remitted if the person did three hundred days of public penance according to the discipline of the ancient Church. Just how much that may be only God can know.

In God's plan of salvation not a word of prayer, not a tear of sorrow or a twinge of pain offered to Him is wasted. Every bit of satisfactory merit which a person may gain and which is not needed to satisfy for his own sins is added to the total fund of satisfactions upon which the Church may draw for the needs of her children. This great reservoir of accumulated satisfactions is available to us for paying the debt of temporal punishment which is due for our sins. It is called the spiritual treasury of the Church. The Church is the custodian of this treasure and the dispenser of its contents.

As the foundation of her spiritual treasury, the Church has the infinite satisfactory merits of Jesus Christ Himself. Because Jesus is God, everything that He did and suffered was of infinite value. By His life and death He established an inexhaustible store of satisfactory merit, sufficient for the needs of mankind until the end of time. To this treasury have been added the satisfactions of our Blessed Mother (which she did not need herself), the satisfactions of the saints which were beyond their own needs, and the extra satisfactions of all members of Christ's Mystical Body.

It is upon this spiritual treasury of satisfactory merit that the Church draws when she grants indulgences. This is how an indulgence works: to the Act of Faith which we learned as children (and to the Acts of Hope, of Love, and of Contrition, as well) the Church has attached an indulgence of three years. In effect the Church says to us, "If you are free from mortal sin and if you recite the Act of Faith thoughtfully and devoutly, then I your Mother the Church will offer to God from my spiritual treasury whatever satisfactions are necessary to atone for as much of the temporal punishment due to your sins, as you yourself would atone for if you did public penance for three years."

Each prayer and good work to which an indulgence is attached is like a check which the Church places in our hands. With this check we can draw upon the spiritual bank account of the super-abundant satisfactions of Christ and the saints and with these satisfactory merits make payment on our own debt to God.

Indulgences which are keyed to the ancient practice of public penance are called *partial* indulgences. These indulgences are measured in terms of days or years: one hundred days, three hundred days, three years, seven years, ten years. However, sometimes the Church gives us a blank check on her spiritual treasury. She does so when she grants what we call a *plenary* indulgence. In this instance the Church says to us, "Fulfill these conditions which I have laid down, and I your Mother the Church will dip into my spiritual treasury and will offer to God whatever satisfactions are needed to wipe out completely your own debt of temporal punishment." If we were to gain fully a plenary indulgence and were to die immediately afterwards, we would be with God in heaven immediately, without any need for atonement in purgatory.

In practice, we seldom can be certain that we have gained a plenary indulgence in its fullness. To gain a plenary indulgence completely, it is necessary that we be completely detached from all deliberate sin. This means that we have true sorrow for all venial sins as well as mortal, and that we be resolved to avoid all deliberate venial sins, as well as mortal, in the future. It is not often that we can be confident that our renunciation of sin is so all-embracing. However, in granting a plenary indulgence, the Church does so with the understanding that if we are not properly disposed to receive the indulgence fully, then we shall gain the indulgence at least partially according to the perfection of our dispositions.

Besides this special requirement for the full gaining of a plenary indulgence, there are other conditions which we have to fulfill in order to gain an indulgence. It already has been pointed out that the first essential is that we be in the state of sanctifying grace at the time we gain the indulgence.

However, a person sometimes can *begin* to gain an indulgence even with mortal sin upon his soul, but he must be in the state of grace at the time the indulgenced work is finished. For example, if an indulgence is granted for a visit to a church, plus confession and Holy Communion, a person might be in the state of mortal sin when he makes the prescribed visit to a church but still would gain the indulgence when he received worthily the sacraments of Penance and the Eucharist.

It also is necessary to have at least a general intention of wanting to gain the indulgence, since the Church does not force indulgences upon us. A *general* intention is sufficient. Thus, if on each Sunday morning I make the intention, "Gracious God, I want to gain all the indulgences that I can during this week, and always," then whatever indulgences are attached to the prayers or good works I say or do during the week will be gained by me, even though I don't happen to think about the indulgence at the time—even if I don't happen to know about the indulgence. Even better than once a week is the practice of making this intention every morning as a part of our morning prayers.

It scarcely needs emphasizing that another condition for gaining an indulgence is that we carry out exactly, according to the time, place and manner prescribed, all the requirements which the Church lays down for the gaining of any particular indulgence.

Plenary Indulgences

When we consider the great number of plenary indulgences which the Church makes available to us, it is evident that it will be doubly our own fault if we have to suffer in purgatory before our entrance into heaven. Plenary indulgences are so numerous and the works prescribed for them are so easy that only the rankest kind of spiritual sloth could lead a person to neglect them or ignore them.

All prayers and devotions to which indulgences have been attached (partial as well as plenary) are published in an official book of the Church called *The Raccolta*.[1] *The Raccolta* is a translation into English of the official Manual of Indulgences of the Church, the original being in Latin. *The Raccolta* can be purchased at any Catholic book store. As a companion volume to the Daily Missal, *The Raccolta* is the finest prayer book that we could own. It contains prayers and devotions for every need and occasion, and every prayer and devotion has been approved and indulgenced by the Church.

Most plenary indulgences can be gained only once during the day. In this they differ from partial indulgences, which can be gained as often in the day as one performs the prescribed work unless the directions specifically state otherwise. Thus, if I devoutly say, "My Jesus, mercy!" a hundred times during the day, then a hundred times I gain an indulgence of three hundred days. On the contrary, a plenary indulgence can be gained only once during the day unless the directions specifically state otherwise. When a plenary indulgence may be gained many times during the same day, it is called a "toties quoties" indulgence. Freely translated, this Latin phrase means, "as often as you do it." An example is the plenary indulgence which may be gained for the souls in purgatory on All Souls' Day. For every visit made to a church on that day, with the Our Father, Hail Mary, and Glory be to the Father recited six times for the intentions of the Pope at each visit, we may gain a plenary indulgence for the suffering souls.

One further requirement for gaining this "toties quoties" indulgence is that we receive the sacraments of Penance and Holy Eucharist. This, indeed, is a requirement for the gaining of almost all plenary indulgences. In *The Raccolta* and in other prayer books we notice that the directions for gain-

[1] Published by Benziger Brothers, New York, N. Y. Current price, $3.85.

ing the plenary indulgence for a certain prayer or devotion almost always will read, "under the usual conditions." The "usual conditions" required for the gaining of most plenary indulgences are four: (1) Visit a church or public chapel. Some classes of persons, such as Sisters or boarding-school students, may make their visit to a semi-public chapel. (2) Pray for the intentions of the Holy Father. While there is no top limit on the number or kind of prayers we may offer for the Holy Father, a minimum of one Our Father, Hail Mary, and Glory be to the Father has been established unless the directions call for more, as on All Soul's Day. (3) Confession. The confession required for the gaining of a plenary indulgence may be made at any time within eight days before the day on which we perform the indulgenced work, on the day itself, or within eight days after. (4) Communion. Our Holy Communion for the gaining of a plenary indulgence may be received at any time from the day before we perform the indulgenced work until the eighth day after. Obviously, any person who is in the habit of going to confession at least every two weeks and is receiving Holy Communion at least once a week already is fulfilling the confession-Communion requirements for the gaining of plenary indulgences calling for the reception of these sacraments.

It follows that anyone interested in paying off his own debt of temporal punishment and in helping the suffering souls in purgatory will make bi-weekly confession and weekly Holy Communion his own minimal practice. If we make it our further policy always to pray for the Pope each time we assist at Mass or otherwise visit the church, then we already have done most of the work necessary for the gaining of whatever plenary indulgences may become available to us from day to day.

In fact the Canon Law of the Church explicitly states that anyone who regularly receives the sacrament of Penance every two weeks or receives Holy Communion "almost daily" (interpreted as meaning at least five times a week) is automatically eligible for all plenary indulgences which call for "the usual conditions," as long as the other requirements are fulfilled. However, for a jubilee indulgence a special confession is necessary.

It should be observed that we cannot apply the indulgences which we gain to other living persons. In this matter each of us has to work off his own debt. However, we *can* apply most indulgences to the souls in purgatory. In fact, *all* indulgences granted by the Holy Father, unless the contrary is expressly stated, may be applied to the suffering souls.

Since the Church has direct authority over her living members, the indulgences which we gain for ourselves are absolutely certain in their effects provided we have fulfilled all the necessary conditions. Such is the teaching of a considerable number of reliable theologians. The Church, however, does not have direct authority over the souls in purgatory. Indulgences offered for them are offered by way of suffrage—that is, as a petition to God begging Him to apply the indulgence to the particular soul or souls for whom it is gained and offered. Whether or not the indulgence is applied to that soul or souls rests with the mercy of God. We can hope that the specified soul will receive the indulgence which we have gained for him; but, since we cannot know for sure, the Church allows us to offer more than one plenary indulgence for the same departed soul.

We may safely assume, most of us, that we constantly are getting ourselves into debt with God. We do not lead the sinless lives of angels. Even though our sins may not be big sins, there still is penance to be done for them—here or hereafter. It will be nobody's fault but our own if we carry our debt into the hereafter. Below are listed some of the easily gained indulgences with which we can, day by day, keep our account paid up.

The indulgences attached to the recitation of the Rosary are as numerous as we might expect in a devotion centered on her who is "the refuge of sinners." For the recitation of five decades of the Rosary the Church grants an indulgence of five years, even if the beads have not been blessed. If this recitation is in company with others, it is an indulgence of ten years that is gained. If this recitation (with others) is performed three times during any one week of the month, a plenary indulgence may be gained, under the usual conditions, on the last Sunday of the month.

If the Rosary beads have been blessed by a priest delegated to attach the *Crozier*, the *Dominican*, and the *Apostolic* indulgences, then our Rosary has become a real treasure-house of indulgences. The *Crozier* blessing grants us an indulgence of five hundred days for each Our Father and Hail Mary that we say on the beads, even though we may not say a complete Rosary. The *Dominican* blessing enables us to gain another indulgence of one hundred days on each bead, plus various indulgences if we pray the Rosary regularly over a period of time or in company with others. The *Apostolic* indulgences attached to a Rosary by the proper blessing include a whole list of indulgences which have been granted by the Pope for the recitation of the Rosary—including a plenary indulgence for one who is dying and has the Rosary on his person. Finally, if we say the Rosary in the presence of the Blessed Sacrament (whether exposed on the altar or reserved in the tabernacle), we are granted a plenary indulgence each day that we do so, provided that we receive the sacraments of Penance and Holy Communion, as explained previously.

The Way of the Cross is another easy bypass around purgatory. Each time we make the Way of the Cross (even several times in the same day) we gain a plenary indulgence. If we also receive Holy Communion that same day, we gain a second plenary indulgence for that same Way of the Cross. If for some reason we are unable to complete the Way of the Cross, then we gain an indulgence of ten years for each station we have visited. These indulgences are gained whether we make the Way of the Cross privately or with others.

It is easily understandable why the Church has so richly endowed the Way of the Cross with indulgences. No one can devoutly follow Our Lord on His agonized journey without being moved to deeper sorrow for his own sins, which made such suffering necessary, and to renewed resolutions of improvement.

To gain the indulgences of the Way of the Cross, it is not necessary to say any vocal prayers. What is required is that we move from station to station and, as we do so, *meditate* on Christ's sufferings. This means to *think about* the significance of what Jesus is undergoing for us and to draw from His sufferings some lesson for ourselves. For example, as we think about Jesus stripped of His last and only possession—His clothes—we may become a little ashamed of our own acquisitiveness and of our blindness to the needs of others.

We may spend a few minutes or we may spend half an hour in "making the stations." As long as we make the rounds and meditate on our Lord's Passion, we gain the indulgences. When the Way of the Cross is made publicly by a group (as in the parish during Lent), it is sufficient that one member of the group go from station to station, but each must do his own meditating. In making the Way of the Cross, we do not need a book. If we have a sluggish imagination, a book may help; but our own thoughts will be best.

The most easily gained plenary indulgences of all are those which the Church has attached to two prayers—under the usual conditions of confession, Holy Communion, visit to a church, and prayer for the Pope. One of these prayers is the beautiful Prayer before a Crucifix, "Look down upon me, good and gentle Jesus . . .," which is familiar to most of us and which must be recited before an image of our crucified Savior. The other prayer, for some reason, is less familiar to Catholics, although just as meaningful. It is the Prayer to Christ the King, and is given here in full for those who might wish to copy it and place it in their prayer books:

"O Christ Jesus, I acknowledge Thee King of the Universe. All that has been made has been created for Thee. Make full use of Thy rights over me. I renew the promises I made in Baptism, when I renounced Satan and all his works and pomps; and I promise to live a good Christian life; and especially I promise to undertake to help, to the extent of my means, to secure the triumph of God and of Thy Church. Divine Heart of Jesus, I offer Thee my efforts to obtain that all hearts may acknowledge Thy sacred royalty, and that so the kingdom of Thy peace may be established throughout the entire universe. Amen." (*Plenary indulgence once daily, under the usual conditions.*)

CHAPTER XXXIII

Extreme Unction

Sacrament of the Sick

In His merciful efforts to bring us safely to Himself in heaven, God seems to have gone to the very limit. Jesus has given us the sacrament of Baptism, in which original sin and all pre-Baptismal sins are cleansed from the soul. Allowing for mankind's spiritual weakness, Jesus also gave us the sacrament of Penance, by which post-Baptismal sins could be forgiven. As though He were impatient lest a soul be delayed a single instant from its entry into heaven, Jesus gave to His Church the power to remit the temporal punishment due to sin, a power which the Church exercises in the granting of indulgences. Finally, as though to make doubly sure that no one, except through his own deliberate fault, would lose heaven or even spend time in purgatory, Jesus instituted the sacrament of Extreme Unction.

The catechism defines Extreme Unction as "the sacrament which, through the anointing with blessed oil by the priest, and through his prayer, gives health and strength to the soul, and sometimes to the body, when we are in danger of death from sickness, accident, or old age."

The name "Extreme Unction" became attached to this sacrament only towards the end of the twelfth century. In earlier times it was known simply as the "Anointing of the Sick" or as "Prayer-Oil." The present name of the sacrament (Extreme Unction means "Last Anointing") does not signify that this is positively the last anointing that a person may receive and that he should be expected to die after having received it. This is a mistaken notion that has led some people to have a superstitious fear of Extreme Unction—the fear that if they receive Extreme Unction, then surely they are going to die. The term "last anointing" has a purely liturgical significance. This anointing is ordinarily the last in sequence of the four anointings which a Christian may receive: Baptism, Confirmation, Holy Orders—with Extreme Unction in the fourth place. The term does not mean *last —period*.

In his Gospel St. Mark (6:12–13) gives us an indication of this sacrament of the sick when he tells us that the apostles, going forth, "preached that men should repent, and they cast out many devils, and anointed with oil many sick people, and healed them." However, the classical description which the Bible gives of the sacrament of Extreme Unction is found in the Epistle of St. James (5:14–15): "Is any one among you sick? Let him bring in the presbyters [priests] of the Church, and let them pray over him, anointing him with oil in the name of the Lord. And the prayer of faith will save the sick man, and the Lord will raise him up, and if he be in sins, they shall be forgiven him."

The oil used in administering the sacrament of Extreme Unction is called Oil of the Sick. It is one of the three Holy Oils blessed by the bishop of the diocese at his cathedral on Holy Thursday morning, the other two Holy Oils being Holy Chrism and the Oil of Catechumens, which is used in Baptism. Oil of the Sick is pure olive oil—nothing being added except the blessing of the bishop. Its appropriateness as part of the outward sign of Extreme Unction is evident from the healing and strengthening effects which are characteristic of olive oil.

In the administration of the sacrament of Extreme Unction there are certain introductory and follow-up prayers which the priest recites when time permits. However, the essence of the sacrament lies in the actual anointing and the short prayer which accompanies the anointing. In giving the sacrament, the priest traces a small cross with Oil of the Sick on the eyes, ears, nostrils, lips, and hands of the sick person; in other words, he anoints the five bodily senses of sight, hearing, smell, taste, and touch. If it is not inconvenient to uncover the feet, the priest also traces a cross on these agents of human action.

As he anoints each sense organ in turn, the priest recites this prayer: "By this holy anointing and His most loving mercy may the Lord forgive you whatever wrong you have done by the use of your sight (of hearing, of smell, of taste and speech, of touch, of power to walk)." It is reported that a puzzled parishioner once asked his pastor how it was possible to sin with one's nose. "By sticking it into other people's business," was the answer of the Irish padre. More seriously, reflection will tell us that the nose often plays a part in sins of intemperance—both in food and in drink—and in other sins of sensuality. The role of the feet in carrying a person to the scene of sin is obvious.

While the anointing of the particular bodily senses must be performed if at all possible, it is not absolutely essential for the valid giving of the sacrament. If the priest judges that there is not time for the five- or six-fold unction (for example, if the sick person seems to be drawing his last breath), then a single anointing on the forehead with the prayer, "By this holy anointing and His most loving mercy may the Lord forgive you whatever wrong you have done," will suffice. If time permits afterwards, the priest will follow up with the other anointings; but this might not be possible in times of disaster when many people are in need of Extreme Unction with but one or few priests to minister to them.

When faced with the danger of death, a person normally will experience a feeling of great anxiety. This is to be expected. God has planted in human nature a strong attachment to life which we commonly call the instinct for self-preservation. He has done so precisely in order to assure that we take due care of our physical well-being and do not expose ourselves to unnecessary danger to our life. We need not feel ashamed, therefore, nor convicted of lack of faith if we find ourselves apprehensive when the shadow of death looms over us. To counteract this fear of death when it needs to be counteracted, and to remove all *cause* for fear, God has given us the sacrament of Extreme Unction.

In common with all the sacraments, Extreme Unction confers sanctifying grace. It is an *increase* in sanctifying grace that Extreme Unction gives, since it presupposes that the recipient already is free from mortal sin. Thus there is intensified in the soul that supernatural life, that oneness-with-God, which is the source of all spiritual strength as it is also the measure of our capacity for the happiness of heaven.

Besides this increase in sanctifying grace Extreme Unction gives its own special *sacramental* grace. The primary purpose of the special grace of Extreme Unction is to comfort and to strengthen the soul of the sick person. This is the grace that quiets anxiety and dissipates fear. It is the grace which enables the sick person to embrace God's will and to face the possibility of death without apprehension. It is the grace which gives the soul the strength to face and conquer whatever temptations to doubt, despondency, or even despair may mark Satan's last effort to seize this soul for himself. Doubtless many who read this have already received Extreme Unction, perhaps even several times. If so, they know by experience, as does the writer, what peace of mind and confidence in God this sacrament bestows.

This spiritual tranquillity and strength is further increased by the second effect of Extreme Unction. This is the preparation of the soul for entrance into heaven by the forgiveness of venial sins and the cleansing of the soul from the remains of sin. If we are so blessed as to receive the sacrament of Extreme Unction in our last illness, we may have every confidence that we shall enter into the happiness of heaven immediately after death. We hope that our friends still will continue to pray for us after death, since we never can be sure of the adequacy of our own dispositions in receiving this sacrament; and if we do not need the prayers, someone else will profit by them. Yet we should have a high degree of confidence, once we have received Extreme Unction, that we shall look upon the face of God moments after our soul leaves our body. The soul has been cleansed from all that might hold it back from God, from venial sins and from the temporal punishment due to sin.

The "remains of sin" from which Extreme Unction cleanses the soul include that moral weakness of soul which is the result of sin, both of original sin and our own sins. This weakness—even to the point of spiritual indifference—is likely to afflict that person especially who has been a habitual sinner. Here again, the soul of the sick person is tempered and prepared against the possibility of any last-moment conflict with the world, the flesh, and the devil.

Since Penance is the sacrament by which God intends our mortal sins to be forgiven, a sick person who has mortal sins to confess must receive the sacrament of Penance before he receives the sacrament of Extreme Unction. However, it is a comfort to know that Extreme Unction does forgive mortal sin also if the critically ill person is unable to receive the sacrament of Penance. This could happen, for example, if Extreme Unction were administered to an unconscious person who had made an act of imperfect contrition for his mortal sins before losing consciousness.

It is plain that the principal purpose of the sacrament of Extreme Unction is a spiritual one: to prepare the soul for death, if death is to eventuate. However, there is a secondary and conditional effect of Extreme Unction: the recovery of bodily health by the sick or injured person. The condition under which this secondary effect can be expected to operate is stated by the Council of Trent: "When it is expedient for the soul's salvation." In other words, if it will be *spiritually* good for the sick person to recover, then his recovery can with certainty be expected.

The recovery, however, will not be a sudden miraculous recovery. God does not multiply marvels unnecessarily. Whenever possible He works through natural causes. In this instance, recovery will be the result of the powers of nature, stimulated by the graces of the sacrament. By eliminating anxiety, abolishing fear, inspiring confidence in God with resignation to His will, Extreme Unction reacts upon the bodily processes for the physical betterment of the patient. It is evident that we have no right to expect this physical result from Extreme Unction if the priest is not called until the body is hopelessly ravaged by disease.

But perhaps "hopelessly" is not a good word. Every priest who has had much experience in caring for the sick can recall some remarkable and unexpected recoveries that have followed after Extreme Unction.

When To Call the Priest

Every Catholic who has reached the age of reason can and should receive the sacrament of Extreme Unction when in danger of death from sickness, accident, or old age. Since the purpose of Extreme Unction is to comfort the soul in anxieties and heal the effects of sin and to strengthen the soul against the possibility of sin, it is plain that this sacrament is not for infants. Neither is it for mentally afflicted adults who have lacked the use of reason their whole life long. Such persons have not committed sin and cannot commit sin; Extreme Unction would have no effect upon them.

The danger of death must be present in the body of the person, whether the danger be due to illness or wounds or to the debility of advanced years. Extreme Unction cannot be administered to a soldier before he goes into battle, even though he does face the danger of death. Neither may the sacrament be administered to a criminal before his execution. Danger of death from such outward perils does not qualify one for Extreme Unction.

Unfortunately, it sometimes happens that a person who does have the right to the Last Anointing dies without it because of the carelessness or the misdirected love of those who are in charge of the patient. Carelessness enters in when there is ignorance or misunderstanding of the purpose of Extreme Unction. The sacrament is not just for those who are gasping out their last breath. It is for anyone whose condition is such that death is probable; for any type of sickness or injury which a doctor might term critical; in fact for a physical condition which some doctors might term merely serious. Where there is any doubt as to the person's condition, he should be given the benefit of the doubt. For example, if the victim of a highway accident seems to be seriously hurt, the priest will not wait for the results of X-rays and other examinations before administering Extreme Unction.

A basic principle to be followed by family, friends, or any others who may find themselves responsible for a sick person is to *call the priest soon enough*. Soon enough, that is, so that Extreme Unction may have its full effect, physical as well as spiritual, upon the patient. And what is "soon enough"? A good rule of thumb to follow is that any time a person is sick enough to have a doctor, he is sick enough for the priest to be advised of his illness; people do not ordinarily call in a doctor for a minor malady.

When the priest is notified, he may ask for details concerning the patient's condition. He may decide that a hurry-up visit and immediate anointing are not indicated. But every pastor likes to know who are ill or bedridden in his parish. As a good shepherd he likes to visit the disabled members of his flock if only to impart a blessing and speak a cheerful word. Even when Extreme Unction does not seem to be called for, the priests of the parish do want to bring Holy Communion to those who are confined to their homes for any considerable length of time. We should never fear that the priest will resent being asked to call upon a sick member of our family, even though the sickness is not "unto death."

Just as bad as delaying Extreme Unction through ignorance of its purpose is the postponement of the sacrament through mistaken love. This happens when those close to the sick person think that it will be a shock to him or her if the priest is called. "We didn't want to frighten Mother by telling her how bad off she was." Many a priest has had to restrain his rising blood pressure as he has listened to some such explanation at three o'clock in the morning by the bedside of an unconscious person who should have received Extreme Unction a week or more ago.

To realize how uncharitable it is to keep a sick person ignorant of his critical condition, we have only to ask ourselves, "Would *I* wish to be told if I were in danger of dying?" Ninety-nine out of one hundred of us will answer "Yes!" to that question. No matter how good our lives may be, we feel that we could put a little more pressure into our prayers if we knew that Judgment might be near.

And *we don't have to die* just because we have received Extreme Unction. Whatever anxiety we may feel when advised that our condition is critical will quickly be stilled and more than stilled by the graces of the sacrament. The fear of Extreme Unction as a harbinger of death is a superstition that harks back to the Middle Ages. Church historians tell us that in the Middle Ages this misconception of Extreme Unction was so prevalent that a person who recovered after being anointed was treated like a person who literally had returned from beyond the grave. If married, he was not allowed to continue his conjugal relations; he was not allowed to take an oath; legally he was dead.

One further point needs noting with respect to calling the priest. That is the fact that Extreme Unction will have its spiritual effects as long as the soul still is present in the body if the person had the state of grace or sorrow for sin before losing consciousness. We never can be sure when the soul separates itself from the body. The fact that breathing and heart action have stopped is no guarantee that the soul is gone. For this reason the Church allows the priest to administer Extreme Unction up to several hours after apparent death has occurred. In case of sudden death, therefore, as by accident or heart attack, the priest should be called. Unless and until decomposition has set in, the soul still may be present. The priest still can administer conditional Extreme Unction.

A member of your family is sick. The illness seems rather serious; or at least it is a disability (such as a broken hip) which is going to mean house-confinement for more than just a few days. You notify your pastor of the state of affairs and he says that he will call on the sick person. What preparations will you make for the priest's coming?

Obviously, if the priest is going to begin with just a friendly call because the illness does not seem dangerous ("I'll drop in this afternoon to see Grandma"), then no special preparations are necessary for his coming. If, however, the priest says, "I'll come over tomorrow morning after the seven o'clock Mass to bring Grandma Holy Communion," some preliminaries are called for.

In this instance, a small table should be placed beside the bed or chair of the sick person. If no such table is available, the top of the dresser or chest of drawers will do. The table (or substitute) should be covered with a clean white linen cloth. On the table should be a crucifix flanked by two wax candles. There should be a sprinkler-bottle of holy water; or, lacking such a bottle, a small dish of holy water with a sprig of blessed palm that the priest can use as a sprinkler. There also should be a glass of plain water, a spoon and a clean napkin.

The candles should be lighted before the priest arrives. One of these candles (or a third lighted candle) should be carried by the person who goes to the door to admit the priest. As he enters the home the priest will say, "Peace to this house." The one admitting the priest will answer (if he knows the answer), "And to all who live here." The priest is led silently to the sickroom. He will kneel and place upon the table the burse containing the Sacred Host, then will rise to sprinkle the invalid and the room with holy water. Other members of the family who may be in the sick room should kneel as the priest enters. After the sprinkling and its accompanying prayer, the priest will nod to the others present, and while the priest hears the sick person's confession, they should leave the room, closing the door as they leave.

When the priest reopens the door, the family should re-enter and kneel. If the sick person himself or herself is unable to recite the Confiteor, one of the others present should do so. After giving the sick person Holy Communion, the priest will rinse out the pyx (the small gold case in which the Sacred Host was contained) with a spoonful of water. As this water cannot be poured down an ordinary drain, the priest will be grateful if there is a plant in the room, so that he can pour this water into the earth of the flower pot.

The priest will not do this, however, if he has further Communion-calls to make, with Sacred Hosts still remaining in the pyx. In this event, when he is ready to leave he will make the sign of the Cross over the sick person with the burse containing the Blessed Sacrament. Then, led by someone bearing a lighted candle, he should be conducted silently to the door. In cases of prolonged illness when the priest will be coming often to administer the sacraments, it will be commendable for the family to buy a copy of the *Collectio Rituum* at a Catholic book store. In this book are contained all the prayers (in English as well as in Latin) that are used on sick calls. A member of the family then can make the proper responses to the prayers instead of leaving the priest to answer himself.

If it is a dangerous illness that occasions the calling of a priest, he doubtless will come prepared to administer the Last Rites. This involves a little added preparation to those already described for Holy Communion. On the bedside table, besides the items already mentioned, there should be a saucer containing six balls or pieces of absorbent cotton with which the priest will wipe away the Holy Oil of the anointing. Another dish should contain a slice of bread cut into squares and a slice or two of lemon with which the priest will cleanse the Holy Oil from his fingers after the anointing. A dish of water and a small towel also will be appreciated by the priest.

The Last Rites administered to a person dangerously ill include the sacraments of Penance, Extreme Unction, and Holy Viaticum, plus the Apostolic Blessing (sometimes called the Last Blessing), which carries with it a plenary indulgence for the very moment of death. In the new English Ritual the term "Extreme Unction" is no longer used; instead, the sacrament of the sick is called the "Holy Anointing." We may hope that this less frightening and less archaic name becomes more widely used.

"Viaticum" is a Latin word which means "traveling-companion." Holy Viaticum is simply Holy Communion given to one who is in danger of death. Ordinarily, in administering Holy Communion the priest says, "May the Body of our Lord Jesus Christ preserve your soul unto everlasting life." In administering Holy Communion as

Viaticum, the priest says, "Receive, my brother (sister), this food for your journey, the Body of our Lord Jesus Christ, that He may guard you from the malicious enemy and lead you into everlasting life." As Holy Viaticum, Holy Communion may be given at any hour of day or night, even though the sick person may have received "ordinary" Holy Communion previously on that same day as an act of devotion, and no matter how recently he may have eaten.

In cases of sudden urgency, of course, we should not delay in calling the priest in order to prepare the sick room. The sick person's need is more important than candles and holy water. The priest will not complain if things are not ready.

CHAPTER XXXIV

Holy Orders

What Is a Priest?

To know what a priest is we have to know what a sacrifice is. Nowadays the word "sacrifice" is used in many different ways. But in its strict meaning, its original meaning, a sacrifice is the offering of a gift to God by a group, through the agency of someone who has the right to represent the group. The purpose of such an offering is to give *group* worship to God; that is, to acknowledge God's supreme lordship over mankind, to thank Him for His blessings, to atone for human sin, and to beg for His benefits. It is not that God *needs* our gifts. Everything that exists was made by God in the first place. Even a mountain of diamonds would of itself have no value in God's eyes. Until Jesus gave us Himself as the perfect gift in the sacrifice of the Mass, nothing that man could offer to God was really worthy of God.

Nevertheless it pleased God, from the very beginning of human history, to have man "act out" his feelings towards God by means of sacrifice. From all that God had given, man would take the very best (whether it was a lamb or a bullock or fruit or grain) and offer it back to God—destroying it upon an altar to symbolize the act of giving. These were only "token" gifts—like the Christmas necktie which a poor man might give to his rich and generous uncle. But the gifts expressed, better than could words, the deepest sentiments of the human heart towards God. "O almighty God," the gift would say, "I know that all which I have, I have from You. I thank You for Your bounty. I beg Your forgiveness for not serving You better. Please be good and merciful to me anyway." Sacrifice, in short, is prayer in action. It is the prayer-in-action of a group. And the one who offers the sacrifice in the name of the group is the priest.

Since men have offered sacrifice to God from the very beginning of the human race so also have there been priests from the very beginning. In the first period of Biblical history—the age of the Patriarchs—it was the father of the family who was also the priest. It was the father of the family who offered sacrifice to God for himself and his family. Adam was priest for his family; so were Noah and Abraham and all the other family heads priests for their families. In the time of Moses, however, God directed that the priesthood of His chosen people, the Jews, should henceforth belong to the family of Aaron of the tribe of Levi. The oldest son in each generation of Aaron's descendants would be the high priest and the other Levites would be his assistants.

When the Old Law ended with the establishment of the New Law by Christ, the priesthood of the Old Law also came to an end. The New Law of love would have a new sacrifice and a new priesthood. At the Last Supper Jesus instituted the Holy Sacrifice of the Mass. In this new sacrifice the gift offered to God would not be a mere token gift, such as a sheep or an ox or bread and wine. The gift now, for the first time and always, would be a gift worthy of God. It would be the gift of God's own Son; a gift of infinite value, even as God Himself is infinite. In the Mass, under the appearances of bread and wine, Jesus would daily renew the once-and-forever offering which, upon the cross, He made of Himself to God. In the Mass He would give to each of us, His baptized members, the opportunity to unite ourselves with Him in that offering.

But who would be the human priest who would stand at the altar—the human agent whose hands and whose lips Christ would use for the offering of Himself? Who would be the human priest to whom Christ would give the power of making the God-Man present upon the altar, under the appearances of bread and wine? There were eleven such priests, to begin with. (It is not certain that Judas was present at the time the Apostles were made priests.) At the Last Supper, as we know, Jesus made His Apostles priests, when He gave them the command (and with the command, the power) to do what He had just done. "Do this," He said, "in remembrance of Me" (Luke 22:20).

It was this power, the power to offer sacrifice in the name of Christ and of Christ's Mystical Body, His Church (which means you and me united to Christ by Baptism), which made the Apostles priests. To this power of changing bread and wine into His Body and Blood, Jesus on Easter Sunday night added the power to forgive sins in His name. "Receive the Holy Spirit," He said; "whose sins you shall forgive, they are forgiven them; and whose sins you shall retain, they are retained" (John 20:22–23).

This power of the priesthood which Christ conferred upon His Apostles was not to die with them. Jesus came to save the souls of *all* people who ever would live, down to the end of the world. Consequently, the Apostles passed their priestly power on to other men in the ceremony which we now call the sacrament of Holy Orders. In the Acts of the Apostles we read of one of the first (if not the first) ordinations by the Apostles: "And the plan met the approval of the whole multitude, and they chose Stephen, a man full of faith and of the Holy Spirit, and Philip and Prochorus and Nicanor and Timon and Parmenas and Nicholas, a proselyte from Antioch. These they set before the Apostles, and after they had prayed they laid their hands upon them" (Acts 6:5-6).

It was as deacons that these men were ordained, not yet as priests. But it gives us the picture of the Apostles sharing, and passing on to others, the sacred power which Jesus had bestowed upon them. As time went on, the Apostles consecrated more bishops to carry on their work. These bishops in turn ordained other bishops and priests, and these bishops in *their* turn, still others. So that the Catholic priest of today can truly say that the power of his priesthood has come down, in the sacrament of Holy Orders, in an unbroken line from Christ Himself.

Nineteen hundred and more years have elapsed since Jesus elevated the eleven Apostles to the priesthood on Holy Thursday night. (It is uncertain whether Judas still was present.) Since then, there may have been times in the Church's history when there were enough priests for all the needs of Christ's Mystical Body, but that time certainly is not now. Priests, priests, and more priests—this is one of today's most urgent needs. Priests are needed here in our own country, where so many parishes remain understaffed and souls so often are meagerly cared for because of lack of priests. The need is even greater in mission lands, where whole villages will plead for a priest to come to them and no priest can be given. We may be sure that God, Whose interest in souls is supreme, is not at fault here. We may be sure that He is calling to the priesthood many young men who, for one reason or another, are not heeding His voice.

No young man should make a choice of his vocation in life without first asking himself, "Could it be that God wants me to be a priest?" Notice, the question is not, "Do I want to be a priest?" but rather, "Does God want me to be a priest?" It is a question that should be asked and pondered in prayer—and pondered and prayed about, over a reasonable length of time. Obviously God does not want every young man to be a priest. There are other vocations to be filled—notably that of parenthood. But a man will be the happier in Christian marriage and parenthood if he first has made sure that he is not closing his ears to God's invitation to spiritual fatherhood.

What are the signs of a vocation? Actually a vocation is the "call" of the bishop. When a bishop notifies a young man, at the end of his seminary course, that he should prepare to receive the sacrament of Holy Orders, *that* is the essential factor of a vocation. To answer that call it is necessary that the man be in the state of grace and that he be of exceptionally good character. It is necessary that he should have completed the necessary course of study: four years of high school, four years of college, and four years of theology.

It is necessary that he be twenty-four years of age; without a dispensation, Holy Orders cannot today be administered at a younger age. It is necessary that he be the child of validly married Catholic parents. The Church sets great store by the thoroughly Catholic home life of candidates for the priesthood. It is the spirit of faith and love for God in which the child grew up that will most notably mold the later character of the man. However, the Church will grant a dispensation for the son of a mixed marriage to become a priest—even for an illegitimate child to become a priest—if all other factors are favorable. Finally, the candidate for Holy Orders must have the right intention: the intention of dedicating himself to the service of God in the priesthood—in order to sanctify his own soul by laboring for the souls of others. No other motivation than this should be in the heart of a man who kneels to receive the sacrament of Holy Orders.

However, this is the *end* of the road to the priesthood, of which we have been talking. What about the beginning of the road? How can a boy tell, and how can he begin? In the first place, there will be no special revelation, at least not normally. God will not hit a boy over the head and say: "I want you to be a priest!" God has given us our reason and He expects us to use it. He will illumine our reason and guide us gently if we give Him the chance in prayer; but He expects us to use the guideposts He already has provided.

Let the boy ask himself: "Do I have reasonably good health?" There is no need to be a superman, but a sickly constitution is not likely to persevere through twelve years of study beyond the eighth grade. Let the boy also ask himself, "Do I have a reasonably fair ability to study and to learn?" There is no need to be a genius, but the studies in the seminary are stiffer than the average high school and college outside. A consistently bad report card would point away from the likelihood of a vocation.

Then let the boy ask himself: "Do I go to confession often and do I receive Holy Communion frequently?" If the answer is no, this is a defect that quickly can be remedied; just start receiving more often now. Finally, the boy should ask himself: "Do I live habitually in the state of sanctifying grace; do I avoid mortal sin?" If the answer to this is negative, this defect also can quickly be remedied, with the help of prayer and the sacraments. For a boy to consider the priesthood, it isn't necessary to be a saint. If that were necessary, we would have very few priests. But it is necessary that he want to be better than he is. Good health, intelligence, and virtue—these gifts of nature and grace are prerequisites to a call to the priesthood.

If a boy can answer yes to the above four questions, if he has finished or is finishing the eighth grade, and if he can find in his heart the generosity to offer himself to God —then by all means he should talk to his pastor about the possibility of going to the seminary. And the parents, when the boy mentions his thoughts to them, should give the boy every encouragement. They should not push him, but they should encourage him. More than one vocation has been lost because of the false prudence of parents who said, "Wait until you're through high school," or "Wait until you finish college." As though there should be any waiting when God is calling! There is no danger that any boy will be "pressured" into staying in the seminary. On the contrary, he will have to prove that he has the goods in order to survive.

This is what the boy can do, and what his parents can do. What *all* of us can do is to make a daily intention, in our prayers and our Masses, for present priests and seminarians —with a special plea that still more boys may hear God's voice and head towards the altar.

What Is Holy Orders?

There are two notable ways in which the sacrament of Holy Orders differs from the other sacraments. One is the fact that Holy Orders can be administered only by a bishop. Only a bishop has the power to ordain priests. An ordinary priest cannot pass his power on to another. The second way in which Holy Orders differs from other sacraments is that Holy Orders is not received all at once. When we are baptized, we are completely baptized by the single pouring of water. When we are confirmed, we are completely confirmed in a single ceremony. Holy Orders, however, is given by degrees, by successive steps.

The Catechism defines Holy Orders as "the sacrament through which men receive the power and grace to perform the sacred duties of bishops, priests, and other ministers of the Church." It is that phrase, "other ministers," which sometimes puzzles children as they study their Catechism. Here in America the word "minister" is the title usually given to clergymen of the Protestant churches. Many are surprised to learn that there are ministers in the Catholic Church also.

Actually the word "minister" (originally a Latin word) simply means "one who serves." In the sense that Pope, bishops, and priests are servants of their respective flocks, all of them might be called ministers. However, the phrase "other ministers" in the Catechism definition refers to the ranks of the clergy below the level of priest. Perhaps this will be clearer if we follow a young man through the various steps that lead him to the priesthood.

After he has graduated from high school and finished his four-year college course, the young man headed for the priesthood will enter a theological seminary. During or after the first year of his theology course he will receive the *tonsure*. In the ceremony of tonsure, the bishop clips a bit of hair, in the form of a cross, from the crown of the young man's head, while the young man himself states his purpose of giving himself to the service of the Lord. The young man is now a *cleric*—one who is set aside and dedicated to the service of God in the Church.

During the course of his next two years of study, the seminarian will receive the four *minor orders:* porter, lector, exorcist, and acolyte. Like the tonsure, these four minor orders probably are not a part of the sacrament of Holy Orders; they are a *preparation* for Holy Orders. These minor orders go back to at least the third century of Christian history. In those ancient times it was the custom of bishops to delegate men for certain church duties which did not require the fullness of the power of the priesthood. Certain men, called acolytes, were designated to serve the priest at the altar for the celebration of Holy Mass. Others, called exorcists, were empowered to cast out evil spirits. Still others, called lectors (which is Latin for "readers"), were assigned to read the Epistles and Scripture lessons at Mass. Porters, finally, were charged with guarding the church doors against intruders and unauthorized persons— an important duty in the ages of persecution. Nowadays, of course, the seminarians (except for acolytes and lectors) do not exercise these duties; but the minor orders themselves still remain as steps to the priesthood.

When well advanced in his theological studies (usually at the end of his third year of theology), our young man will be ordained a subdeacon. Subdeaconship is the first of the three *major* orders; the other two are deaconship and priesthood. It is when he is ordained a subdeacon that the young man makes his solemn vow of chastity. From then on, he is obliged to recite the Divine Office every day. Next to the Mass itself, the Divine Office is the most important of the liturgical prayers of the Church. It is made up of psalms, Epistles, and Gospels from the Bible, and other sacred readings and prayers compiled by the Church. Every priest, from subdeaconship on, and every religious who has made solemn vows, is obliged to the daily recitation of the Divine Office. The praying of it takes about an hour each day, and this is what a priest is doing when you see him "praying his breviary." The breviary is the book in which the prayers of the Divine Office are contained. When he is reciting the Divine Office, the priest or religious is a mouthpiece of the Church. He is praying, not in his own name, but as the representative of the entire Mystical Body of Christ. It is in your name and mine that the priest is offering this act of adoration and praise to God.

When he becomes a subdeacon, our young man has completed his preparatory steps to the priesthood. Although it is one of the three major orders, subdeaconship probably is not a part of the *sacrament* of Holy Orders. Like tonsure and the four minor orders, subdeaconship also was instituted by the Church early in her history. It had its origin, apparently, in the Church's early need for men who would dedicate themselves completely, and for life, to responsible duties below the level of administering the sacraments.

Today, a subdeacon's principal active office is to assist, with a deacon, at the celebration of a Solemn High Mass. The subdeacon, in vestments which match those of the officiating priest, chants the Epistle of the Mass and otherwise ministers to the celebrant at the altar.

And now, as his fourth and last year of theology begins, the seminarian is nearing the top of the steps. He is ready for the actual sacrament of Holy Orders.

Like a flower developing from bud to full bloom, so does the sacrament of Holy Orders unfold itself through three stages as it confers successively the powers of deacon, priest, and bishop. By the time a seminarian begins his fourth and last year of theological studies, he has completed the preparatory steps. He has received the four minor orders (acolyte, exorcist, lector or reader, and porter or doortender) and the first major order of subdeaconship. With subdeaconship he has made his solemn vow of perpetual chastity and has assumed the duty of praying the Divine Office daily. And now, in his final year of study, the seminarian is ready to begin to receive the sacrament of Holy Orders.

Deaconship, priesthood, and bishopric are the three stages in the sacrament of Holy Orders as it was instituted by Christ. At each stage, as in every sacrament, there is an increase in sanctifying grace. At each stage there is the imprinting of a character upon the soul; each successive character, like a progressively brighter sun, enveloping and containing the one that has gone before. In that character are rooted the right and the power that belong to the order which is being received. For the deacon it is the right to baptize, to preach, and to administer Holy Communion. For the priest it is the power to change bread and wine into the Body and Blood of Christ and to forgive sins. For the bishop, who alone has the complete fullness of the priesthood, it is the power to confirm and to ordain—to pass the power of the priesthood on to others in the sacrament of Holy Orders. Then, besides the increase in sanctifying grace and the priestly character with its accompanying power, there is the special sacramental grace which gives to the one ordained a claim upon God for whatever actual graces he may need in the faithful discharge of his office.

Nowadays we do not find any deacons actively at work outside the seminaries. It is for only a few short months that a man remains a deacon. These months are spent in the seminary preparing for the second and most awesome grade of Holy Orders—the priesthood. The deacon of today has no opportunity to administer Baptism and very little opportunity to preach. In the seminary he may be called upon occasionally to assist in distributing Holy Communion and occasionally to assist the priest in the offering of Solemn High Mass; that will be the extent of his deaconly duties. In the Church at present the power of the deacon remains to a great extent a latent and unused power—this power which comes to the candidate for Holy Orders when the bishop places his hands upon the candidate's head and says the words by which the power of the deaconship is conferred.

But the day of his ordination to the priesthood comes quickly for the young deacon. On the appointed day the bishop again places his hands upon this same head, a moment later praying, "We beseech Thee, Almighty Father, invest this Thy servant with the dignity of the priesthood. . . ." This time the Holy Spirit imparts that tremendous and almost unbelievable power to call Jesus Christ Himself down upon the altar—and to forgive, in Christ's name, the sins of men.

For most, this second step in the sacrament of Holy Orders will be their last. No priest would or could wish for more. As he bends each morning over the bread and the wine, lending his lips to Christ as he speaks Christ's words, "This is My Body. . . . This is My Blood," the priest time and again feels all but crushed by the sense of his own unworthiness, by the consciousness of his human weakness. He *would* be crushed, too, if it were not for the grace of the sacrament of Holy Orders, which God infallibly gives to those who humbly ask it.

It is, of course, this power to offer sacrifice, this power to offer the Perfect Gift to God in the name of God's people, that distinguishes a priest from a Protestant minister. It would not be incorrect to call a priest a minister; he is a minister, a servant of Christ and of Christ's flock. He is a preacher, too, and might rightly be called a preacher, as he delivers God's message of salvation Sunday after Sunday. However, while it would be correct enough to call a priest a minister or a preacher, it would not be correct to call a Protestant minister a priest. The minister does not have the power to offer sacrifice, which is precisely what makes a priest a priest. Indeed, Protestant ministers—except the clergy of the High Episcopalian Church—do not even believe in such a power. The High Church—or Anglican—clergy do consider themselves priests, but unfortunately they are mistaken. There is no one who can impart to them the power of the priesthood.

The line of succession by which the power of the priesthood has come down to us, from Christ to the Apostles to bishop to bishop to bishop, was broken centuries ago when the Anglican Church rejected the whole idea of the Mass and a sacrificing priesthood. In later times High churchmen have revived the idea of the Mass, but they have no bishops who are true successors of the Apostles, no bishops who themselves have any of the power which the sacrament of Holy Orders gives. This is not said in any spirit of prideful disdain—it is just a sad fact of history; one that should move us to renewed prayer that our separated brethren may return to the one true fold.

Bishops—and Others

The third and top step of the sacrament of Holy Orders is that of bishop. When a new bishop is needed to head a diocese or to perform some other high-level work of the Church, the Holy Father as Peter's successor designates the priest who is to be raised to the episcopacy. This priest then receives his third "laying on of hands" from a bishop (deaconship and priesthood have gone before) and himself becomes a bishop. To his previous power to offer Mass and to forgive sins there is now added the power to administer Confirmation in his own right and the exclusive power which only a bishop possesses: the power to administer the sacrament of Holy Orders, the power to ordain other priests and to consecrate other bishops.

At this final imposition of hands from the consecrating bishop (who normally is assisted by two other bishops, called "co-consecrators"), the new bishop receives the Holy Spirit for the last time. The Holy Spirit came to him for the first time in Baptism and gave him the power to share with Christ in offering sacrifice and the power to receive grace from the other sacraments. The Holy Spirit came again in Confirmation and conferred upon him the power to share with Christ His office of prophet—the power to spread the faith by word and by deed. The Holy Spirit came once more with new power and grace in deaconship and in priesthood. And now, as he becomes a bishop, he receives the Holy Spirit for the last time; there is no further Christ-sharing power left which God can give to man. For the last time his soul is marked with a character—the full and complete character of the sacrament of Holy Orders—the character of bishop.

It is in his power to perpetuate himself, the power to ordain priests and to consecrate other bishops, that the essence of the order of bishop lies. It is a power that he never can lose. Just as a priest can never lose his power to change bread and wine into our Lord's Body and Blood, even though he may leave the Church and become an apostate priest, so, too, a bishop can never lose his power to ordain other priests and bishops, not even if he were to abandon the Catholic Church. It is here that we find the principal difference between the Orthodox churches and the Protestant churches.

The Protestant churches, as we have previously mentioned, do not believe in the Mass or in a priesthood empowered to offer sacrifice—and therefore do not believe in the sacrament of Holy Orders. We noted that High Church members of the Episcopalian and Anglican faith do believe in the Mass and the priesthood. However, real priests and bishops ceased to exist in the Anglican church back in the sixteenth century. At that time the leaders of the Anglican church eliminated all reference to the Mass and the power of sacrifice from their ordination ceremony. Without the intention of ordaining sacrificing priests, the sacrament of Holy Orders is invalid; it is *not* Holy Orders. In fact that is true of any sacrament. If a priest speaks the words, "This is My Body. . . . This is My Blood," in the presence of bread and wine (at table, for example), the bread and wine are not consecrated unless the priest has the *intention* of consecrating. Whoever gives a sacrament must have the intention of doing what the sacrament is supposed to do, or the sacrament is invalid. That is how true priests and bishops died out, in the Anglican church, once the intention of ordaining sacrificing priests and bishops was taken out of the ordination service.

Matters are different, however, with the so-called Orthodox churches, such as the Greek Orthodox, the Russian Orthodox, the Rumanian Orthodox, and so on. A thousand years and more ago, when all the Christian world was Catholic, the church leaders in some countries broke away from their union with Rome. They refused to obey the Pope as the head of the Church. When this happened, it was because of political rivalry and bitter personal resentments. However, as the church leaders of these nations turned their backs on Rome, they still continued to believe all the truths which the Catholic Church taught. They still believed in the Mass and all the sacraments. Their bishops remained true bishops, even though they had severed their allegiance to the Pope. These bishops continued to ordain priests validly, and to consecrate other bishops as their successors. With the power of the priesthood thus passed on, down through the centuries, the Orthodox churches still have the Mass and the sacraments. There are sixteen branches of the Orthodox church in all. Because of their rejection of the Pope, they are non-Catholic churches, and Catholics may not attend their services. However, they are not Protestant churches; we term them "schismatic" or separated churches.

The Orthodox churches should not be confused with the Eastern *Catholic* churches. Most of us who are Catholics belong to the Latin rite—our liturgy is in the Latin language. But there are large groups of Catholics in some of the countries of Eastern Europe and Asia, who have had the Mass and the sacraments in their own language from the very beginnings of the Church; for example, the Greek Catholics and the Armenian Catholics. Many of their ceremonies also are somewhat different from ours. But they believe in the Pope as the head of the Church and are just as truly Catholics as you or I. It is quite permissible for Latin-rite Catholics to assist at Mass in a church of the Eastern rite, and to receive Holy Communion there under the appearances of both bread and wine. Eastern or Western, we are one in Christ.

Deacon, priest, bishop; these are the three steps in the sacrament of Holy Orders. Above the order of bishop there is no further spiritual power that God gives to men. Then what about the Pope? Does he not have more power than an ordinary bishop? And what about cardinals and archbishops? Where do they come into the picture?

No, the Pope does not have any more spiritual power than any other bishop. He does have more *authority*, more extensive jurisdiction than any other bishop. Because he is the bishop of Rome, the successor of St. Peter, the Pope has authority over the entire Church of Christ. He makes laws for the entire Church. He designates the priests who are to become bishops, and assigns bishops to their dioceses. He also enjoys a very special privilege which Jesus conferred on St. Peter and St. Peter's successors: the privilege of infallibility. By this divine privilege God preserves the Holy Father from error whenever he makes a definitive pronouncement to the universal Church on matters of Christian faith or moral conduct, using the fullness of his teaching authority. But the Holy Father's essential priestly power is no greater than it was on the day when he was first consecrated a bishop.

The office of cardinal has nothing whatever to do with priestly power. The cardinalate is a position of honor, quite independent of Holy Orders. The cardinals are simply the Pope's personal advisers; they are the Papal "cabinet officers." Theoretically, a cardinal does not even have to be a priest. Nowadays it is only priests and bishops who are chosen as cardinals, but there was a time in the Church when laymen also were appointed to this office. The title of cardinal is a very ancient one in the Church, but it was Pope Nicholas II in the year 1059 who made the College of Cardinals pretty much what it is today—giving the cardinals the right to elect a new Pope when the Holy See falls vacant.

To understand the office of archbishop, we need to know a little about the physical make-up of the Church. The whole world is divided up into dioceses or the equivalent of dioceses. (In missionary lands the divisions are called "vicariates" or "prefectures" instead of dioceses.) There are in the neighborhood of two thousand such divisions in the Church today. Each diocese has definite geographical boundaries, just as states and counties have definite boundaries. Everyone living within the boundaries of a certain diocese belongs to that diocese. Each diocese is divided into parishes, each parish also having its geographical boundaries; and each person living within those boundaries belongs to that parish—whether he is "registered" or not. The only person who could truthfully say, "I don't belong to any parish," would be a confirmed and constant vagabond who had no fixed home anywhere.

At the head of each diocese is a bishop. The bishop who rules over a diocese is called the *Ordinary* of the diocese. The title of Ordinary distinguishes a ruling bishop from a *titular* bishop. A titular bishop is one who does not have a diocese of his own to rule. When he is consecrated a bishop, he is given title to an extinct diocese—usually a diocese embracing some city in Asia or Africa which ceased to exist centuries ago. A titular bishop may be assigned to assist the Ordinary of a large diocese, in which case he is called an *auxiliary* bishop. Or he may be engaged in some non-diocesan work, such as head of a Catholic university or papal delegate.

Several adjacent dioceses are grouped together to form a *province* in the Church. The principal diocese of the province is called an *archdiocese*, and the Ordinary of that principal diocese is called an *archbishop*. The archbishop is not "boss" over the other dioceses in his province; each bishop is the ruler of his own diocese. But the archbishop does have the precedence in honor and does have certain duties, such as calling meetings of the bishops of the province and presiding over such meetings. And, just as there are titular bishops, so also there are titular archbishops who do not head an archdiocese. To them the Pope has given the title of archbishop as a mark of honor because of the important work in which they are engaged or the meritorious work which they have done.

Coming back now to the organization of the Church within the diocese, we find that most dioceses are divided into several deaneries, each deanery comprising several adjacent parishes. One of the pastors within that territory is appointed as dean by the bishop, and to the dean the Ordinary delegates many of his lesser tasks of supervision. This, then, is the hierarchical organization of the Church: several parishes make a deanery; several deaneries constitute a diocese; several dioceses comprise a province; and all the provinces of the world make up the Universal Church.

At this point someone may say, "But what about monsignors? Where do monsignors fit in?" The title of Monsignor, with the right to wear a purple cassock instead of black, is an honor conferred on a priest by the Holy Father, usually at the request of the bishop in whose diocese the priest labors. Usually the priest to whom such an honor comes is a member of the bishop's "official family"—chancellor, secretary, vicar-general, Propagation of the Faith director, and so on; or he is a pastor whose exceptional work seems to merit special recognition. The bestowal of the monsignorship puts upon a priest the seal of his bishop's high approval but does not give any increase of priestly power or authority.

CHAPTER XXXV

Matrimony

God Made Marriage

The simplest form of living creature is the cell. A living cell reproduces itself by a process of fission, of division. The cell increases in size, then "pinches itself together" in the middle and splits apart into *two* living cells. This process goes on over and over again, as the cells increase and multiply.

In planning the human race, God could have provided for the propagation of mankind in some similar fashion. Under such a plan, each human being would grow wider and wider, with a double set of organs gradually forming. At the proper moment the two halves of the person would split apart—and there would be two human beings instead of one.

It is a whimsical thought, obviously. But it serves to bring home to us the fact that God didn't *have* to make the human race male and female as He did. God didn't *have* to share His creative power with His own creatures and make the beginning of a new human life depend upon the free co-operation of a man and a woman with Himself. There is a limitless number of other ways in which God could have arranged for the multiplication of human beings, had He chosen to do so.

But God didn't do it any other way. He chose to make man male and female, and to give him the power, in partnership with Himself, to produce new human life. By the act of intimate union which we call sexual intercourse, man and woman would fashion a physical image of themselves; and into this new body so wondrously begun God would infuse a spiritual and immortal soul. It is God, then, Who bestowed upon humans the power of procreation—as the sexual faculty is called. It is God Who planned and Who gave to men and women their genital organs. It is God Who (to guarantee the perpetuation of the human race) attached to the use of those organs a high degree of physical pleasure. Since God is the author of sex and since all that God does is good, it follows then that sex in itself is something good. Indeed, because of its close relationship with God Who is a partner to the reproductive act, sex is not merely something good, it is something sacred and holy.

This is a point that needs emphasizing, this basic *sanctity* of sex. When the sense of the sacredness of sex is lost, the sanctity of marriage also is forgotten. Sex becomes a plaything, an exciting tool for pleasure rather than an instrument of God. Easy divorce and casual remarriages; prostitution and marital infidelity; these are some of the evils which follow when sex is twisted from its context in the divine scheme of things. And even righteous people can suffer from a warped concept of sex. The distorting effects of original sin often make it difficult to confine the sexual drive within the channel established by God—the channel of true marriage. Even pious people can make the mistake of confusing the misuse of sex with the procreative act itself; by a false sort of logic they come to regard sex as a degrading and defiling thing rather than as a magnificent gift of

God. More than one marriage has been robbed of complete happiness by such a mistaken state of mind.

To assure the right use of the procreative power God founded the institution of marriage: the lifelong and irrevocable union of one man and one woman. The necessity of such a union is apparent, since it is essential not only that children be born but that they be lovingly reared and cared for by the father and mother who bring them into the world. Our juvenile courts and mental hospitals bear daily witness to the evils that follow when the unity and permanence of marriage are forgotten.

But it was not merely for the purpose of peopling the earth that God instituted marriage. "It is not good that the man is alone," said God as Adam slept in Eden. "I will make him a helper like himself." It is God's design that man and woman should complete each other, draw strength from each other, contribute to one another's spiritual growth. It is in the lifelong espousal of one man and one woman, wherein minds and hearts as well as bodies are fused into a new and richer unity, that this purpose of God is achieved.

It was as a unique and permanent union that God established marriage when He gave Eve to Adam in Paradise. This uniqueness and permanence was strictly enforced by God throughout Biblical history, with two exceptions. After the Deluge, God permitted the Patriarchs, such as Abraham and Jacob, to have more than one wife so that the earth might be more quickly repeopled. Later, after the Jews escaped from the slavery of Egypt, God permitted them to divorce and remarry on the grounds of proven adultery; although, as Jesus later on pointed out to the Jews, it was only because of "the hardness of their hearts" that God relaxed His strict law even to this extent.

With the coming of Jesus, these exceptions to the oneness and the permanence of marriage were ended. Up to the time of Christ, marriage, although a sacred union, was still only a civil contract between a man and a woman. Jesus, however, took this contract, this exchange of marital consent between man and woman, and made the contract a conveyer of grace; He made marriage a sacrament, the sacrament of Matrimony among Christians. Matrimony is defined as "the sacrament by which a baptized man and a baptized woman bind themselves for life in a lawful marriage and receive the grace to discharge their duties."

It is not hard to understand why Jesus made marriage a sacrament—the sacrament of Matrimony. From man's beginning marriage was a sacred union. It was God's instrument for the begetting, the rearing, the education, and the moral training of successive generations of human beings. Marriage was a "natural," we might say, for elevation to the holy rank of a sacrament. Besides the priesthood, there is no state in life that *pleads* for grace as demandingly as does marriage.

No matter how well matched they may be, it is not easy for any two people to live together day in and day out, year after year, with their inescapable faults and personality defects grating upon each other; and to help one another grow in goodness and nobility in spite of those faults—little by little adjusting to one another so that the faults of one "fit in" to the perfections of the other and unity arises from the very differences of the two persons. This is a beautiful evolution, like the emergence of the butterfly from its chrysalis; but it is not easy.

No matter how selfless a couple may be, it is not easy for them to face the prospect of responsible parenthood, with all the sacrifices that entails. Especially it is not easy to face the prospect of an ultimate judgment, in which they will have to answer to God for the souls of the children who have been entrusted to them. If ever there was a state of life which called for grace, this is it.

And, in Christ's new plan for mankind, there was a further need for grace in marriage. It would be upon parents that Jesus must depend for the continual replenishment of His Mystical Body: that union-in-grace whereby all baptized Catholics are one in Christ. From now on, for Christian parents it would not be enough to beget, rear, educate, and train offspring. From now on Jesus would expect parents to form and nurture the souls of their children in the pattern of sainthood. Without guiding grace and strengthening grace, this would be a hopeless task.

It is no wonder, then, that Christ made marriage a sacrament. Just *when* He did so, during his public life, we do not know. Some think that it may have been at the marriage feast at Cana. Others think it may have been at the time He instructed the Pharisees: "Have you not read that the Creator, from the beginning, made them male and female, and said, 'For this cause a man shall leave his father and mother, and cleave to his wife, and the two shall become one flesh'? Therefore now they are no longer two, but one flesh. What therefore God has joined together, let no man put asunder" (Matthew 19:4–7). However, such speculations as to the exact time at which Jesus made marriage a sacrament are rather fruitless. It is enough for us to know, by the constant and unbroken tradition of the Church, that Jesus did so transform the marriage bond.

A sacrament, as we know, is an outward sign that confers an inner grace. In Matrimony, the outward sign is the exchange of marital consent on the part of a baptized man and a baptized woman. In other words the couple who are getting married administer the sacrament of Matrimony to each other. It is not correct to say (although we often do) that "John and Mary were married by the priest." More correctly we should say, "John and Mary married each other in the presence of the priest." The priest cannot administer the sacrament of Matrimony; only the contracting couple can do that. The priest is simply the official witness, representing Christ and Christ's Church. The priest's presence is normally essential; without him there is no sacrament and no marriage. But he does not confer the sacrament.

The rare case in which a priest's presence is not required for the sacrament of Matrimony is not practical for us, but it is interesting. If a baptized couple wish to marry but it will be impossible for them to reach a priest for thirty days or more, the Church legislates that they may exchange marital consent in the presence of two witnesses and it will be the sacrament of Matrimony. This could happen, for example, in a country under persecution, such as Russia; or in a missionary country where a priest is seen but seldom in outlying parts. If one of the parties to the proposed marriage should be in danger of death, then even the thirty-day clause does not hold; if a priest cannot be had, the couple may marry each other in the presence of two witnesses; and it *is* the sacrament of Matrimony that they receive.

Aside from these exceptional cases, a Catholic cannot validly contract marriage except it be in the presence of a priest. The competent priest to preside at a marriage is the pastor of the parish in which the marriage takes place, or the bishop of the diocese—or a priest delegated by such a pastor or the bishop. A Catholic who attempts to enter into marriage before a minister or a civil magistrate (such as a judge or a justice of the peace) is not really married at all. He commits a grave sin by going through such a ceremony; and the couple will be living in habitual mortal sin as long as they continue to cohabit. Two non-Catholics who are married by a minister or a civil magistrate are genuinely married. If the two are unbaptized, theirs is a "natural" marriage, such as was marriage before Jesus instituted the sacrament of Matrimony. If both non-Catholics are baptized, however, their marriage is a sacrament. For a Catholic, there just isn't any other way to marry validly except to receive the sacrament of Matrimony. When Jesus institutes a sacrament, He requires that His followers use it.

Matrimony Has Special Graces

If a husband (or a wife) is having a bad day, perhaps discouraged under the pressure of an acute domestic problem, tempted to self-pity, with the awful feeling that it was a mistake ever to get married—*that* is one good time to remember that Matrimony is a sacrament. It is a good time to remember that he (or she) has an absolute right to whatever grace may be needed in this emergency; whatever grace may be needed to strengthen human weakness and to guide to a solution of the problem. To Christian spouses who do their human best to make theirs a truly Christian marriage, God has pledged His grace, when needed and as needed. God will not default on His pledge.

Since Matrimony is a sacrament, we know that it gives grace. Like every sacrament, it gives two kinds of grace. First of all there is the increase in *sanctifying* grace, imparted at the very moment that the sacrament is received. As the just-wed couple turn away from the altar, their souls are spiritually stronger, spiritually more beautiful than when they came to the altar a few moments earlier. It is essential, of course, that they present themselves to receive this sacrament with souls which already are in the state of sanctifying grace. The purpose of Matrimony is not to forgive sin. For a person to receive this sacrament with a mortal sin upon his soul would be a sacrilege, a grave sin. The marriage still would be a true and valid marriage; but it would be a most unhappy beginning for what is designed to be a partnership with God.

Besides this increase in sanctifying grace—which all "the sacraments of the living" confer—Matrimony gives its own special grace, its *sacramental* grace. This consists in a claim upon God for whatever actual graces the couple may need, through the years, to make a happy and successful marriage. For its full effectiveness this grace needs the co-operation of both partners to the marriage. The grace is intended for that single entity, that "one-from-two," which a married couple have become. But if one partner should prove derelict to Christian duty, the other spouse still can count on exceptional graces of strength and wisdom.

To be more specific, the sacramental grace of Matrimony perfects the natural love of husband and wife; elevates this love to a supernatural level which far surpasses mere mental and physical compatibility. It gives to marital love a *sanctifying* quality, making it an instrument for growth in holiness and marriage a path to sainthood. The special grace of Matrimony also imparts conscientiousness in the begetting and rearing of children and prudence in the innumerable problems consequent upon family life. It enables husband and wife to adjust to one another's shortcomings and to bear with one another's faults. This is only a little of what the grace of Matrimony will accomplish for those who, by their co-operation, give God a chance to show what He can do.

Four hundred years ago the Council of Trent, in propounding the Catholic doctrine on the sacrament of Matrimony, said: "The grace which would perfect that natural love (of husband and wife) and confirm that indissoluble union and sanctify the married, Christ Himself merited for us by His Passion; as the Apostle St. Paul indicates, saying, 'Husbands, love your wives as Christ loved the Church.' " It seems to me that it should be a wonderfully inspiring thought to a Christian husband and wife to realize that Jesus was thinking of them as He suffered His Passion; to realize that one of the things for which Christ died was the graces they would need in marriage. Equally inspiring should be the knowledge that the Holy Spirit inspired St. Paul to compare marriage to the fruitful, grace-filled union and interchange between Christ and His Spouse, the Church.

In addition to the conferring of grace, another effect of the sacrament of Matrimony is the forging of the marriage bond, a moral change wrought in the souls of the married couple. It is only the three sacraments whose fundamental objective is the worship of God—Baptism, Confirmation, and Holy Orders—which work in the soul that *physical* change which we call the "character" of the sacrament. These are the three sacraments by which we share, in varying ways, in the priesthood of Christ. However, theologians have not hesitated to compare the marriage bond to these sacramental characters and even to term it a *quasi-character*.

It is from this "quasi-character," this matrimonial bond, that result the two properties of marriage: *unity* and *indissolubility* (such a jaw-breaker!). By the unity of marriage is meant that a man can have only one wife, and a woman only one husband. They are *two* in one flesh, not many in one flesh. The unity of marriage is opposed to polygyny (many wives) and polyandry (many husbands). Since Christ's time, monogamy (one spouse) must be the rule without exception.

By the indissolubility of marriage is meant that marriage is a *permanent* union. Once a man and woman are completely united in a consummated Christian marriage, there is no power on earth, not even the Pope, who can dissolve the bond. "What therefore God has joined together, let no man put asunder" (Matthew 19:6). The Church does have the power, under very special circumstances, to dissolve a marriage that was not a sacramental marriage (for example, the marriage of two unbaptized persons when one of the parties has later been baptized), and to dissolve a sacramental marriage that never has been consummated. But even the marriage of two validly baptized Protestants is a sacramental union which, once consummated, the Church herself cannot break. The state laws which permit divorce with remarriage are meaningless as far as God is concerned. The divorced person who remarries, and his or her new partner, are living in habitual adultery if the previous marriage was valid; legalized adultery, but adultery nonetheless.

There are times when the unbreakableness of the marriage bond seems to result in a great hardship. We are thinking of such instances as that of a husband whose wife becomes mentally ill. She is judged incurable and will never return from the hospital where she is confined. The husband is left with several small children on his hands, yet he cannot remarry so long as his wife still lives. Or we think of the wife who is obliged, for the safety of herself and her children, to separate from a drunken and abusive husband. The children need a father, but she cannot remarry so long as her husband still lives. Or we think of the husband or wife who is deserted by a spouse who is just plain "no good"; and the innocent party is left to struggle singlehanded in rearing the family or to live a solitary and a lonely life. There can be no remarriage so long as the deserter lives.

That is, there can be no remarriage for such persons so far as God is concerned. They can, of course, secure a civil divorce (with the consent of the bishop) if it is necessary to protect themselves against a vicious or a deserting spouse. But the civil divorce cannot break the marriage bond. If such persons enter into a civil union with a new spouse, it means that they cut themselves off from God's grace and live in habitual sin. They barter their eternal happiness for the sake of the few years of added comfort which their second "marriage" may bring. Even this comfort must be tainted by the knowledge that they have separated themselves from God.

We feel a great pity for persons caught in such a dilemma. We are tempted to ask, "*Why* is God so adamant against any breaking of the marriage bond? Why doesn't He make some provision for especially deserving cases?" The answer is that God, once He decided to create the human race male and female and to have men and women co-operate with Him in peopling the earth and heaven too, was compelled to make marriage a permanent union in order to fulfill His purposes. (When we say "decided" and "compelled," we are speaking of God in purely human terms.) If children were to reach adulthood in the full nobility which God willed them to have—children of God and images of Him— it was essential that they should have the emotional, mental, and spiritual stability which could be achieved only by growing up with their own parents. (The writer, whose principal work is with children from broken homes, can bear witness to the harmful effects of step-parentage.)

Moreover, even where there are no children to consider, the secondary purpose of marriage still demands a permanent union. The secondary purpose is the mutual completion which a man and a woman are destined to find in one another—the enrichment and growth which results from their fusion into a new unity, one from two. This is a purpose that never could be fulfilled if the marriage bond were temporary or terminable.

That is why we say that the indissolubility of the marriage bond flows from the *natural* law, even aside from any positive decree on the part of God. It is based on the very *nature* of man as he is.

Yes, someone may say, that is all true. But couldn't there be a dispensation in cases of exceptional hardship? Unfortunately, there can be no exceptions if God's plan is to succeed. When a man and a woman know that "this is for life," that they *have* to make a go of their marriage—then ninety-nine times out of a hundred they will. If adultery were grounds for severing the marriage bond with the right to remarry, or brutality or desertion, then how easy it would be to provide the grounds. We have seen that very result exemplified in our own country, as our divorce-and-remarriage rate grows and swells. No, this is a case where God must hold the line firmly or God's cause is lost.

It is a case where an individual (an innocent deserted mother, for example) is sometimes called upon to suffer for the common good. Those who say that the innocent should not have to suffer are saying in effect that virtue should be practiced only when virtue is easy. By this principle it would be quite all right for a Catholic caught in a Communist land to deny his Faith if it would keep him out of prison. By this principle martyrs would be fools, and goodness would simply depend upon how low the pressure was.

As for the deserted wife or lonely husband, God knows

their problems better than anyone else. He can be depended upon to give the needed courage and strength and help if given the chance. The abandoned children need a father, yes; but they do not need a stepfather more than they need God. God will be doubly a Father to them. Surely He can be given credit for caring at least as much as we.

One practical conclusion that flows from all this is that a Catholic should never, in good conscience, keep company with a divorced person whose true wife or husband still lives. Such company-keeping is of itself ordinarily a grave sin, even though marriage is not intended. The occasion of sin, the danger of eventual involvement, is always present.

It may be well to repeat that the marriage of two non-Catholics, by civil magistrate or minister, is a true and valid marriage, a *permanent* union. The divorced non-Catholic may feel that he is free to marry, but God holds otherwise. The Catholic who keeps company with such a divorced person is, in effect, turning his back upon God.

Foresight Makes Happy Marriages

"I'm going to have to drive it a long time; I want to make sure I get a *good* car." How often we hear a man say that as he sets out to buy a new car. He doesn't impulsively buy the first car that catches his eye. He is not misled by glamorous appearance or flashy performance. He visits several showrooms, talks with salesmen, reads their literature. He discusses the various makes of cars with his friends and weighs their opinions. Gas mileage, riding comfort, ease of handling, cost of upkeep—it is these considerations, and not the quantity of chrome stripping, that finally determine his choice.

The same is true of the lucky woman who goes out to buy a fur coat. "I'll have to wear it the rest of my life," she says; "I don't want to make any mistake about this." She shops around carefully, tries on many coats, seeks advice, and finally buys the one that fits best, will wear best, and best suits her figure—for the money she can spend.

It is a sad but observable fact that people sometimes will exercise more care in choosing a car or a coat than they will exercise in choosing a husband or a wife; in spite of the fact that this is a lifelong, unbreakable union (for better or for worse) into which they are entering. More than that, it is a *vocation* which they are choosing, a state of life upon which will depend their own salvation and that of their children. Before pronouncing his vow of chastity and accepting a call to the priesthood, a young man will give several years of prayerful thought, under competent spiritual guidance, to the wisdom of his choice. Yet, in spite of the fact that the marriage vow is just as permanent and just as binding as the vow of celibacy, a young man or woman sometimes will enter into marriage after a few months (or even weeks) of acquaintance, with a partner whose sole recommendation is one of physical attraction. When the physical attraction burns itself out, there is nothing left but ashes—and long dreary years ahead.

For the wise person who feels that marriage is his or her vocation, what *are* some of the elementary steps in the choice of a life partner? A most basic precaution, obviously, is to choose a Catholic partner. A husband and wife who cannot kneel at the altar and the Communion rail together, who cannot live by a shared set of moral principles, who cannot pray the same prayers together with their children, begin their married life under a terrific handicap. And the only way for a person to make sure of marrying a Catholic is, of course, to have dates with none but Catholic companions. The problem of mixed marriages is as simple as that. If Catholic boys dated none but Catholic girls, and Catholic girls none but Catholic boys, how could there be any mixed marriages? The trap that catches many is the casual just-this-once date with a non-Catholic companion. "Oh, Mother, don't be silly. It isn't that serious. I don't have to marry him just because I go out with him once or twice!" The words sound familiar, do they not? The catch is that little by little it does become serious. The heart becomes deeply involved, and the head goes out the window. Another mixed marriage goes down in the parish register. "He's better than lots of Catholic boys I know" is the stubborn defense. That well may be; but then it isn't a good idea to marry a bad Catholic boy either.

The fundamental moral principle that governs all company-keeping, is that it is justified only so long as it is part of one's search for a partner in the sacrament of Matrimony. Close and frequent companionship between persons of the opposite sex poses moral dangers that are too real to excuse dating "just for fun," just for the sake of having a date. This does not mean that every boy will marry the first girl he goes with or that every girl will marry her first date. The whole purpose of courtship is to get well enough acquainted so that each party can reach an intelligent answer to the question: "Can I live happily and holily with this person in Christian marriage—forever?" Several may be weighed in the balance and discarded before the right one is found.

What the fundamental moral principle of company-keeping does mean is that no two people should go steadily together unless both are free, willing, and able to get married if they should decide to do so. This plainly rules out steady dating on the part of adolescents—a widespread evil in our present American culture. Youths of high school age cannot reasonably expect to marry for several years to come. To place themselves without justification in the proximate occasion of serious sin by "going steady" is, objectively, a grave sin. No Catholic boy is so strong, and no Catholic girl is so good, that some danger is not present.

Adolescence is, at best, a period of emotional conflict for most youths. They are in a no-man's-land, no longer children, not quite adults. They are torn between the desire for the independence of maturity and the reluctance to relinquish the security of childhood. They are troubled by the newly awakened feelings and urges of their glandular development. Parents who put added strain upon this emotional tension by encouraging or complacently accepting the steady dating of their children do the youngsters a great disservice. Mary and her Joe may look cute together; their romance may be "just too sweet for words"—but it still isn't good.

When it comes to marriage, Mother and Dad cannot do the choosing for their son or daughter. It is son or daughter who will have to live with the spouse they choose, and it is son or daughter who must make their own decision. However, unless Mother and Dad are complete morons, they have learned a lot about human nature during the course of years. At the age of forty or fifty they can penetrate beneath the surface of a shallow charm and spot a phony much more accurately than can a youth of twenty.

It is a wise young man (or woman) who talks things over with Dad and Mother before entering into a definite engagement for marriage. It is an *un*wise son or daughter who dismisses any parental expression of misgivings with a resentful, "Well, I like him (her); that's all that matters to me." Admittedly, parents can be prejudiced. It is hard for a father to admit that any fellow is good enough for his daughter; it is hard for a mother to think that any girl will take as good care of her son as she has. But, by and large, parents are aware of their own prejudices and do try to be objective in their judgments. More so, usually, than the young person who is in the grip of what seems to be love.

If parental bias does seem totally unreasonable, there is a disinterested third party to whom the prudent youth can readily turn for guidance—his pastor or his confessor. Indeed, in view of the fact that marriage is a life-vocation with such important and lasting consequences, it would seem mere good sense for *anyone* bent upon a happy marriage to talk it over with his or her confessor.

Through all this counsel-taking and decision-making there will run, for a genuinely Catholic youth, a continual vein of prayer. Parents can be mistaken, one's confessor can be mistaken, but God cannot be mistaken. Asking God for enlightenment in the making of such a serious choice and listening to God's answer in occasional quiet moments of meditation before the tabernacle would seem to be elementary steps in any courtship.

Frequent confession and Holy Communion will be a part of this program of prayer. With a happy marriage the hoped-for outcome, both partners in the courtship will want to do their utmost to deserve God's full blessing upon their eventual union. Even with the best of intentions, the close companionship of an engaged or steady-dating couple presents a danger to the virtue of chastity. In saying that, we are not casting reflections on the characters of good Catholic young men and women. We simply are admitting that fallen human nature is fallen human nature; it is only the fool who thinks that he or she has no breaking-point. For a dating couple, frequent confession and Holy Communion are the best safeguard against chiseling on God—the best guarantee against tarnishing the beauty and holiness of Matrimony by pre-marital liberties to which the couple have no right. The couple who seek a truly happy marriage will come to the altar secure in the knowledge that they have kept their desire for each other under the control of reason and grace. Only when they have effected their partnership with God in marriage will they seek that oneness-in-flesh which can be so noble an act when it is a part of God's creative plan and so irreverent a defiance of God when it is filched against His will.

Prudent counsel and prayer and pre-marital purity—with a Catholic partner. These are the foundation stones of a happy, lasting, and enriching marriage. They will be climaxed, if at all possible, by marriage at a Nuptial Mass. The Nuptial Mass is not the sacrament of Matrimony. The sacrament of Matrimony is received when the couple exchange their marital consent in the presence of the priest and two other witnesses. It still will be the sacrament of Matrimony even if the Nuptial Mass does not follow; even if *no* Mass follows.

However, no bride and groom who are seeking all the grace they can obtain for the fulfillment of their vocation will want to forego a Nuptial Mass. The Nuptial Mass is a special Mass with a very special blessing which the Church provides in her liturgy for those who are embarking upon the holy vocation of marriage. There is a special Mass of Ordination in the liturgy for the young man who is offering himself to God in the priesthood. There is a special Mass of Consecration for the offering of a new church edifice to God. It is not surprising, then, that there is a Nuptial Mass for the couple who are dedicating themselves to God as co-operators in His work of creation and redemption, as a little "church-within-a-church" in the Mystical Body of Christ. It is a measure of the importance which the Church attaches to the sacrament of Matrimony.

It can happen that a couple receive the sacrament of Matrimony at a time when they may not have a Nuptial Mass. For example, a couple might have some reason for wishing to be married during Lent or Advent. In such an instance, the couple should arrange to have a Nuptial Mass offered and to receive the nuptial blessing at some later date when it can be managed. Normally and ideally, the Nuptial Mass follows immediately upon the reception of the sacrament of Matrimony; but it does not have to.

A Catholic couple, both esteeming marriage as a vocation under God, receiving the sacrament of Matrimony after a chaste courtship in which prayer and the sacraments have kept God close, kneeling together to receive Holy Communion at their Nuptial Mass—there is a marriage upon which they, and all who love them, can pin their hopes.

CHAPTER XXXVI

The Sacramentals

Agents of Grace

The word "sacramental" looks very much like the word "sacrament." Indeed the word "sacramental" means "something like a sacrament." Yet there is a big difference in meaning between the two words. A sacrament is an outward sign instituted by Christ for the purpose of giving grace to souls. A sacramental also is an outward sign; but the sacramentals have been instituted by the Church and do not of themselves give grace. Rather, they *dispose* us for grace by arousing in us sentiments of faith and love which make a claim upon God for answering grace. Whatever grace we may obtain through the use of sacramentals comes to us because of our own interior dispositions and because of the power of the Church's prayers which back up the sacramentals.

This may be more clear if we examine one of the sacramentals most familiar to us: holy water. Holy water is plain tap water in which a little table salt has been mixed. The Church (through the priest) blesses first the salt and then the water, with a final blessing of the combined ingredients. In blessing the salt the Church prays that it "may bring health of soul and body to all who make use of [it], and . . . may put to flight and drive away from the places where [it is] sprinkled every apparition, villainy, and turn of devilish deceit, and every unclean spirit. . . ."

Over the water the Church prays that it may "become an agent of divine grace in the service of Thy mysteries, to drive away evil spirits and dispel sickness, so that everything in the homes and other buildings of the faithful that is sprinkled with this water may be rid of all uncleanness and freed from every harm. Let no breath of infection, no disease-bearing air, remain in these places. May the wiles of the lurking Enemy prove of no avail. Let whatever might menace the safety and peace of those who live here be put to flight by the sprinkling of this water, so that the healthfulness obtained by calling upon Thy holy name may be made secure against all attack."

Then, after the salt has been mixed with the water, the Church begs God "to look with favor on this salt and water which Thou hast created. Shine on it with the light of Thy kindness. Sanctify it by the dew of Thy love, so that, through the invocation of Thy holy name, wherever this water and salt is sprinkled it may turn aside every attack of the unclean spirit and dispel the terror of the poisonous serpent. And wherever we may be, make the Holy Spirit present to us who now implore Thy mercy."

And that is holy water. The Church has taken two common elements of man's daily life and has made them instruments of grace. Not *conveyers* of grace, not direct carriers of grace as are the sacraments. Only the personal power of Jesus Himself could do that. But with all the power that is hers as Christ's Mystical Body the Church speaks to God a covering plea for all those who will devoutly use this water blessed in Christ's name.

When we then use this holy water devoutly, we place

ourselves under this widespread prayer of the Church, like a child who seeks protection from the rain under the outspread umbrella of his mother. Our own interior faith in God's loving providence and our own interior acknowledgment of our complete dependence upon God are the personal dispositions which make the Church's prayer effective for us. That is the twofold source of grace which the sacramental occasions: the interior dispositions of the user, the prayer of the Church.

Some sacramentals are *things*, and some are *actions*. Besides holy water there are many things which the Church blesses and by her blessing sets aside to be used for religious purposes. Included is the wide range of things which we call objects or articles of devotion: candles, ashes, palms, crucifixes, medals, Rosaries, scapulars, images of our Lord, the Blessed Mother, and the saints.

Sacramentals which are *actions* are the various blessings and exorcisms which the Church imparts through her bishops and priests. Some of these blessings are of a dedicatory nature, as when the Church blesses a chalice, an altar, Mass vestments, or some other thing that is to be set aside and used exclusively for divine worship. Other blessings are simply invocative, bespeaking God's bounty and protection in regard to the thing or person which is blessed, such as the blessing of a home, of an automobile, of fields and crops, of infants, and of the sick. Few people know how many blessings the Church has provided in her armory of sacramentals. There is a blessing—which means an official prayer with all the power of Christ-in-His-Church behind it—for almost every major need or tool of human living.

A very special kind of sacramental action is an exorcism, in which the Church, in Christ's name, commands the devil to leave the body of a person of whom he has taken possession. Before Jesus died upon the Cross, Satan's power over man and nature was much greater than it is now. That is why diabolical possession was much more common before

Calvary than it is now. By His death Jesus redeemed man and broke the dominion of Satan. It is rarely—and for good reasons of His own—that God now permits diabolical possession.

That is why the Church, before allowing an official exorcism, is very careful to determine that it is a real case of possession and not just a mental disturbance. Only a priest appointed by the bishop may perform such an exorcism solemnly, and then only after a period of fasting and prayer in preparation for the attack upon the Father of Lies. When such an exorcism does take place we seldom hear of it, as the Church insists on complete secrecy on the part of all who are involved in it.

The sacramentals most commonly used in a Catholic home are the crucifix, holy water, and blessed candles. The sacramental most commonly used on the person is the Carmelite scapular—or its replacement, a scapular medal.

In the homes of Catholics who strive to make their faith a vital force in their lives, the crucifix holds a prominent place. It hangs upon the wall or stands upon the mantel of the principal room of the house; its replica also may be found in the bedrooms. The value of the crucifix as an aid to prayer and to Christian living is obvious. There is no symbol which so vividly reminds us of the infinite love of God for man as does the image of God's own Son skewered to the cross that we might have eternal life. Nothing could better move us to sorrow for our sins than this visual presentation of Jesus paying the price of our sins. Nothing could better buoy us up in our daily trials and discouragements than this image of the agonized Christ giving meaning and value to suffering.

In a font that hangs just inside the bedroom door or in a sprinkler bottle upon the dresser, there will be holy water also, in a Catholic home. The significance of water—the universal cleanser—as a symbol of the purifying power of God's grace needs no elaboration. The value of holy water as a sacramental has been discussed already. It is rather surprising that more Catholics are not to be seen of a Sunday morning filling their bottles with holy water from the container that is to be found in the rear of most churches.

The Catholic home will possess two blessed candles tucked away in an easily accessible drawer. Better still, perhaps they stand in candlesticks flanking a crucifix upon a chest or mantel. The use of lamps or candles as accessories to religious worship seems to have been a universal practice in man's history. Even among pagans, and of course among the ancient Jews by God's own designation, candles played an important part in religious ceremonies. In the early Christian Church, candles or other lights were a necessity, as the Holy Sacrifice was offered in the pre-dawn darkness or in the blackness of the catacombs. It is not surprising that the connotation of the candle as a symbol of Christ the Light of the world, who "has visited us, to shine on those who sit in darkness and in the shadow of death, to guide our feet into the way of peace" (Luke 1:78–79), should have impressed the imaginations of the early Christians.

The Church very soon sanctified this symbolism by definitely prescribing the use of candles in divine worship: they must burn at Mass, in the administration of most of the sacraments, and at many other religious ceremonies. If a priest brings Holy Communion to a sick person, Christ the Light of the world meets Christ in the Eucharist at the door, and candles burn upon the bedside table. Blessed candles may burn beside the crucifix as the household kneels for family night prayers or the family Rosary. Blessed candles may be lit in times of severe storms or deep trouble as a reminder of God's providence and as an act of faith in His loving care. On baptismal anniversaries the candles may burn upon the supper table as a reminder of the light of faith which was enkindled at the baptismal font for the one who celebrates. There are many reasons why blessed candles are to be found in Catholic homes.

With the possible exception of blessed Rosary beads, the *personal* sacramental most used by individuals is the Carmelite scapular. This consists of two rectangular pieces of brown woolen cloth (the sewed-on pictures are not essential) connected by two strings or ribbons and worn over the shoulders. Most of us were enrolled in the brown scapular at the time of our first Holy Communion—probably without much understanding of what it was all about.

The custom of wearing scapulars goes back to the Middle Ages. At that time lay people frequently were allowed to join the religious Orders as "oblates" or associate members. These oblates shared in the prayers and good works of the monks and were allowed to wear the monastic scapular. The monastic scapular (from the Latin word "scapula," meaning "shoulder blade") is a long panel of cloth which slips over the monk's head and hangs down, front and back, over his tunic. For the sake of convenience, the scapulars worn by lay members of the religious Orders gradually were made smaller and smaller, until they developed to the irreducible minimum of today's scapulars.

There are eighteen different kinds of small scapulars in use among Catholics today, each stemming from a different religious Order. However, the brown scapular of the Carmelite Order, whose special patroness is Our Lady of Mount Carmel, is the one most commonly worn. The popularity of the brown scapular is due partly to a vision ascribed to St. Simon Stock, thirteenth-century Superior General of the Carmelite Order. Our Blessed Mother is said to have promised St. Simon that no one who died clothed with her scapular would die in the state of mortal sin.

St. Simon's vision is a pious tradition and not a matter of faith, not something which we have to believe. But whether the vision is authentic or not, we must remember that many Popes have encouraged and have indulgenced the wearing of the brown scapular as an act of devotion to our Blessed Mother; we thereby place ourselves under her motherly protection; and those who have been properly enrolled do share in the Masses, prayers, and good works of the Carmelite Order. Once enrolled in the scapular, it is permissible to substitute for it a scapular medal which is worn or borne constantly upon the person, a badge and a reminder of one's dedication to the Mother of God.

CHAPTER XXXVII

Prayer

The What and Why of Prayer

Perhaps not often enough do we think of the great privilege that is ours in being able to speak with God in prayer. It is rather horrible to try to imagine what life would be like if God had chosen to wrap Himself in the mantle of His majesty, leaving man to shift for himself. If there were no intercommunication between us and God, we would be like rudderless and radioless ships adrift in the middle of the ocean; without direction, without guidance, without hope.

Prayer is defined as "the lifting up of our minds and hearts to God." We lift our minds to God when we direct our attention to God, just as we direct our attention to any person we are addressing when we have something important to say and are eager to get our message across; just as we focus our attention on any person who has something important to tell us, whose meaning we do not want to miss. We raise our hearts to God when we let our will go out in an act of love to God; much as a husband, watching over

535

the top of his newspaper as his wife feeds the baby, lets his will go out in an act of love (perhaps unspoken) to both of them.

The need for prayer (and without prayer there is no salvation) is rooted in man's very nature as a creature of God and as the recipient of His bounty. God made us, body and soul. We belong to Him one hundred percent. Every good thing that comes to us has its source in God; we depend upon Him for the very air we breathe.

Because of this relationship to God, we *owe* God the duty of prayer. Prayer is an act of justice, not merely an act of piety. Prayer is a debt that we must pay, not merely a graceful gesture that we choose to make.

First of all, we must acknowledge God's infinite majesty, His supreme dominion as the Lord and Master of all creation. This is the first and most essential purpose of prayer. Adequate adoration of the Godhead was the first intention in the mind of Jesus Christ as He offered Himself upon the Cross; as it was the first intention to be expressed in His own prayer: "Hallowed be Thy name." This must be the first intention in our prayers too.

We also must acknowledge God's infinite goodness by thanking Him for the innumerable favors and benefits He has bestowed on us. For every grace in our lives that we consciously recognize as coming from God, there are ten thousand others that we shall not know about until, in eternity, we see God's total plan for us. We are like little children who recognize their mother's love when she feeds their hunger and binds their wounds; and recognize their father's love when he gives presents and plays with them on the floor; but are totally unaware of all the precautions and the safeguards, the foresight and the planning, the worry and the sacrifices that are lavished upon these little unobservant imps. So we owe God gratitude, more for the gifts we do not know about than for the ones we can recognize. This is the second purpose of prayer.

Since we are God's very own, down to the last fractional inch of us, we owe God our complete and absolute loyalty. We are the work of His hands even more than a watch is the work of its maker. There is nothing that He has not the right to ask of us. If we choose to disobey God, the malice of our act is far greater than that of the most un-natural son who would raise his hand against a loving and sacrificing mother. If the angels had bodies, surely they would shudder to behold the depth of ingratitude involved in sin. It follows, then, that the third purpose of prayer must be to acknowledge our sinfulness, to beg God's pardon for our rebellions, and to make atonement (here rather than hereafter) for the debt of punishment that we have incurred.

In the last place—and only in the last place—the purpose of prayer is to ask God for the graces and favors we need, for ourselves and for others. If we ignore the three other purposes of prayer and see prayer only as a means of twisting God's arm for what we want, then our prayer will hardly be prayer at all. We need not be surprised if it falls back to earth like a misfired rocket without reaching its destination. It is true that a prayer of petition is better than no prayer at all. There is in it at least a minimum of adoration, since by it we do acknowledge that good things come from God. However, if all our prayers were of the "give-me" type, we should fail sadly in our duty to God.

When we offer prayers of petition, asking God for our needs, we are not of course telling God something that He does not already know. God knows what we need far better than we know it ourselves; He has known all our needs from all eternity. A prayer of petition for ourselves focuses our attention on our own necessity and keeps alive our aware-ness of God's goodness; in prayer of petition for others, we are given opportunity for limitless acts of charity. It is for these reasons, and not to jog His own memory, that God wants us to offer prayers of petition. God knows what we want, but He wants us to know it too; and He wants us to care enough to ask.

Adoration, thanksgiving, repentance and petition: these are the four purposes of prayer.

It might be observed that when we pray to our Blessed Mother and the saints we really are adoring God. We are honoring God by honoring these, His mother and His most beloved friends. We are praising God in reverencing these masterpieces of God's grace. We are pleasing God when we beg the intercession of these fellow members, now triumphant in heaven, of the Mystical Body of Christ. It is God's will that we *should* acknowledge our oneness in Christ our Head, that we should acknowledge our interdependence one upon another here upon earth and our dependence upon our Mother and our brethren in heaven.

We are not angels. We are creatures composed of a spiritual soul and a physical body. It is this *whole* man—body and soul—which owes adoration to God. As we might expect, then, the basic form of prayer is that which we call *vocal* prayer, in which mind and heart and vocal organs unite in offering to God the praise, thanksgiving, repentance, and petition which are His due.

Vocal prayers need not be *audible* prayer. We may, and often do, pray silently, but moving our lips and tongue as when we recite the Rosary privately. But if we make use of words as we pray, even though we speak the words silently, our prayer still is classed as vocal prayer. Sometimes, too, actions may take the place of words in prayer. A reverent genuflection to Jesus in the Blessed Sacrament, for example, or a wordless sign of the cross, or an inclination of the head at the sound of the Holy Name: such bodily gestures as these are prayer by action and are classified as vocal prayer even though no word is spoken.

Vocal prayer must necessarily be audible prayer when a group prays together. God did not make humans as solitary individuals to live in independent seclusion one from the other. He made us to be *social* beings, members of a group mutually dependent one upon the other: members first of the family group and then of the larger group composed of many families, the community.

Group prayer (sometimes called corporate prayer) is especially pleasing to God. From man's beginning, group prayer has been expressive of our oneness in God, of the bond of fraternal charity which should unite all men of good will. For Catholics corporate prayer has the added significance of our oneness in the Mystical Body of Christ. This is a unity which gives to our group prayer far more power than the mere sum of the prayers of the individuals in the group. The prayer of the group is in a special sense the prayer of Christ: "For where two or three are gathered together for My sake, there am I in the midst of them," says Jesus (Matt. 18:20). That is why the prayers of a family praying together, or of a congregation praying together, are so effective with God, so pleasing to God.

Many corporate prayers such as the Rosary or novena prayers recited in common are the prayers of an unofficial group and are classified as private prayers. However, when Christ's Mystical Body, His Church, officially prays in His name for all His members, we call that *liturgical* prayer. The Mass is a liturgical prayer. The Divine Office, which a priest is obliged to recite daily, is a liturgical prayer. The sacraments and the consecrations and official blessings imparted by the Church—all these are liturgical prayers. Liturgical prayer is always group prayer, even when only one person seems to be involved—for example, the priest reciting the Divine Office—because in liturgical prayer it is the whole Church which prays. It is Christ in His Mystical Body (including you and me) who prays, even though He may be praying through a single designated individual.

Besides vocal prayer there is a higher form of prayer which we call *mental* prayer. The most widely used form of mental prayer is termed *meditation*. In mental prayer, as the name suggests, the mind and heart do all the work, without benefit of vocal organs and without use of words. It is not the same as silent vocal prayer, in which words still play a part. We might say that the essence of mental prayer lies in this: that we let God talk to us, instead of ourselves talking to God as we do in vocal prayer.

In the form of mental prayer known as meditation, we simply meditate on (that is, think about or "chew over") some truth of faith, or incident in the life of Christ or of His saints. We do so, not to increase our knowledge (that would be study) but to increase our faith and hope and love, trying to apply to ourselves in a practical way the truth or the incident upon which we meditate. The New Testament is an ideal source book for meditation, although almost any good spiritual book will provide the springboard we need for our thoughts. We all practice some degree of mental prayer, as when we meditate on the mysteries of the Rosary or on the sufferings of Jesus in the Way of the Cross. But for real growth in holiness and for the guidance from God which all of us need, we should try to give some time each day to formal meditation; perhaps fifteen or twenty minutes in the privacy and quiet of our bedroom.

Beyond meditation there is a still higher form of mental prayer: the prayer of contemplation. In contemplation the mind ceases its activity and simply fixes itself upon God in an act of love, content to gaze upon God, as it were, in His infinite lovableness; leaving it to God to do whatever work is to be done in the soul. If you think that this type of prayer is beyond your reach, just think back to the last time you knelt or sat in church, just gazing at the tabernacle with a quiet mind. Without any words or effort at ordered thought, you experienced a feeling of peace, refreshment, and renewed strength. You were practicing the prayer of contemplation.

The truth is, most of us talk too much *to* God; we don't give God enough chance to talk to us.

Prayer That Reaches God

Not many of us have had the privilege of a personal interview with the President of the United States or the privilege of a private audience with the Holy Father. But it is not hard for us to imagine how attentive we should be under such circumstances; attentive to the words which we ourselves would speak, attentive to each word spoken by the distinguished personage. It hardly needs emphasizing, then, that in addressing the infinitely august Personage who is God, attention to what we are doing is the first requisite if our prayer is to be more than a sham.

There is no spiritual magic in mere words, no matter how lengthily the words may be multiplied. In introducing His own prayer, the Our Father, Jesus said: "But in praying, do not multiply words, as the Gentiles do; for they think that by saying a great deal, they will be heard. So do not be like them" (Matt. 6:7–8). Our Lord is not discouraging quantity in prayer, but He is condemning quantity at the expense of quality. One decade of the Rosary devoutly prayed will count more with God than five decades rattled off in thoughtless haste. It is possible to have a compulsive neurosis in the matter of prayer, to feel that certain prayers and a certain number of prayers *must* be got through, even when the available time does not permit their recitation with attention and devotion.

So we begin our prayers by directing our attention to God, by forming in our mind the intention of praying well and of keeping our mind fixed, if not on the words we say, at least on Him to whom they are addressed. It is important to begin with this intention because, unless we are in a rare spiritual mood, our mind will wander before we have progressed very far. Prayer is hard work. The human mind does not take kindly to intense concentration. The difficulty of continuous attention is doubled if our mind is troubled by worry or anxiety or weakened by illness or lack of rest. And of course we may expect that Satan will be doing his best to direct our attention elsewhere as we try to pray.

None of this need trouble us, however, if we have begun with a sincere purpose of being attentive and if we reach out to bring our wandering mind back to its task whenever we catch it in its act of vagrancy. It is only when our distractions are voluntary, stemming from a careless distinterest in what we are doing, that our prayer ceases to be prayer. God asks of us only that we do our best. He knows our difficulties and does not hold us accountable for what we cannot help.

Indeed, the more we are bothered by involuntary distractions, the more pleasing to God is our prayer because of the greater effort involved. A difficult deed done for God always is more meritorious than the same deed done easily. This, incidentally, is also the answer to a person who excuses himself from prayer on the score that he doesn't *feel* like praying, doesn't feel in the mood. The less one feels like praying, the more pleasing to God will be the prayer that is offered under such a handicap. Prayer must not depend upon our mood. It is a duty we owe to God, not an occupation indulged in for our own pleasure.

Besides the effort to pray with attention, we must bring to prayer a spirit of humility, a consciousness of our complete dependence upon God, of our utter helplessness without Him. Prayer and pride are mutually exclusive terms; they cannot co-exist. Prayer comes very hard to the proud person who feels himself to be self-sufficient and in need of no one's help. To bow the head and bend the knee and acknowledge his own nothingness in God's sight is painful to such a one. In this fact we find one of the reasons why pride so often leads to loss of faith.

In prayer of petition a third requirement is that we have a genuine and deep desire for the graces we beg of God. It is to be feared that we sometimes ask for graces out of a sense of duty, without really wanting the graces we ask for. Our prayer in such an instance is merely a sop to our own conscience and is not really prayer at all. Thus the bibulous man may pray for the grace of temperance without really wanting, in his heart, to abandon his excess. The unchaste youth may pray for chastity without really wanting to give up his deviations, or—what amounts to the same thing—without doing his part by avoiding the occasions of sin. We have no right to ask God for grace if we are not willing to do our part, at least to remove the obstacles that may hinder the operation of grace.

As a final example, we cite the person who might pray for an increase in charity without really wanting to give up the pleasure of malicious gossip, without really wanting to make peace with "that impossible person" in the office, without really wanting to see the Negro as a brother under God.

Along with pride (to which it is allied), lack of charity interposes a tremendous obstacle to fruitfulness in all prayer. We cannot expect our prayers to find favor in God's sight if we look with disfavor and disdain upon any soul which God has made, any soul for which Christ has died. A prayer that is weighted down by habitual uncharitableness has little chance of reaching God.

In catechism class a priest once asked a child, "Does God always answer our prayers?" "Yes, Father," the youngster answered. "Then why don't we always get what we pray for?" the priest continued. After a puzzled moment the child replied, "God always answers our prayers, but sometimes He answers yes and sometimes He answers no."

The young theologian deserved an "A" for effort, but his answer was incomplete. God never answers a prayer—a *real* prayer—with a simple no. Sometimes God answers, "No, not what you ask for; it would hinder rather than help you towards heaven. I shall give you something else, something much better, in place of what you ask for." Even ordinary human wisdom follows this pattern. If three-year-old Tommie is suddenly struck by the beauty of the shiny fork in his mother's hand and begs to play with it, mother will not give Tommie the fork, however much he may beg. But if she is a wise mother, she does not simply say no. She gives Tommie a mixing spoon to play with, or an old pan to pound on. At the moment Tommie may feel cheated, but he would bless his mother if he understood.

Sometimes we humans pray for things which we are so sure would be good for us: a better job, or better health, or the blessing of a baby in the home. Yet God may know otherwise. In His infinite knowledge He sees the effect, upon ourselves and upon others, of every least change in our circumstances. A better job now may mean eventually a decline in virtue. Better health may mean a loss of much needed merit which now is being gained by sufferings patiently borne for ourselves or others. A child in this particular home may one day mean the loss of a soul. Whatever it is that we ask for, God will not give it unless it in some way works to our true advantage, unless it contributes to (or at least will not detract from) the destiny for which God made us: eternal happiness with Himself in heaven.

This is true even of spiritual favors for which we pray. I may be tormented by fierce temptations of one kind or another, temptations which seem to put me in danger of sinning any minute and which sap my spiritual energy. "Oh," I think, "if only I could be relieved of these temptations and find interior peace, how much better I could pray, how much better I could practice my faith!" And so I beg God for the grace of chastity or temperance or patience or charitableness. But in God's plan my way to sanctity and to heaven is over the rough path of day-by-day struggle and conquest. I pray for deliverance from temptation, and in answer I simply get the grace I need to meet the next temptation that comes along.

This was St. Paul's experience; we need not be surprised if it is ours. "There was given me a thorn for the flesh," St.

Paul tells us (2 Cor. 12:7–9), "a messenger of Satan to buffet me. Concerning this I thrice besought the Lord that it might leave me. And He has said to me, 'My grace is sufficient for thee, for strength is made perfect in weakness.' Gladly therefore I will glory in my infirmities, that the strength of Christ may dwell in me." If we cannot glory gladly in our infirmities, it may be God's will at least that we bear with our weakness patiently to the end.

We come then to the fourth quality which must characterize real prayer. We must pray not only with attention, with a sense of our own helplessness and dependence upon God, with a genuine desire for what we ask of Him; we also must pray with a loving trust in God's goodness. This means to pray with a childlike confidence that God hears us and that He will answer us. With this confidence is combined a complete submission to God's superior wisdom. He loves us and wants what is best for us. If what we ask is unwise, we are quite willing to leave the choice of a substitute to Him. *But we do believe that He hears and that He will answer*. If we do not believe that with all our heart, then our prayer is not prayer at all.

There is only one kind of prayer that we can offer unconditionally. That is when we pray that we may get to heaven and for the grace we need in order to get there. When this is the burden of our prayer, we know absolutely that what we want also is what God wants. His will and our will are coinciding. Our prayer in this instance certainly will be answered, provided that it possesses the fifth and last quality which prayer must have: perseverance. The man who never quits praying for grace and salvation is the man who is certain to go to heaven.

Perseverance is essential to all prayer. We shall not grow discouraged if we remember that whatever God does He does in His own way and in His own best time. We may be praying for the repentance or conversion of someone dear to us. We are tempted to discouragement because we see no sign of change in the person. Then we remember that it is the person's salvation that is the basic thing, not necessarily an outward conversion that will give comfort to us. If God chooses to answer our prayer by giving the person the grace to make an act of perfect contrition in the last moment of his life—well, God's will be done. Even though, regarding our prayers for others, God has not given us the same assurance of infallible efficacy that He has given concerning our prayers for ourselves, our confidence should endure.

Indeed, not until we reach heaven and then know all that God has done shall we be aware of all the gifts and graces that have come to us in response to prayers which, at the time, seemed to go unanswered. Sometimes we can see the substitute answer here and now; quite often, not.

For Whom Shall I Pray?

First and before all, I shall pray for myself, for the grace to live and die in the state of grace. Does that sound selfish? It isn't. It is the *right* kind of self-love, the kind of self-love God wants us to have. Under God each of us is the keeper of his own soul, with the primary responsibility of achieving the eternal union with Himself for which God made us. If we fail in that responsibility, we have failed in everything. All other petitions fade into insignificance compared to the importance of our prayer for a happy death—for "the grace of final perseverance," as it is called. No day should begin without some such plea as this: "Give me, O God, the graces I need to do Your will here and to be happy with You hereafter."

Allied to our prayer for a happy death should be the intention of accepting our death from the hand of God with complete resignation. In *The Raccolta* (the Church's official book of indulgenced prayers), we read: "The faithful who at any time in their lives, from a sincere spirit of love of God and with at least a contrite heart, express their intention of accepting calmly and gladly from the hand of God whatsoever manner of death it may please Him to send them, together with all its pain, anguish and suffering, may gain: an indulgence of 7 years; a plenary indulgence at the hour of death, if they have made such an act at least once in their lifetime, after having fulfilled the usual conditions" (confession, Holy Communion, visit to a church or public chapel, prayer for the Holy Father). If we have not already done this, let us do it now.

The right kind of self-love—the urgent desire to live and die in the grace of God—also is the measure of our love for our neighbor: "Love thy neighbor as thyself." Consequently, prayers for the spiritual welfare of one's neighbor take precedence over prays for temporal favors for self. Jesus already has answered the question, "Who is my neighbor?" My neighbor is anyone in need whom I can help. In matters spiritual, that embraces the entire world—and the souls in purgatory.

There are, however, varying degrees of obligation to be considered in my prayers for my neighbors. Our first duty is to those closest to us; spouses must pray for each other, parents for their children, children for their parents and for each other. Another step removed, we must pray for our relatives and our friends—and very especially for our enemies if we have any. Gratitude dictates that we pray for our benefactors, particularly for our spiritual benefactors: our Holy Father the Pope, our bishop, our pastor, and other priests of the parish. In our effort to pray according to the mind of Christ, we shall pray for His Church, for all bishops, priests and religious, through whom Christ's work on earth must be done.

We shall pray for our country and for the officials who govern it, that they may direct wisely our nation's destiny in accordance with God's will. We shall pray (if our conscience is at all sensitive) for all who may have suffered any harm at our hands, especially for those who may have suffered spiritually through our bad example, our neglect, or our failure in charity. "Dear God, let no soul suffer or be lost through any fault of mine," is an orison that should rank high on our list. And of course we shall pray for the souls in purgatory, our neighbors who have to depend upon us so completely in their sufferings.

Perhaps we even may have sufficient generosity of heart to make the Heroic Act of Charity. The Heroic Act of Charity consists in offering to God in favor of the souls in purgatory all the indulgences we may gain and all the satisfactory works we may perform during our own lifetime, as well as all the indulgences that may be gained and all the prayers and satisfactory works offered for us by others after our death. It is the grand act of love for the suffering souls. For their sake we are willing to go into eternity naked and empty-handed and abandon ourselves completely to the mercy— and the justice—of God. It is easy to see why this is called the Heroic Act of Charity.

This does not, of course, deprive us of the cleansing grace of the Sacrament of Extreme Unction, nor indeed of any graces which we receive during life. Grace is a personal gift of God which cannot be transferred to another. It is only the satisfactory value, the atoning value of our prayers and good works (and of those of others for us), that we surrender to the suffering souls. But that is a lot.

A person who has made the Heroic Act may gain a plenary indulgence (applicable only to the souls in purgatory) every time he receives Holy Communion, provided he has fulfilled the other conditions of confession, visit to a church or public oratory, and prayer for the Pope. He may gain a similar plenary indulgence on any Monday of the year when he assists at Holy Mass and offers the Mass for the holy souls, if he fulfills the usual conditions. No special formula is prescribed for the making of the Heroic Act. It is enough simply to tell God that we do offer for the souls in purgatory all the indulgences we may gain and all the satisfactory works we may perform, as well as those that shall be offered for us after death, and to keep the intention fresh in our mind by renewing it from time to time.

There are so many to pray for. Missionaries, sinners and unbelievers, besides all the others we've mentioned. A practical suggestion is to write down on a card or sheet of paper a list of all the people for whom we wish to pray and cast a quick eye over it each morning at the time of our morning prayers. If caught short, "For all on my list," will suffice.

Tom and his wife, so the story goes, were returning home from shopping. As they passed a church the wife suggested, "Tom, let's stop in and make a visit." "What's the use?" Tom answered. "We haven't got our prayer books."

It doesn't sound like a true story, admittedly. It seems hardly possible that any adult Catholic would be so naïve as to think that he could not talk to God in his own words. Some of our best prayers, we know, are those that pour out of our hearts spontaneously to God, without any thought as to the niceties of rhetoric. In fact some of our very best praying is done when we use no words at all but just fix our minds upon God with loving attention and invite God to talk to us.

But there are some basic prayers that we ought to know by heart. When we kneel in the morning, still half-drugged with sleep, it is good to be able to speak familiar words that rise easily to our lips. At nighttime, too, we often are grateful for memorized prayers that put little strain on a tired brain. Likewise, when driving the car or working at some monotonous task, remembered prayers can be repeated and still leave a bit of the mind attentive to the job in hand.

In such instances, freed from the necessity of thinking how to say it, we can give our attention to the meaning of what we say. However, it should be noted that even when we make use of memorized prayers it is not essential that we advert to the actual meaning of all the words we use. We have enlisted our vocal organs in the service of God but it suffices for good prayer if our conscious mind simply directs itself to God with sentiments of faith and trust and love.

The basic prayers which should be standard equipment for every Catholic are the Our Father, the Hail Mary, the Apostles' Creed, the Confiteor, the Glory be to the Father, and the Acts of Faith, Hope, Love, and Contrition.

The Our Father is the perfectly formulated prayer, given to us by Jesus Himself when His disciples asked Him, "Lord, teach us to pray." The greater part of the Hail Mary also comes from the inspired pages of the Gospels; we cannot better address Mary than in the words with which God Himself addressed her, through the archangel Gabriel and St. Elizabeth.

The Apostles' Creed, in which we renew our allegiance to the principal mysteries of our Christian faith, goes back to the Church's beginnings and is one of the most ancient of our prayers. The Confiteor, in which we at one and the same time confess our sinfulness and beg the intercession of all the angels and saints, is a prayer which the Church uses often in her liturgy, notably as a preparation for Mass and for Holy Communion; it is a good prayer for us at any time. The value of the Glory be to the Father as a simple prayer of praise and adoration of the Most Blessed Trinity is evident. Evident also is the need to exercise, through the recitation of the Acts of Faith, Hope, and Love, the three divine virtues which were infused into our soul at Baptism. The Act of Contrition we also need, to make explicit our sorrow for our sins and our desire for God's forgiveness.

Since nothing that we do has any eternal significance unless God is working with us, it is customary for us to begin and end our prayers with the sign of the cross. The sign of the cross is both an appeal to God to make our prayers worth while and an act of faith in two of the most important truths of the Christian religion: the Blessed Trinity and the Redemption. When we say, "In the name of" (singular, not plural), we express our belief in the oneness of God. When we say, "the Father, and of the Son, and of the Holy Ghost," we state our faith in the fact that in the one God there are three Divine Persons. And as we trace a cross from forehead to breast and from shoulder to shoulder, we signify our conviction that by His death on the cross Jesus Christ has redeemed mankind.

We learned as children in catechism class that we ought to pray in the morning when we get up and at night before we go to bed, before and after our meals, and in time of temptation. Morning and night and mealtimes are good memory helps, pegs, we might say, upon which to hang our prayer-duty.

However, the real answer to the question, "When should we pray?" is, "Always." Jesus Himself gave us that answer ("And He told . . . them . . . that they must always pray and not lose heart"—Luke 18:1) and the apostles in their Epistles have repeated that answer. We pray always when we dedicate our every moment to God and to the doing of His will. No day should begin without an offering of our day to God.

It can be in our own words: "O my God, all that I do, say, think, and suffer today I want to do, say, think, and suffer for love of You." Then must follow an attempt to make our day acceptable to God, a real effort to identify our will with His. Perhaps during the day we can occasionally renew our morning offering, especially in moments of stress. Just a reminder to ourselves, "This is for God," will ease some rather heavy burdens.

It is not a sin to miss our morning prayers. But we lose—and lose more than we ever can regain—if we start our day without having offered it to God.

CHAPTER XXXVIII

The Our Father

The Best Prayer

If we want to learn to do something well, we ask—if we can—an expert's advice. It was with commendable wisdom, then, that one of His disciples asked Jesus, "Lord, teach us to pray." Christ's answer to that request was made not just to the disciple but to all mankind, to you and to me. His answer was the prayer which we commonly call the Our Father, as found in its entirety in the sixth chapter of St. Matthew's Gospel.

The Our Father rightly is called the Lord's Prayer. It is given to us by our Lord Himself, who is God. Who should know better than God the kind of prayer God wants us to address to Him? It is no wonder that the Church makes such constant use of the Lord's Prayer, both in the Mass and in other liturgical rites. It is no wonder that the Lord's Prayer is the favorite of Christians everywhere. Because we use it so often, it is important that we understand the richness of meaning in the words that we say.

"Our Father," we begin, "who art in heaven." In these

few words there are encapsuled a whole complex of thoughts and sentiments. There is the awesome privilege of being able to address so familiarly as Father the infinitely great and holy God, the Lord of all creation. There is the thought of His love for us, for each of us individually. Out of His love for me He made me—because from all eternity He loved the image of me in His divine mind and wanted me with Him in heaven. There is His love for me by which He united me to Himself through sanctifying grace and made me not merely His servant but His beloved child.

There is His love for me which moves Him to watch over me ceaselessly, going before me and following after me with His grace, trying by every means possible—short of taking away my freedom—to bring me safely to Himself in heaven. Sometimes we forget how *personal* is God's interest in us. We let ourselves unconsciously fall into human ways of thinking about God. There are more than two and a half billion people on earth; God's attention to me (we may let ourselves feel) is bound to be somewhat divided, spread pretty thin. In feeling so, we have let ourselves forget that God is infinite, that numbers mean nothing to Him. Even if I were the only person on the whole earth, God could not be more intensely and lovingly attentive to me than He is right now. It is of this that I remind myself as I say, "Our Father who art in heaven."

The word "Our" is an important word, too. The Lord's Prayer is a prayer of perfect charity: of love for God, to whom we offer ourselves unreservedly; of love for our fellow men, for whom we beseech the same graces and favors which we ask for ourselves. It is a prayer of Christian unity, of oneness-under-God, a prayer whose recurring theme of "our" and "we" and "us" reminds us that this is not a prayer to be said with a selfish heart.

"Hallowed be Thy name," we continue, as we perform the primary duty of all prayer: the adoration and praise of God. The whole purpose of our existence is that we may give

glory to God as the work of His hands and as living testi-
monies to His goodness and His mercy and His power. To
the mute voice of inanimate nature which gives glory to
God by its very existence we add the more noble praise of
free hearts and tongues. There is more than an echo here
of the song of the angels on Christmas night: "Glory to God
in the highest!"

Yet we are not content with the praise that God is receiving. In our love for Him we shall not be content until all
men everywhere shall be His faithful subjects and shall join
in a universal and everlasting paean. So we pray, "Thy kingdom come." We pray that God's grace may find its way into
the hearts of all men, to establish there His dominion of love.
We pray that Christ's words may be realized: that "there
shall be one fold and one shepherd"; that Christ's visible
kingdom on earth, His Church, may become the haven of
all mankind. We pray, too, for the advent of His kingdom in
heaven; that we and all for whom Jesus died may reign with
Him there in His eternal glory. The hearts and hands of
missionaries all over the world are fortified as millions of us
daily pray, "Thy kingdom come!"

"Thy will be done on earth, as it is in heaven." May everyone everywhere on the face of this earth obey Thee as willingly and joyfully, O God, as do the angels and saints in
heaven. These are such easy words to say, especially when it
is the other fellow's complete obedience to God that we
pray for. But to put the words into action in the life of the
one person we can most directly control—ourselves—may
take some doing. Obviously, the words "Thy will be done"
are pointless unless we really mean them. Making the words
effective in our own personal life will mean an end to mur-
murings, complaints, and self-pity. It will mean a mental
throwing back of the shoulders and a chin-up approach to
each day and the inevitable annoyances and disappointments
which so often catch us off balance. "Thy will be done"
means for me, "Whatever You want, God, I want too, no

matter how much it may hurt; I'll trust to Your grace to see me through."

The Lord's Prayer has begun by focusing, as every good prayer should, upon what is due to God: His glory and praise—His glory especially through man's doing His will. Now, and only now, do we turn to our own needs.

Good parents know the needs of their children for food, clothing, shelter, toys, books, picnics, and all the rest. Nevertheless, parents are pleased when a child acknowledges the source of what comes to him so easily. Parents are pleased when a child asks for something, even though it is something which he already is slated to get. In this parents do but reflect the paternal love of God of which they are agents and the human exemplars.

It is no surprise to us, then, that the second part of the Lord's Prayer concerns itself with the needs of the one who prays. And with what beautiful simplicity does Jesus phrase it! Left to ourselves we could so easily jabber on endlessly, "Please, God, give us enough food and decent clothes and a comfortable house and a reasonably good car and good health and success in our work and new glasses and bridge-work and a pleasant vacation and . . . oh, yes, the graces we need to lead good lives and especially to overcome this confounded temper of mine and. . . ."

It could develop into quite a long litany. But Jesus calmly cuts right across the whole of it and compresses it all into seven words, "Give us this day our daily bread." The word "bread" here is symbolic of all our needs, spiritual as well as physical. We can add our own personal litany if we will. Our detailed list will be a continuing acknowledgment of our dependence upon God and will be pleasing to Him as a consequence. But when we say, "Give us this day our daily bread," we really have said it all.

The word "daily" is a key word here, underscored by "this day." It is as though Jesus wanted us to remember, every time we recite the Our Father, that beautiful passage from His Sermon on the Mount: "Therefore I say to you, do not be anxious for your life, what you shall eat; nor yet for your body, what you shall put on. . . . Look at the birds of the air. . . . Consider how the lilies of the field grow. . . . How much more you, O you of little faith!" (Matt. 6:25–30).

"Don't *worry* so," is the message that Jesus folds into the phrase "this day our daily bread"; "Don't worry about whether rain spoils tomorrow's party or whether you lose your job next week or whether that pain will turn out to be cancer. Don't you suppose that God knows the whole story, that He cares, that He will be with you no matter what happens, and that it never will be as bad as you fear? Today's trials are enough for anyone; ask for what you need today; you and God can take care of tomorrow when it comes."

Then comes the really hard part of the Lord's Prayer: "and forgive us our debts, as we also forgive our debtors." It is not hard to ask God's forgiveness for our sins; but sometimes it is very hard to make God's forgiveness of us depend upon our forgiveness of someone else. This is especially true if we have suffered a genuine injury at the hands of another—if we have been betrayed by one whom we thought a friend or if someone has spread tales and damaged our reputation or if we have been treated unjustly by our boss.

Yet we *must* forgive if we expect forgiveness: "For if you forgive men their offenses, your heavenly Father will also forgive you your offenses. But if you do not forgive men, neither will your Father forgive you your offenses" (Matt. 6:14–15). It is here that we put our finger on the very heart of Christian life and practice, in the ability, the willingness to love the sinner even while we detest his sin. "But I say to you," Christ tells us in another place, "love your enemies, do good to those who hate you; and pray for those who persecute and caluminate you, so that you may be children of your Father in heaven, who makes His sun to rise on the good and the evil, and sends rain on the just and the unjust" (Matt. 5:44–45). It is this that marks us as Christ's own. It is this, in a modern phrase, that separates the men from the boys.

The difficulty of practicing this complete charity towards all, even towards our enemies, should convince us of the need we have of God's helping grace if we are to conquer our temptations. And so Jesus places upon our lips the concluding petitions of His prayer: "And lead us not into temptation, but deliver us from evil."

"Lead us not into temptation" is a turn of ancient Hebrew speech which might be paraphrased in our own idiom by saying, "Preserve us from any temptation which might be too big for us and strengthen us with Your grace against the temptations which do face us." Because God, of course, does not lead anyone into a temptation to sin. God sometimes is said to tempt a person, as He tempted Abraham by commanding him to sacrifice his son Isaac. But in such instances the word "temptation" means a trial or a testing— not an allurement to sin. "Let no man say when he is tempted," warns St. James (1:13), "that he is tempted by God; for God is no tempter to evil, and He Himself tempts no one."

"Deliver us from evil." Protect us from all harm, O Father; from physical harm so far as it is in accord with Your will; but especially from any harm that may touch the soul. And so ending, we have said the perfect prayer.

CHAPTER XXXIX

The Bible

Do You Read the Bible?

We can get to heaven without reading the Bible. If that were not so, then people who are unable to read would be in a very hopeless state. If it were necessary to read the Bible in order to get to heaven, most of the people who lived before the invention of printing (about five hundred years ago) also would find heaven closed to them.

We know that Jesus did not make salvation dependent upon the ability to read or to own a Bible. Jesus did not command His Apostles, "Go and write down everything I have said so that the people can read it." Rather did Jesus say, "Go and *preach!* Go and *teach!*" His truths were to be spread (as they had to be spread before the printing press was invented) mainly by the spoken word. It is true that some of the apostles and some of their companions, such as Mark and Luke, did commit to writing many things about the life and doctrines of our Lord. But the oral teachings of the apostles are just as truly the word of God as are their written works which we find in the New Testament of the Bible.

The oral teachings of the apostles have been handed on, from generation to generation, through the Popes and bishops of the Catholic Church. The Latin word for something which is handed on is "traditio"; consequently these oral teachings of the apostles are called the Tradition of the Church. Tradition dating from Christ or His Apostles and the Bible are equally important as sources of divine truths. We must draw upon both of them for a full knowledge of Christ and His teachings. In fact, many parts of the Bible would be difficult to understand aright if we did not have Tradition to guide us in interpreting them.

The oral teachings of the apostles were, of course, eventually put into written form, for the most part by the early Christian writers whom we call the Fathers of the Church. Much of the Tradition of the Church has been enshrined in the decrees of Church Councils and in the *ex cathedra* pronouncements of the Popes. In the last analysis it is only the Church which can separate the wheat from the chaff and say which truths *are* a part of Tradition; the Church in the person of the Pope or a General Council (all the bishops of the world) presided over by him, or of the bishops in union with the Pope teaching in their dioceses throughout the world.

It is not the Bible alone nor Tradition alone, but the Bible and Tradition, as interpreted for us by the living voice of Jesus Christ in His Church, that constitute for Catholics their rule of faith. That is why we see our Protestant brethren as so illogical when they maintain that the Bible and the Bible alone is the means to salvation—the Bible, moreover, interpreted by each individual according to his own understanding of what it says. There is an old saw to the effect that he who tries to be his own doctor has a fool for a physician. Even more truly we might say that he who sets himself up as his own Pope has a fool for a spiritual guide.

To the ignorant, the unwary, and the self-seeking the Bible can be twisted to yield almost any meaning a person may want to read into it. The Bible itself gives us warning on this score. St. Peter, in his second Epistle (3:16), speaking of the writings of St. Paul, says: "In these epistles there are certain things difficult to understand, which the unlearned and the unstable distort, just as they do the rest of the Scriptures also, to their own destruction."

The two points we have been trying to make—the essential importance of Tradition as a complement to the Bible and the necessity of the living voice of Christ in His Church to interpret both of them—are by way of introduction to the real question. Do we read the Bible? We have tried to place matters in proper perspective. But, simply because the Bible is not the single path to salvation, we must not conclude that the Bible has no place in our spiritual lives. The Bible is not everything, but it is a big Something that no Catholic bent on soul-growth can afford to overlook.

We nourish our souls on the Incarnate Word of God, our Lord Jesus Christ present in the Holy Eucharist. We likewise should nourish our minds and hearts on the word of God as it is presented to us in the words of the patriarchs, prophets, and apostles who penned the words of the Bible. It *is* the word of God that they present to us. Although they themselves may not necessarily have been aware of what was happening, God inspired the writers of the biblical books to write what He wanted written. As they wrote, God by a special act of His providence preserved them from making any error in what they wrote. By a further act of His providence God made sure that the books written under His inspiration were preserved, through thousands of years, for successive generations. Finally, through the infallible authority of His Church, God indicated which of all the seemingly holy books that had been written were the ones inspired by Him.

This is the Bible (from the Greek word "biblion," meaning "the book"). It contains seventy-three divisions, or "books," as they are called—some of which have been dropped from some Protestant editions of the Bible. Written by different authors (all inspired by God), the Bible begins with the book of Genesis, ascribed to the patriarch Moses, and ends with the book of the Apocalypse, written by the apostle St. John. God, we might say, has gone to a lot of trouble to give us the Bible. Surely He expects us to read it.

If some public-opinion organization were to conduct a poll of Catholic families as to Bible-ownership and Bible-use, the results might be surprising. Since no such survey has been made (as far as I know), we can only guess that there are more than a few Catholic homes in which no Bible would be found; and probably very many Catholic homes in which the Bible seldom, if ever, is read.

The Church makes extensive use of the Bible in the liturgy. Many parts of the Mass, much of the Divine Office, and a goodly part of other official rites are drawn from the Bible. The Bible also is the treasure-book of all priests who preach; most sermons are an enlargement upon some basic truth found in Sacred Scripture. In view of these facts—but especially in view of the fact that the Bible is God's own inspired word—it is surprising that more Catholics do not read the Bible regularly for their own personal enrichment and spiritual growth.

It is not surprising perhaps that our Protestant neighbors outstrip us in the propagation of the Bible and in the use of it. For the Protestant the Bible is everything; for us it is but a part of our total religious environment. It is an important part, however, and one that is neglected to our own spiritual loss.

We say—and we believe—that the essence of Christian living lies in our effort to develop a Christlikeness in ourselves. Our purpose is to make ourselves over in the image of Christ. We want to learn to see life whole as He sees it, and not live our days in fragmented fashion, with our family life, breadwinning work, recreation, social responsibilities, and personal relationships frequently in conflict one with the other. It is Christlikeness that is the key to an integrated, a sense-making life. This means learning to think as Christ thinks, to judge as He judges, to speak and act as He would speak and act. As this Christlikeness fills our own individual mold and is modified by our own personal characteristics, it will manifest itself in a glorious variety of ways; but the fundamental and unifying principle of Christlikeness will be unmistakable.

We cannot pattern ourselves on Christ unless we know Him well. For such a knowledge there is no better source than the Gospels. Better than any secondhand image that we may get from sermons or spiritual books is the stark and simple picture of Him presented by the four evangelists. Then, in the Epistles of Paul and Peter and James and John, we shall find Christ's teachings elaborated, especially His doctrine and law of charity. Turning back to the Old Testament, we shall find there, in the historical books, God's grand plan for man's salvation, unfolding slowly through eons of time. In the prophetic books we shall see Christ approaching, like a wavering shadow cast on the side of a house. In the books of wisdom we shall find the principles of conduct and right living that God has distilled for mankind from long ages of human experience.

We shall find all this, and more, if we read the Bible regularly and with the prayerful reverence that is due the word of God. We also, if we read for at least fifteen minutes each day, shall gain an indulgence of three years and a plenary indulgence once each month under the usual conditions. The granting of these indulgences was a part of Pope Leo XIII's effort to encourage the reading of the Bible.

We must, of course, read an authorized version of the Bible. There are not two Bibles, the "Catholic" Bible and the "Protestant" Bible. There is only one Bible, as it was inspired by God and written down book by book, age after age, in ancient Hebrew and Greek. The original fragile manuscripts long since have perished, but there still are ancient manuscript copies extant, dating back to early Christian times. It is from these manuscripts, or from the famous Latin translation made by St. Jerome (called the "Latin Vulgate") that modern translations are made into English, French, German and the other modern languages. These are called vernacular *versions* of the Bible.

If the Bible is translated into a modern language such as English by a competent biblical scholar or scholars and is approved by the Pope or by the bishops of the country as being an accurate translation, then that translation of the Bible is called an *approved* version, an authorized version. This means that the version is as free from errors as human care can make it. It is only such *approved* versions that a Catholic may read. Even a translation of the Bible made by a Catholic scholar cannot be used by Catholics unless it has received the official approval of the Church. We can see, then, that in choosing a Bible it is not a case of Protestant versus Catholic Bible; it is a case of a non-approved Bible versus an approved Bible.

Until recently the approved English version of the Bible used by Catholics was the Douay version, a translation which dates back to the end of the sixteenth century. Although it was revised at various later dates, many of its words and terms are archaic now and sound strange to modern ears. Consequently, the bishops of the United States, through the Confraternity of Christian Doctrine, have undertaken to provide us with a completely new English translation of the Bible. A large group of Catholic Biblical scholars have been working at this task for several years. The first fruit of their labors was the Confraternity revision of the New Testament, which is now familiar to most of us as the standard American version of the New Testament. The translation of much of the Old Testament also has been completed and incorporated into the approved editions of the Bible which are sold in America; the old Douay version is being replaced part by part as the scholars progress in their work. Within a very few years the entire Bible as approved by the bishops of the United States will be the Confraternity revision of the Bible.

But there is no need for us to wait until then. If we do not already possess a Bible, the time to provide ourselves with one is *now*.